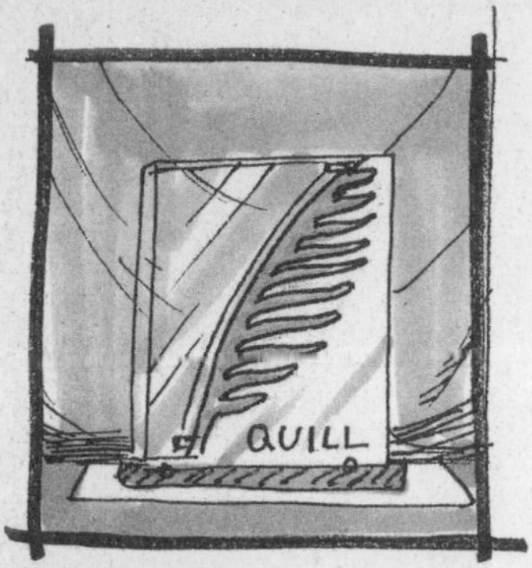
QUILL

Thanks to everyone's support, *Naruto* has now received its first award in the U.S. I was very honored that a Japanese manga was able to win from among so many American comics. I swear to keep working hard on this manga.

—Masashi Kishimoto, 2008

岸本斉史

Author/artist Masashi Kishimoto was born in 1974 in rural Okayama Prefecture, Japan. After spending time in art college, he won the Hop Step Award for new manga artists with his manga **Karakuri** (Mechanism). Kishimoto decided to base his next story on traditional Japanese culture. His first version of **Naruto**, drawn in 1997, was a one-shot story about fox spirits; his final version, which debuted in **Weekly Shonen Jump** in 1999, quickly became the most popular ninja manga in Japan.

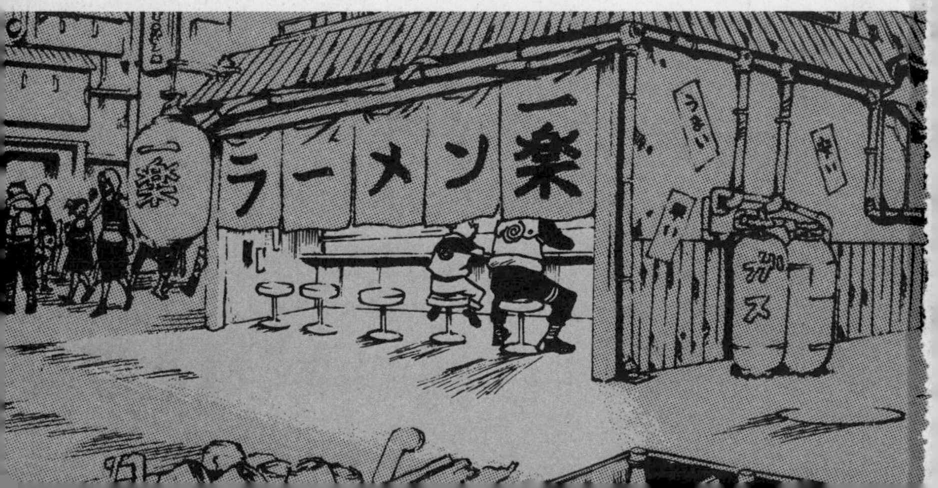
一楽
ラーメン一楽

NARUTO VOL. 41
The SHONEN JUMP Manga Edition

STORY AND ART BY MASASHI KISHIMOTO

Translation/Mari Morimoto
English Adaptation/Deric A. Hughes & Benjamin Raab
Touch-up Art & Lettering/Inori Fukuda Trant
Design/Gerry Serrano
Editor/Joel Enos

Editor in Chief, Books/Alvin Lu
Editor in Chief, Magazines/Marc Weidenbaum
VP, Publishing Licensing/Rika Inouye
VP, Sales & Product Marketing/Gonzalo Ferreyra
VP, Creative/Linda Espinosa
Publisher/Hyoe Narita

Printed in the U.S.A.

Published by VIZ Media, LLC
P.O. Box 77010
San Francisco, CA 94107

SHONEN JUMP Manga Edition
10 9 8 7 6 5 4 3 2 1
First printing, March 2009

SHONEN JUMP MANGA EDITION

NARUTO

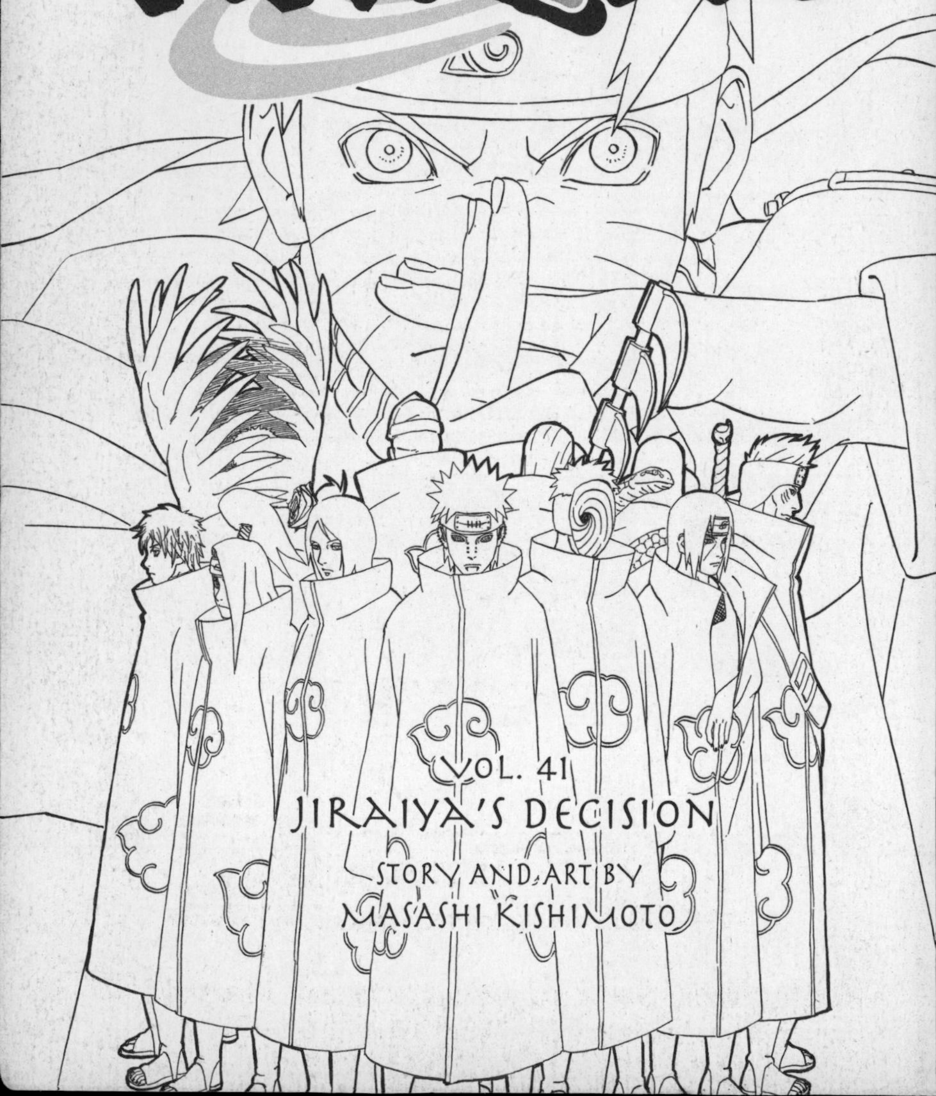

VOL. 41

JIRAIYA'S DECISION

STORY AND ART BY

MASASHI KISHIMOTO

CHARACTERS

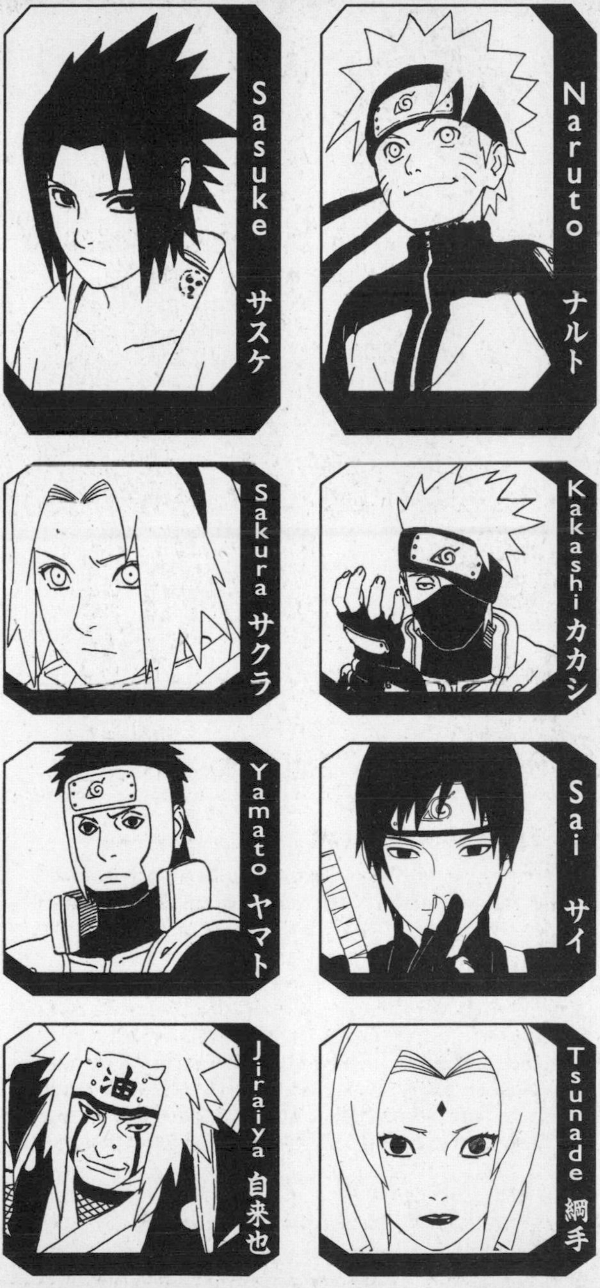
Naruto ナルト
Sasuke サスケ
Kakashi カカシ
Sakura サクラ
Sai サイ
Yamato ヤマト
Tsunade 綱手
Jiraiya 自来也

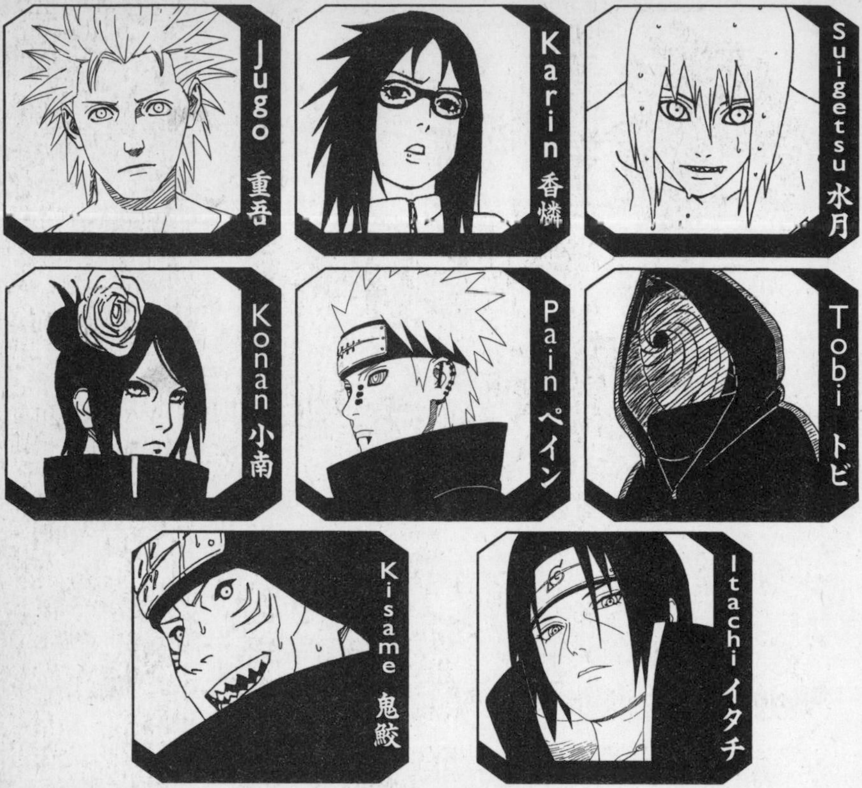
Jugo 重吾
Karin 香燐
Suigetsu 水月
Konan 小南
Pain ペイン
Tobi トビ
Kisame 鬼鮫
Itachi イタチ

THE STORY SO FAR...

Once the bane of the Konohagakure Ninja Academy, Uzumaki Naruto now serves dutifully among the ranks of the Konoha shinobi—an illustrious group of ninja sworn to protect their village from the forces of evil seeking to destroy it from without and within...

After his former classmate, Uchiha Sasuke, is seduced by the evil Orochimaru, Naruto makes it his personal mission to find and save his friend from the darkness growing inside him. Sasuke, however, doesn't want to be found. He only seeks revenge on the man he hates most in the world—the one he blames for murdering his parents—his older brother, Uchiha Itachi. Though Sasuke's quest is temporarily delayed after he comes into conflict with his brother's associates in the insidious organization known as the Akatsuki, at long last he catches up to Itachi...

Meanwhile, Jiraiya infiltrates the Hidden Rain Village on a top-secret mission to gather intelligence on Pain, the Akatsuki's enigmatic leader. Little does he realize he, too, is being watched...

NARUTO

VOL. 41
JIRAIYA'S DECISION

CONTENTS

Number 370: Unease

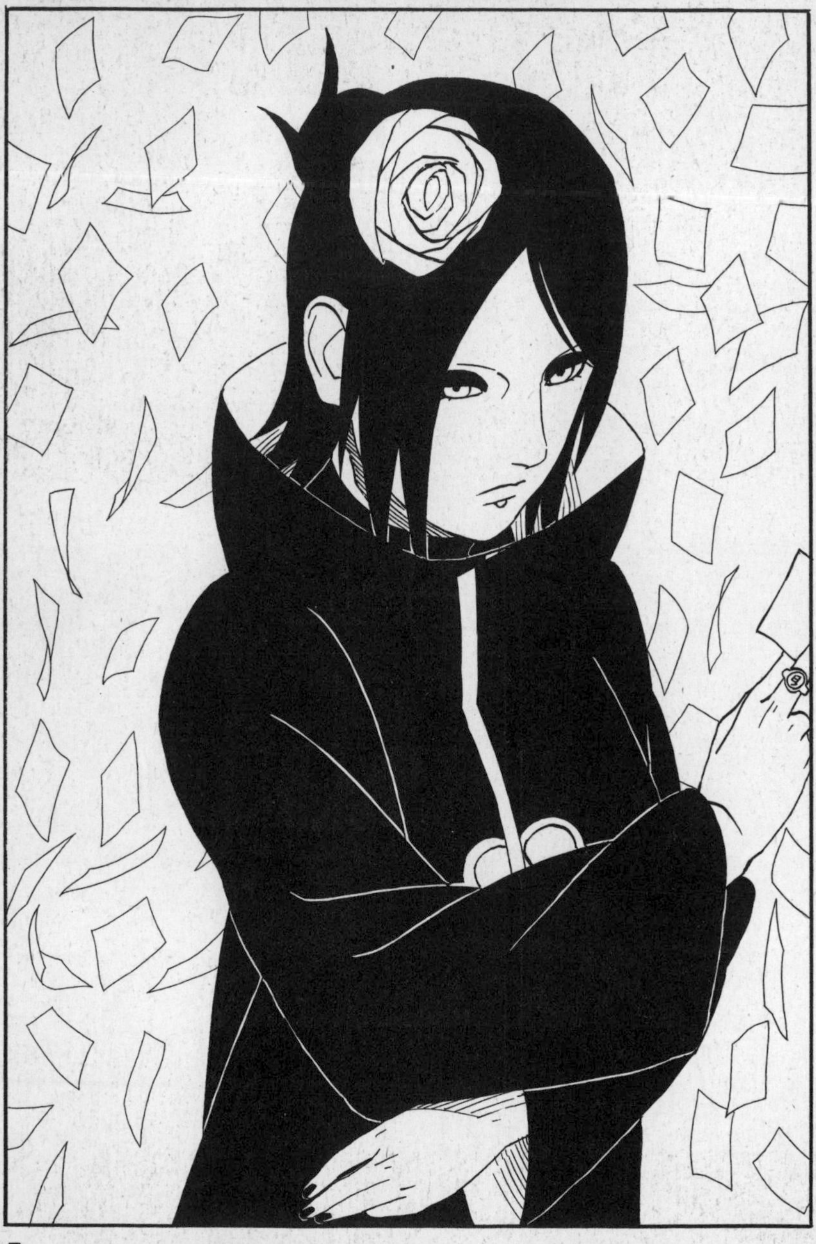

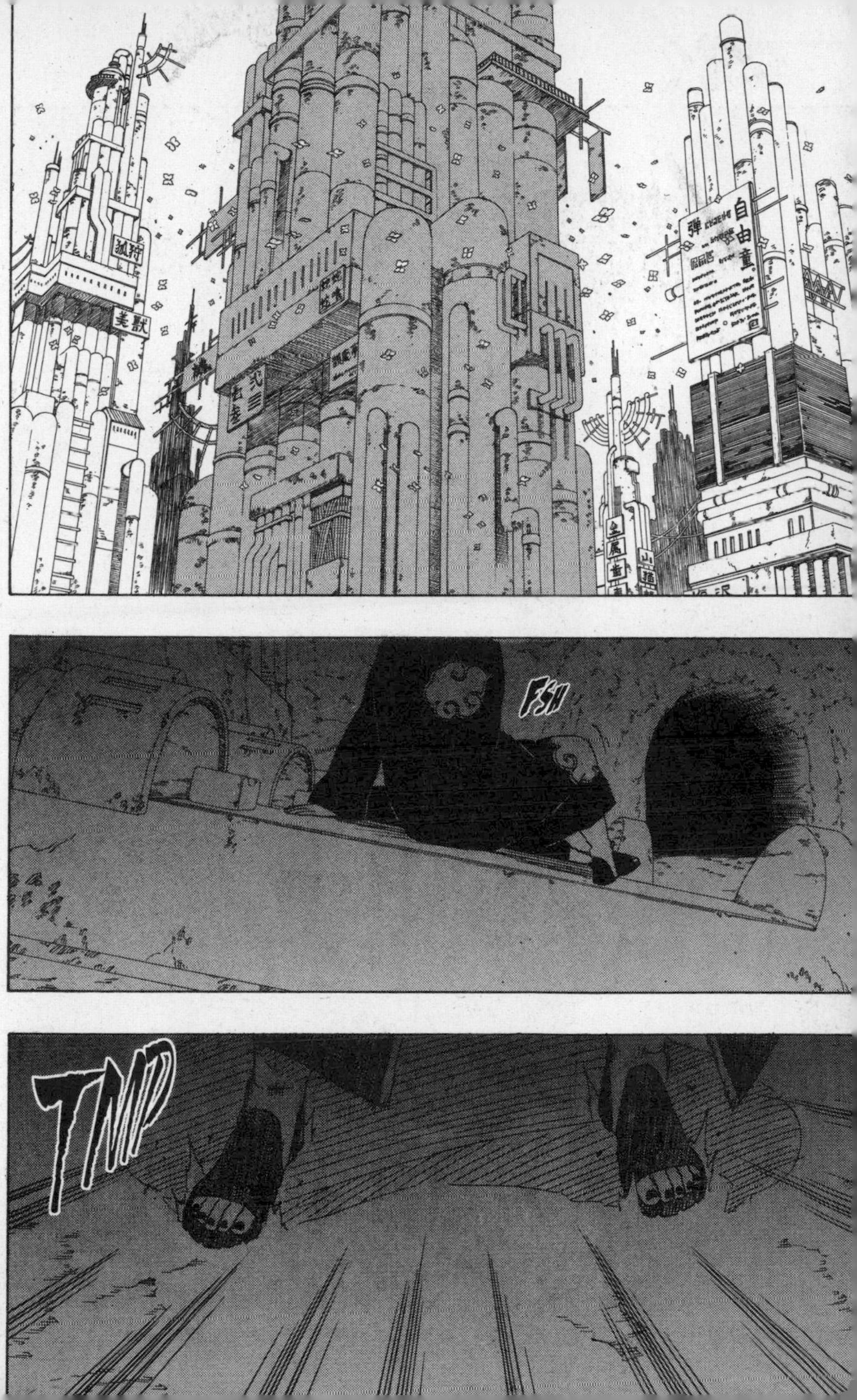
FSH
TMP

READ THIS WAY

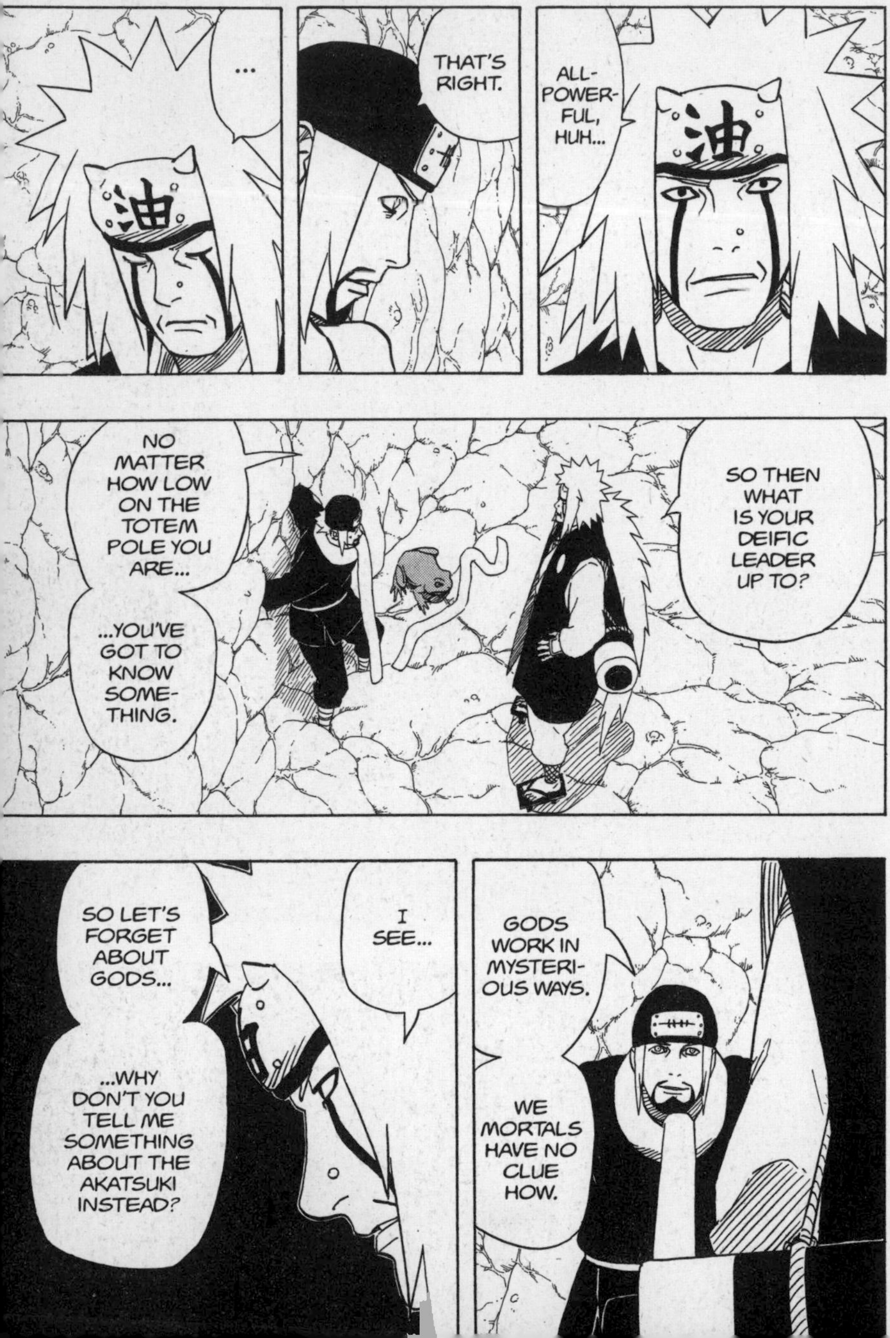
ALL-POWERFUL, HUH...
THAT'S RIGHT.
...
SO THEN WHAT IS YOUR DEIFIC LEADER UP TO?
NO MATTER HOW LOW ON THE TOTEM POLE YOU ARE...
...YOU'VE GOT TO KNOW SOMETHING.
GODS WORK IN MYSTERIOUS WAYS.
WE MORTALS HAVE NO CLUE HOW.
I SEE...
SO LET'S FORGET ABOUT GODS...
...WHY DON'T YOU TELL ME SOMETHING ABOUT THE AKATSUKI INSTEAD?

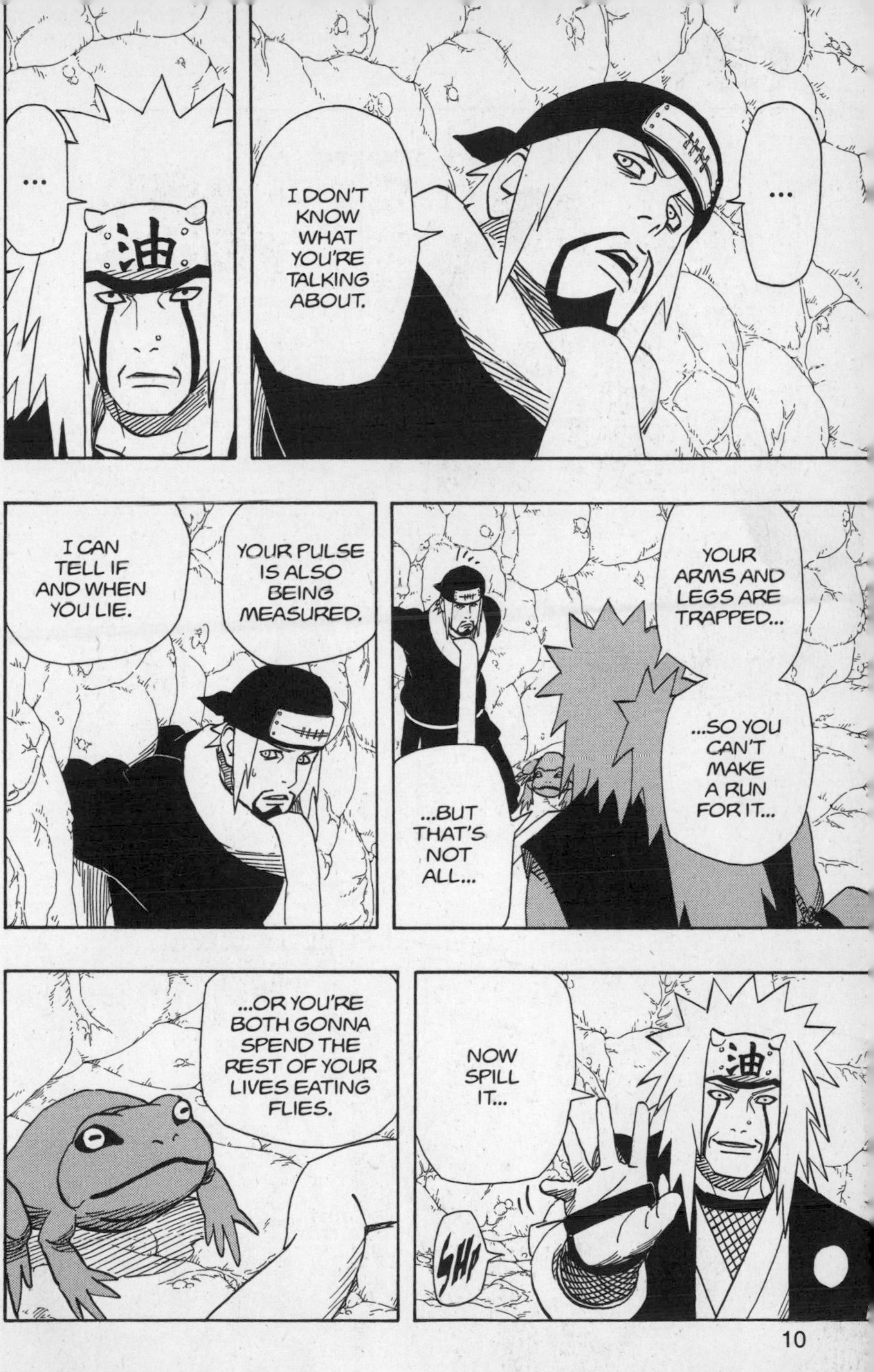
...
I DON'T KNOW WHAT YOU'RE TALKING ABOUT.
...
YOUR ARMS AND LEGS ARE TRAPPED...
...SO YOU CAN'T MAKE A RUN FOR IT...
...BUT THAT'S NOT ALL...
YOUR PULSE IS ALSO BEING MEASURED.
I CAN TELL IF AND WHEN YOU LIE.
NOW SPILL IT...
SHP
...OR YOU'RE BOTH GONNA SPEND THE REST OF YOUR LIVES EATING FLIES.

READ THIS WAY

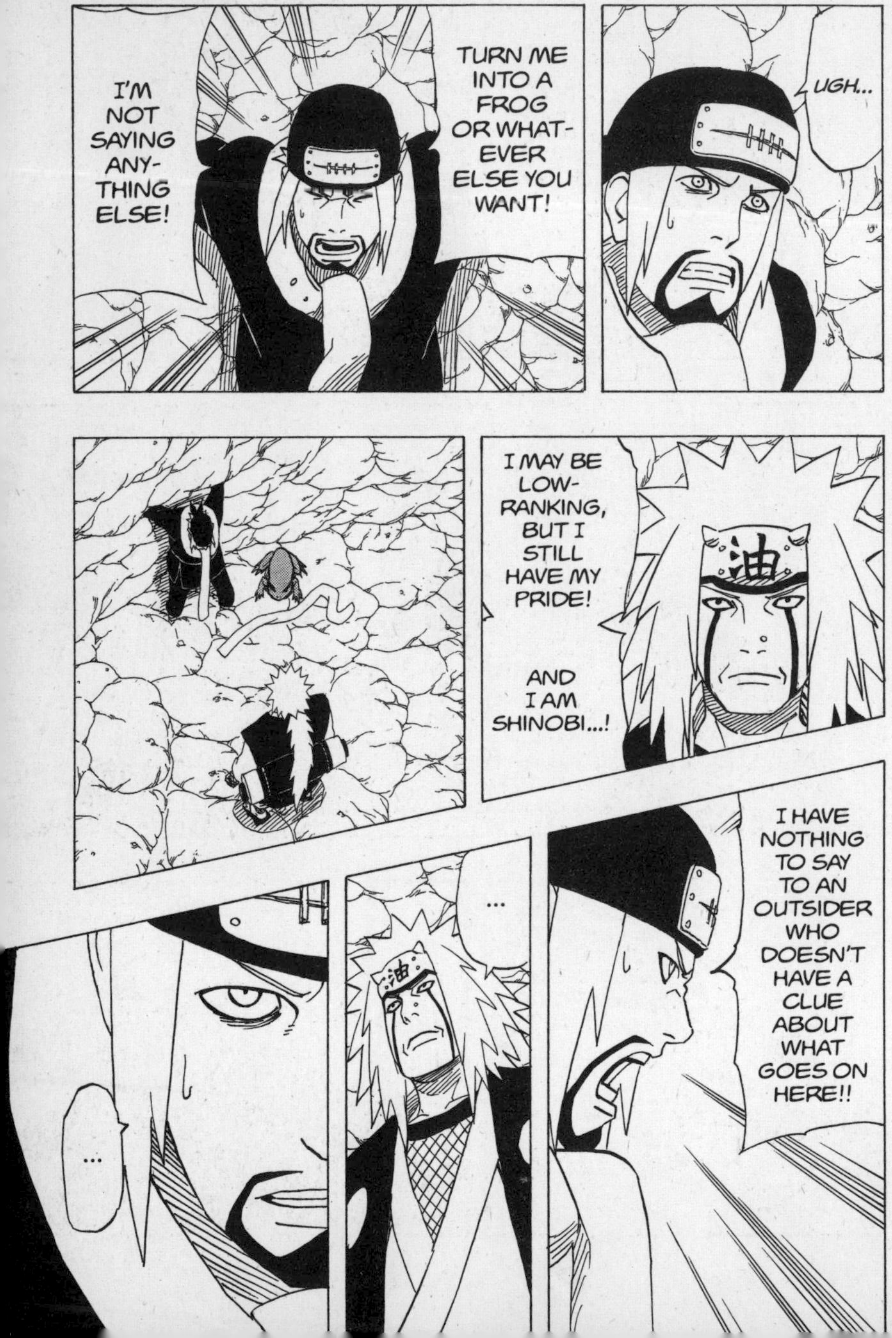
UGH...
TURN ME INTO A FROG OR WHATEVER ELSE YOU WANT!
I'M NOT SAYING ANYTHING ELSE!
I MAY BE LOW-RANKING, BUT I STILL HAVE MY PRIDE!
AND I AM SHINOBI...!
I HAVE NOTHING TO SAY TO AN OUTSIDER WHO DOESN'T HAVE A CLUE ABOUT WHAT GOES ON HERE!!
...
...

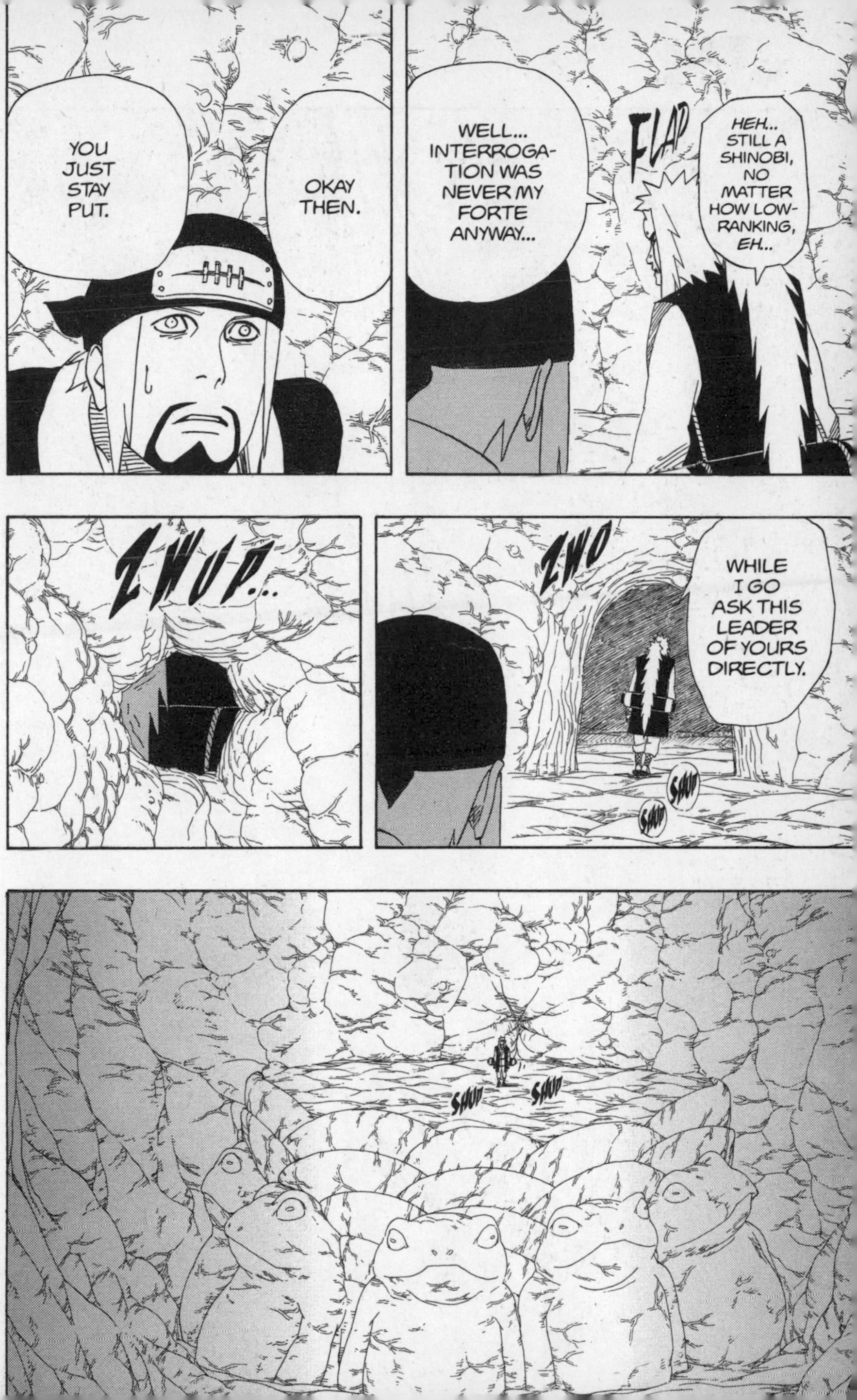
FLAP
HEH... STILL A SHINOBI, NO MATTER HOW LOW-RANKING, EH...
WELL... INTERROGATION WAS NEVER MY FORTE ANYWAY...
OKAY THEN.
YOU JUST STAY PUT.
WHILE I GO ASK THIS LEADER OF YOURS DIRECTLY.
ZWO
SHUP
SHUP
ZWUP...
SHUP
SHUP

READ THIS WAY

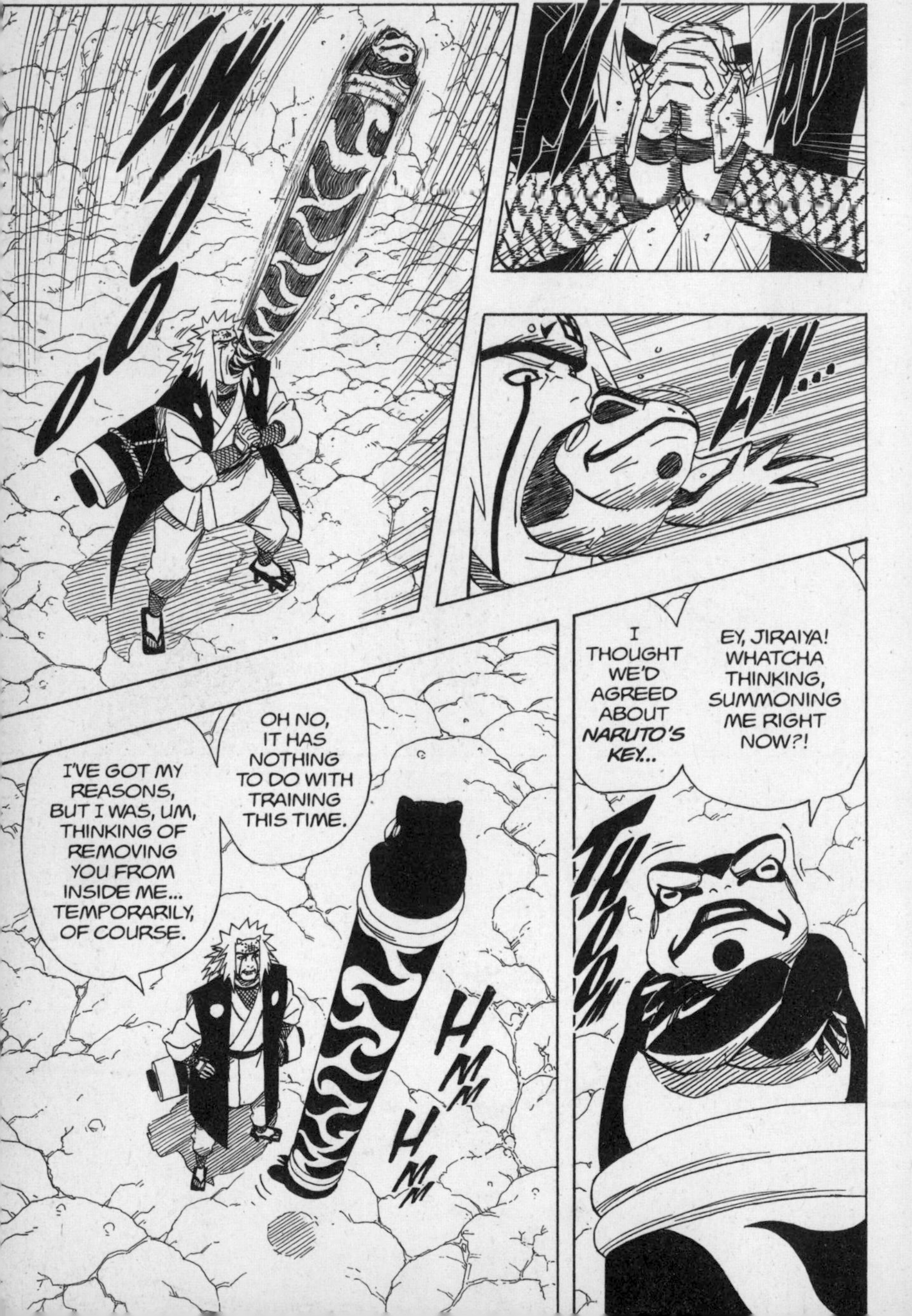
ZW...
ZWOOOOO
EY, JIRAIYA! WHATCHA THINKING, SUMMONING ME RIGHT NOW?!
I THOUGHT WE'D AGREED ABOUT *NARUTO'S KEY*...
OH NO, IT HAS NOTHING TO DO WITH TRAINING THIS TIME.
I'VE GOT MY REASONS, BUT I WAS, UM, THINKING OF REMOVING YOU FROM INSIDE ME... TEMPORARILY, OF COURSE.
HMM HMM

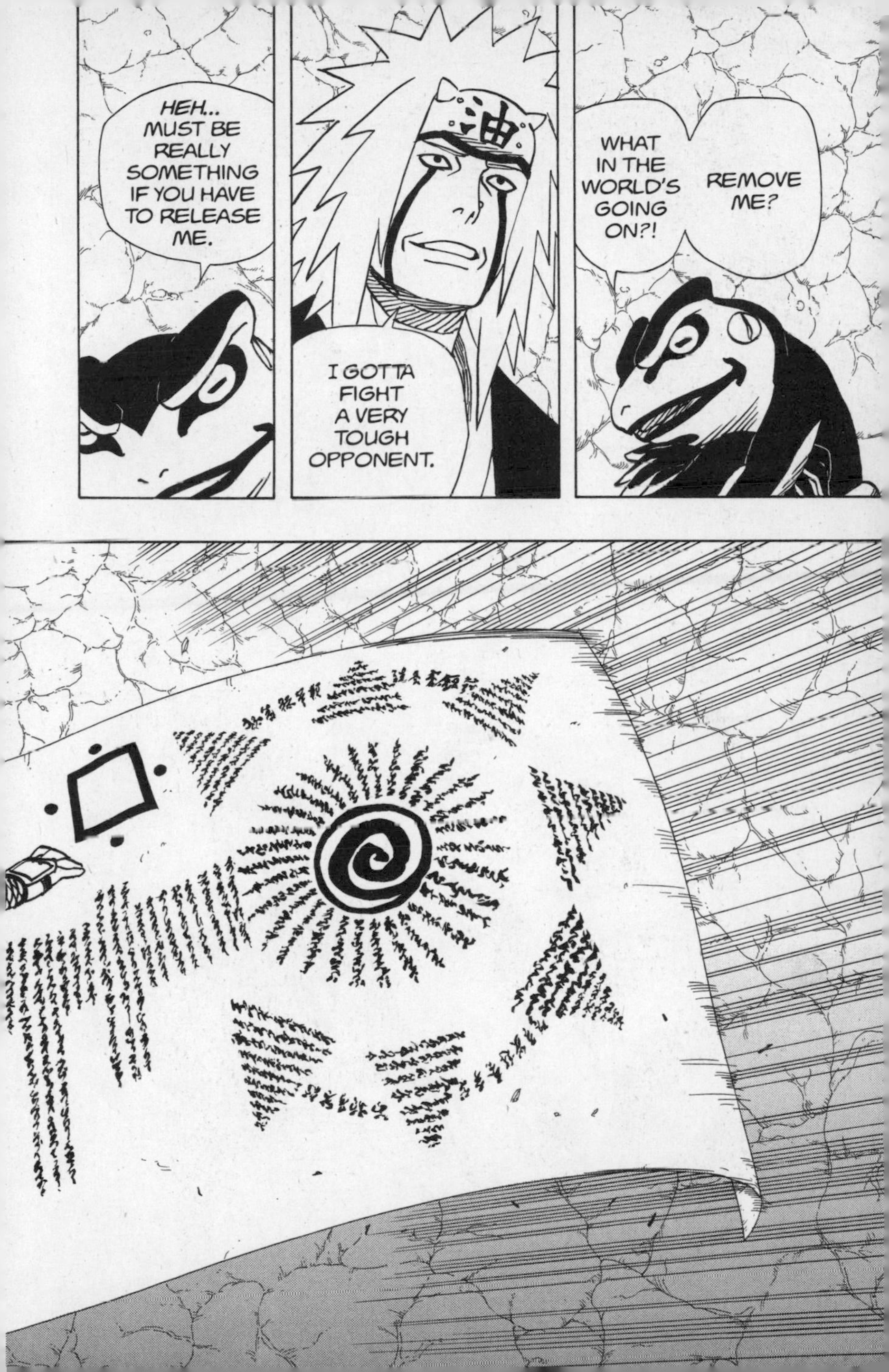
REMOVE ME?
WHAT IN THE WORLD'S GOING ON?!
I GOTTA FIGHT A VERY TOUGH OPPONENT.
HEH... MUST BE REALLY SOMETHING IF YOU HAVE TO RELEASE ME.

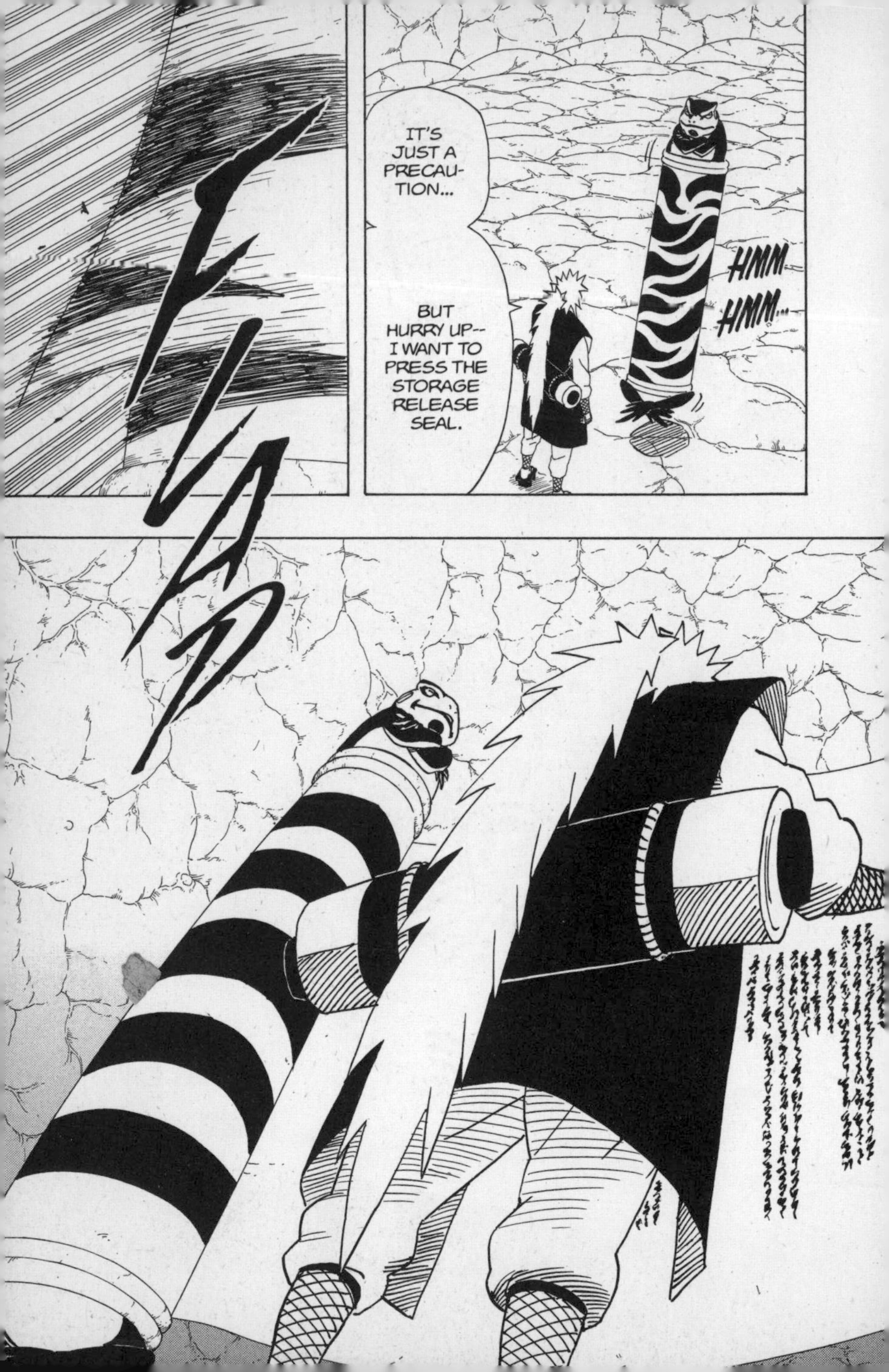
IT'S JUST A PRECAUTION...
BUT HURRY UP-- I WANT TO PRESS THE STORAGE RELEASE SEAL.
HMM HMM...

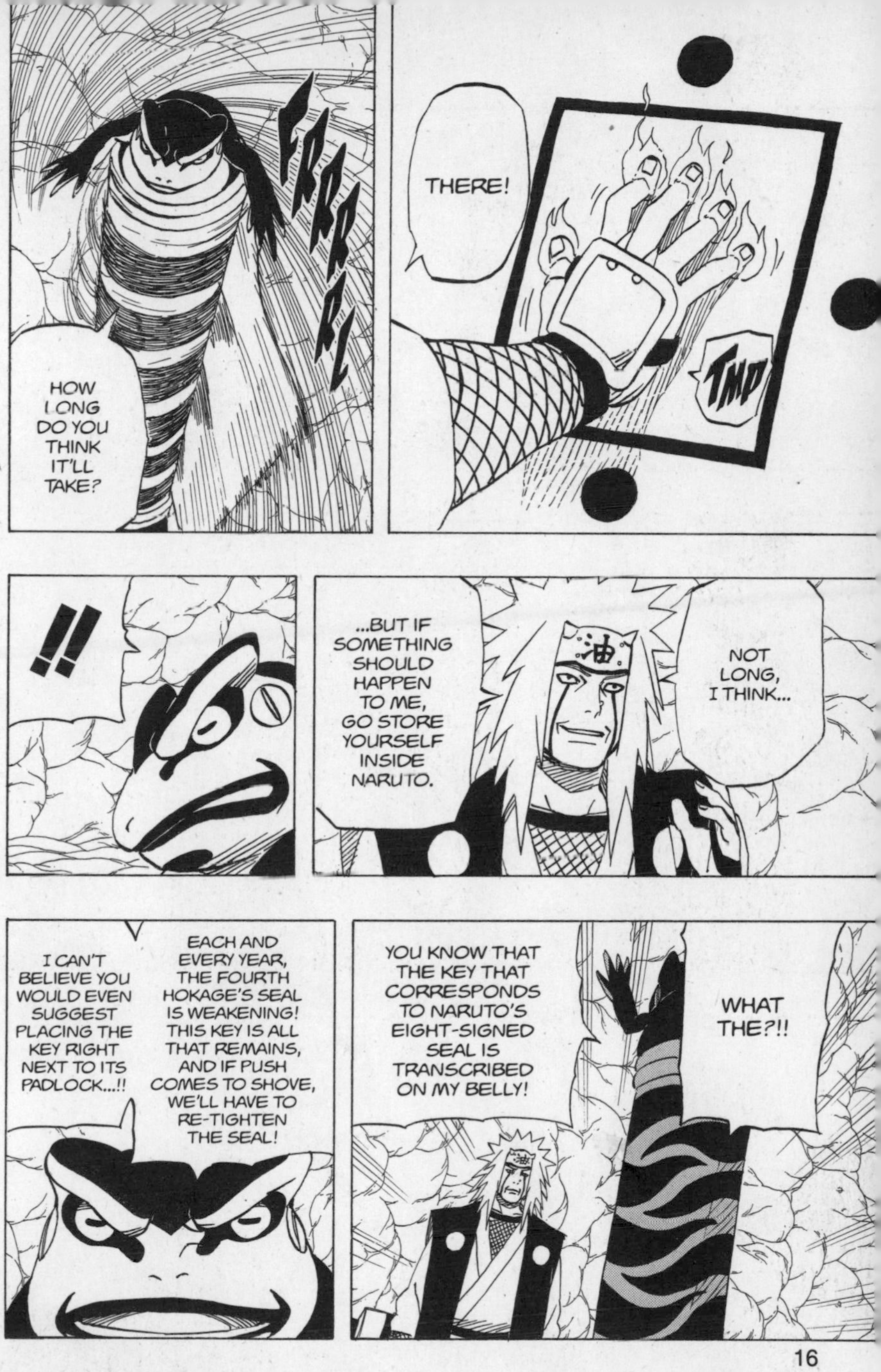
THERE!
TMP
FRRRL
HOW LONG DO YOU THINK IT'LL TAKE?
NOT LONG, I THINK...
...BUT IF SOMETHING SHOULD HAPPEN TO ME, GO STORE YOURSELF INSIDE NARUTO.
!!
WHAT THE?!!
YOU KNOW THAT THE KEY THAT CORRESPONDS TO NARUTO'S EIGHT-SIGNED SEAL IS TRANSCRIBED ON MY BELLY!
EACH AND EVERY YEAR, THE FOURTH HOKAGE'S SEAL IS WEAKENING! THIS KEY IS ALL THAT REMAINS, AND IF PUSH COMES TO SHOVE, WE'LL HAVE TO RE-TIGHTEN THE SEAL!
I CAN'T BELIEVE YOU WOULD EVEN SUGGEST PLACING THE KEY RIGHT NEXT TO ITS PADLOCK...!!

READ THIS WAY

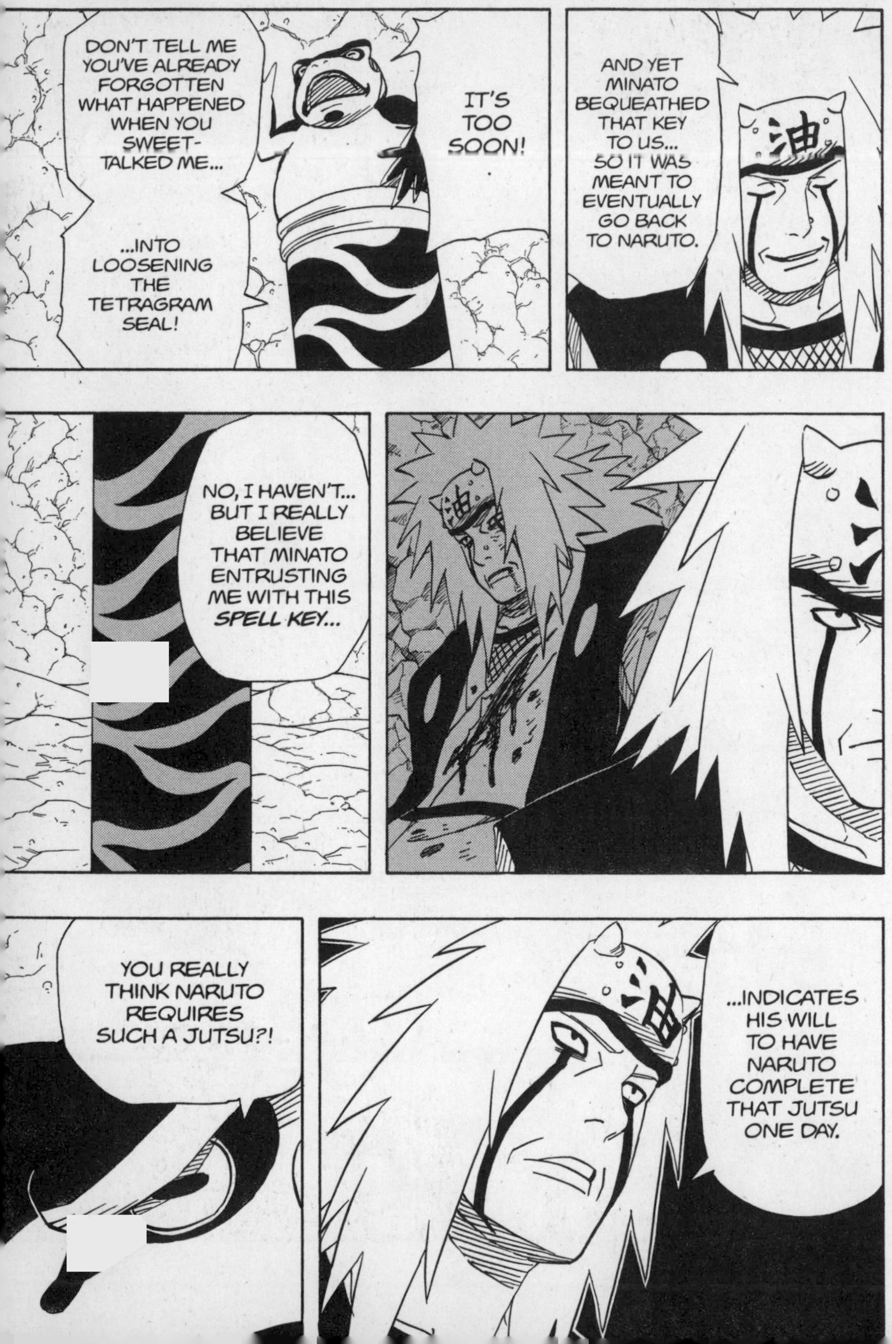
AND YET MINATO BEQUEATHED THAT KEY TO US... SO IT WAS MEANT TO EVENTUALLY GO BACK TO NARUTO.
IT'S TOO SOON!
DON'T TELL ME YOU'VE ALREADY FORGOTTEN WHAT HAPPENED WHEN YOU SWEET-TALKED ME...
...INTO LOOSENING THE TETRAGRAM SEAL!
NO, I HAVEN'T... BUT I REALLY BELIEVE THAT MINATO ENTRUSTING ME WITH THIS SPELL KEY...
...INDICATES HIS WILL TO HAVE NARUTO COMPLETE THAT JUTSU ONE DAY.
YOU REALLY THINK NARUTO REQUIRES SUCH A JUTSU?!

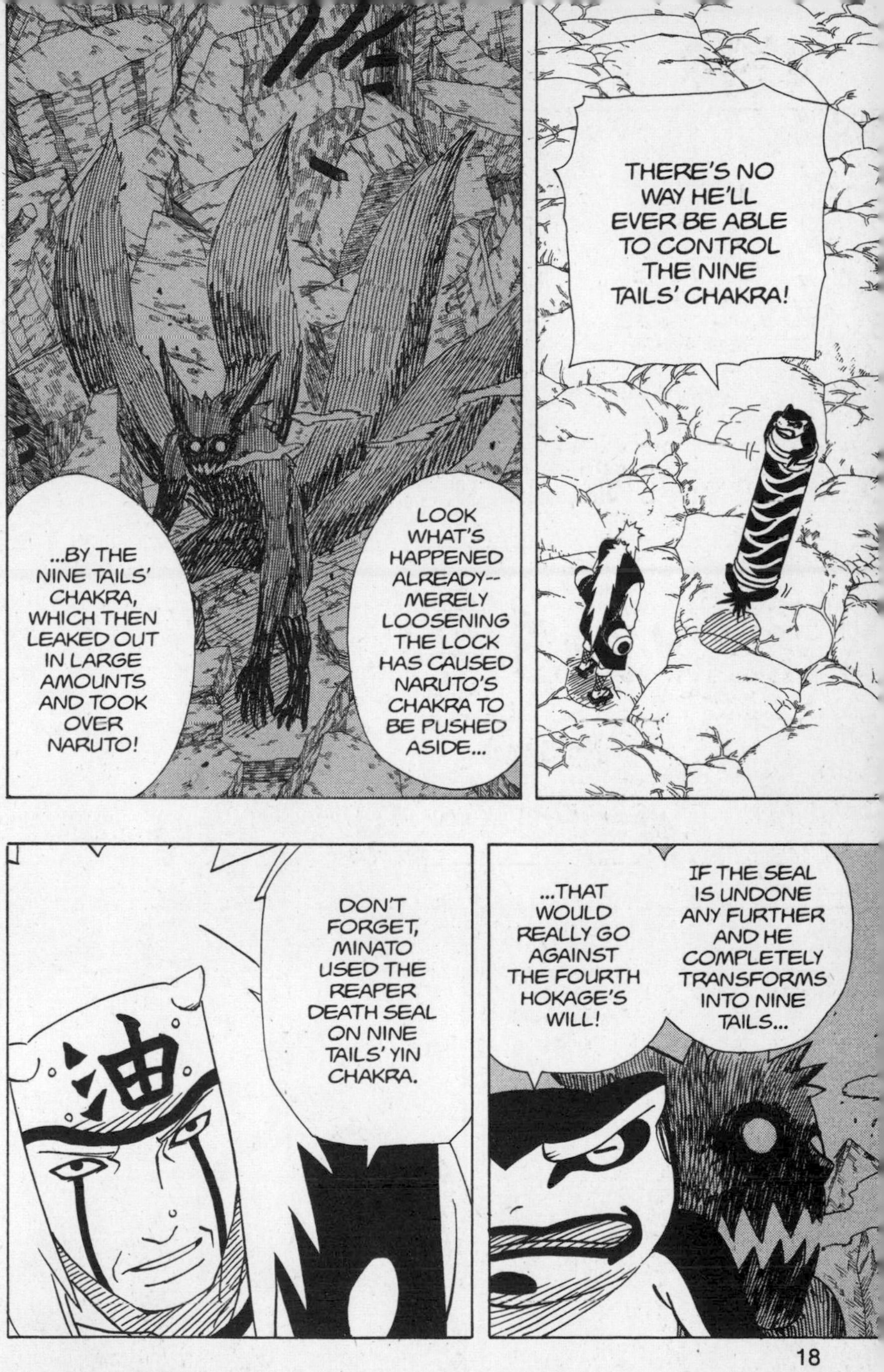
THERE'S NO WAY HE'LL EVER BE ABLE TO CONTROL THE NINE TAILS' CHAKRA!
LOOK WHAT'S HAPPENED ALREADY-- MERELY LOOSENING THE LOCK HAS CAUSED NARUTO'S CHAKRA TO BE PUSHED ASIDE...
...BY THE NINE TAILS' CHAKRA, WHICH THEN LEAKED OUT IN LARGE AMOUNTS AND TOOK OVER NARUTO!
IF THE SEAL IS UNDONE ANY FURTHER AND HE COMPLETELY TRANSFORMS INTO NINE TAILS...
...THAT WOULD REALLY GO AGAINST THE FOURTH HOKAGE'S WILL!
DON'T FORGET, MINATO USED THE REAPER DEATH SEAL ON NINE TAILS' YIN CHAKRA.
油

READ THIS WAY

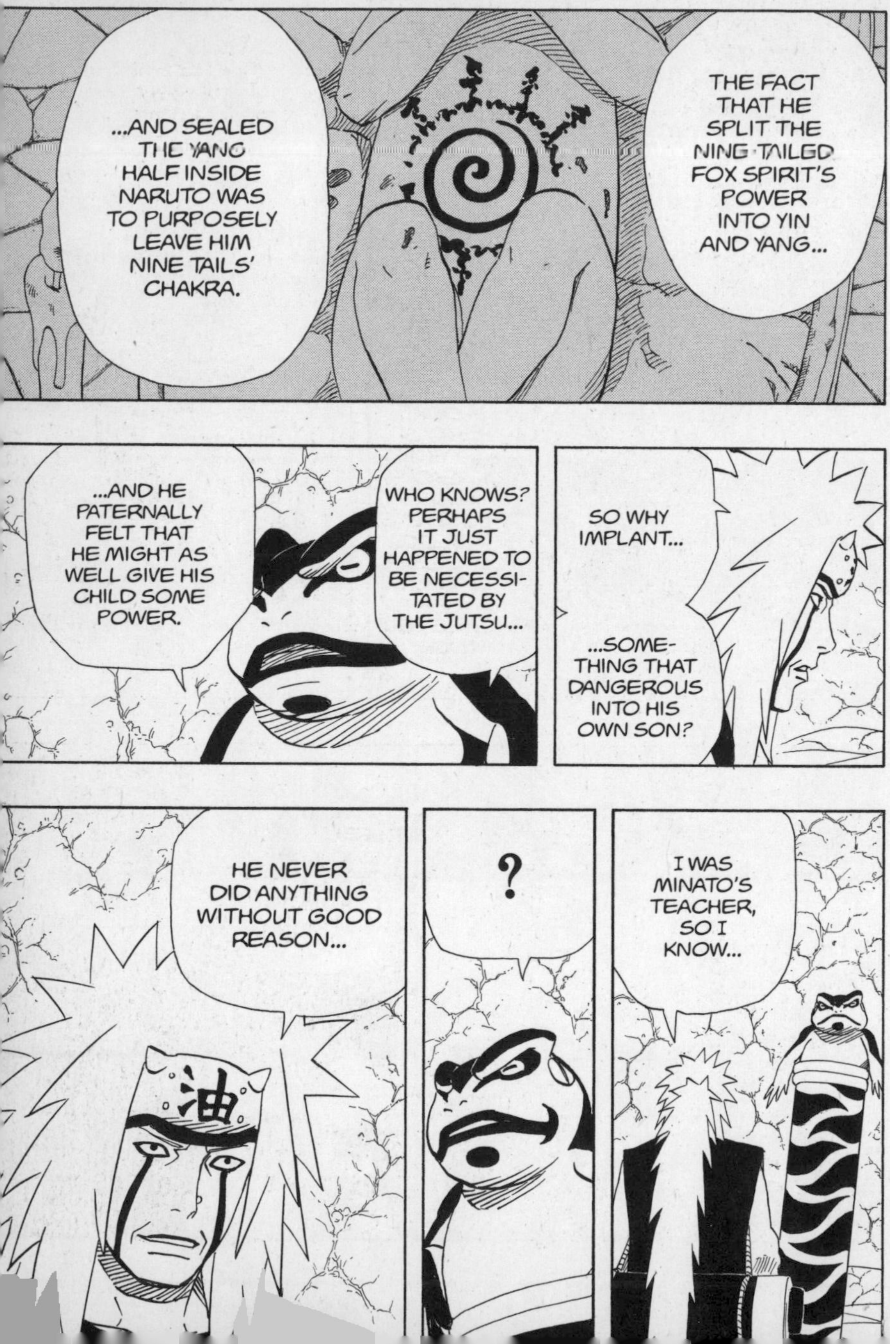
THE FACT THAT HE SPLIT THE NINE-TAILED FOX SPIRIT'S POWER INTO YIN AND YANG...
...AND SEALED THE YANG HALF INSIDE NARUTO WAS TO PURPOSELY LEAVE HIM NINE TAILS' CHAKRA.
SO WHY IMPLANT...
...SOMETHING THAT DANGEROUS INTO HIS OWN SON?
WHO KNOWS? PERHAPS IT JUST HAPPENED TO BE NECESSITATED BY THE JUTSU...
...AND HE PATERNALLY FELT THAT HE MIGHT AS WELL GIVE HIS CHILD SOME POWER.
I WAS MINATO'S TEACHER, SO I KNOW...
?
HE NEVER DID ANYTHING WITHOUT GOOD REASON...
油

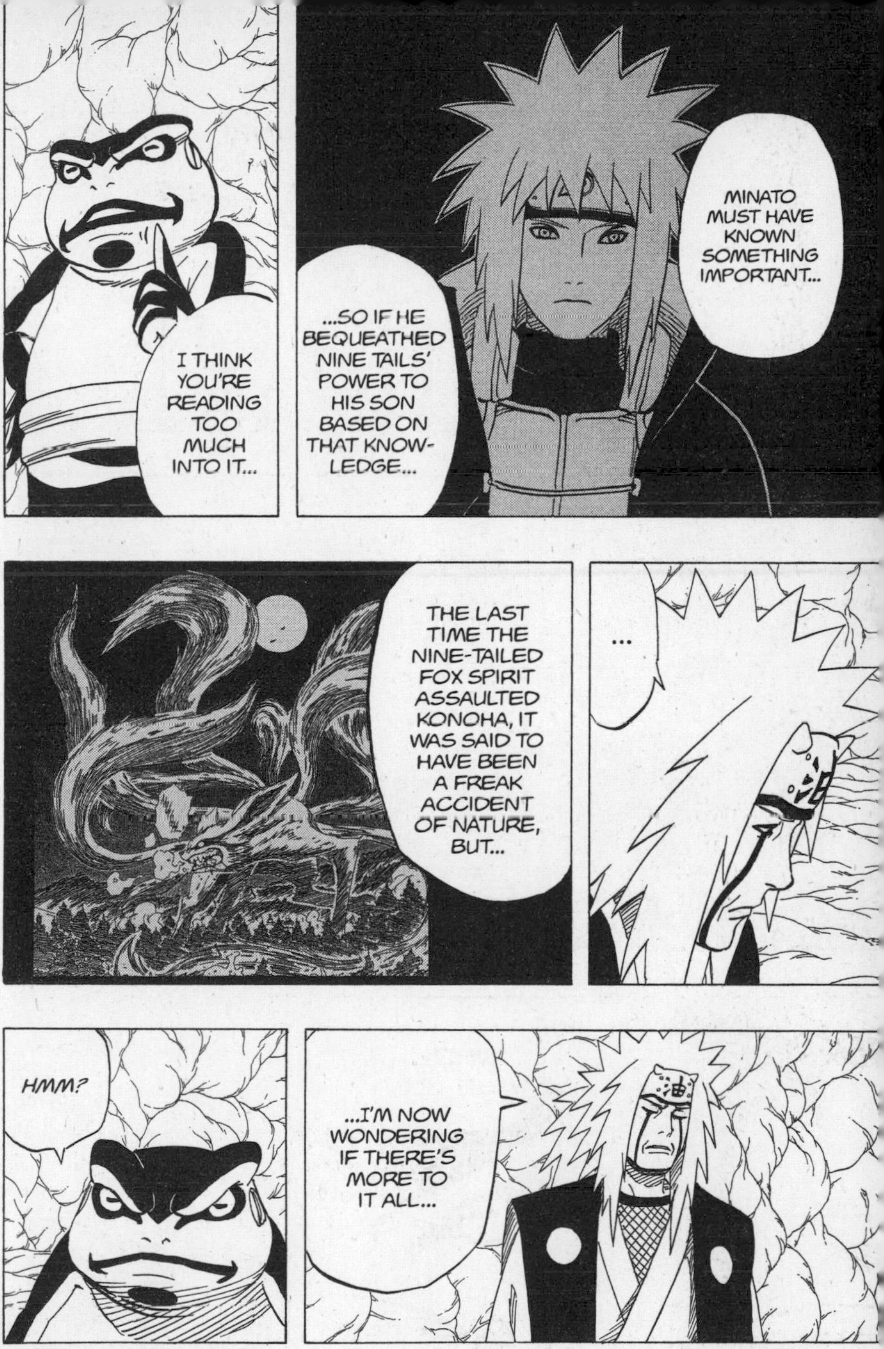
MINATO MUST HAVE KNOWN SOMETHING IMPORTANT...
...SO IF HE BEQUEATHED NINE TAILS' POWER TO HIS SON BASED ON THAT KNOW-LEDGE...
I THINK YOU'RE READING TOO MUCH INTO IT...
...
THE LAST TIME THE NINE-TAILED FOX SPIRIT ASSAULTED KONOHA, IT WAS SAID TO HAVE BEEN A FREAK ACCIDENT OF NATURE, BUT...
...I'M NOW WONDERING IF THERE'S MORE TO IT ALL...
HMM?

READ THIS WAY

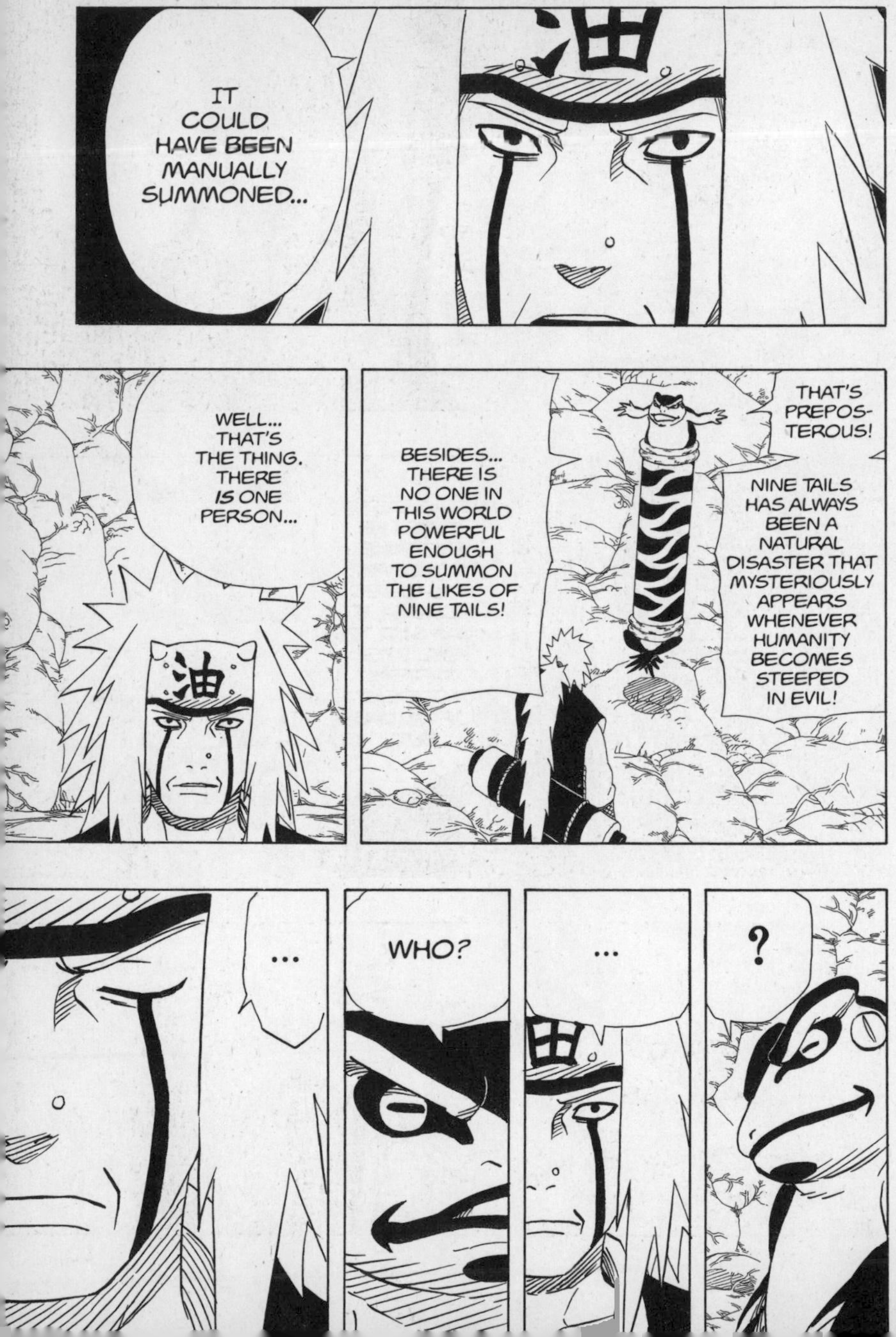

IT COULD HAVE BEEN MANUALLY SUMMONED...
THAT'S PREPOSTEROUS!
NINE TAILS HAS ALWAYS BEEN A NATURAL DISASTER THAT MYSTERIOUSLY APPEARS WHENEVER HUMANITY BECOMES STEEPED IN EVIL!
BESIDES... THERE IS NO ONE IN THIS WORLD POWERFUL ENOUGH TO SUMMON THE LIKES OF NINE TAILS!
WELL... THAT'S THE THING. THERE *IS* ONE PERSON...
?
...
WHO?
...

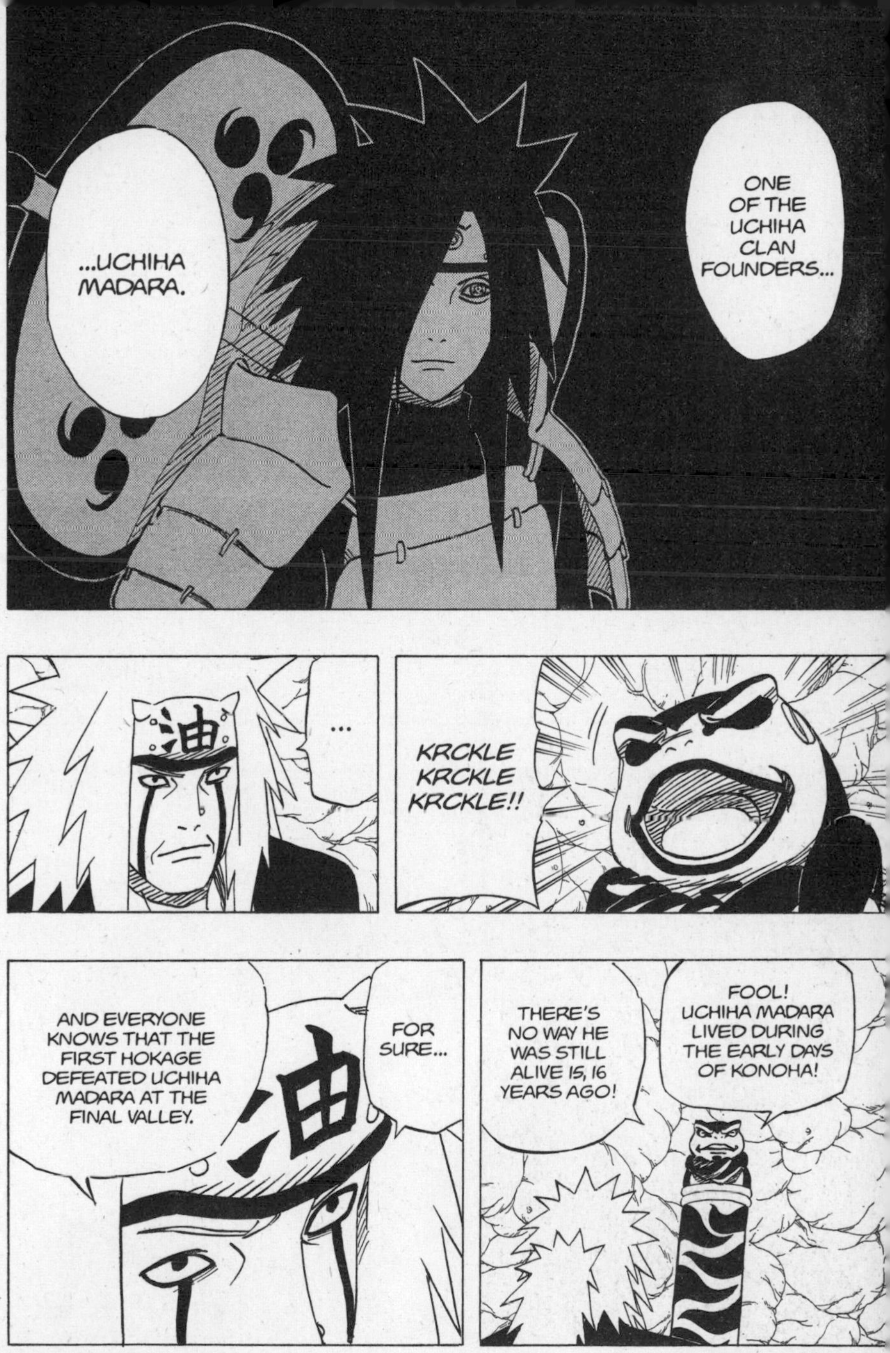
ONE OF THE UCHIHA CLAN FOUNDERS...
...UCHIHA MADARA.
KRCKLE KRCKLE KRCKLE!!
...
FOOL! UCHIHA MADARA LIVED DURING THE EARLY DAYS OF KONOHA!
THERE'S NO WAY HE WAS STILL ALIVE 15, 16 YEARS AGO!
FOR SURE...
AND EVERYONE KNOWS THAT THE FIRST HOKAGE DEFEATED UCHIHA MADARA AT THE FINAL VALLEY.

READ THIS WAY

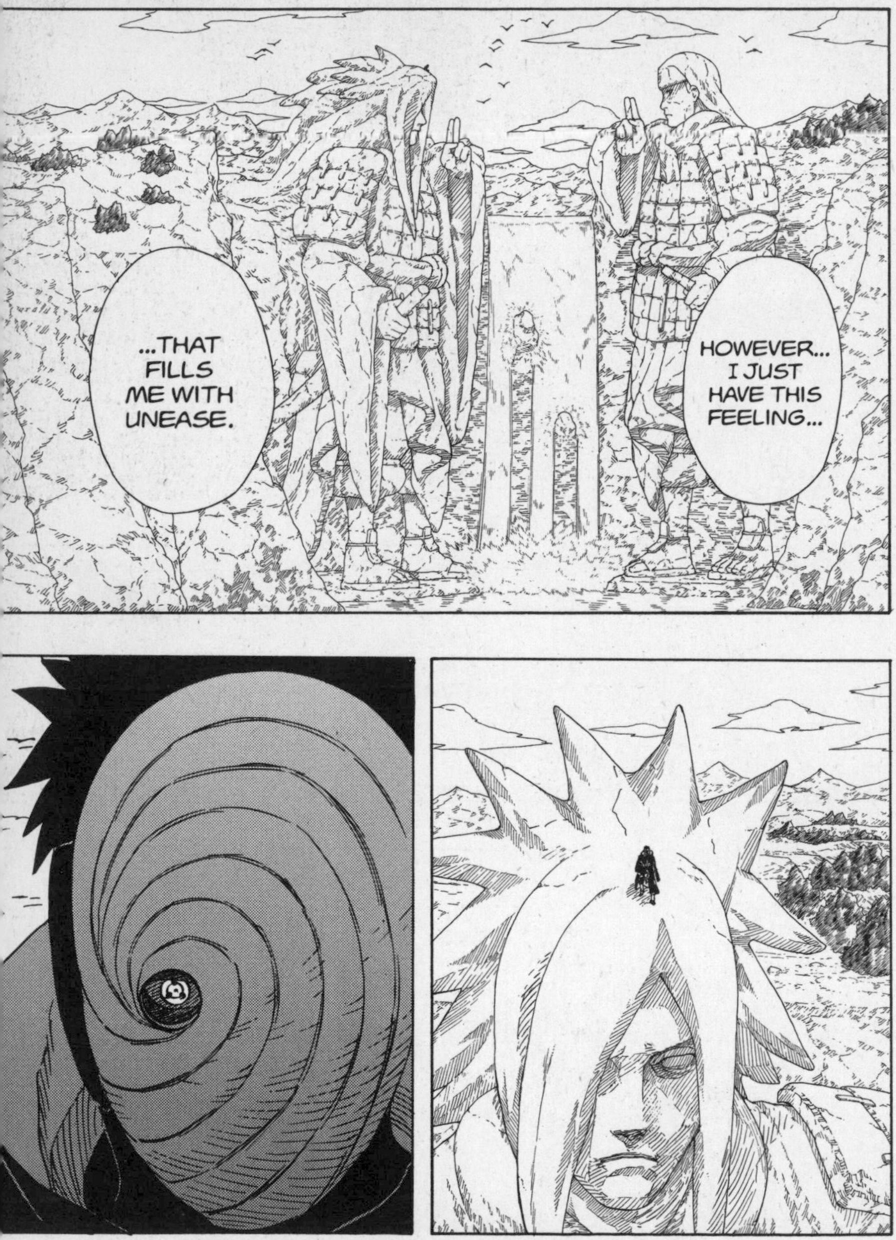
HOWEVER... I JUST HAVE THIS FEELING...
...THAT FILLS ME WITH UNEASE.

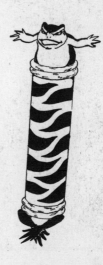

Number 371: Old Acquaintances!!

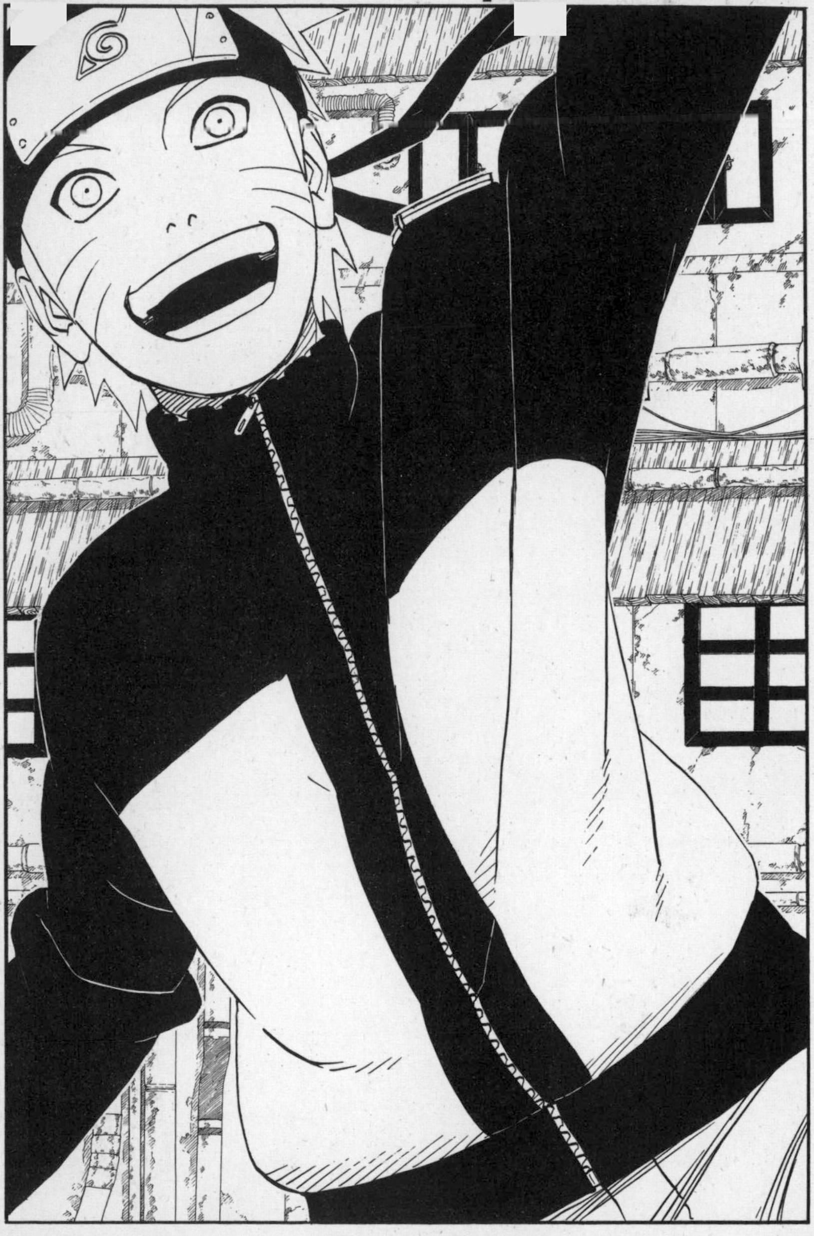

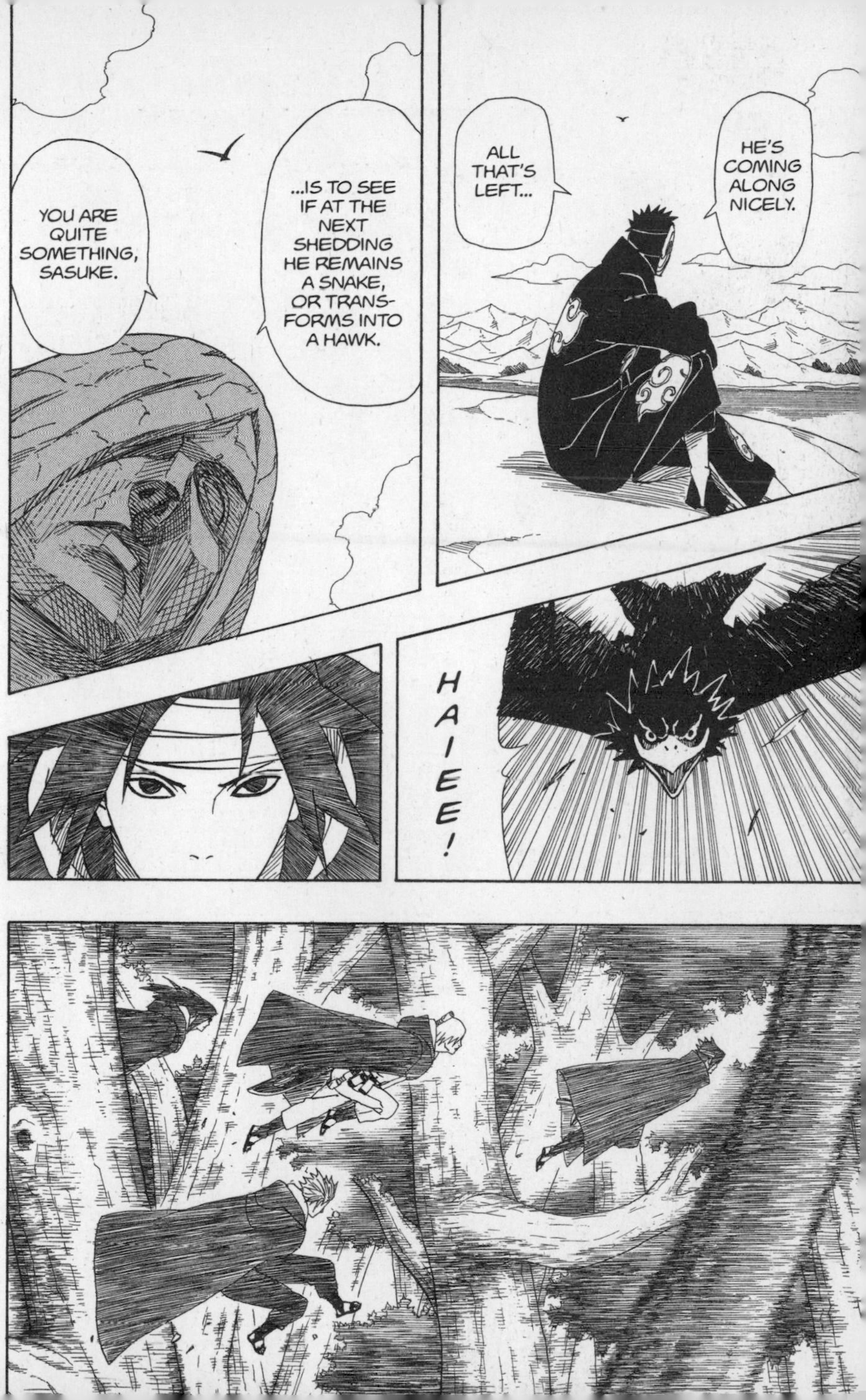
HE'S COMING ALONG NICELY.
ALL THAT'S LEFT...
...IS TO SEE IF AT THE NEXT SHEDDING HE REMAINS A SNAKE, OR TRANSFORMS INTO A HAWK.
YOU ARE QUITE SOMETHING, SASUKE.
HAIEE!

READ THIS WAY

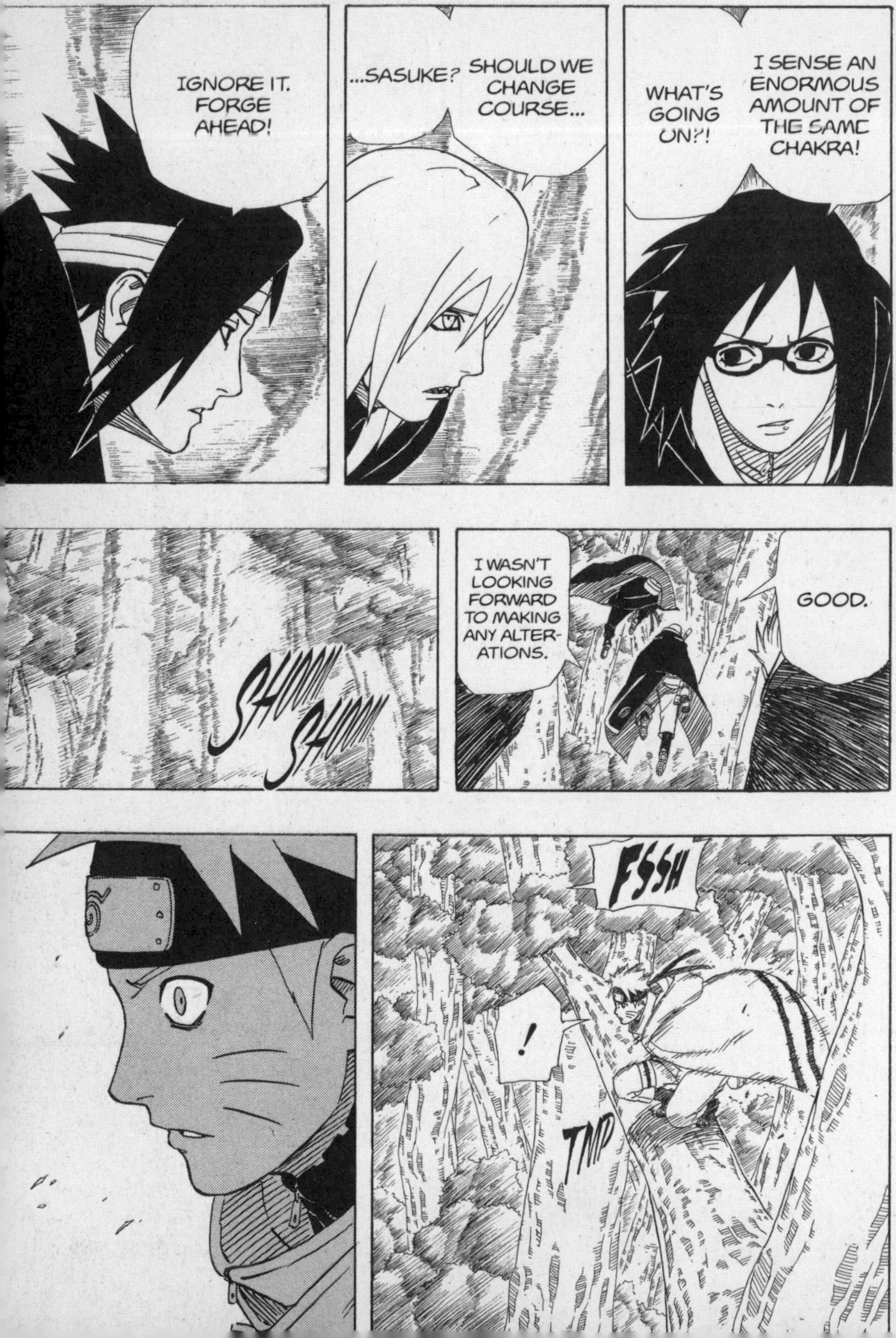
I SENSE AN ENORMOUS AMOUNT OF THE SAME CHAKRA!
WHAT'S GOING ON?!
SHOULD WE CHANGE COURSE...
...SASUKE?
IGNORE IT. FORGE AHEAD!
GOOD.
I WASN'T LOOKING FORWARD TO MAKING ANY ALTERATIONS.
SHOOM SHOOM
FSSH
!
TMP

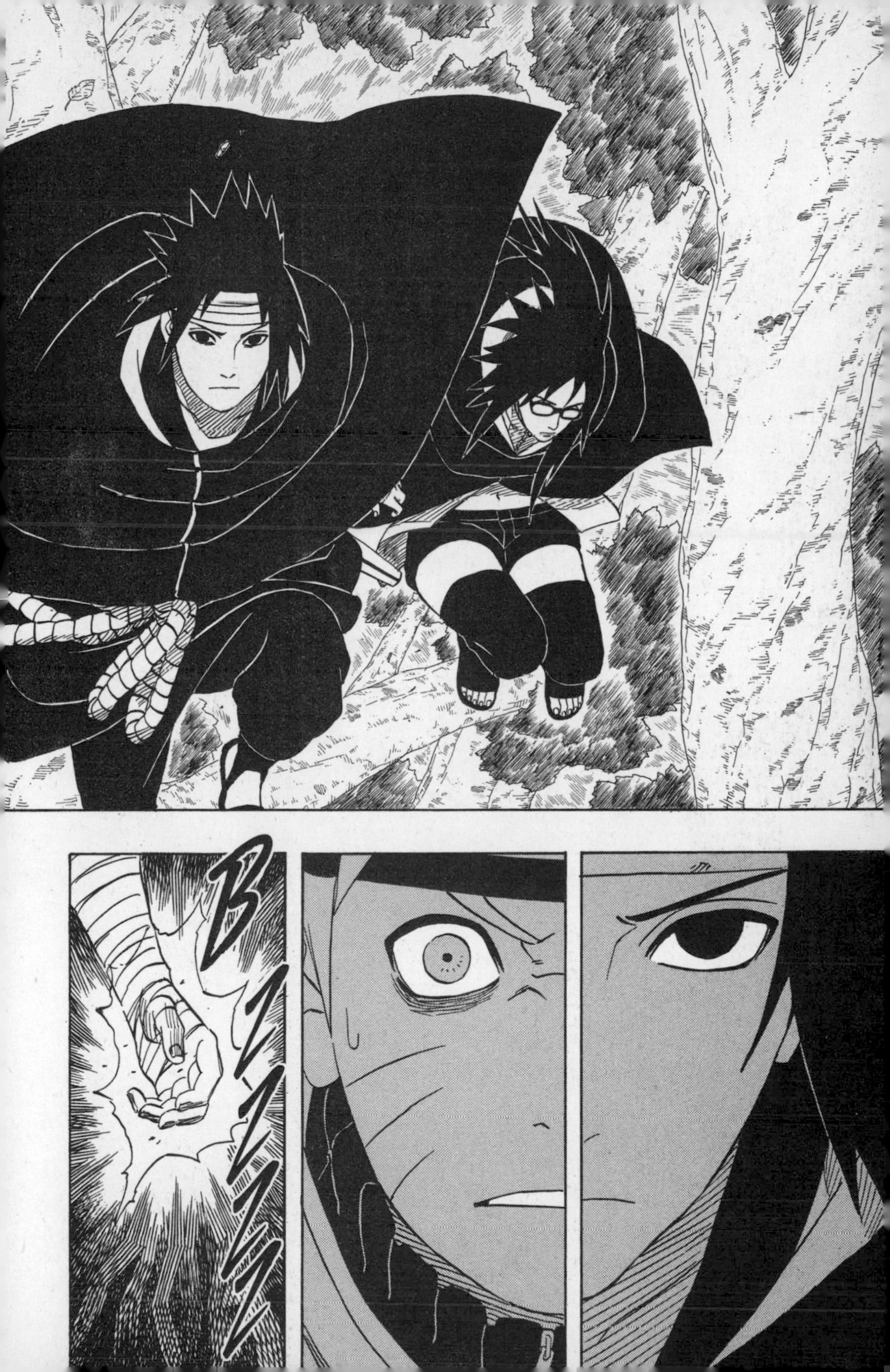
BZZZZZ

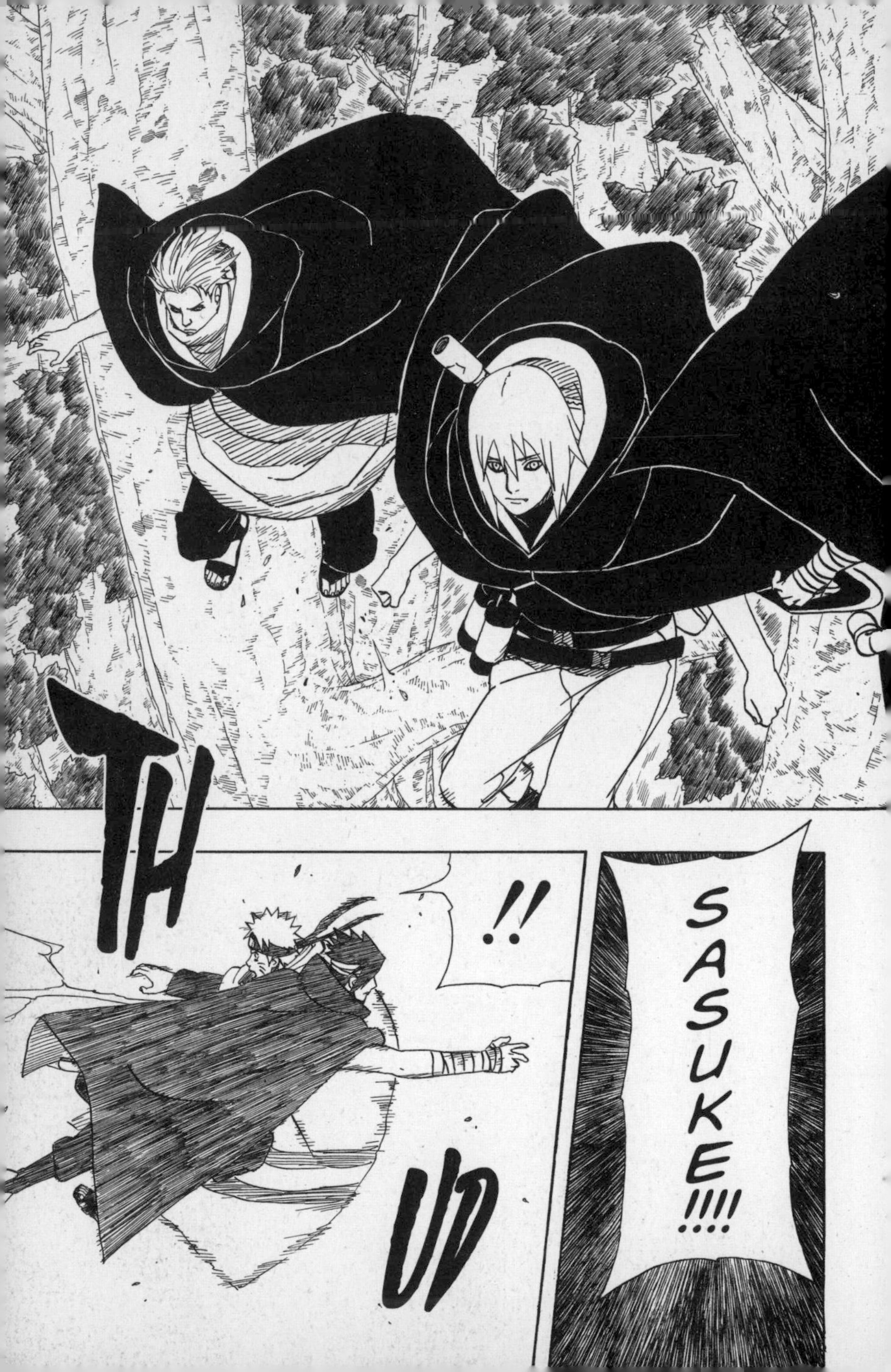
THUD
SASUKE!!!!
!!

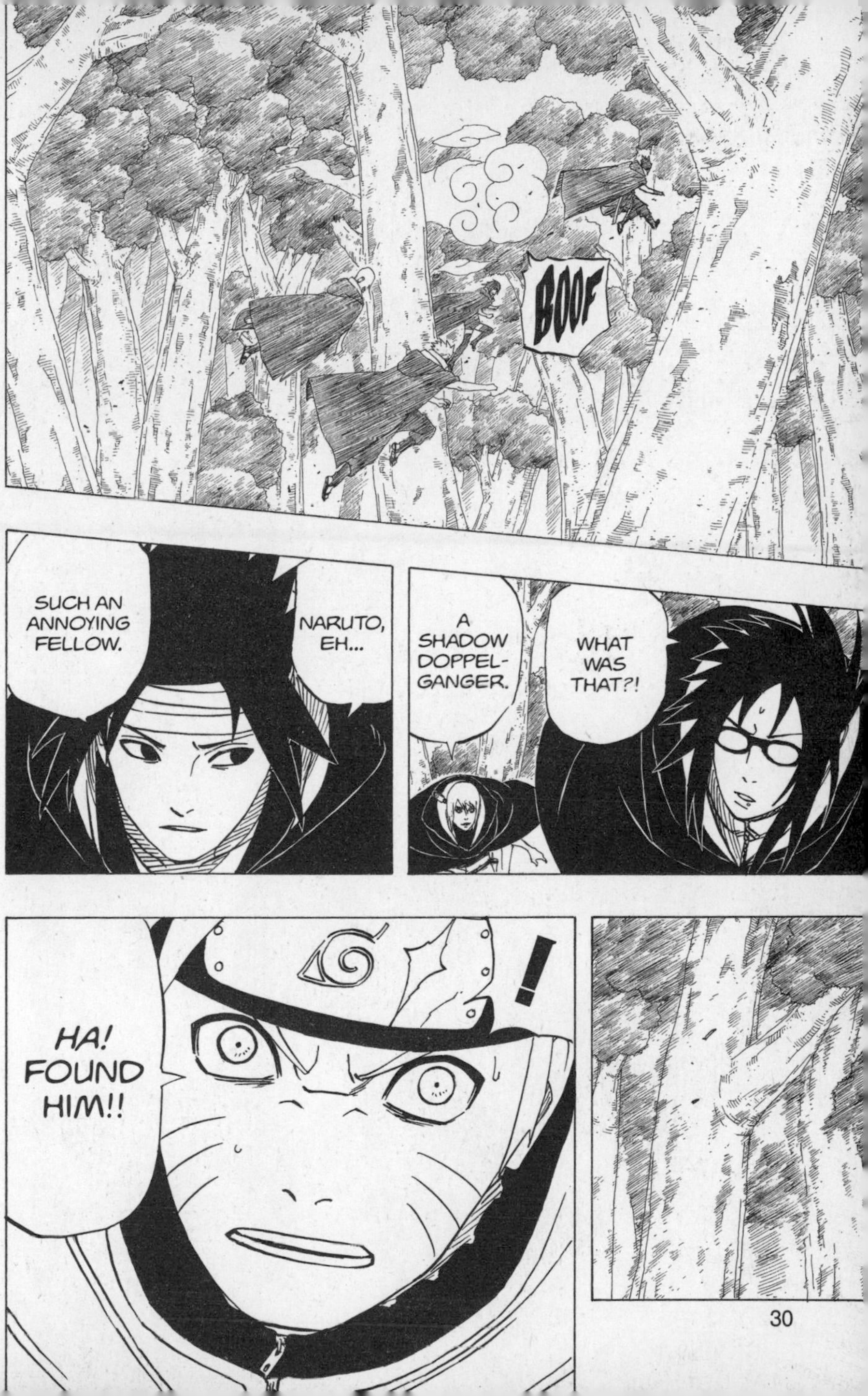
BOOF
WHAT WAS THAT?!
A SHADOW DOPPEL-GANGER.
NARUTO, EH...
SUCH AN ANNOYING FELLOW.
!
HA! FOUND HIM!!

READ THIS WAY

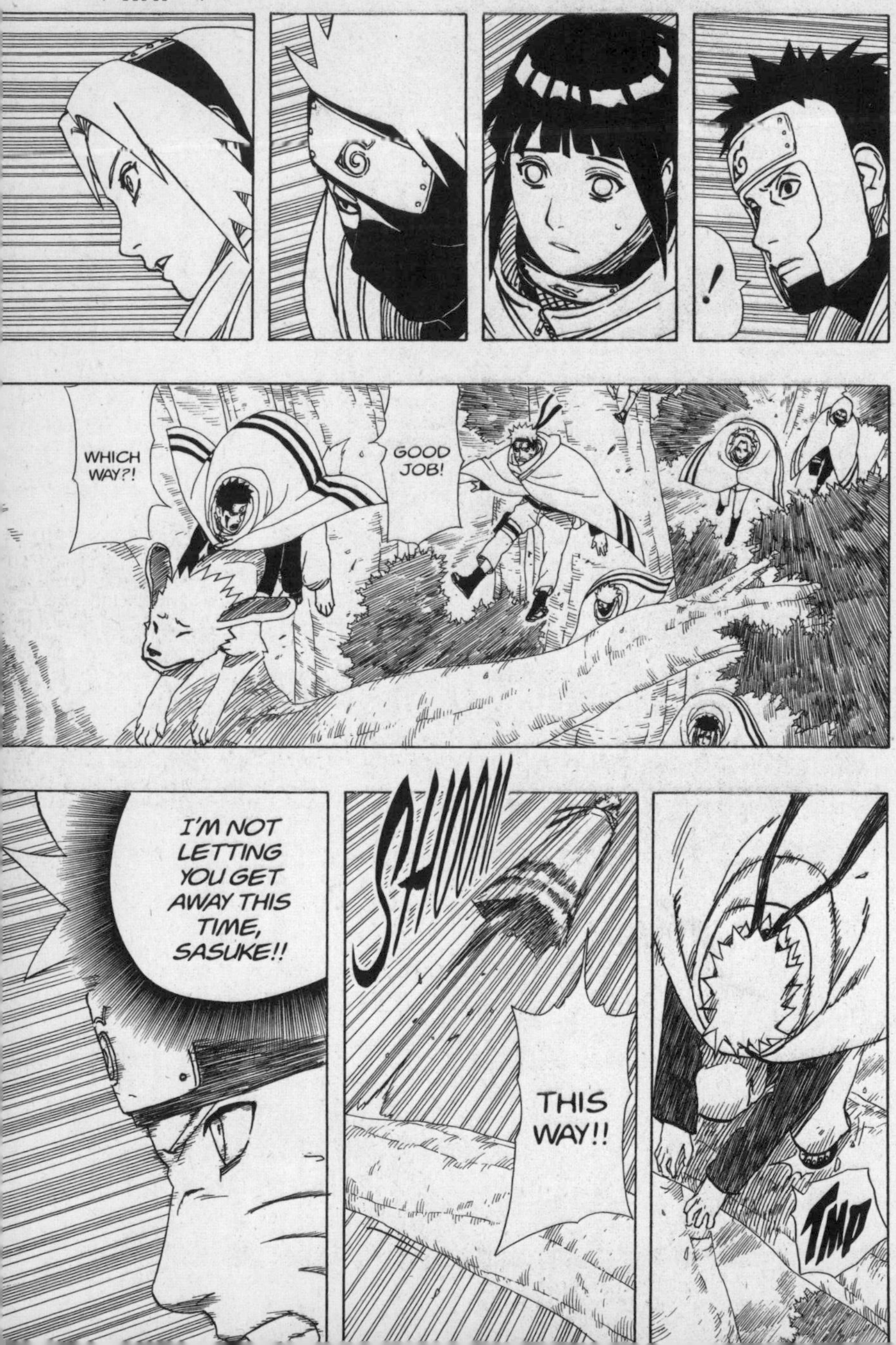
!
GOOD JOB!
WHICH WAY?!
TMP
SHOOM
THIS WAY!!
I'M NOT LETTING YOU GET AWAY THIS TIME, SASUKE!!

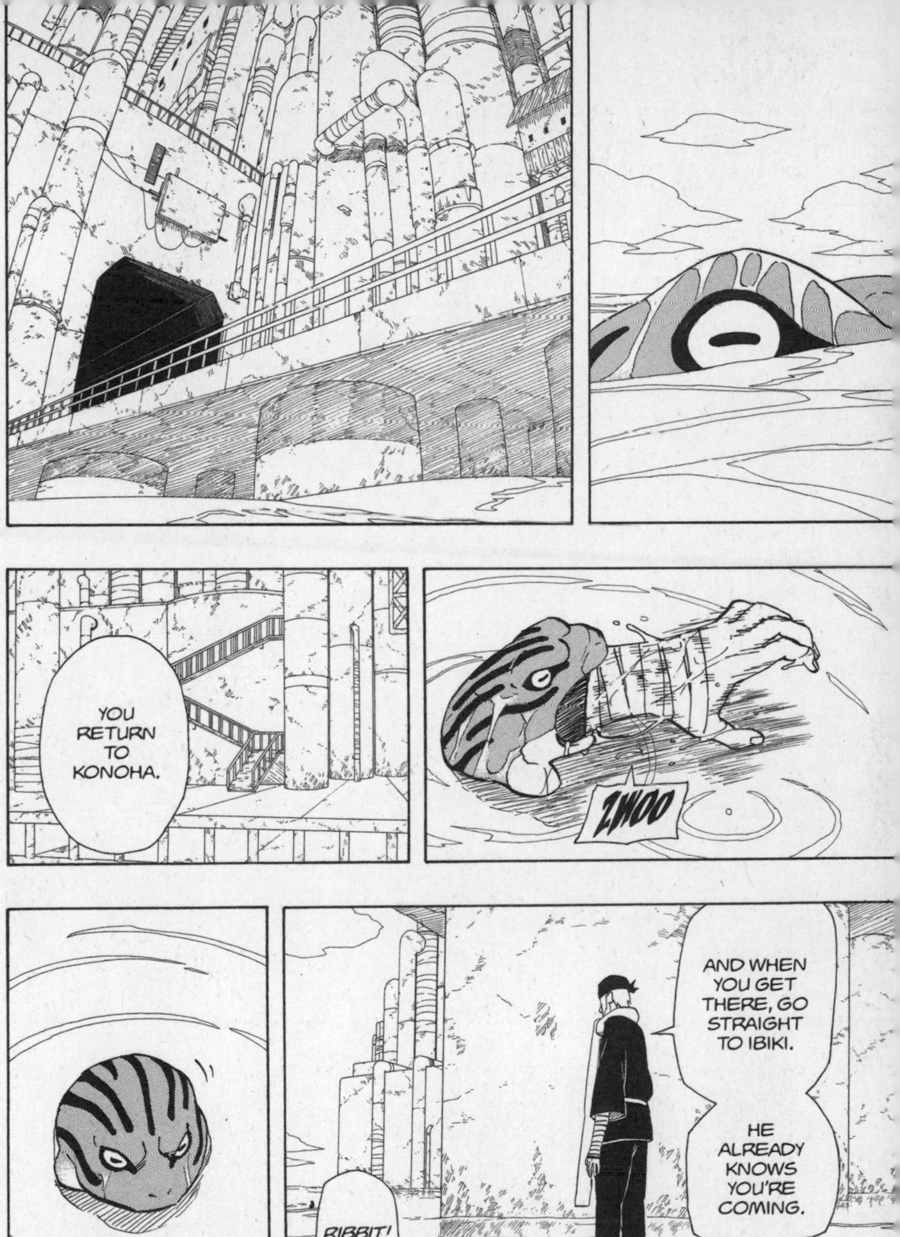
ZWOO
YOU RETURN TO KONOHA.
AND WHEN YOU GET THERE, GO STRAIGHT TO IBIKI.
HE ALREADY KNOWS YOU'RE COMING.
RIBBIT!

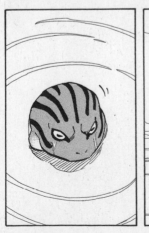

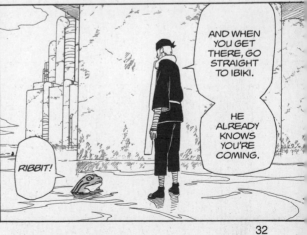

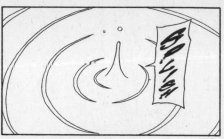

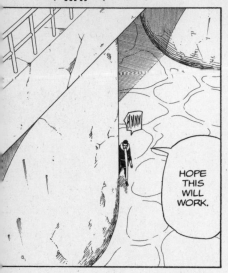

HMM!

HOPE THIS WILL WORK.

SPLISH

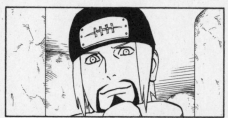

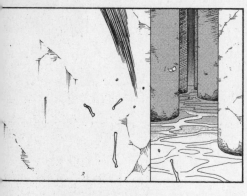

LET'S GO!

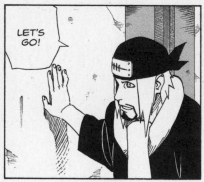

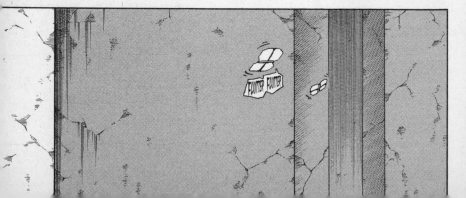

FLUTTER FLUTTER

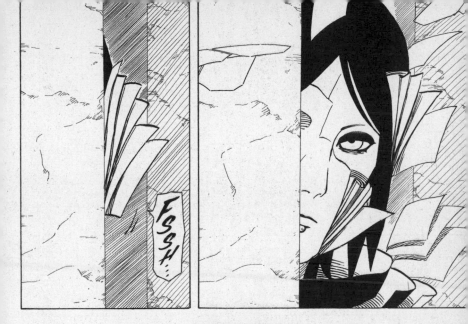

FSSH...

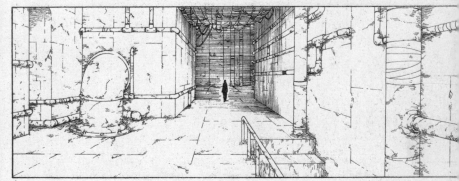

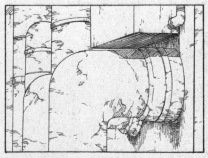

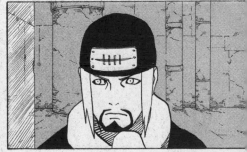

READ THIS WAY

FLAP
ZWOO...
FLAP
FLAP
FLAP
FLAP
FLAP
WELL?
...IT'S JIRAIYA.
...

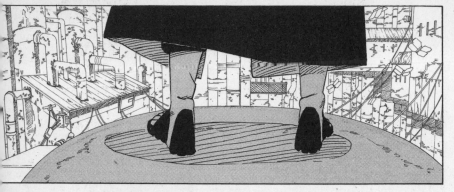

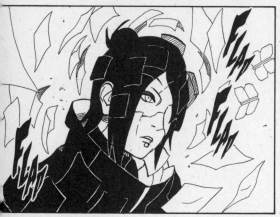

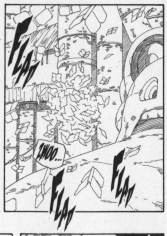

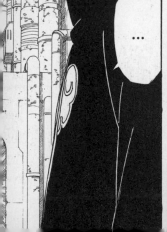

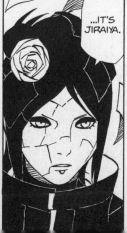

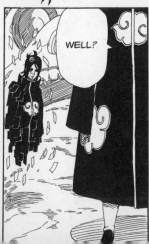

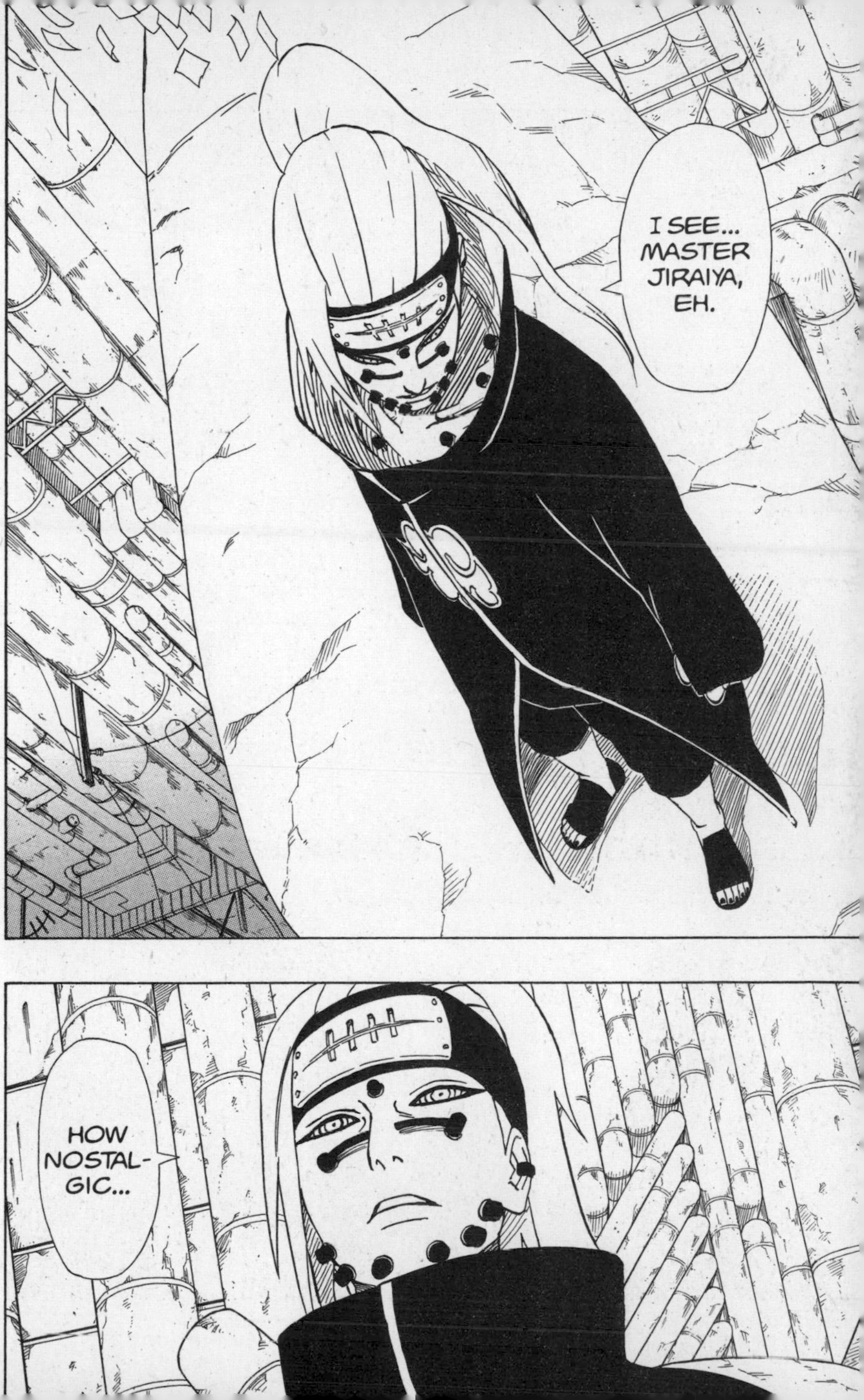
I SEE... MASTER JIRAIYA, EH.
HOW NOSTALGIC...

READ THIS WAY

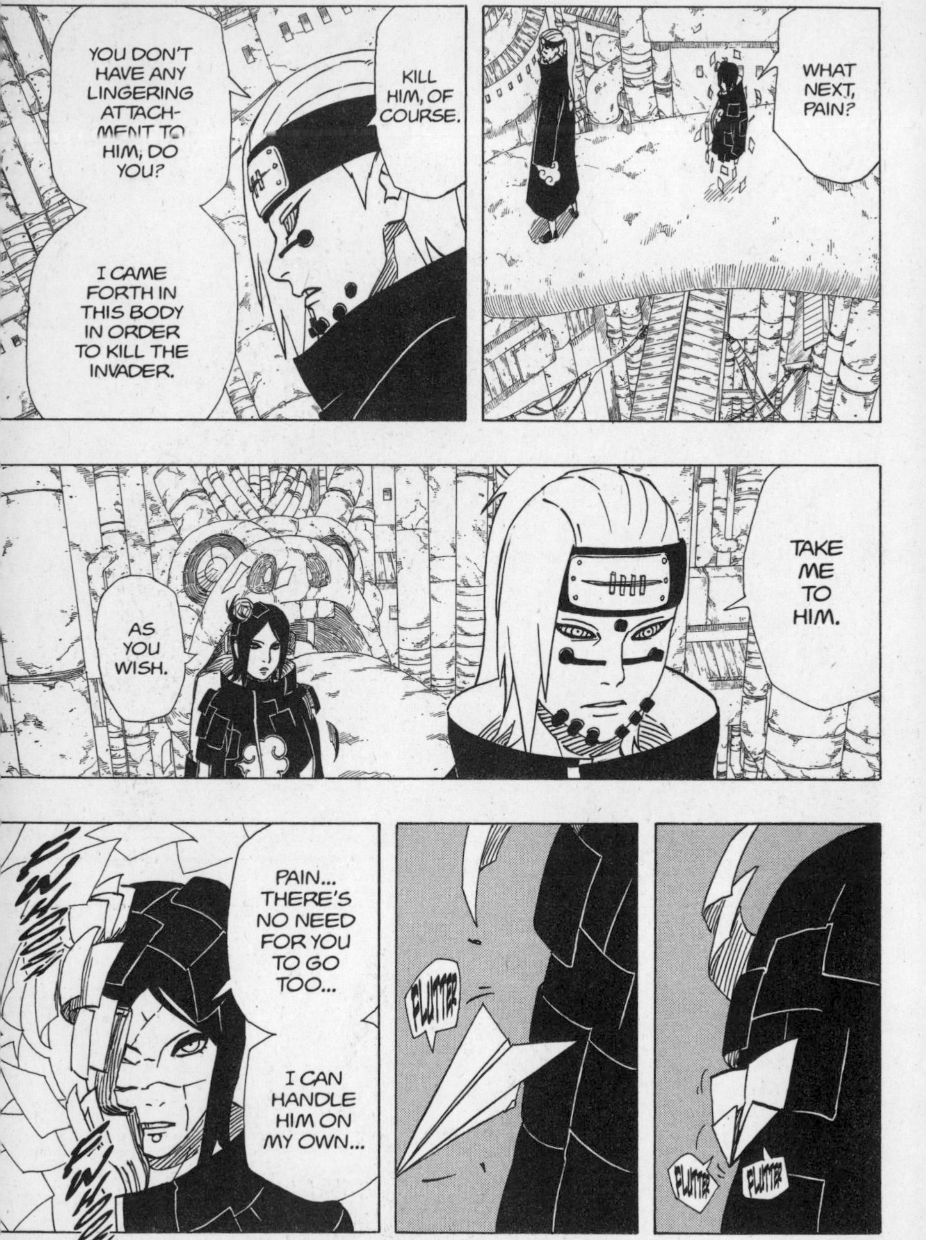
WHAT NEXT, PAIN?
KILL HIM, OF COURSE.
YOU DON'T HAVE ANY LINGERING ATTACH-MENT TO HIM, DO YOU?
I CAME FORTH IN THIS BODY IN ORDER TO KILL THE INVADER.
TAKE ME TO HIM.
AS YOU WISH.
FLUTTER
FLUTTER
FLUTTER
PAIN... THERE'S NO NEED FOR YOU TO GO TOO...
I CAN HANDLE HIM ON MY OWN...

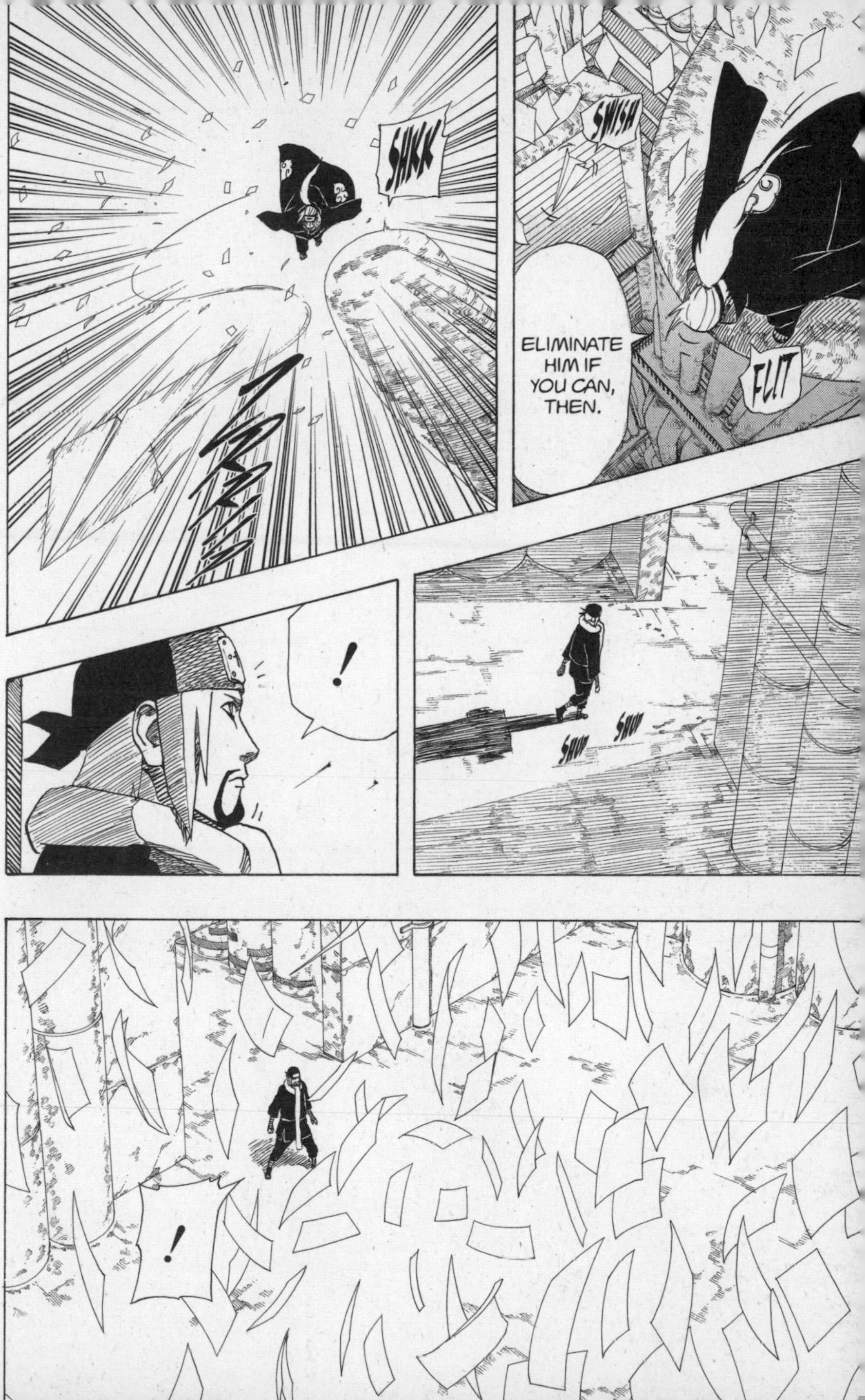
SWISH
ELIMINATE HIM IF YOU CAN, THEN.
FLIT
SHKK
SHU
SHU
!
!

READ THIS WAY

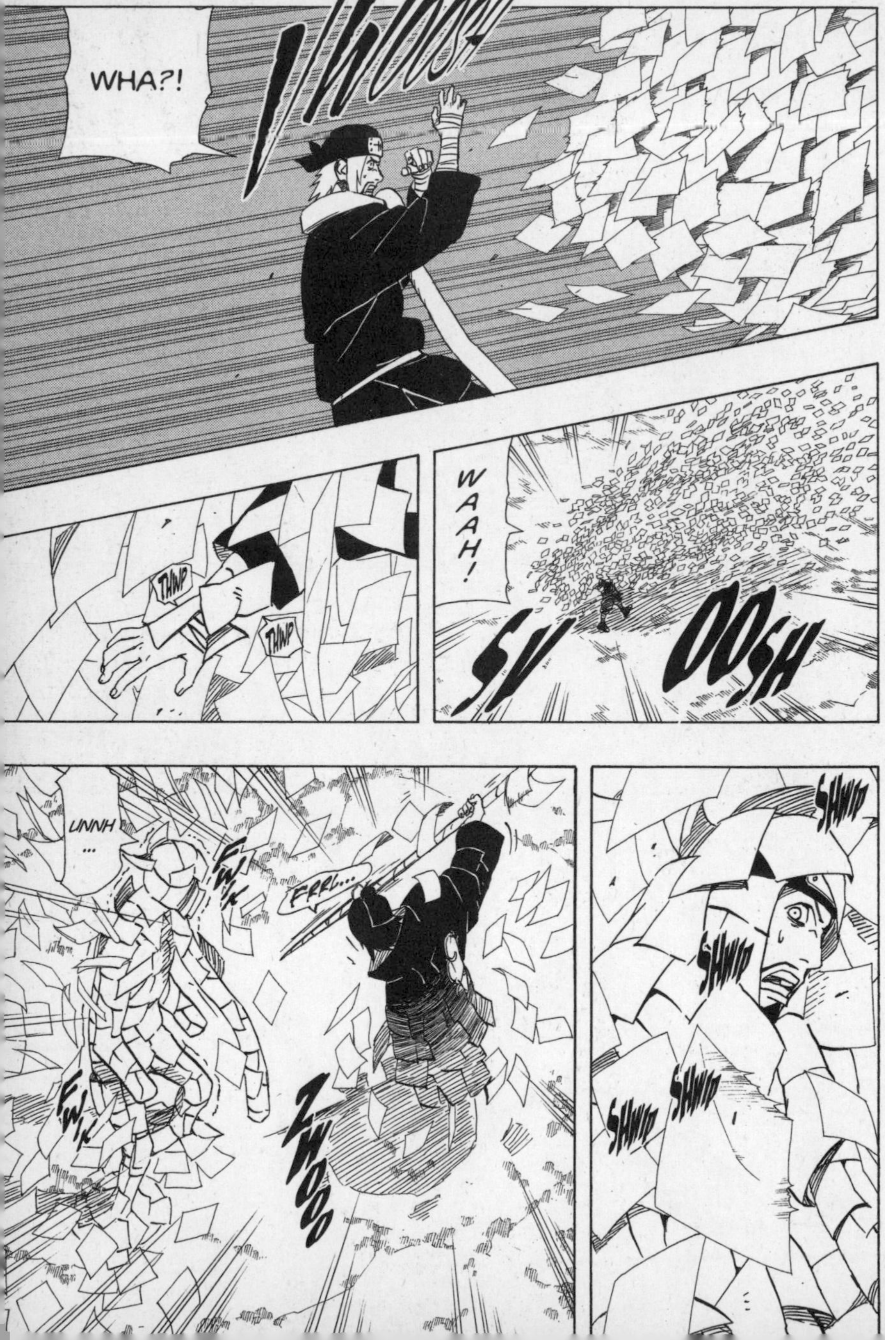

WHA?!
WHOOSH
WAAH!
SWOOSH
THWP
THWP
SHWIP
SHWIP
SHWIP
SHWIP
UNNH ...
FWIK
FRRL...
FWIK
ZWOOO

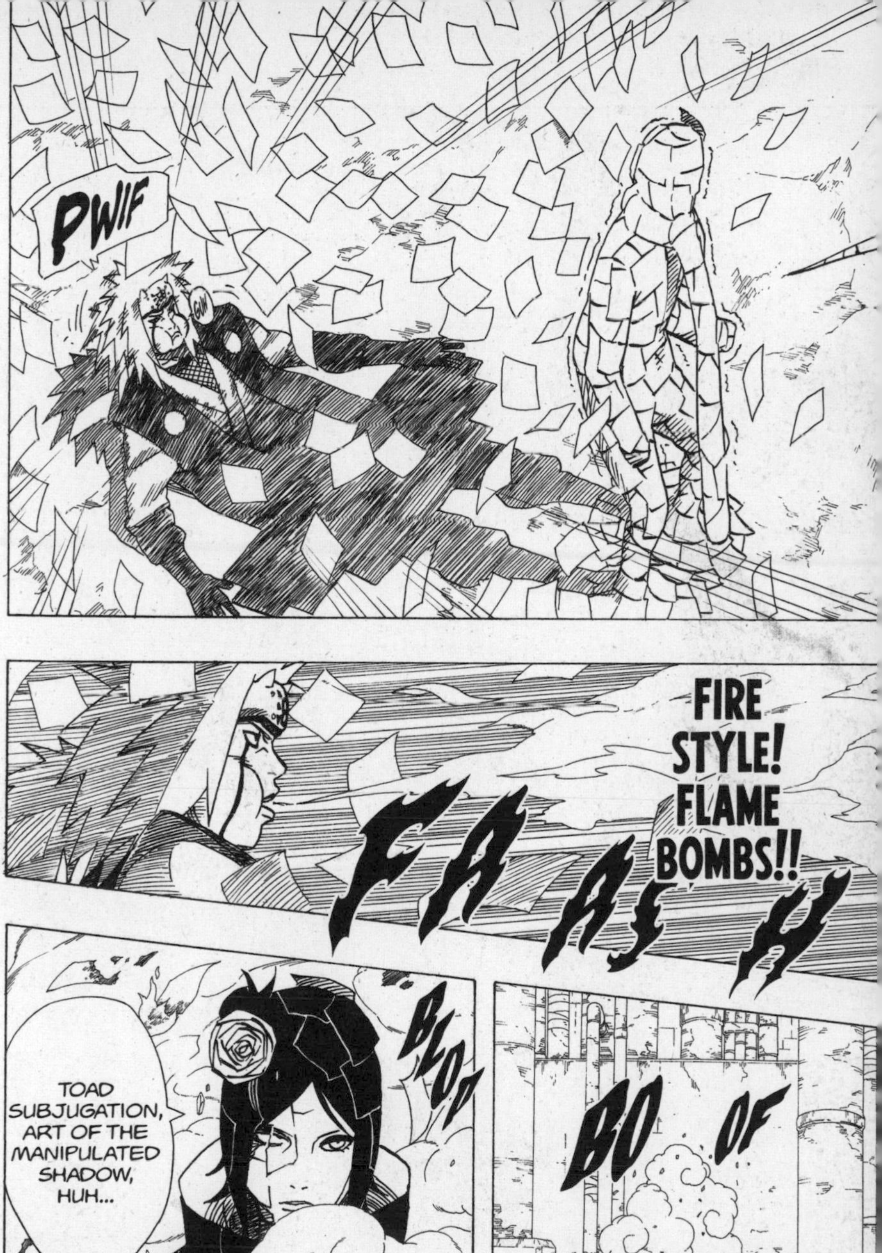
PWIF
GUH
FIRE STYLE! FLAME BOMBS!!
FAASH
BOOF
TOAD SUBJUGATION, ART OF THE MANIPULATED SHADOW, HUH...

READ THIS WAY

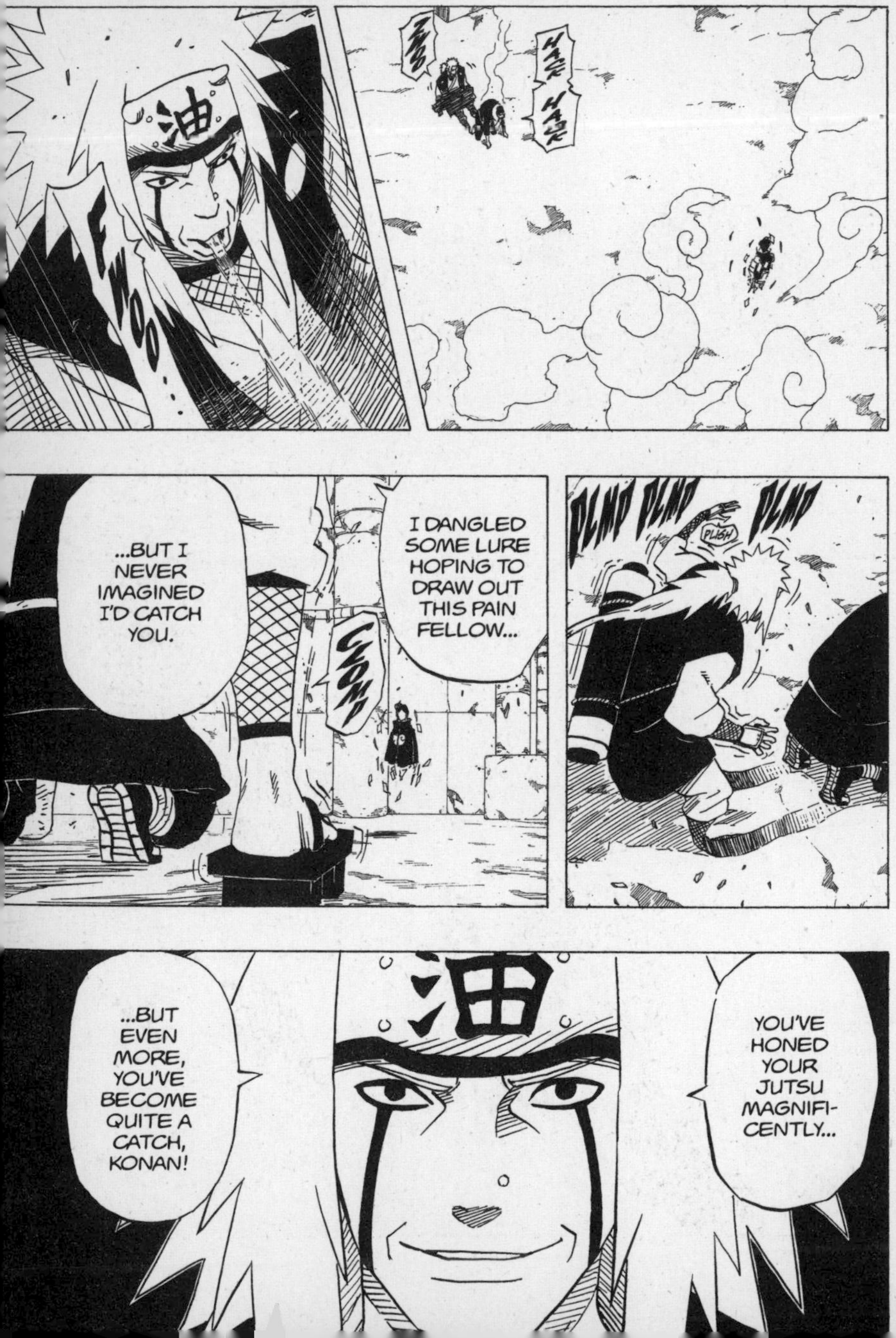
HACK HACK
ZZZ
FWOO
PLMP PLMP PLMP
PLISH
I DANGLED SOME LURE HOPING TO DRAW OUT THIS PAIN FELLOW...
CLOMP
...BUT I NEVER IMAGINED I'D CATCH YOU.
YOU'VE HONED YOUR JUTSU MAGNIFI-CENTLY...
...BUT EVEN MORE, YOU'VE BECOME QUITE A CATCH, KONAN!

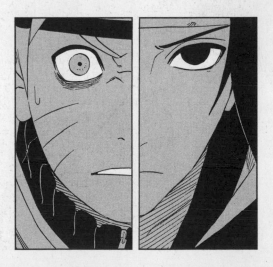

Number 372: The Weeping Land!!

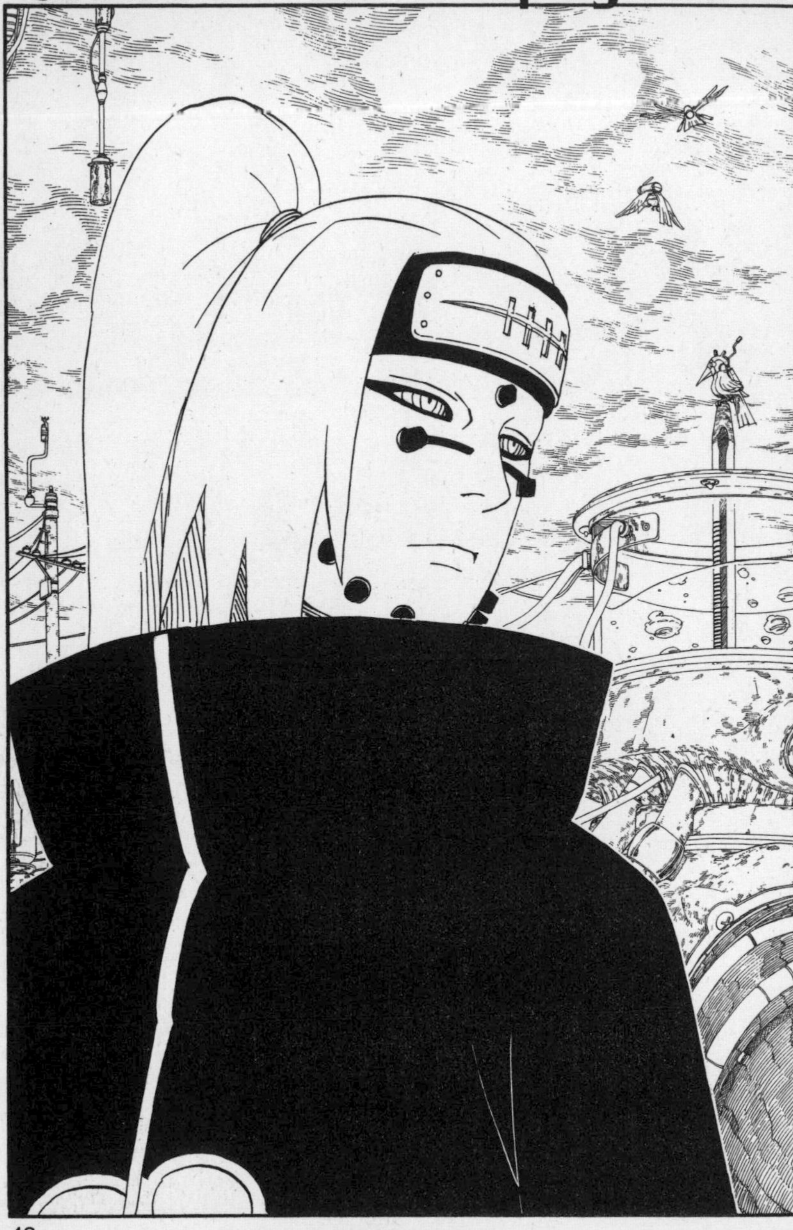

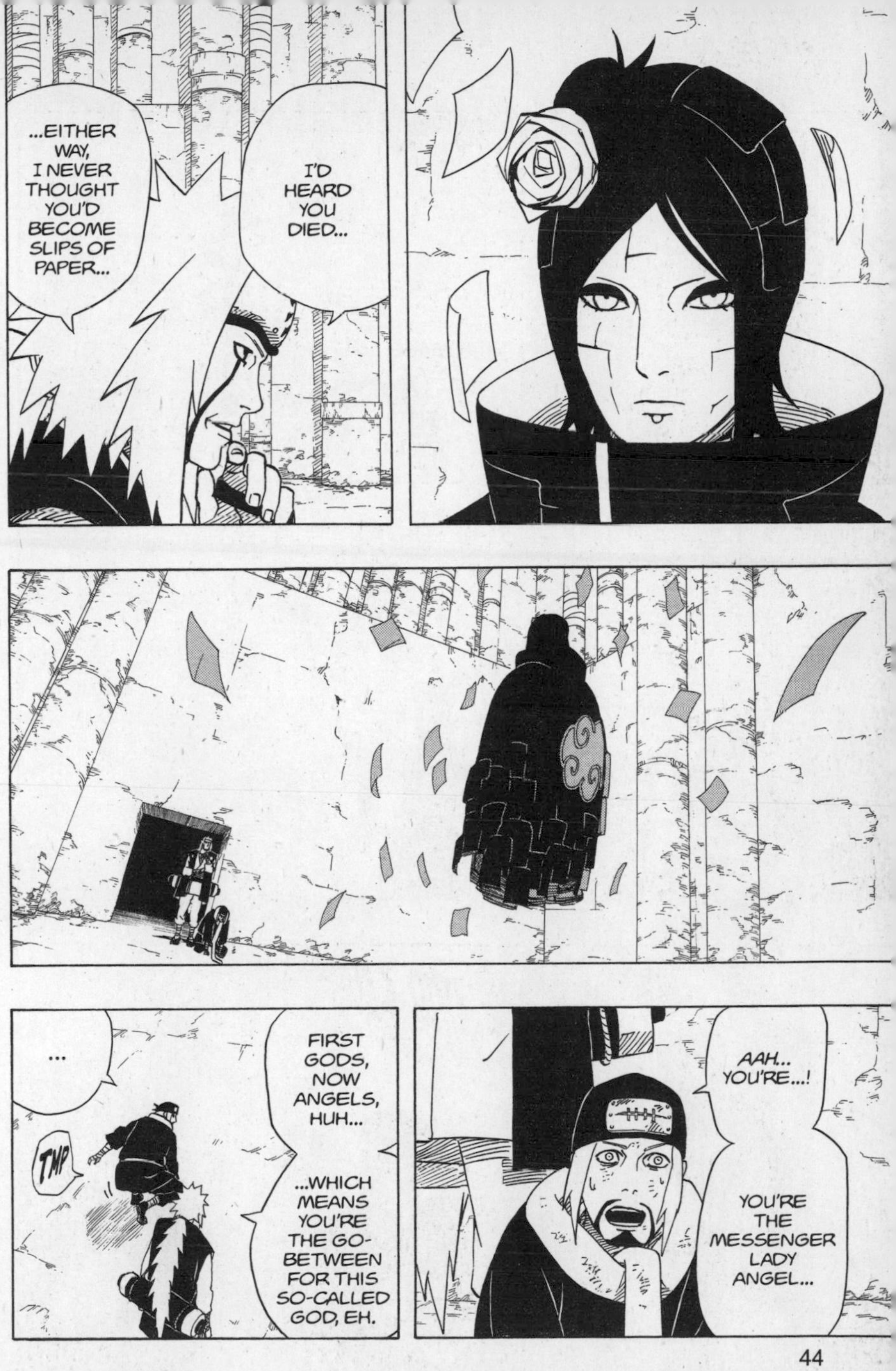
I'D HEARD YOU DIED...
...EITHER WAY, I NEVER THOUGHT YOU'D BECOME SLIPS OF PAPER...
AAH... YOU'RE...!
YOU'RE THE MESSENGER LADY ANGEL...
FIRST GODS, NOW ANGELS, HUH...
...WHICH MEANS YOU'RE THE GO-BETWEEN FOR THIS SO-CALLED GOD, EH.
...
TMP

READ THIS WAY

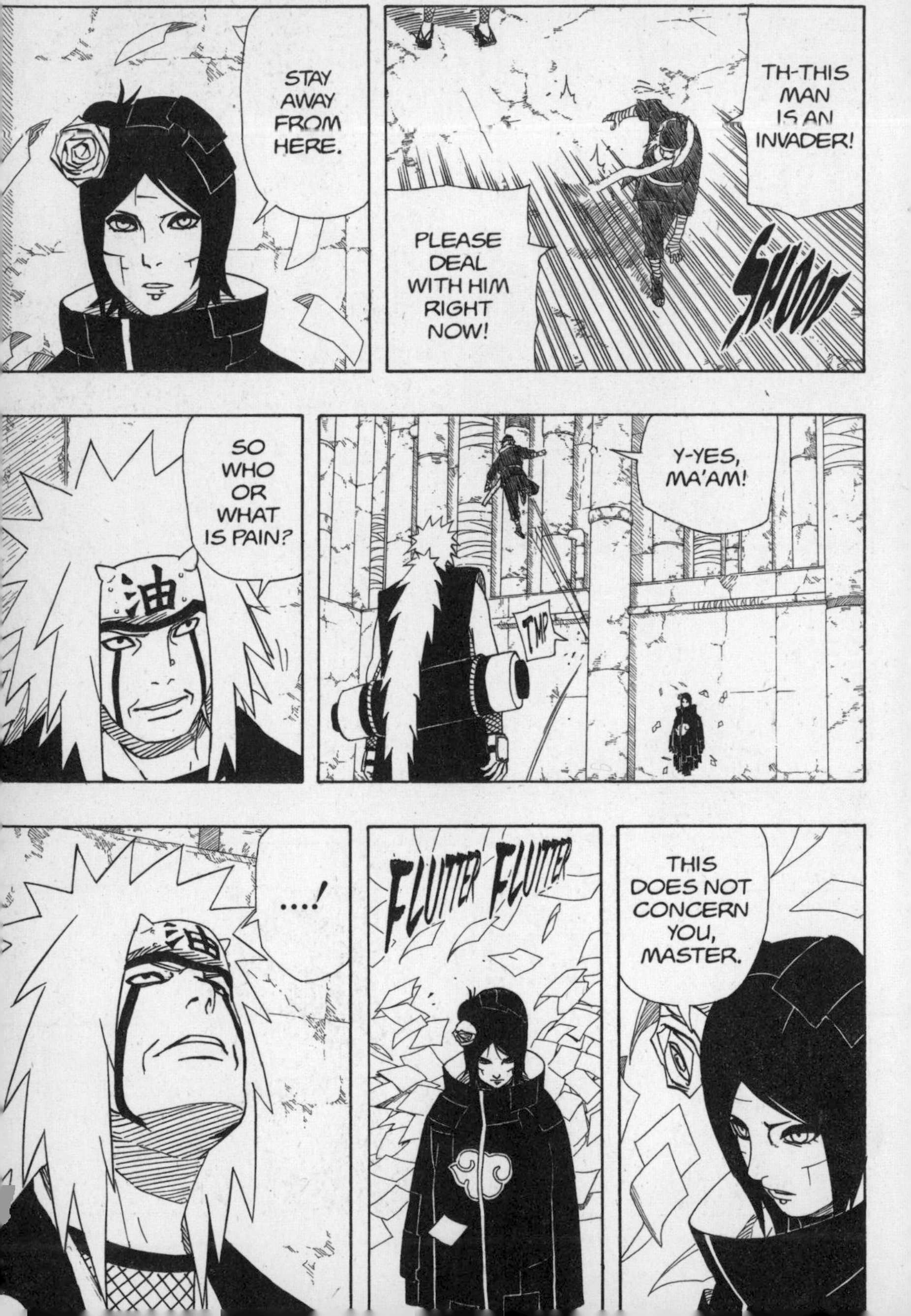
TH-THIS MAN IS AN INVADER!
PLEASE DEAL WITH HIM RIGHT NOW!
SHOOO
STAY AWAY FROM HERE.
Y-YES, MA'AM!
TMP
SO WHO OR WHAT IS PAIN?
油
THIS DOES NOT CONCERN YOU, MASTER.
FLUTTER FLUTTER
...!

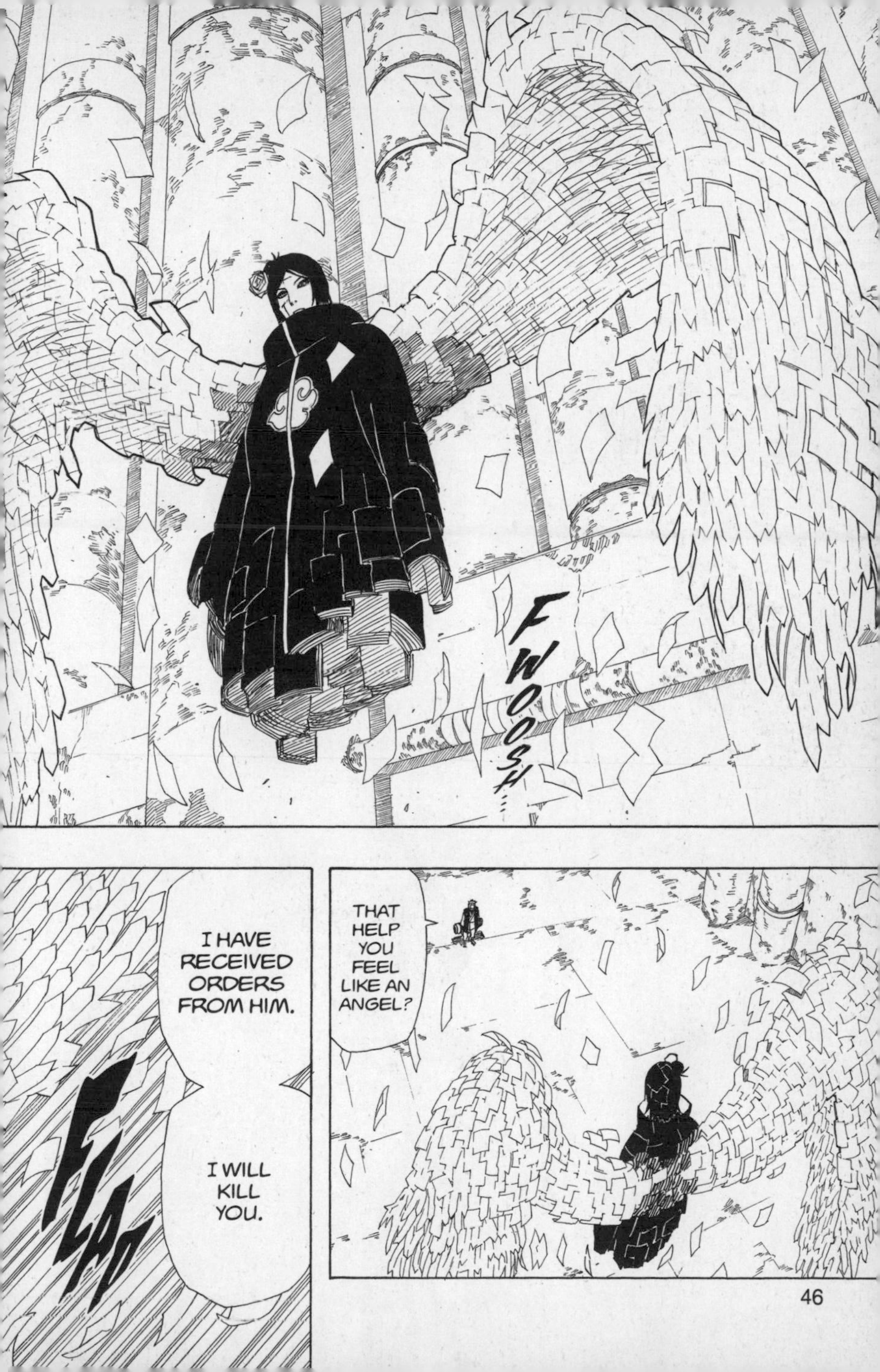
FWOOSH...
THAT HELP YOU FEEL LIKE AN ANGEL?
I HAVE RECEIVED ORDERS FROM HIM.
I WILL KILL YOU.
FLAP

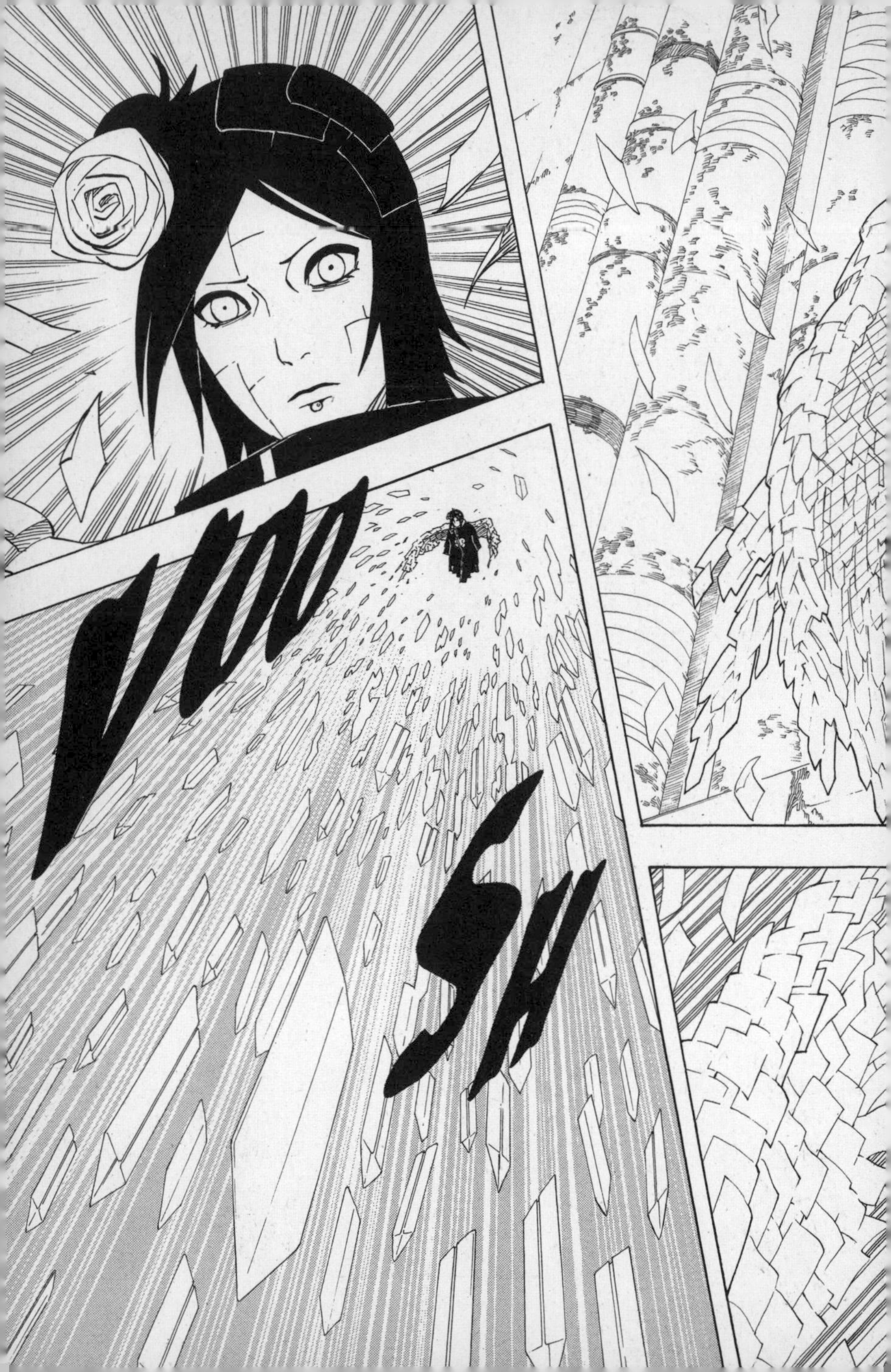
VOOO
SH

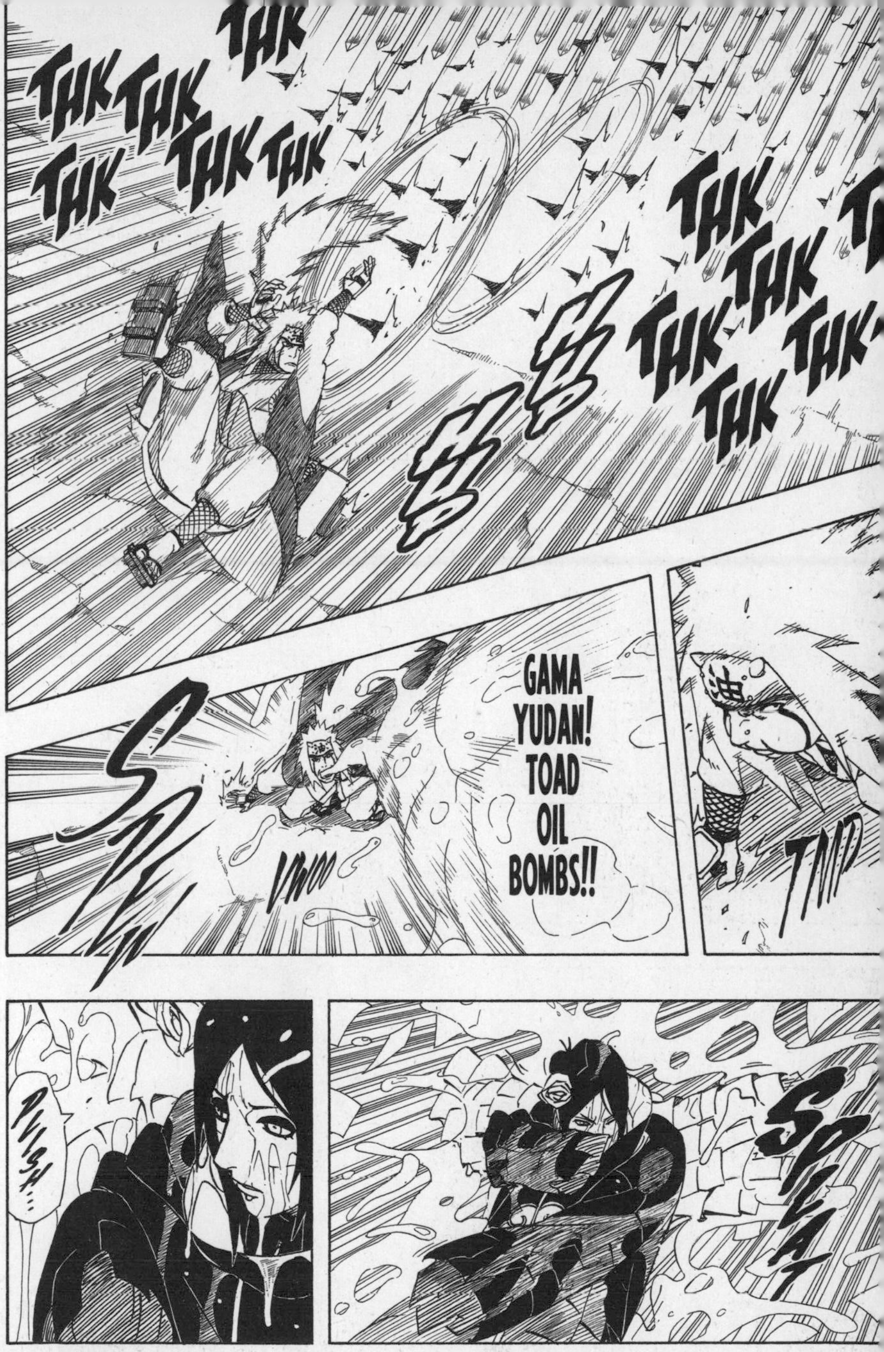
THK THK THK THK THK THK
THK THK THK THK THK THK
TMP
GAMA YUDAN! TOAD OIL BOMBS!!
VWOO
SPLAT

READ THIS WAY

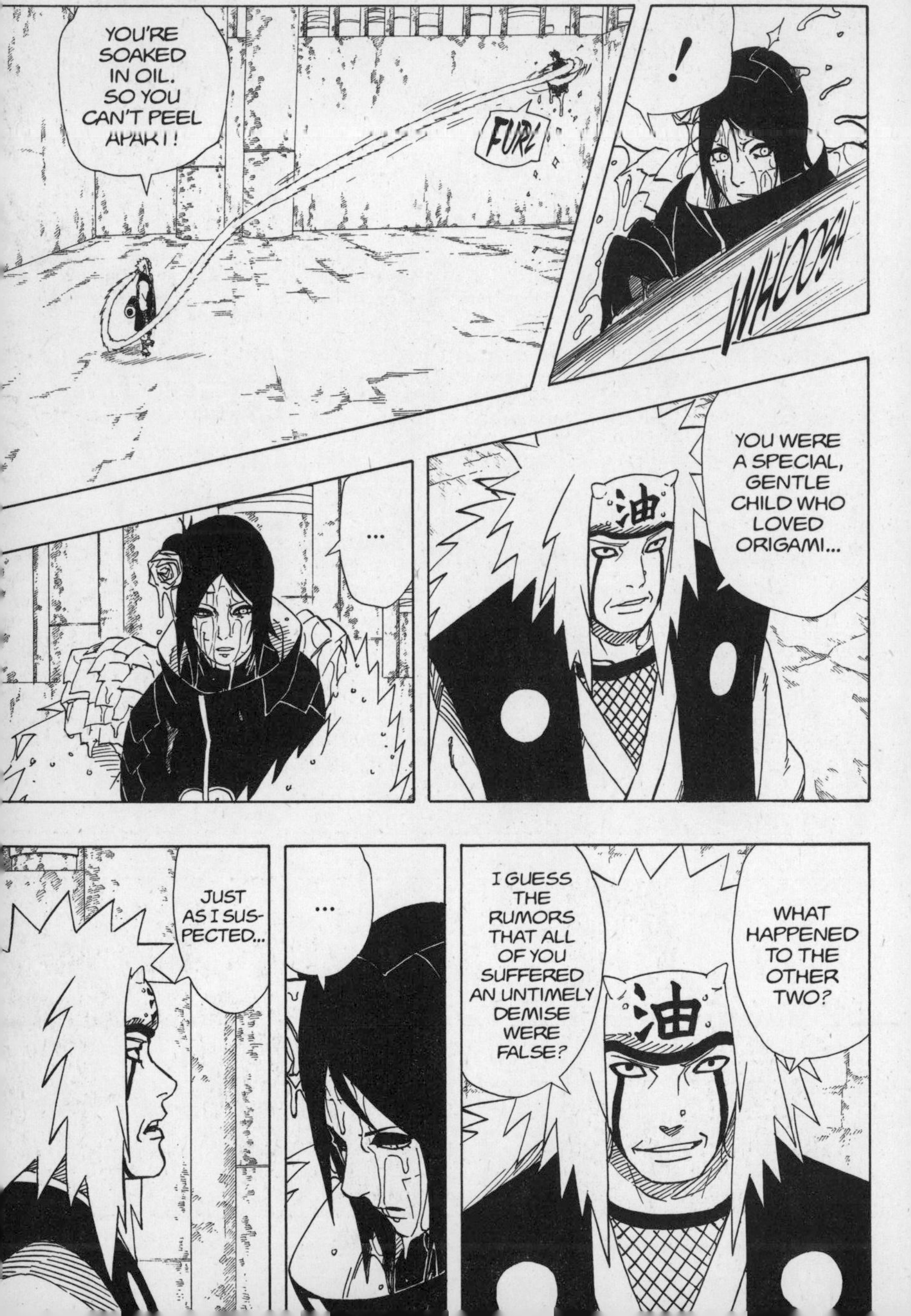
!
WHOOSH
YOU'RE SOAKED IN OIL. SO YOU CAN'T PEEL APART!
FURL
YOU WERE A SPECIAL, GENTLE CHILD WHO LOVED ORIGAMI...
...
WHAT HAPPENED TO THE OTHER TWO?
I GUESS THE RUMORS THAT ALL OF YOU SUFFERED AN UNTIMELY DEMISE WERE FALSE?
...
JUST AS I SUSPECTED...

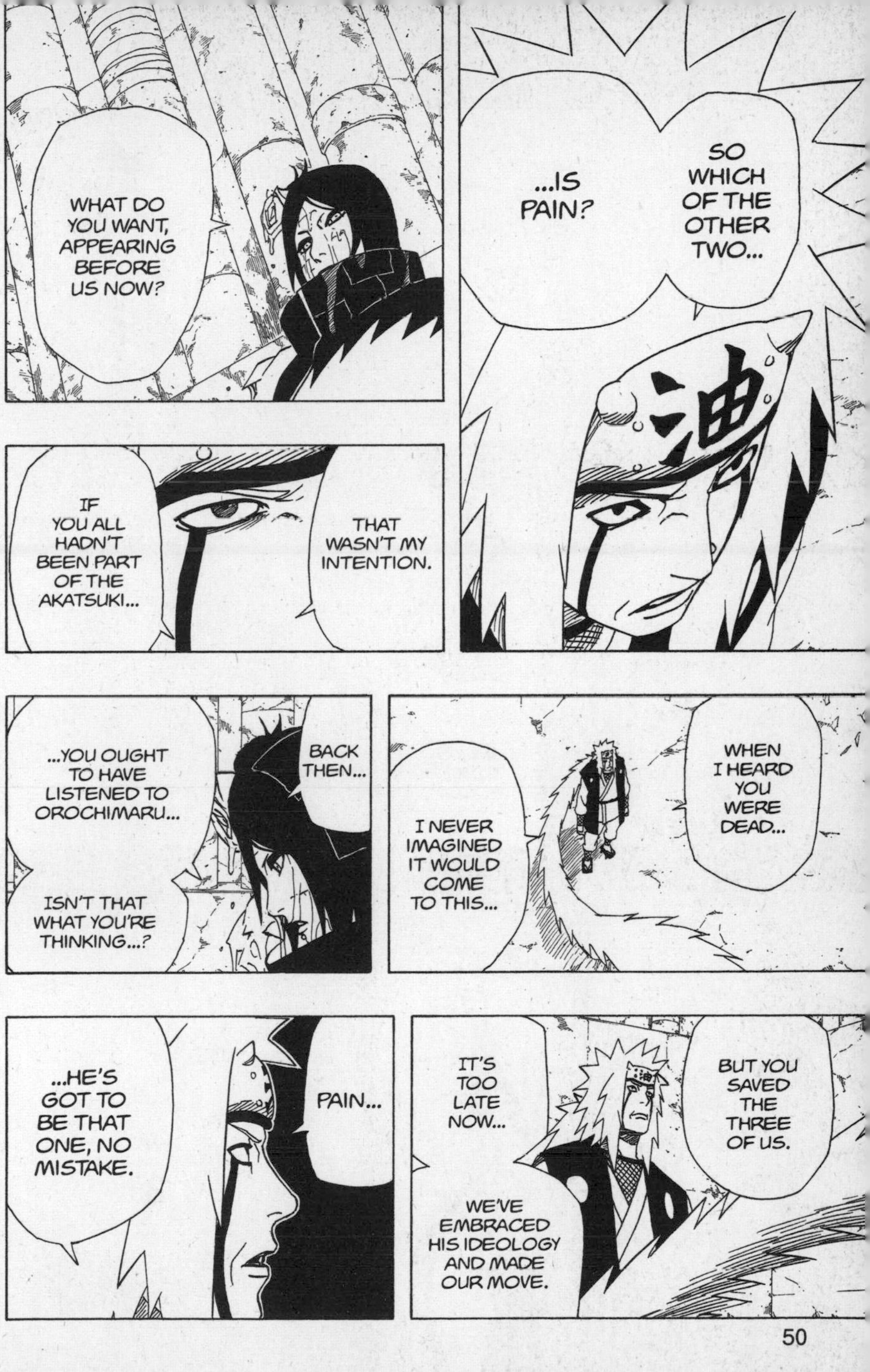
SO WHICH OF THE OTHER TWO...
...IS PAIN?
WHAT DO YOU WANT, APPEARING BEFORE US NOW?
THAT WASN'T MY INTENTION.
IF YOU ALL HADN'T BEEN PART OF THE AKATSUKI...
WHEN I HEARD YOU WERE DEAD...
I NEVER IMAGINED IT WOULD COME TO THIS...
BACK THEN...
...YOU OUGHT TO HAVE LISTENED TO OROCHIMARU...
ISN'T THAT WHAT YOU'RE THINKING...?
BUT YOU SAVED THE THREE OF US.
IT'S TOO LATE NOW...
WE'VE EMBRACED HIS IDEOLOGY AND MADE OUR MOVE.
PAIN...
...HE'S GOT TO BE THAT ONE, NO MISTAKE.

READ THIS WAY

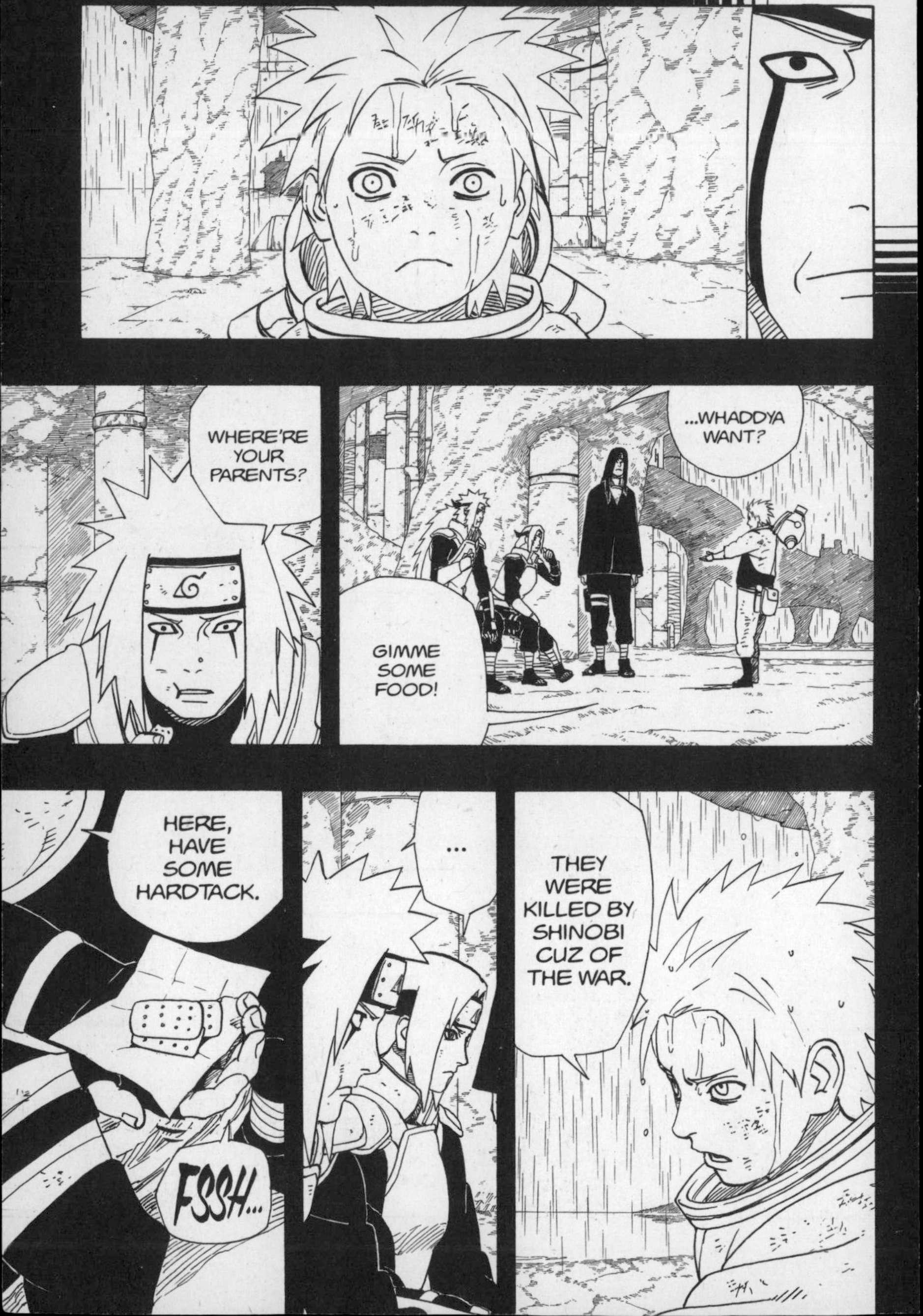
...WHADDYA WANT?
GIMME SOME FOOD!
WHERE'RE YOUR PARENTS?
THEY WERE KILLED BY SHINOBI CUZ OF THE WAR.
...
HERE, HAVE SOME HARDTACK.
FSSH...

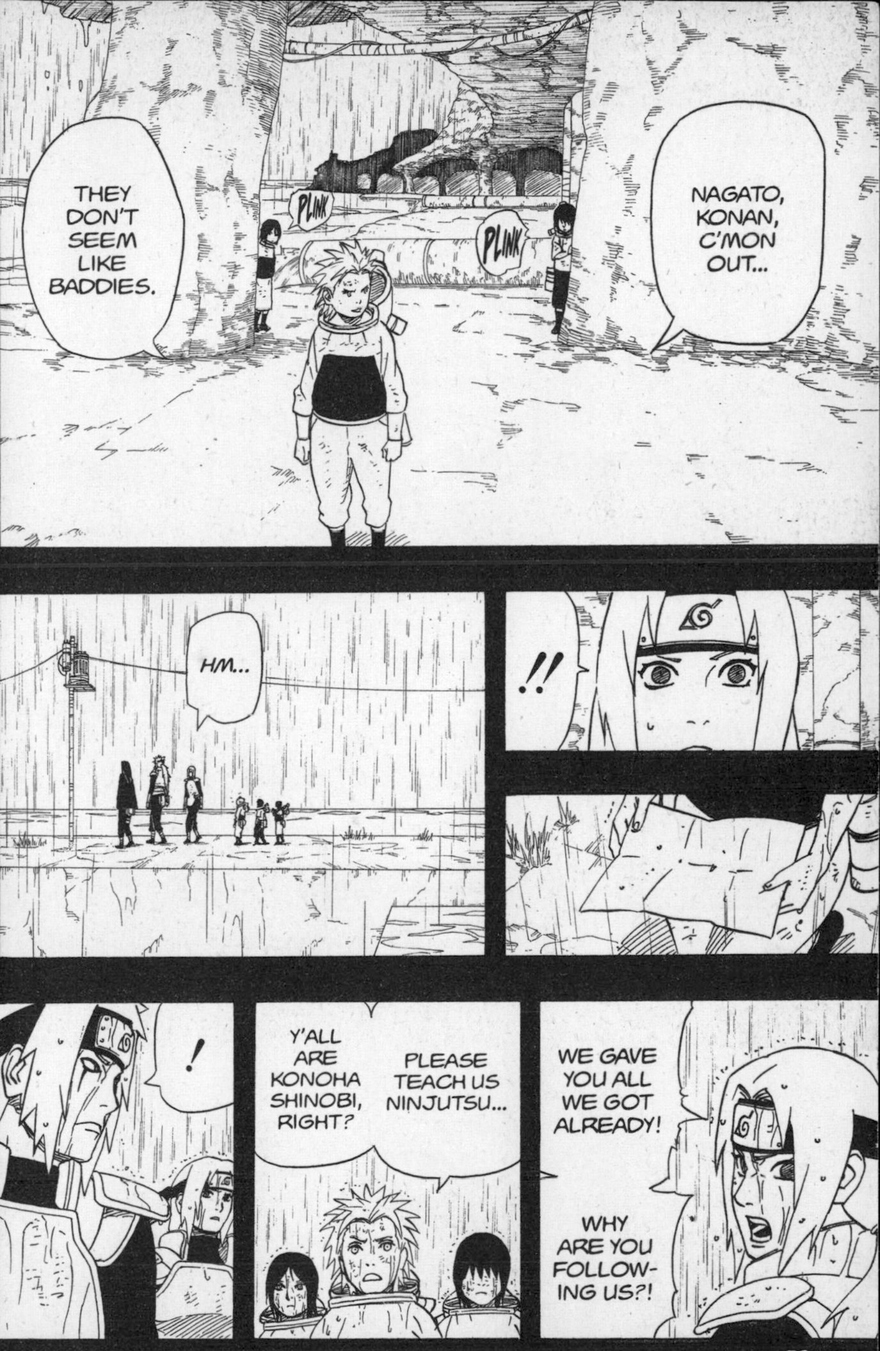
NAGATO, KONAN, C'MON OUT...
THEY DON'T SEEM LIKE BADDIES.
PLINK
PLINK
!!
HM...
WE GAVE YOU ALL WE GOT ALREADY!
WHY ARE YOU FOLLOW-ING US?!
Y'ALL ARE KONOHA SHINOBI, RIGHT? PLEASE TEACH US NINJUTSU...
!

READ THIS WAY

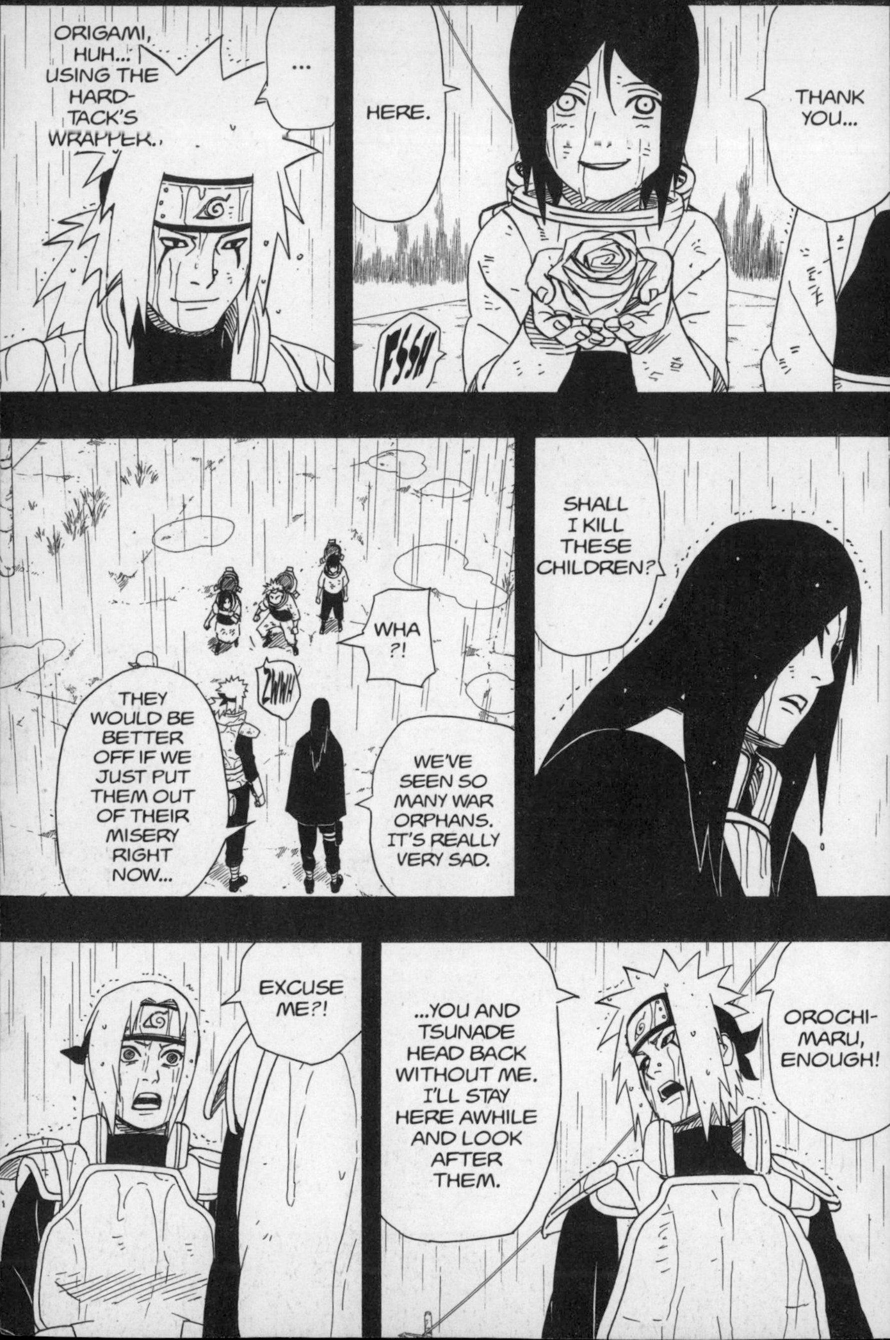
THANK YOU...
HERE.
FSSH
...
ORIGAMI, HUH... USING THE HARD-TACK'S WRAPPER..
SHALL I KILL THESE CHILDREN?
WHA?!
ZWWH
WE'VE SEEN SO MANY WAR ORPHANS. IT'S REALLY VERY SAD.
THEY WOULD BE BETTER OFF IF WE JUST PUT THEM OUT OF THEIR MISERY RIGHT NOW...
OROCHIMARU, ENOUGH!
...YOU AND TSUNADE HEAD BACK WITHOUT ME. I'LL STAY HERE AWHILE AND LOOK AFTER THEM.
EXCUSE ME?!

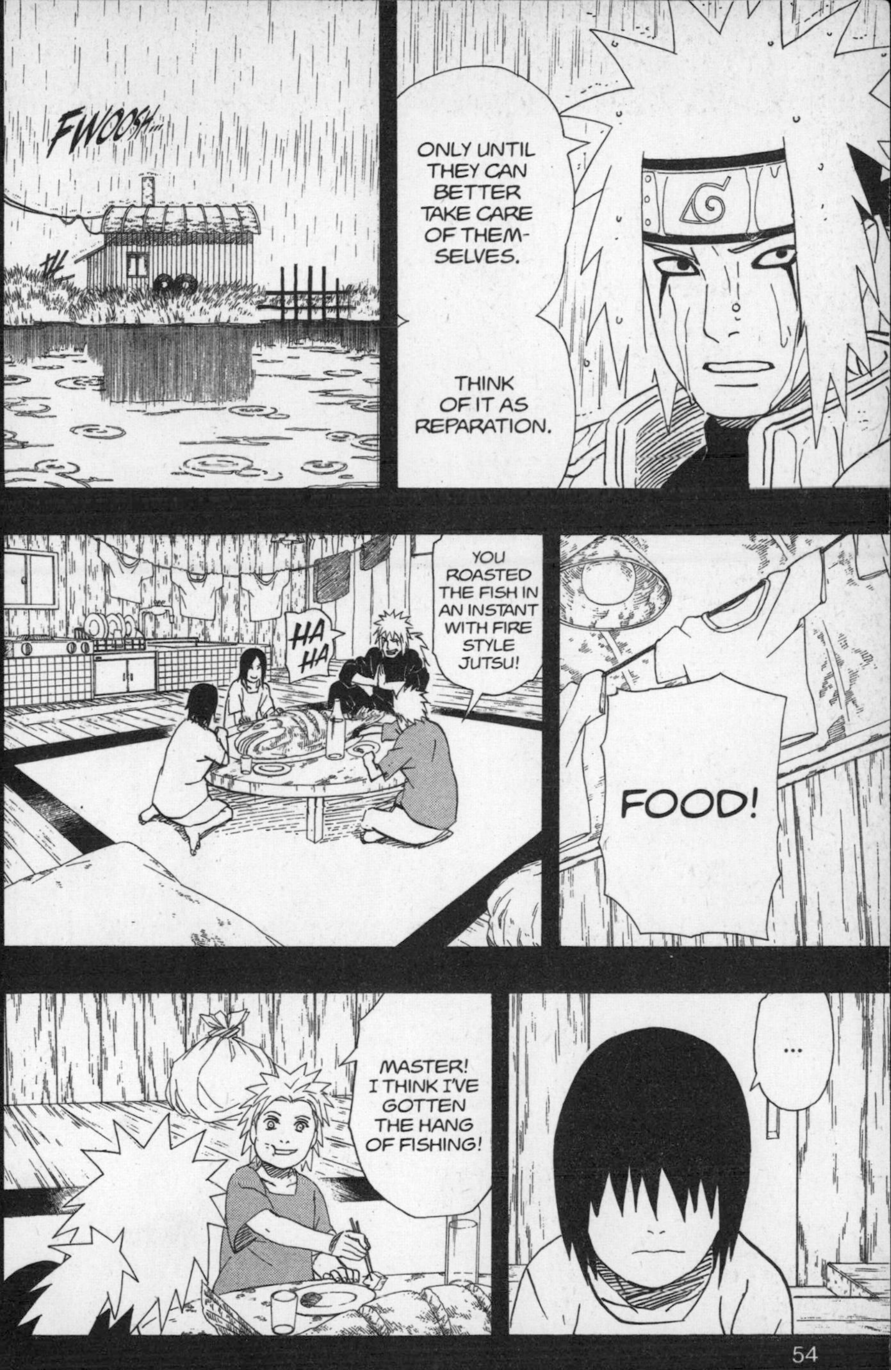
ONLY UNTIL THEY CAN BETTER TAKE CARE OF THEM-SELVES.
THINK OF IT AS REPARATION.
FWOOSH...
FOOD!
YOU ROASTED THE FISH IN AN INSTANT WITH FIRE STYLE JUTSU!
HA HA
...
MASTER! I THINK I'VE GOTTEN THE HANG OF FISHING!

READ THIS WAY

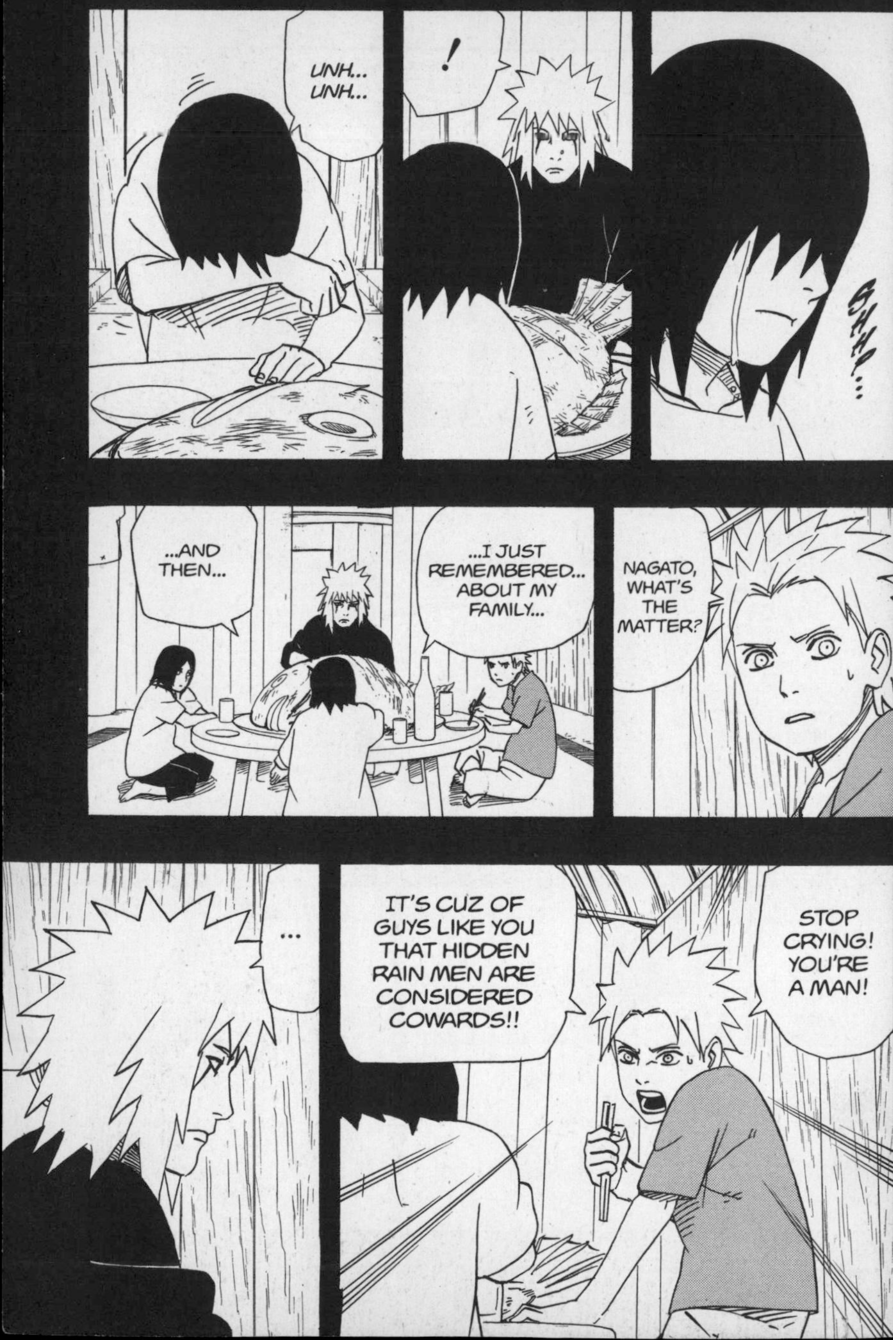
SHHP...
!
UNH... UNH...
NAGATO, WHAT'S THE MATTER?
...I JUST REMEMBERED... ABOUT MY FAMILY...
...AND THEN...
STOP CRYING! YOU'RE A MAN!
IT'S CUZ OF GUYS LIKE YOU THAT HIDDEN RAIN MEN ARE CONSIDERED COWARDS!!
...

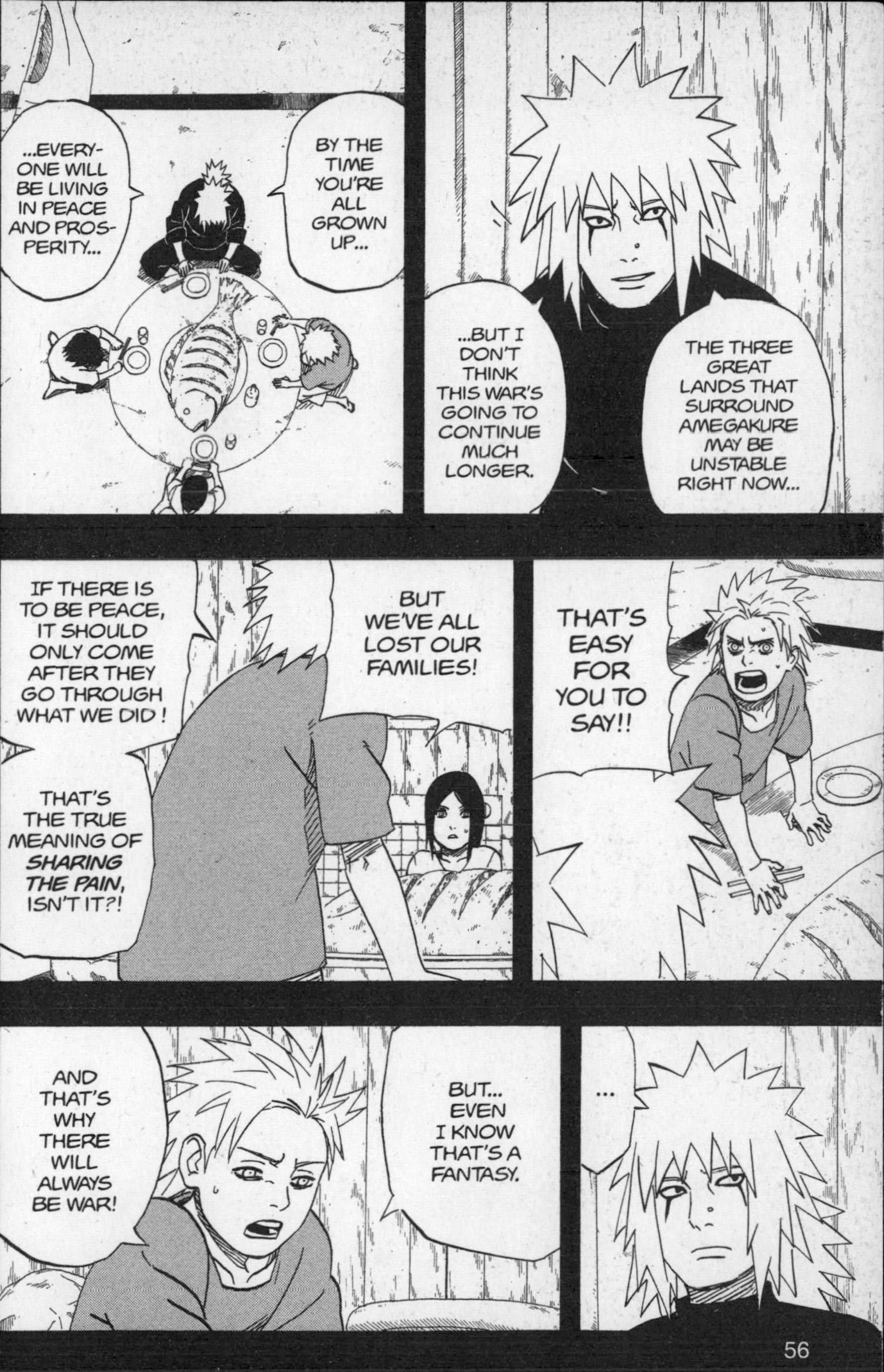
THE THREE GREAT LANDS THAT SURROUND AMEGAKURE MAY BE UNSTABLE RIGHT NOW...
...BUT I DON'T THINK THIS WAR'S GOING TO CONTINUE MUCH LONGER.
BY THE TIME YOU'RE ALL GROWN UP...
...EVERY-ONE WILL BE LIVING IN PEACE AND PROS-PERITY...
THAT'S EASY FOR YOU TO SAY!!
BUT WE'VE ALL LOST OUR FAMILIES!
IF THERE IS TO BE PEACE, IT SHOULD ONLY COME AFTER THEY GO THROUGH WHAT WE DID!
THAT'S THE TRUE MEANING OF *SHARING THE PAIN*, ISN'T IT?!
...
BUT... EVEN I KNOW THAT'S A FANTASY.
AND THAT'S WHY THERE WILL ALWAYS BE WAR!

READ THIS WAY

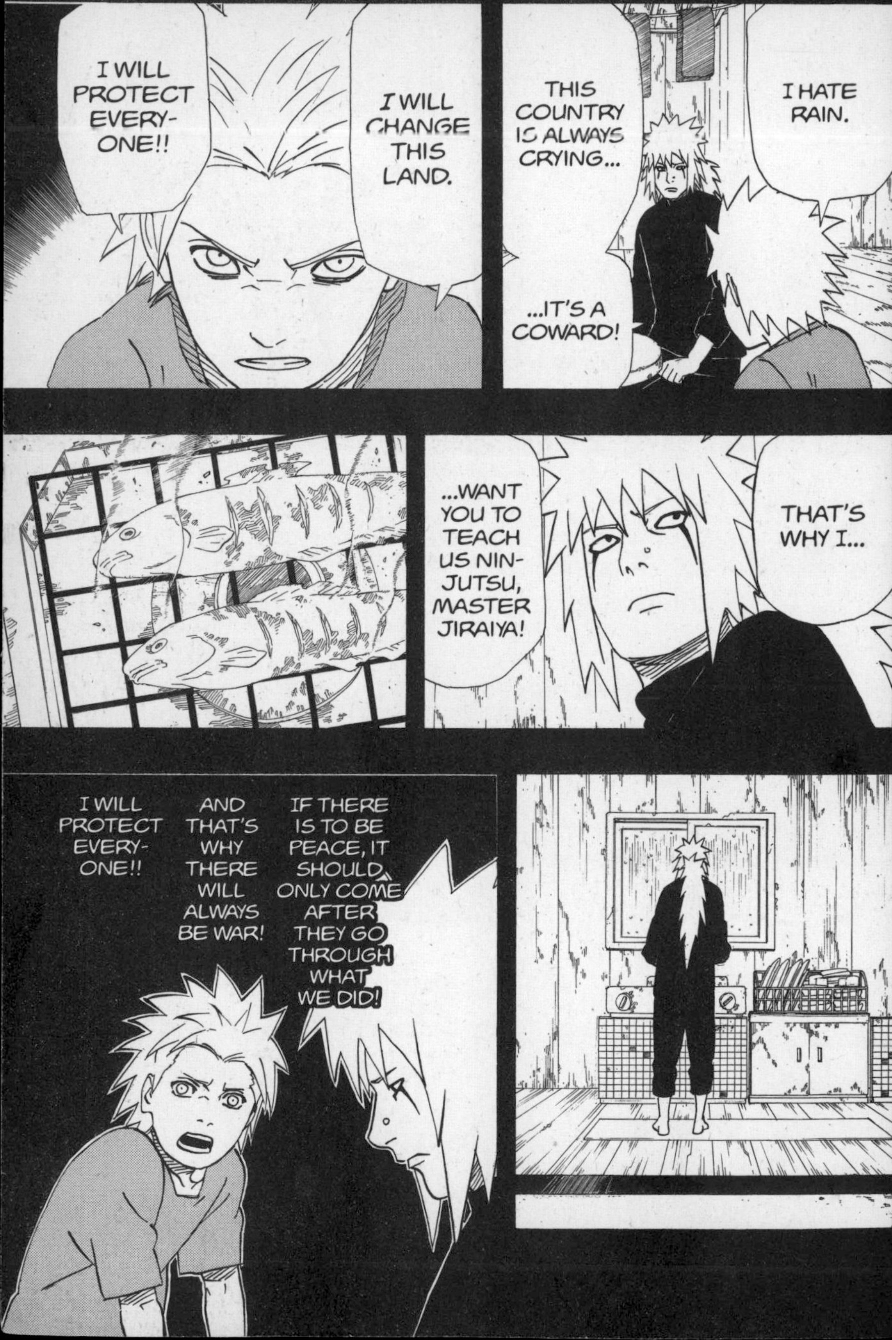
I HATE RAIN.
THIS COUNTRY IS ALWAYS CRYING...
...IT'S A COWARD!
I WILL CHANGE THIS LAND.
I WILL PROTECT EVERY-ONE!!
THAT'S WHY I...
...WANT YOU TO TEACH US NIN-JUTSU, MASTER JIRAIYA!
IF THERE IS TO BE PEACE, IT SHOULD ONLY COME AFTER THEY GO THROUGH WHAT WE DID!
AND THAT'S WHY THERE WILL ALWAYS BE WAR!
I WILL PROTECT EVERY-ONE!!

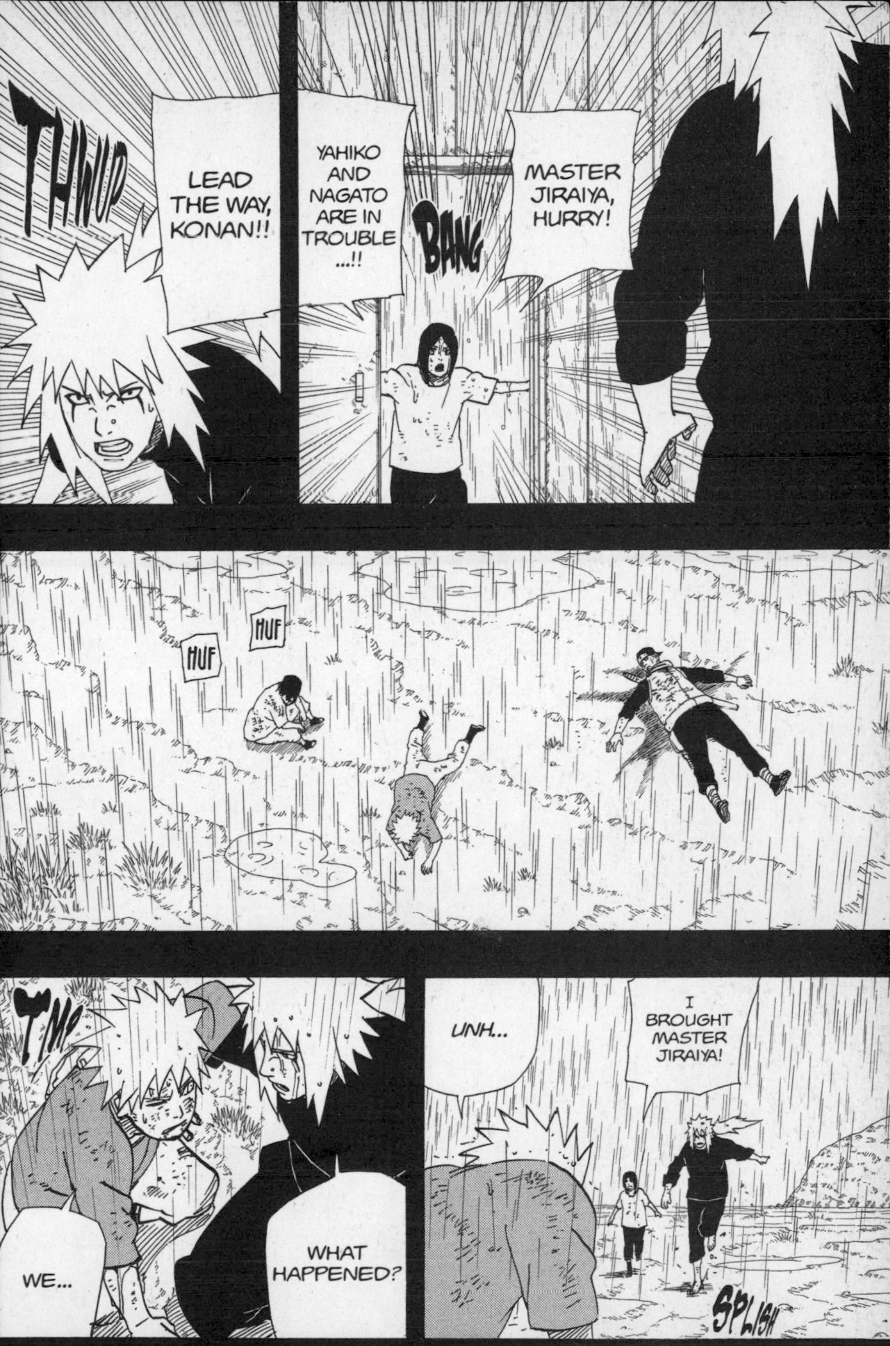
MASTER JIRAIYA, HURRY!
YAHIKO AND NAGATO ARE IN TROUBLE ...!!
BANG
LEAD THE WAY, KONAN!!
THWUP
HUF
HUF
I BROUGHT MASTER JIRAIYA!
UNH...
SPLISH
TMP
WHAT HAPPENED?
WE...

READ THIS WAY

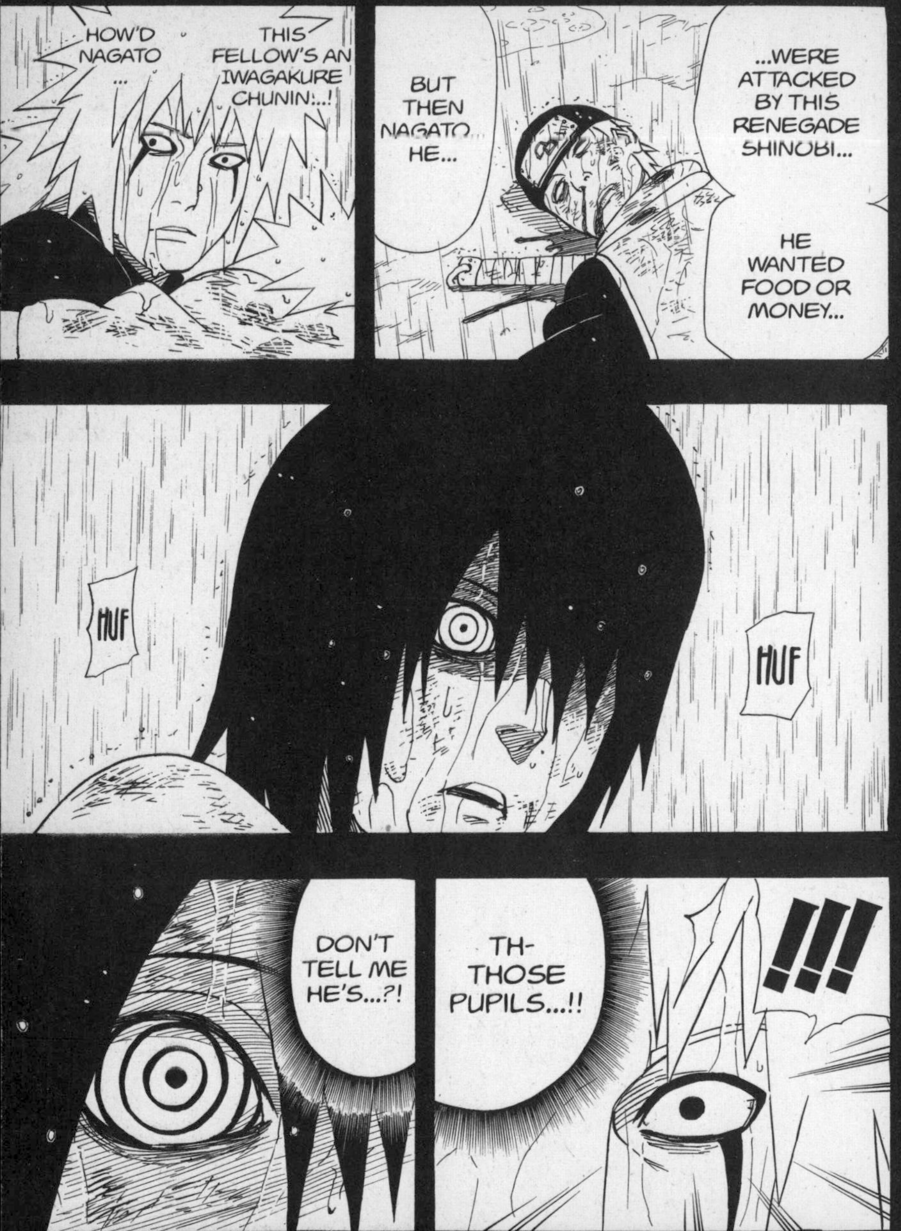
...WERE ATTACKED BY THIS RENEGADE SHINOBI...
HE WANTED FOOD OR MONEY...
BUT THEN NAGATO... HE...
THIS FELLOW'S AN IWAGAKURE CHUNIN...!
HOW'D NAGATO ...
HUF
HUF
!!!
TH- THOSE PUPILS...!!
DON'T TELL ME HE'S...?!

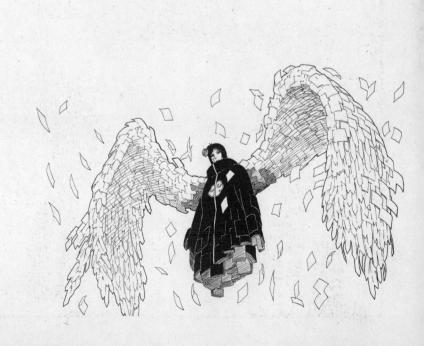

Number 373: Back in the Day...!!

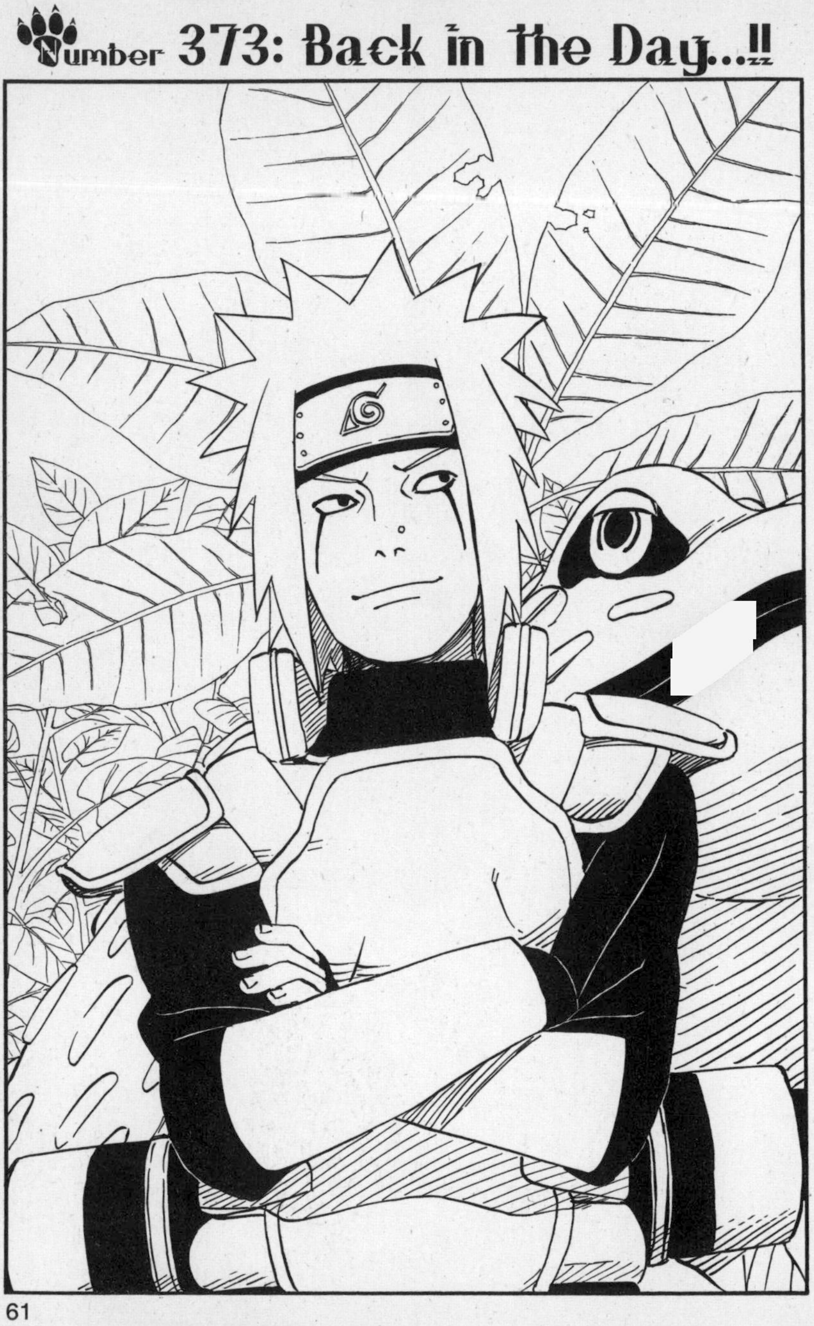

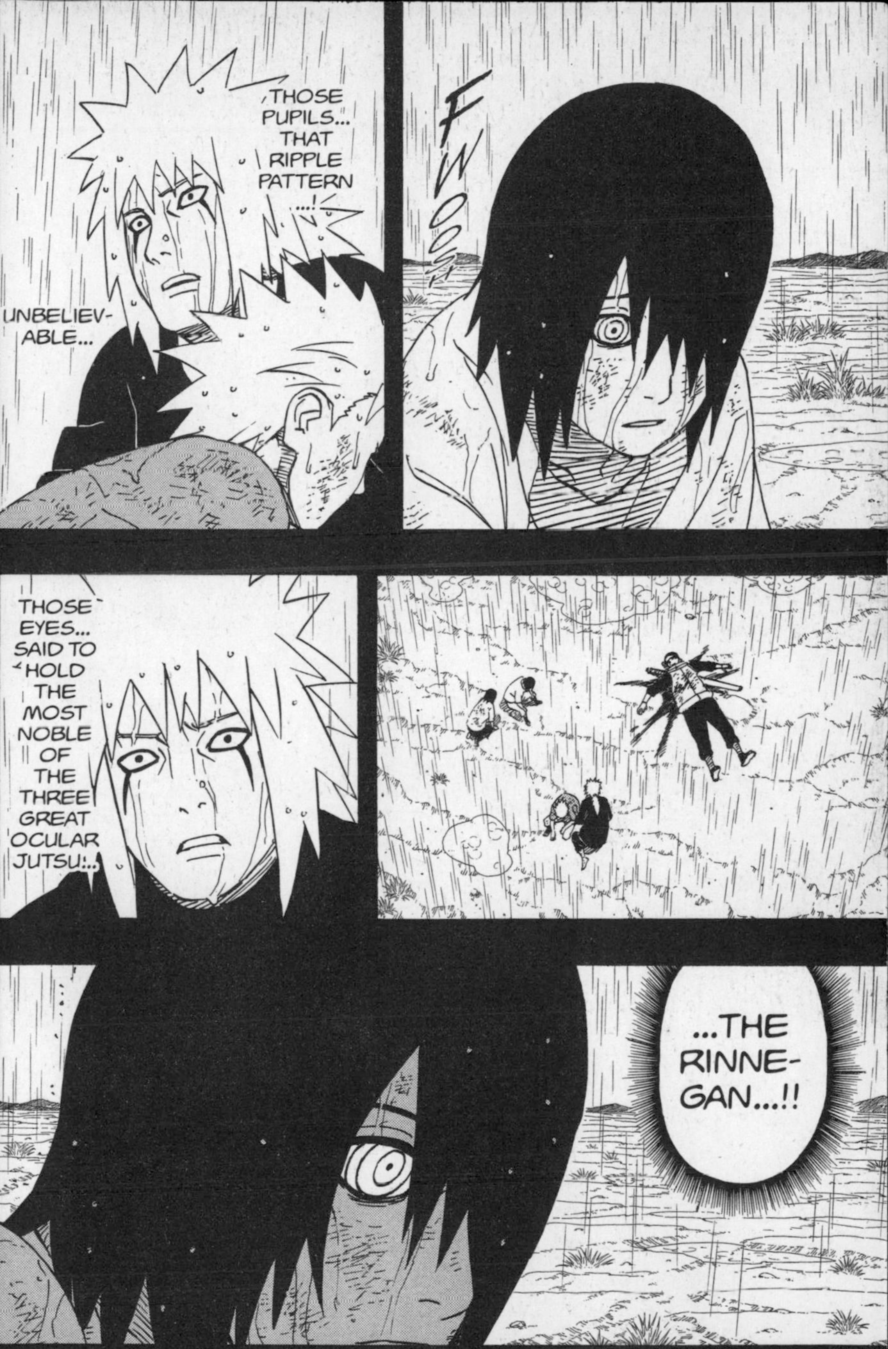
FWOOSH
THOSE PUPILS... THAT RIPPLE PATTERN
....!
UNBELIEV-ABLE...
THOSE EYES... SAID TO HOLD THE MOST NOBLE OF THE THREE GREAT OCULAR JUTSU...
...THE RINNE-GAN...!!

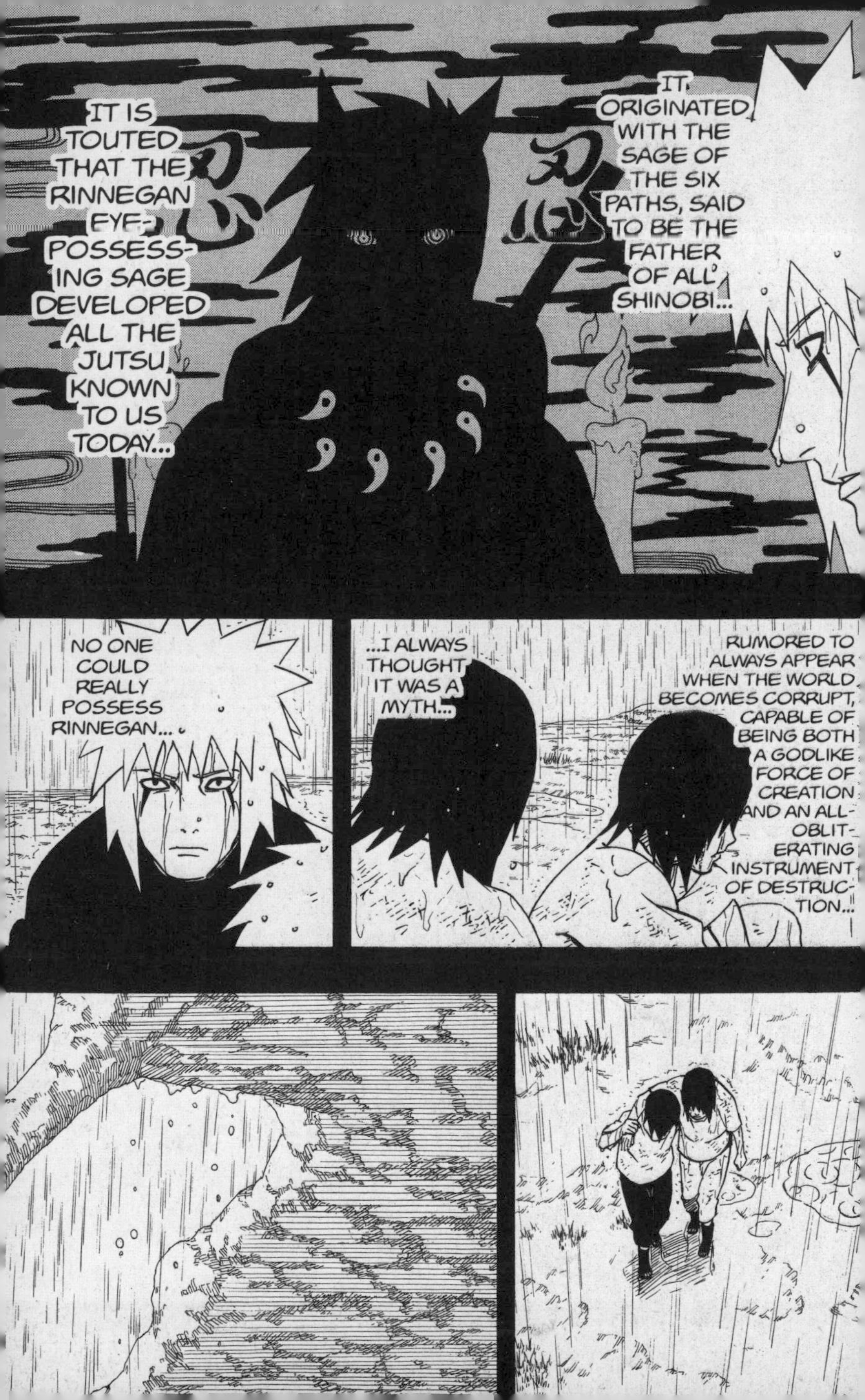
IT ORIGINATED WITH THE SAGE OF THE SIX PATHS, SAID TO BE THE FATHER OF ALL SHINOBI...
IT IS TOUTED THAT THE RINNEGAN EYE-POSSESSING SAGE DEVELOPED ALL THE JUTSU KNOWN TO US TODAY...
RUMORED TO ALWAYS APPEAR WHEN THE WORLD BECOMES CORRUPT, CAPABLE OF BEING BOTH A GODLIKE FORCE OF CREATION AND AN ALL-OBLITERATING INSTRUMENT OF DESTRUCTION...
...I ALWAYS THOUGHT IT WAS A MYTH...
NO ONE COULD REALLY POSSESS RINNEGAN...

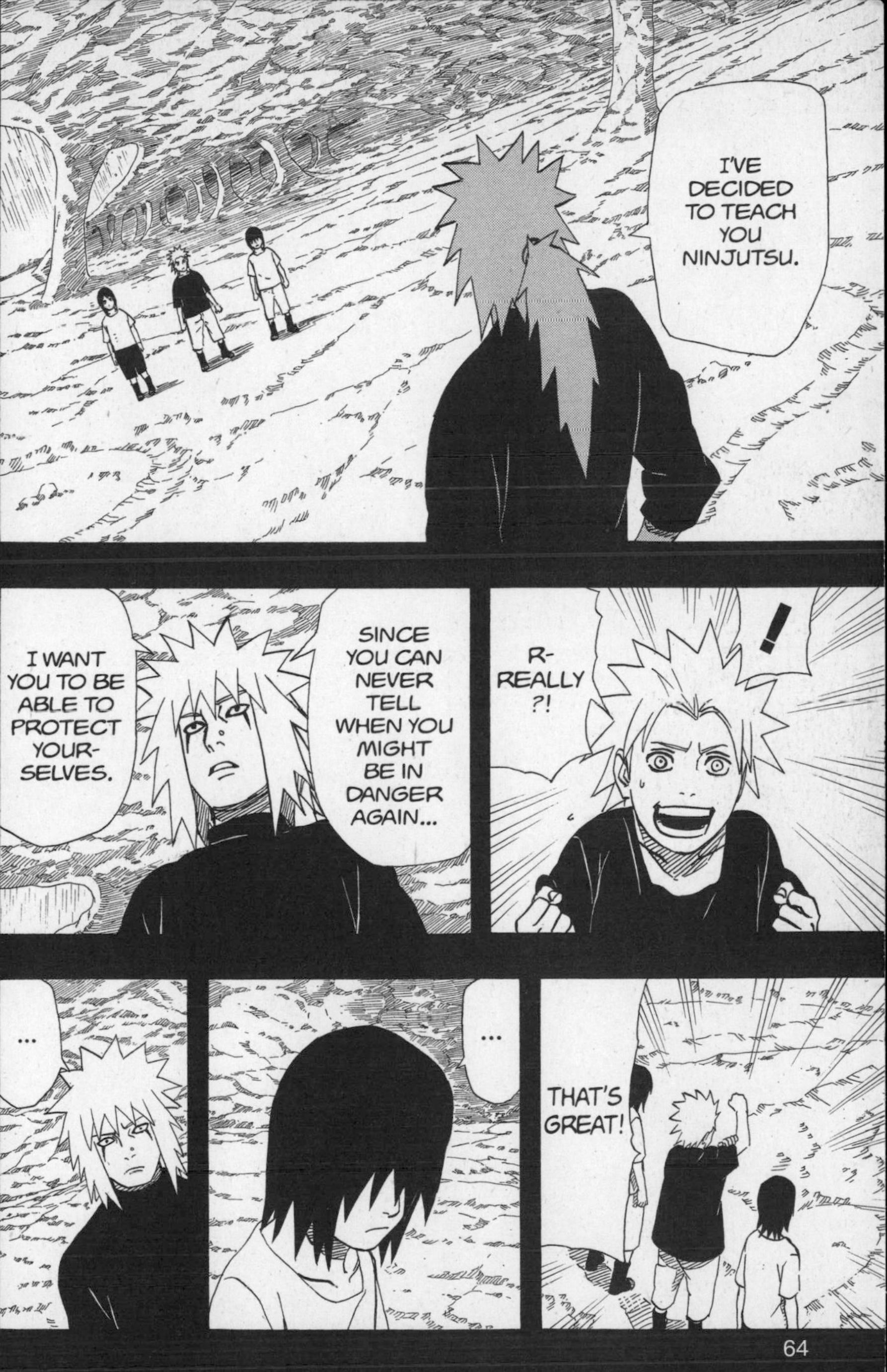
I'VE DECIDED TO TEACH YOU NINJUTSU.
!
R-REALLY ?!
SINCE YOU CAN NEVER TELL WHEN YOU MIGHT BE IN DANGER AGAIN...
I WANT YOU TO BE ABLE TO PROTECT YOUR-SELVES.
THAT'S GREAT!
...
...

READ THIS WAY

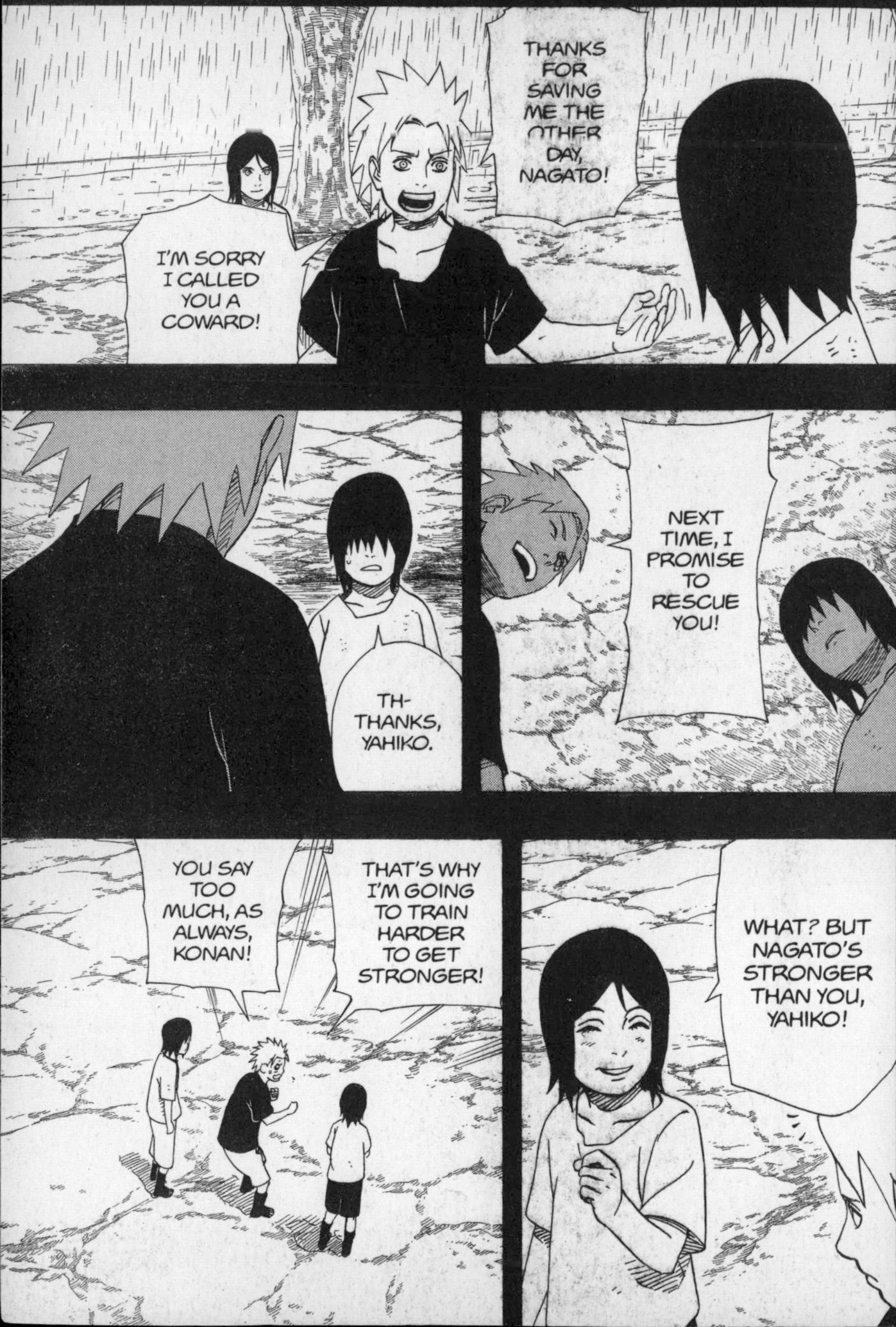
THANKS FOR SAVING ME THE OTHER DAY, NAGATO!
I'M SORRY I CALLED YOU A COWARD!
NEXT TIME, I PROMISE TO RESCUE YOU!
TH- THANKS, YAHIKO.
WHAT? BUT NAGATO'S STRONGER THAN YOU, YAHIKO!
THAT'S WHY I'M GOING TO TRAIN HARDER TO GET STRONGER!
YOU SAY TOO MUCH, AS ALWAYS, KONAN!

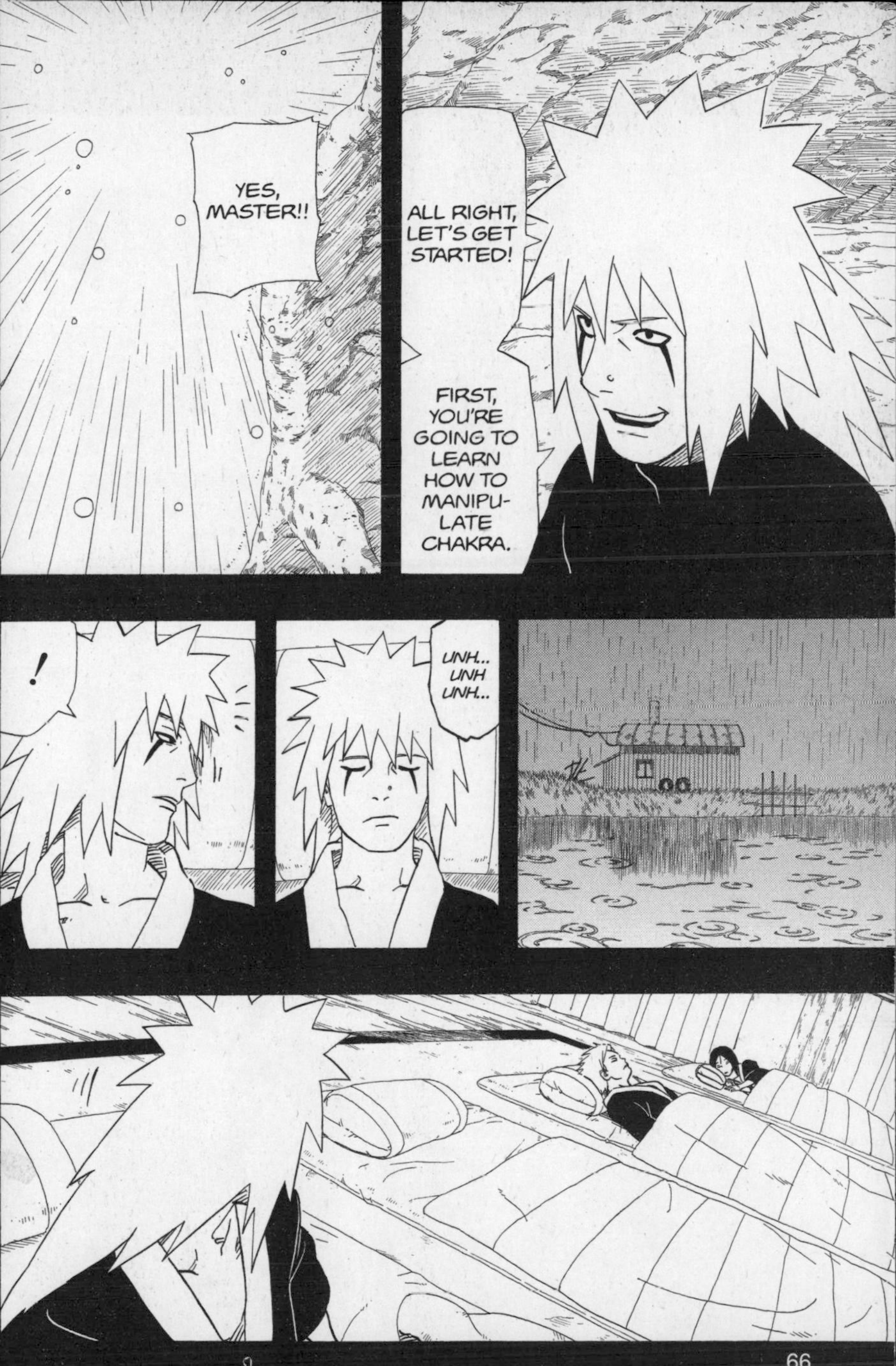
ALL RIGHT, LET'S GET STARTED!
FIRST, YOU'RE GOING TO LEARN HOW TO MANIPU-LATE CHAKRA.
YES, MASTER!!
UNH... UNH UNH...
!

READ THIS WAY

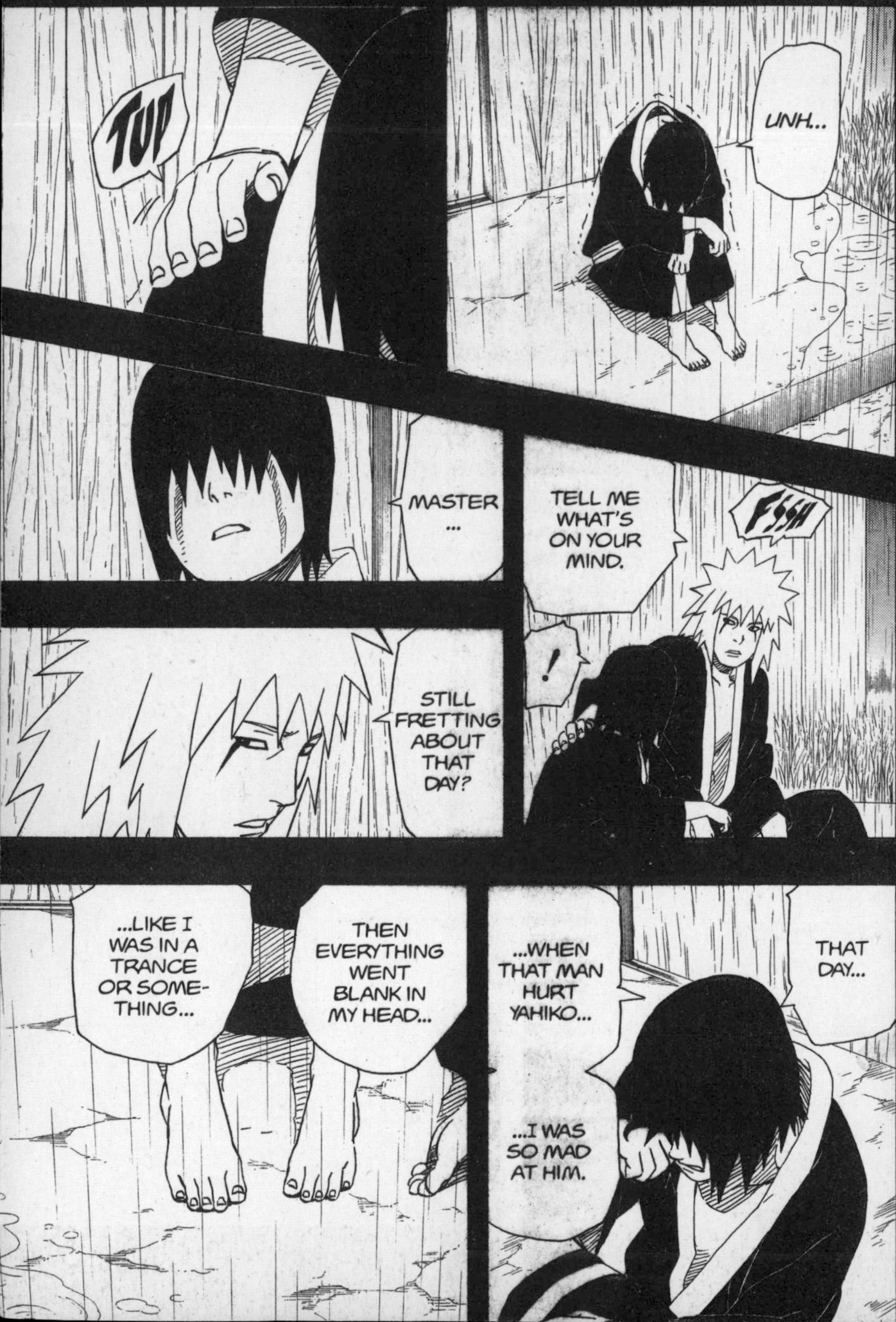
UNH...
TUP
TELL ME WHAT'S ON YOUR MIND.
FSSH
!
MASTER ...
STILL FRETTING ABOUT THAT DAY?
THAT DAY...
...WHEN THAT MAN HURT YAHIKO...
...I WAS SO MAD AT HIM.
THEN EVERYTHING WENT BLANK IN MY HEAD...
...LIKE I WAS IN A TRANCE OR SOMETHING...

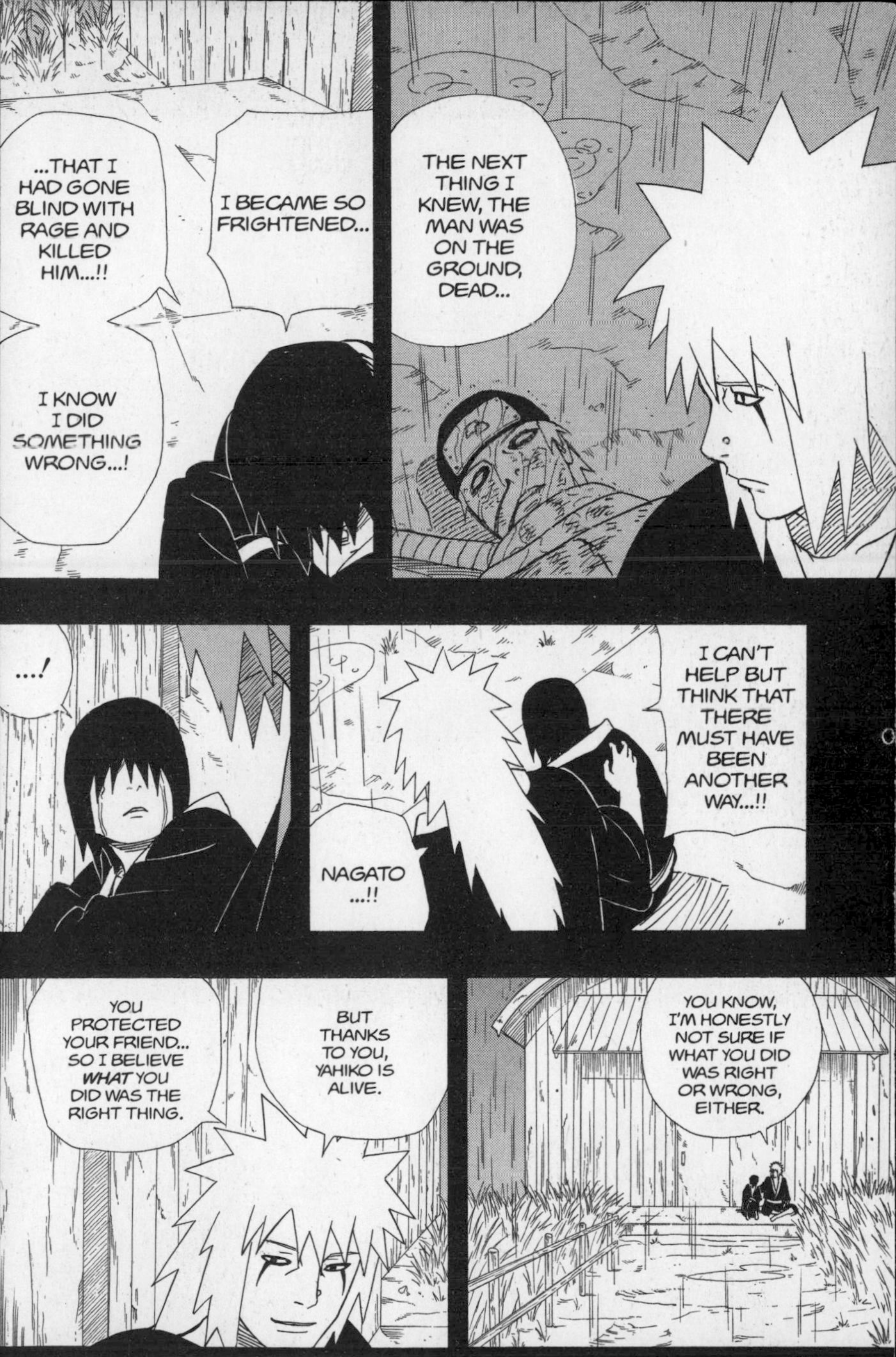
THE NEXT THING I KNEW, THE MAN WAS ON THE GROUND, DEAD...
I BECAME SO FRIGHTENED...
...THAT I HAD GONE BLIND WITH RAGE AND KILLED HIM...!!
I KNOW I DID SOMETHING WRONG...!
I CAN'T HELP BUT THINK THAT THERE MUST HAVE BEEN ANOTHER WAY...!!
NAGATO ...!!
...!
YOU KNOW, I'M HONESTLY NOT SURE IF WHAT YOU DID WAS RIGHT OR WRONG, EITHER.
BUT THANKS TO YOU, YAHIKO IS ALIVE.
YOU PROTECTED YOUR FRIEND... SO I BELIEVE *WHAT* YOU DID WAS THE RIGHT THING.

READ THIS WAY

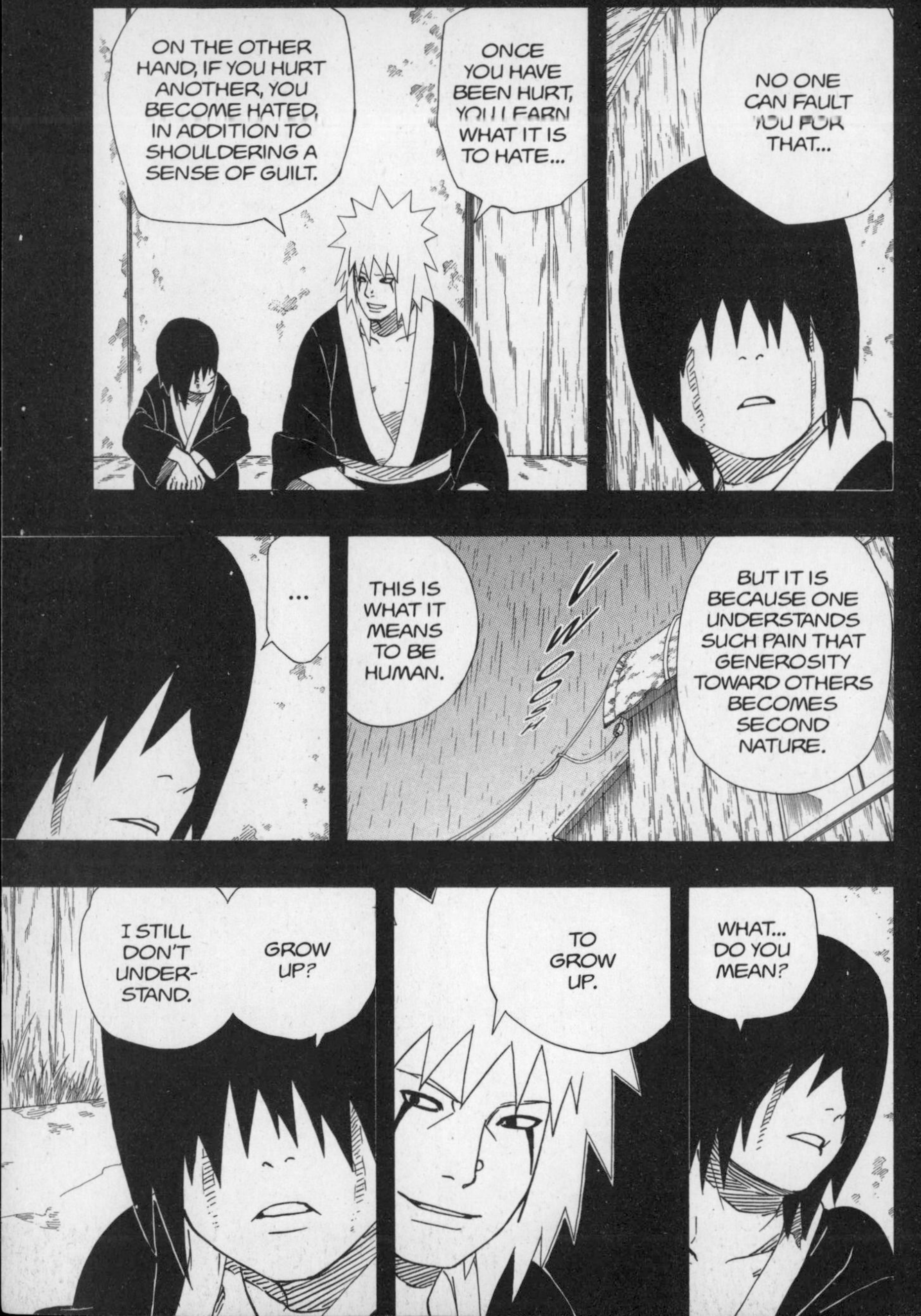
NO ONE CAN FAULT YOU FOR THAT...
ONCE YOU HAVE BEEN HURT, YOU LEARN WHAT IT IS TO HATE...
ON THE OTHER HAND, IF YOU HURT ANOTHER, YOU BECOME HATED, IN ADDITION TO SHOULDERING A SENSE OF GUILT.
BUT IT IS BECAUSE ONE UNDERSTANDS SUCH PAIN THAT GENEROSITY TOWARD OTHERS BECOMES SECOND NATURE.
THIS IS WHAT IT MEANS TO BE HUMAN.
...
WHAT... DO YOU MEAN?
TO GROW UP.
GROW UP?
I STILL DON'T UNDER-STAND.

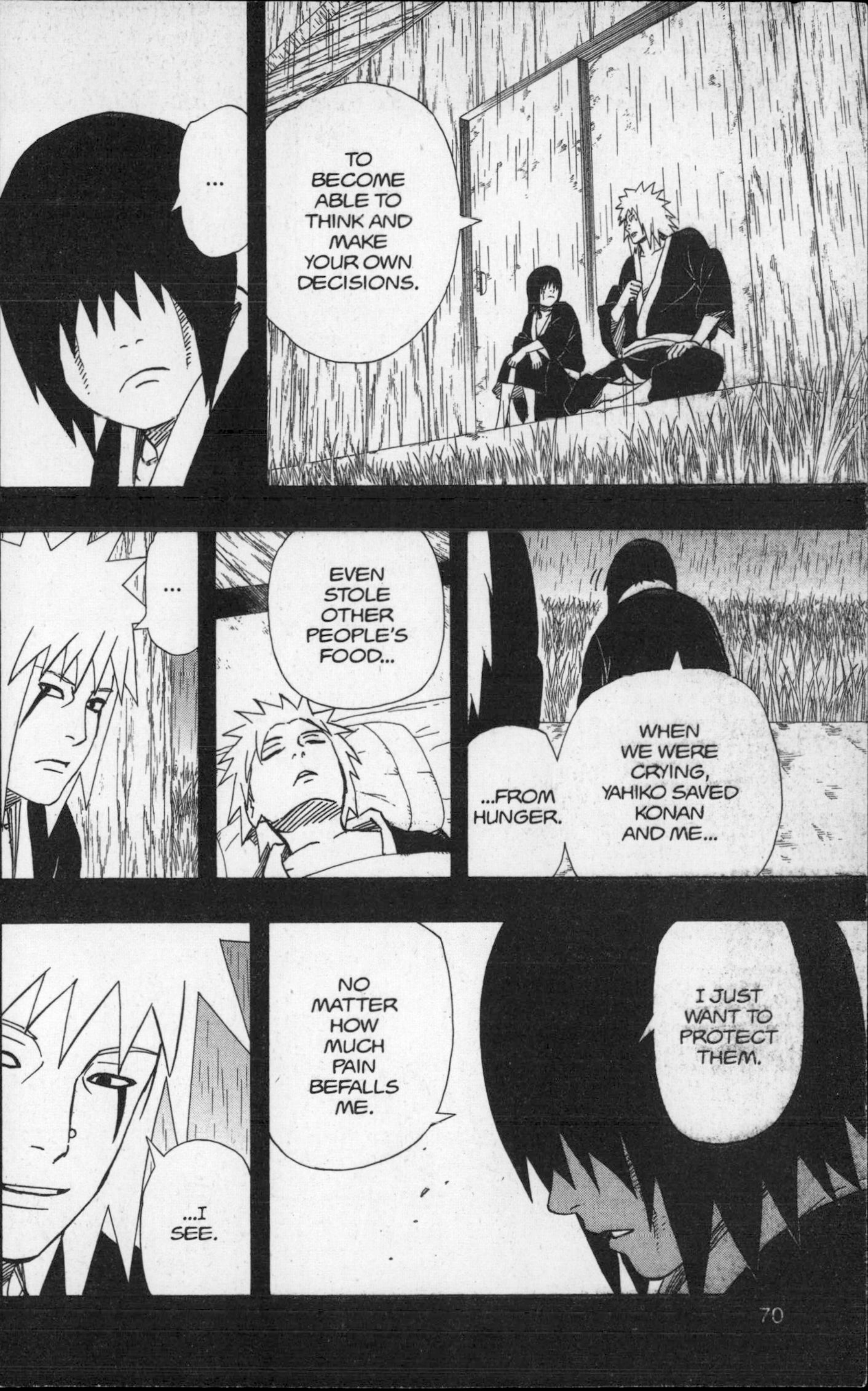
TO BECOME ABLE TO THINK AND MAKE YOUR OWN DECISIONS.
...
WHEN WE WERE CRYING, YAHIKO SAVED KONAN AND ME...
...FROM HUNGER.
EVEN STOLE OTHER PEOPLE'S FOOD...
...
I JUST WANT TO PROTECT THEM.
NO MATTER HOW MUCH PAIN BEFALLS ME.
...I SEE.

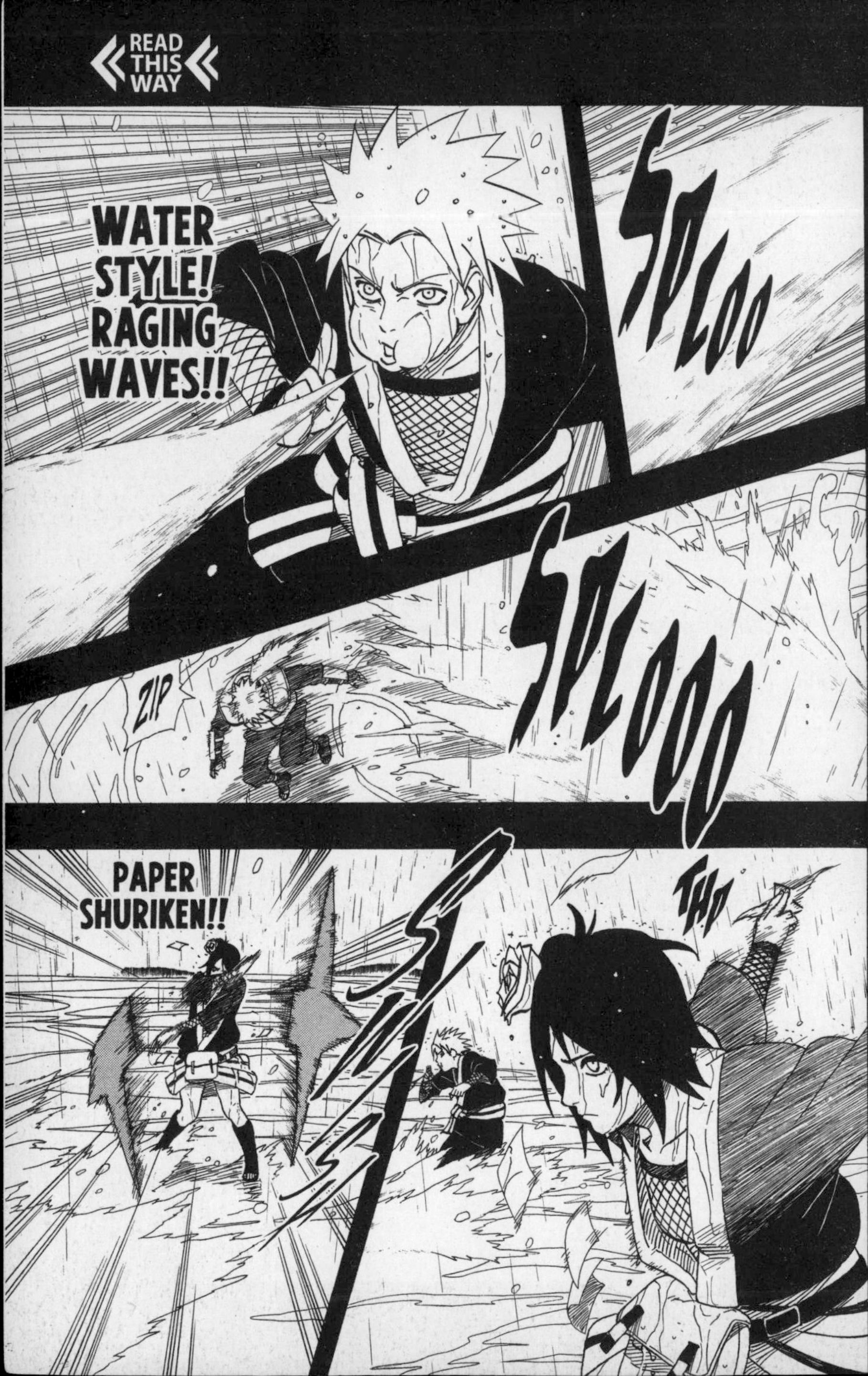
READ THIS WAY
SPLOO
WATER STYLE! RAGING WAVES!!
SPLOOO
ZIP
THP
PAPER SHURIKEN!!
SSSS

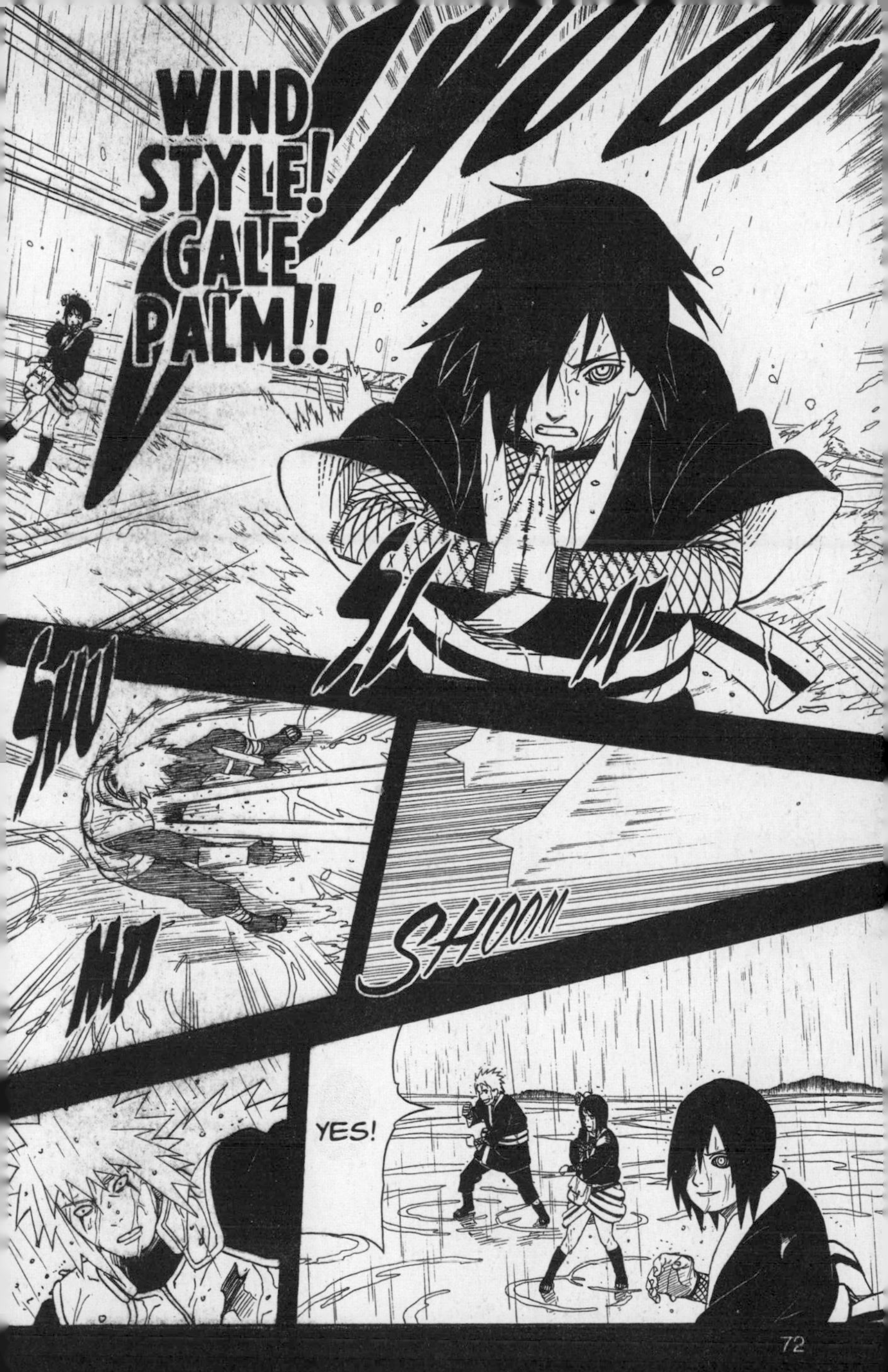
WIND STYLE! GALE PALM!!
SHOOM
YES!

READ THIS WAY

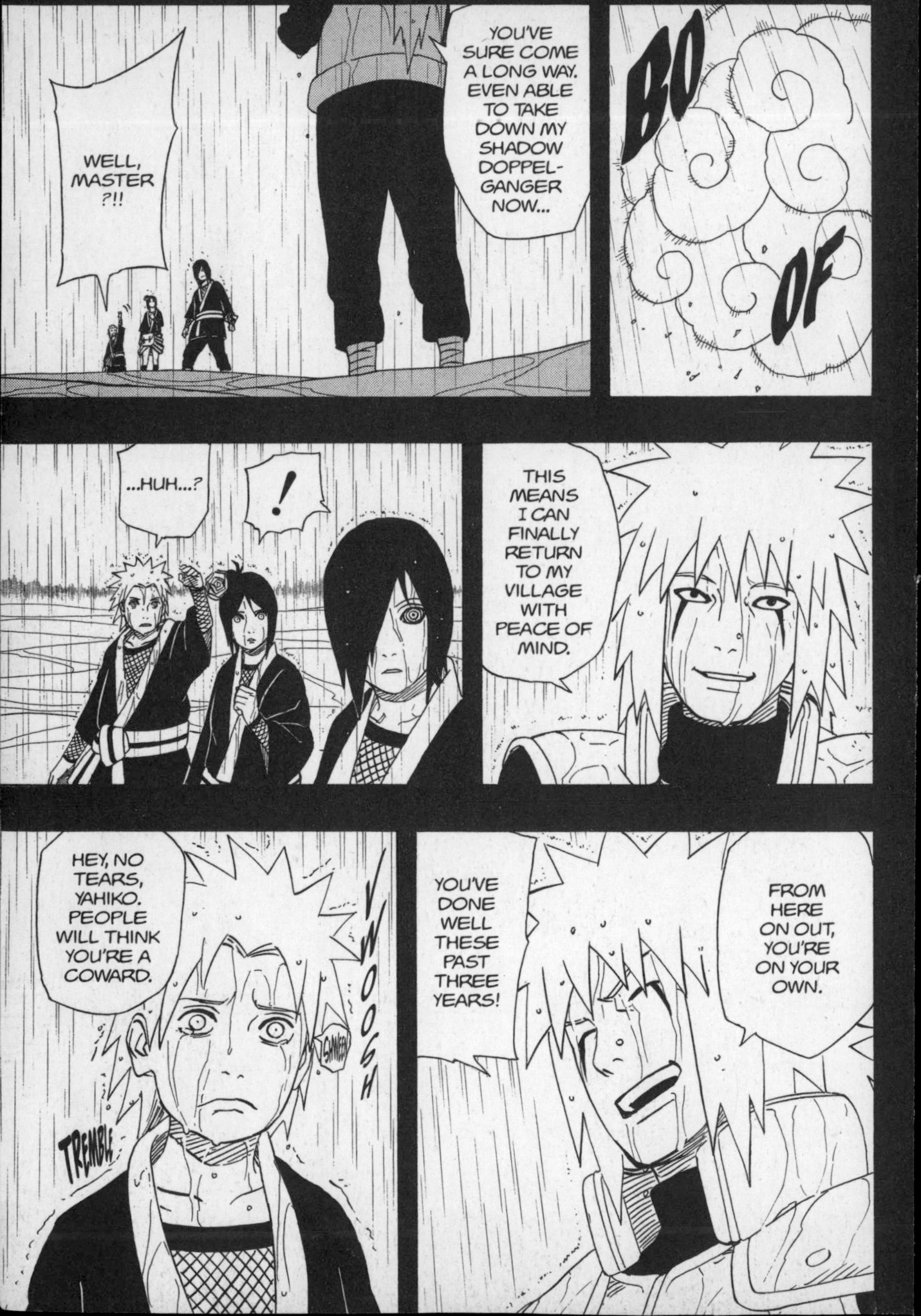
BOOF
YOU'VE SURE COME A LONG WAY. EVEN ABLE TO TAKE DOWN MY SHADOW DOPPEL-GANGER NOW...
WELL, MASTER?!!
THIS MEANS I CAN FINALLY RETURN TO MY VILLAGE WITH PEACE OF MIND.
!
...HUH...?
FROM HERE ON OUT, YOU'RE ON YOUR OWN.
YOU'VE DONE WELL THESE PAST THREE YEARS!
VWOOSH
HEY, NO TEARS, YAHIKO. PEOPLE WILL THINK YOU'RE A COWARD.
TREMBLE

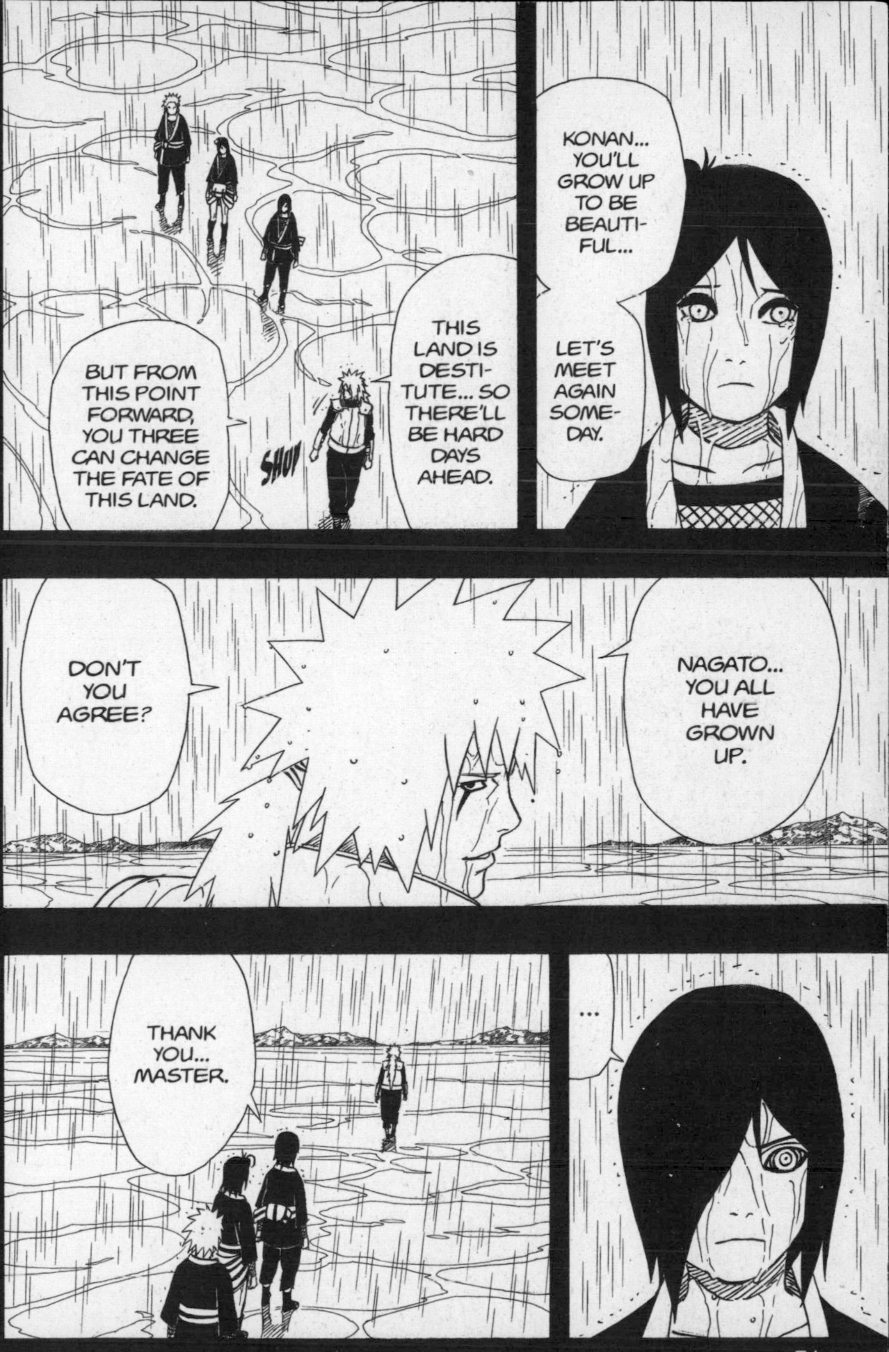
KONAN... YOU'LL GROW UP TO BE BEAUTIFUL...
LET'S MEET AGAIN SOMEDAY.
THIS LAND IS DESTITUTE... SO THERE'LL BE HARD DAYS AHEAD.
SHUP
BUT FROM THIS POINT FORWARD, YOU THREE CAN CHANGE THE FATE OF THIS LAND.
NAGATO... YOU ALL HAVE GROWN UP.
DON'T YOU AGREE?
...
THANK YOU... MASTER.

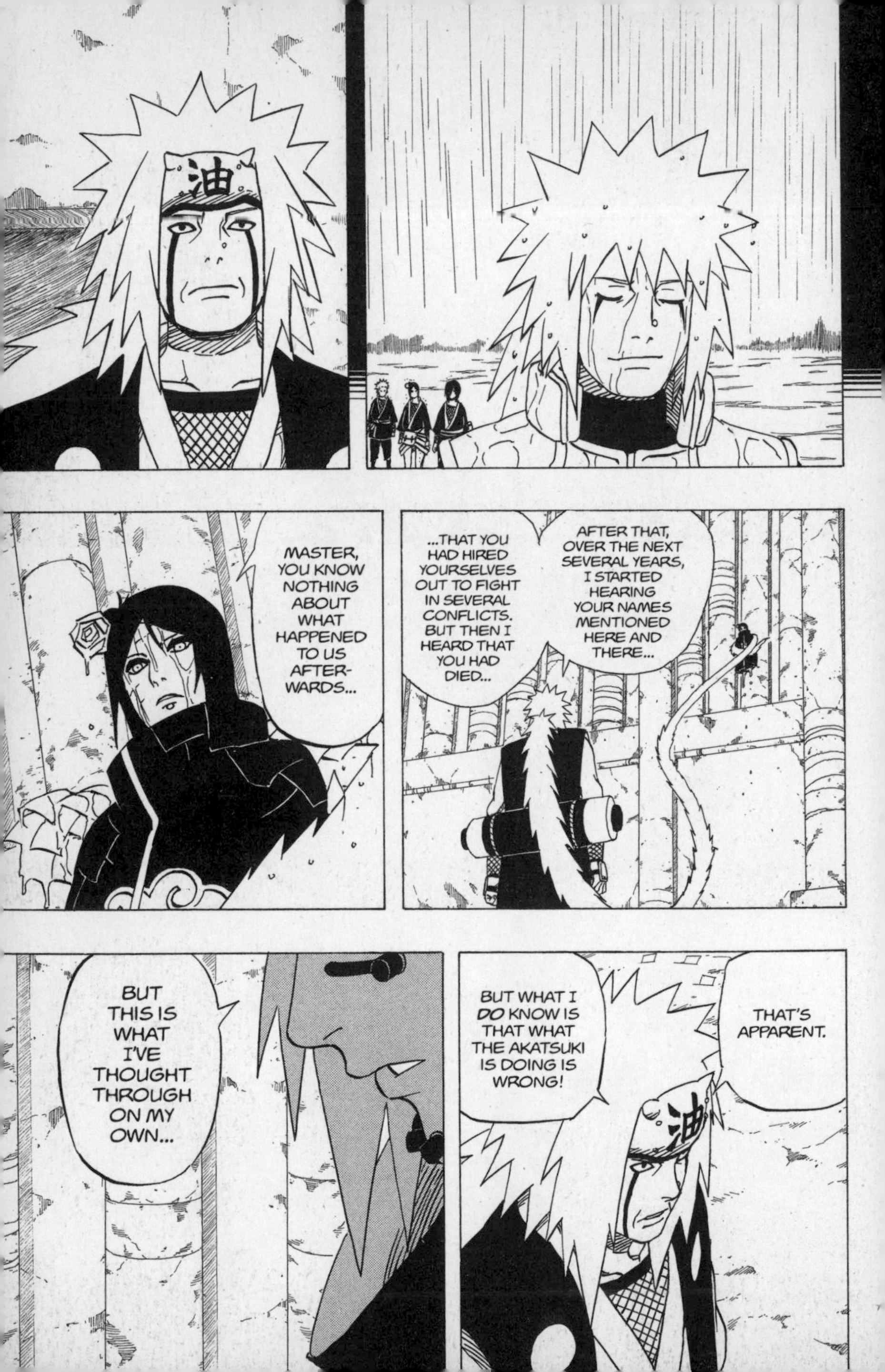
AFTER THAT, OVER THE NEXT SEVERAL YEARS, I STARTED HEARING YOUR NAMES MENTIONED HERE AND THERE...
...THAT YOU HAD HIRED YOURSELVES OUT TO FIGHT IN SEVERAL CONFLICTS. BUT THEN I HEARD THAT YOU HAD DIED...
MASTER, YOU KNOW NOTHING ABOUT WHAT HAPPENED TO US AFTER-WARDS...
THAT'S APPARENT.
BUT WHAT I *DO* KNOW IS THAT WHAT THE AKATSUKI IS DOING IS WRONG!
BUT THIS IS WHAT I'VE THOUGHT THROUGH ON MY OWN...

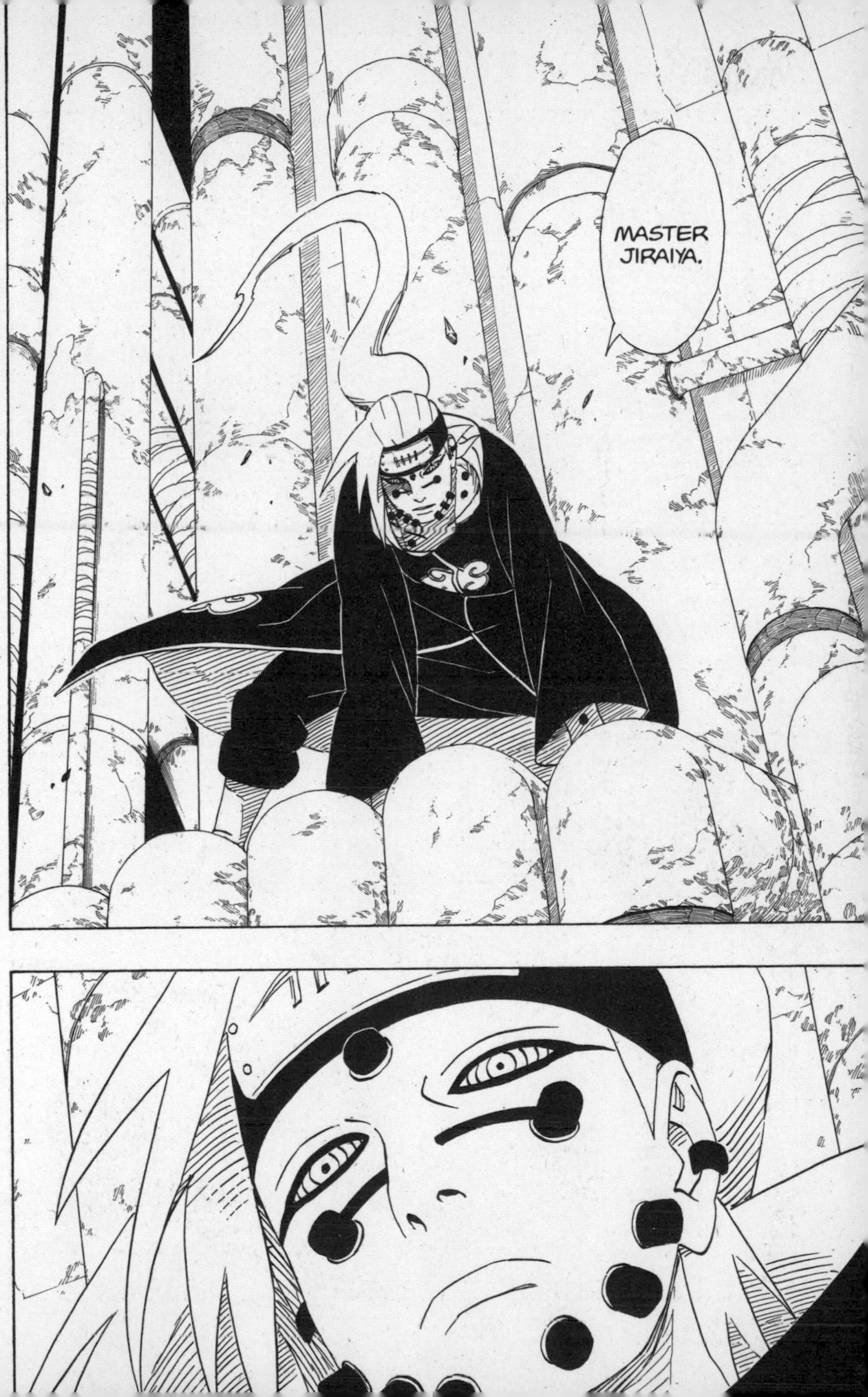
MASTER JIRAIYA.

READ THIS WAY

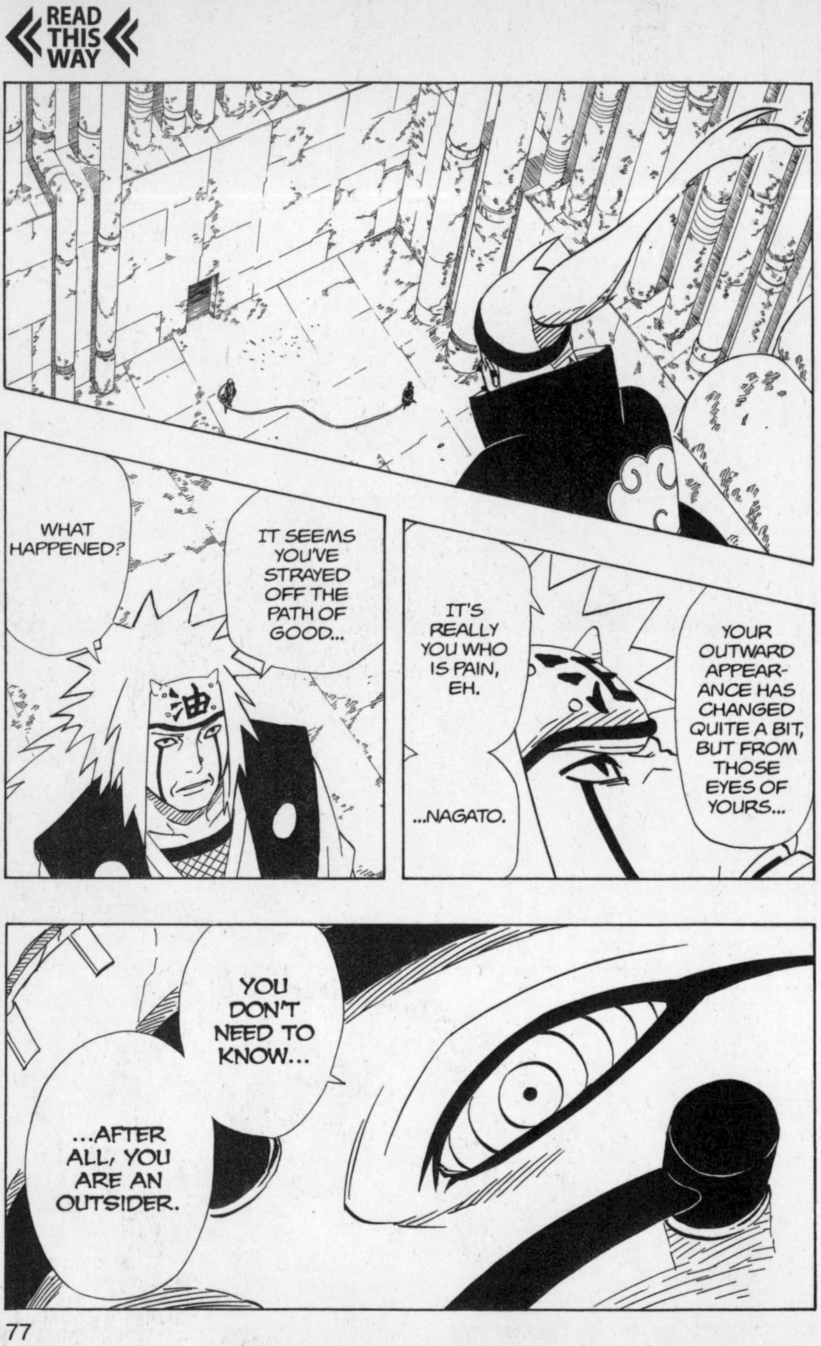
YOUR OUTWARD APPEARANCE HAS CHANGED QUITE A BIT, BUT FROM THOSE EYES OF YOURS...
IT'S REALLY YOU WHO IS PAIN, EH.
...NAGATO.
IT SEEMS YOU'VE STRAYED OFF THE PATH OF GOOD...
WHAT HAPPENED?
YOU DON'T NEED TO KNOW...
...AFTER ALL, YOU ARE AN OUTSIDER.

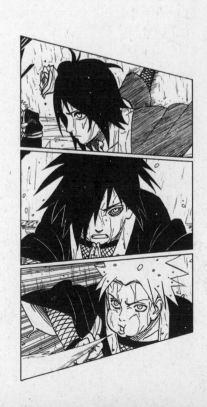

Number 374: Advancement!!

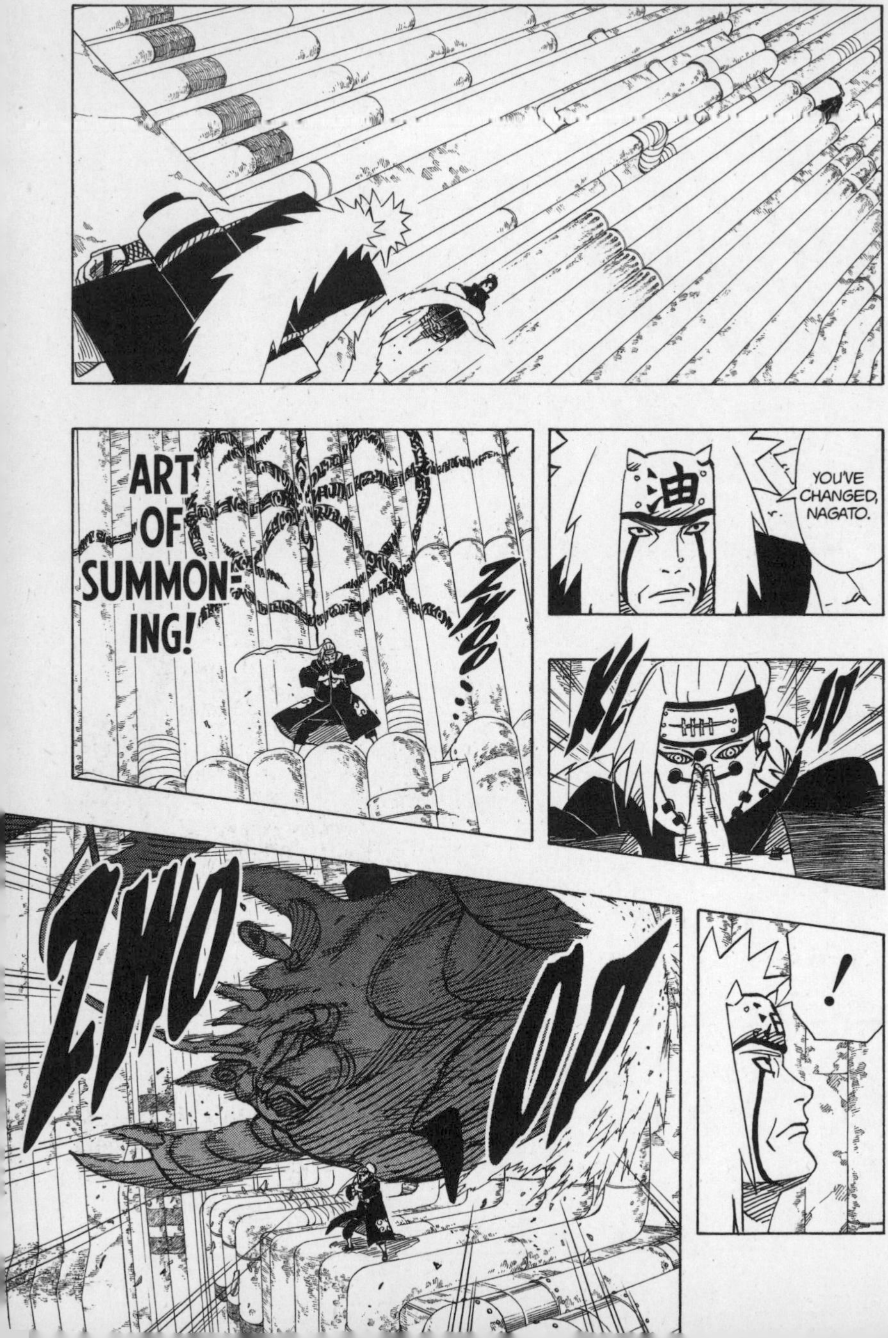
YOU'VE CHANGED, NAGATO.
ART OF SUMMON-ING!
!

Number 374: Advancement!!

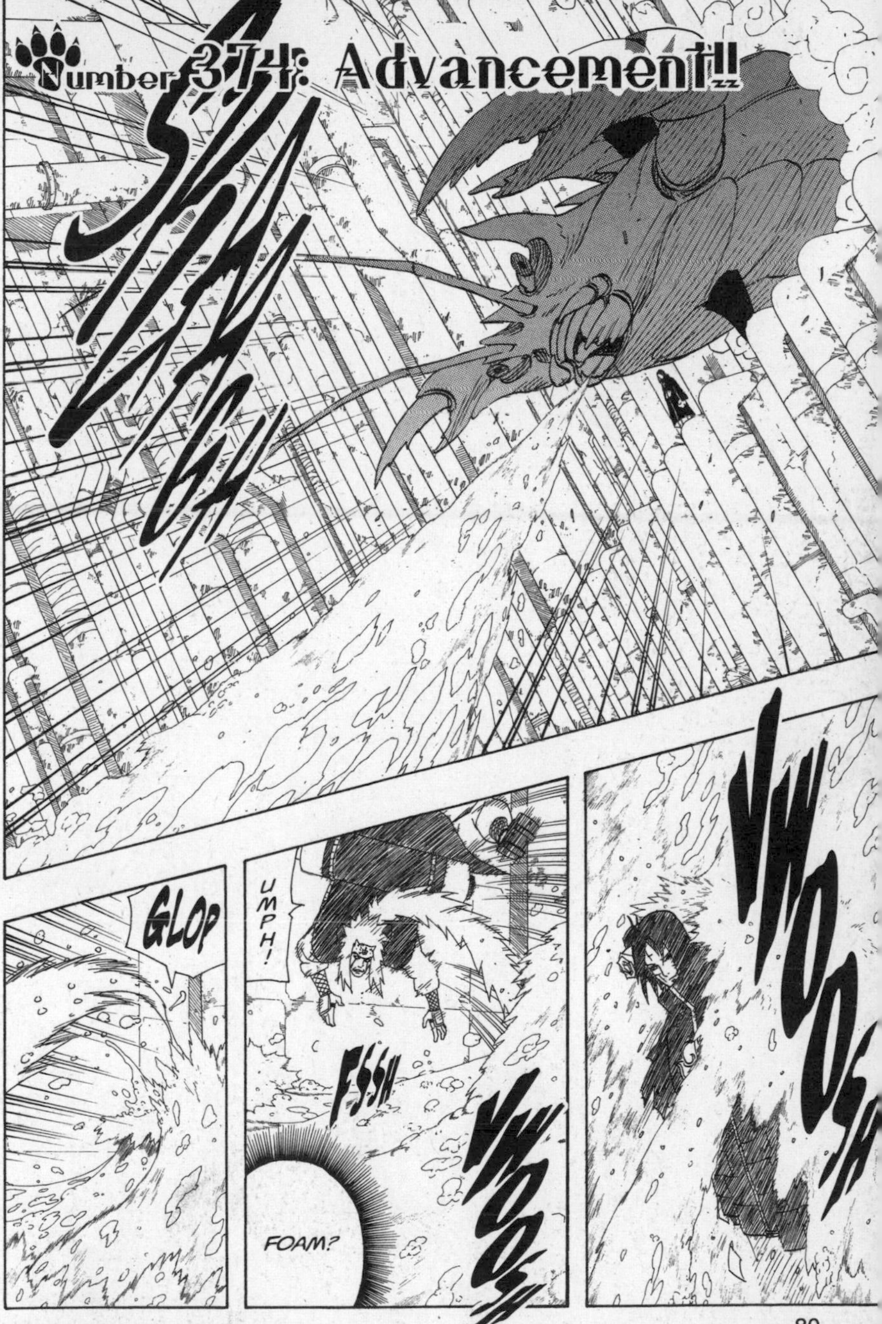
WHOOSH
UMPH!
FSSH
WHOOSH
FOAM?
GLOP

READ THIS WAY

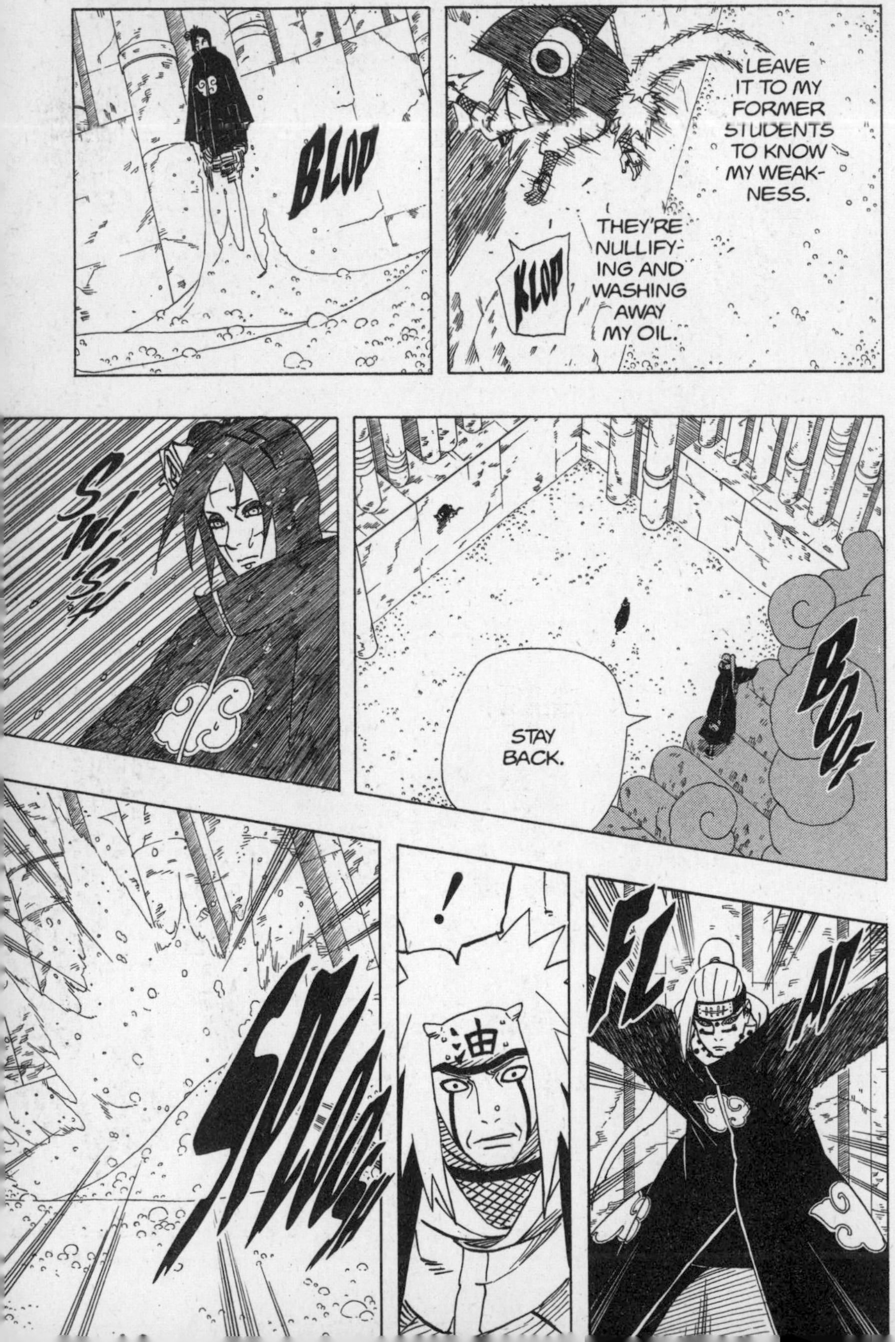
LEAVE IT TO MY FORMER STUDENTS TO KNOW MY WEAKNESS.
THEY'RE NULLIFYING AND WASHING AWAY MY OIL.
KLOP
BLOP
STAY BACK.
BOOF
SWISH
FLAP
!

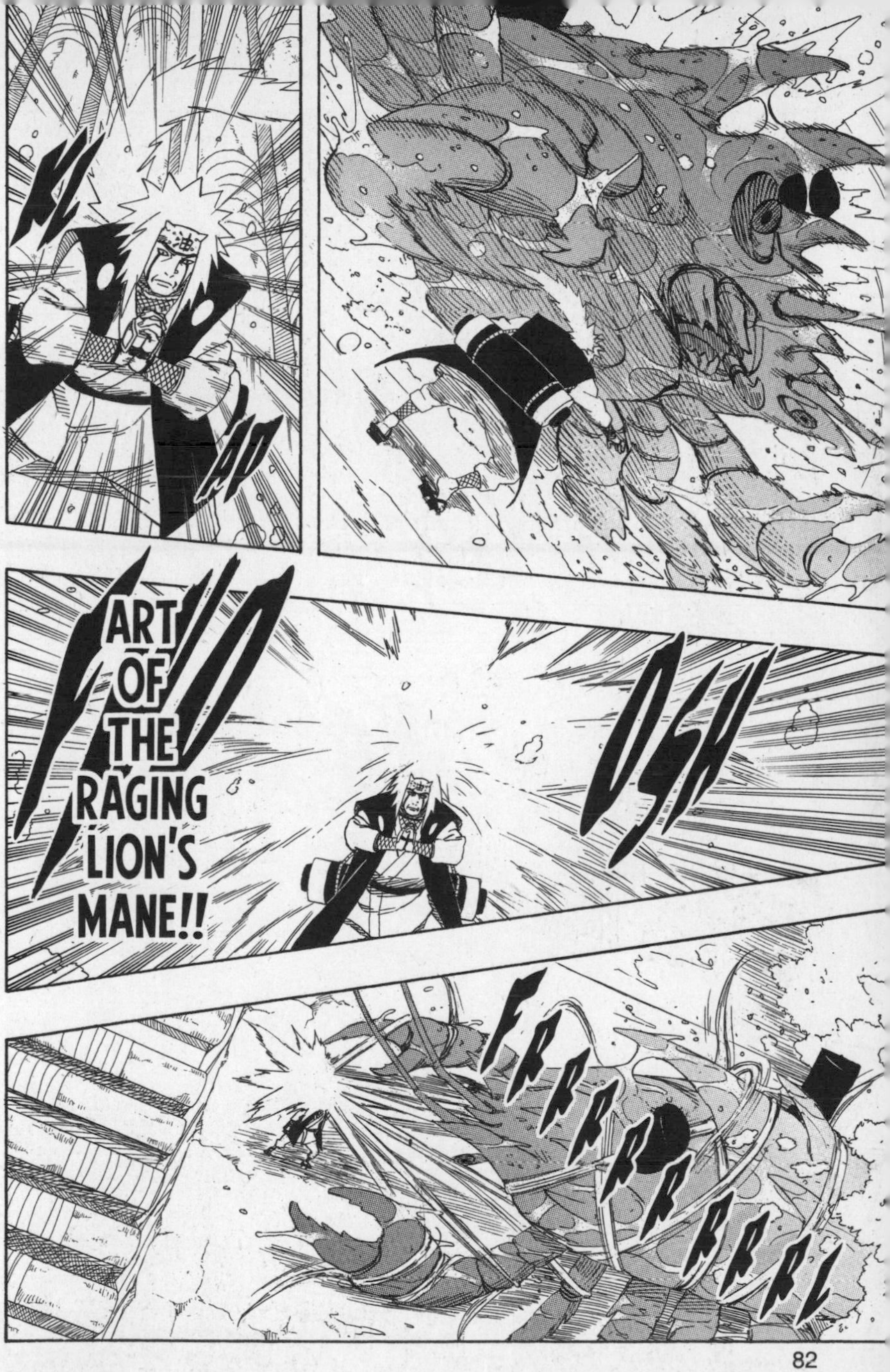
ART OF THE RAGING LION'S MANE!!

READ THIS WAY

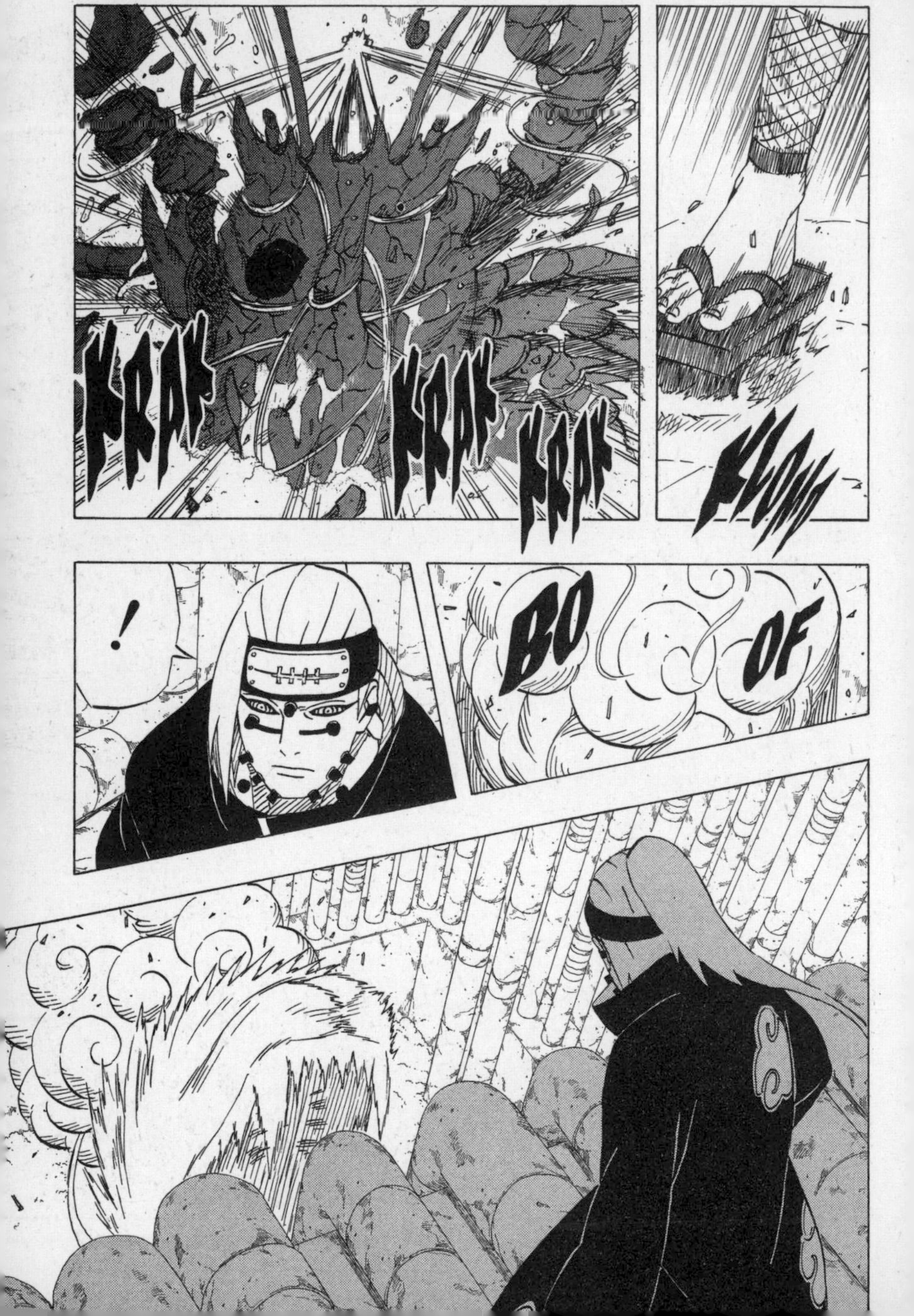
KRAK
KRAK
KRAK
BO
OF
!

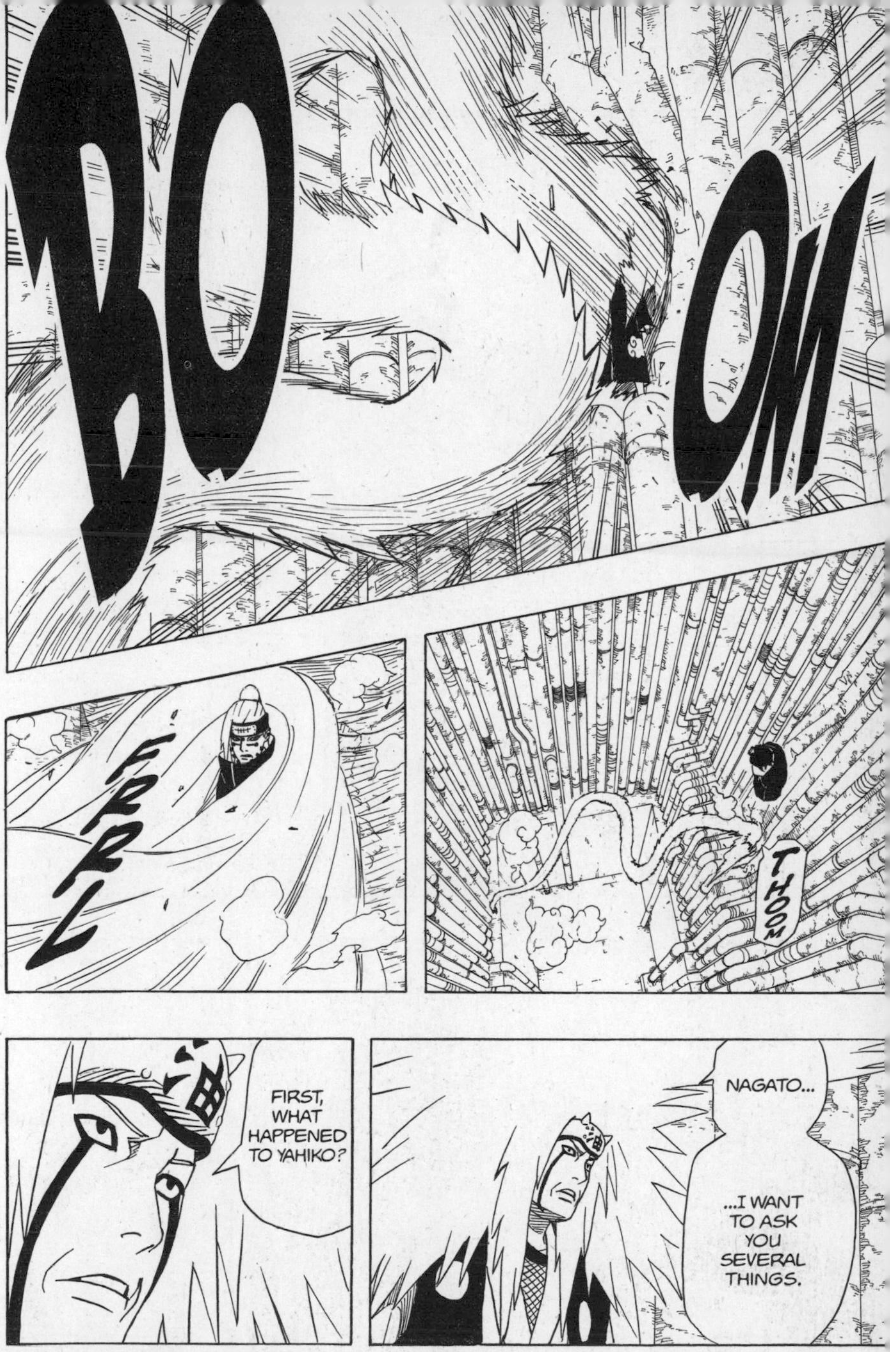
BOOM
THOOM
FRRRL
NAGATO...
...I WANT TO ASK YOU SEVERAL THINGS.
FIRST, WHAT HAPPENED TO YAHIKO?

READ THIS WAY

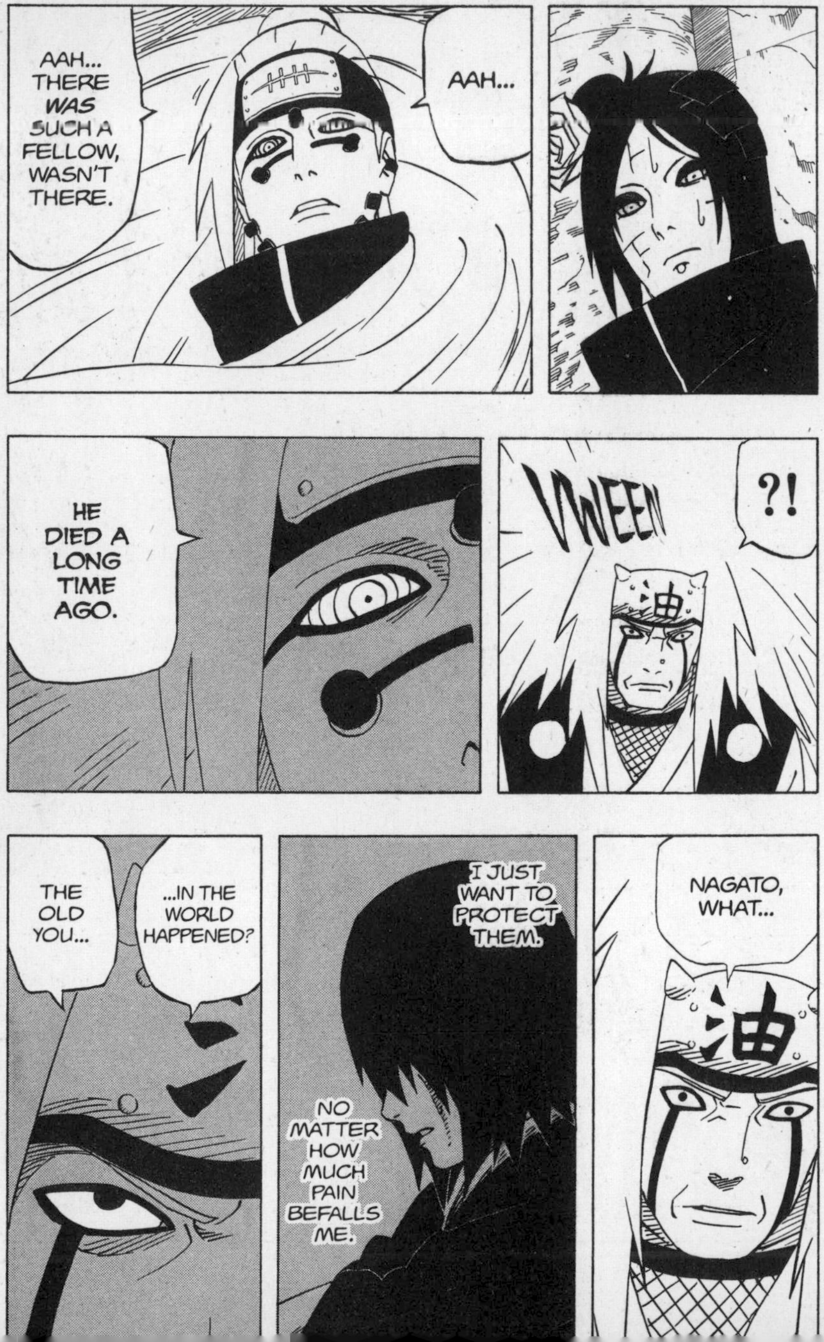
AAH...
AAH... THERE WAS SUCH A FELLOW, WASN'T THERE.
VWEEN
?!
HE DIED A LONG TIME AGO.
NAGATO, WHAT...
I JUST WANT TO PROTECT THEM.
NO MATTER HOW MUCH PAIN BEFALLS ME.
...IN THE WORLD HAPPENED?
THE OLD YOU...

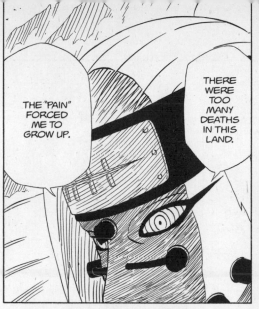

NOTHING...
JUST WAR.
THERE WERE TOO MANY DEATHS IN THIS LAND.
THE "PAIN" FORCED ME TO GROW UP.
WHAT DO YOU MEAN ...?
EVEN INNOCENT, FOOLISH CHILDREN...
...GROW UP IN THE FACE OF PAIN.
UNTIL THEIR THOUGHTS AND BELIEFS ARE THE SAME AS THOSE OF ADULTS.
GROWN-UPS DON'T ABANDON THEIR COMRADES!

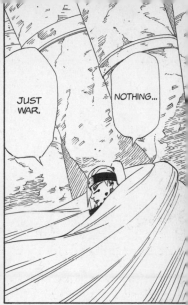

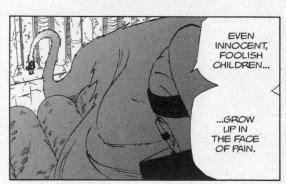

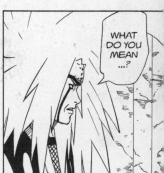

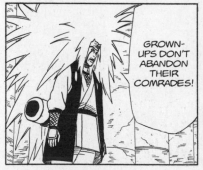

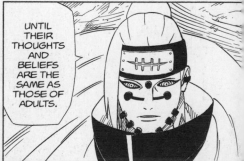

READ THIS WAY

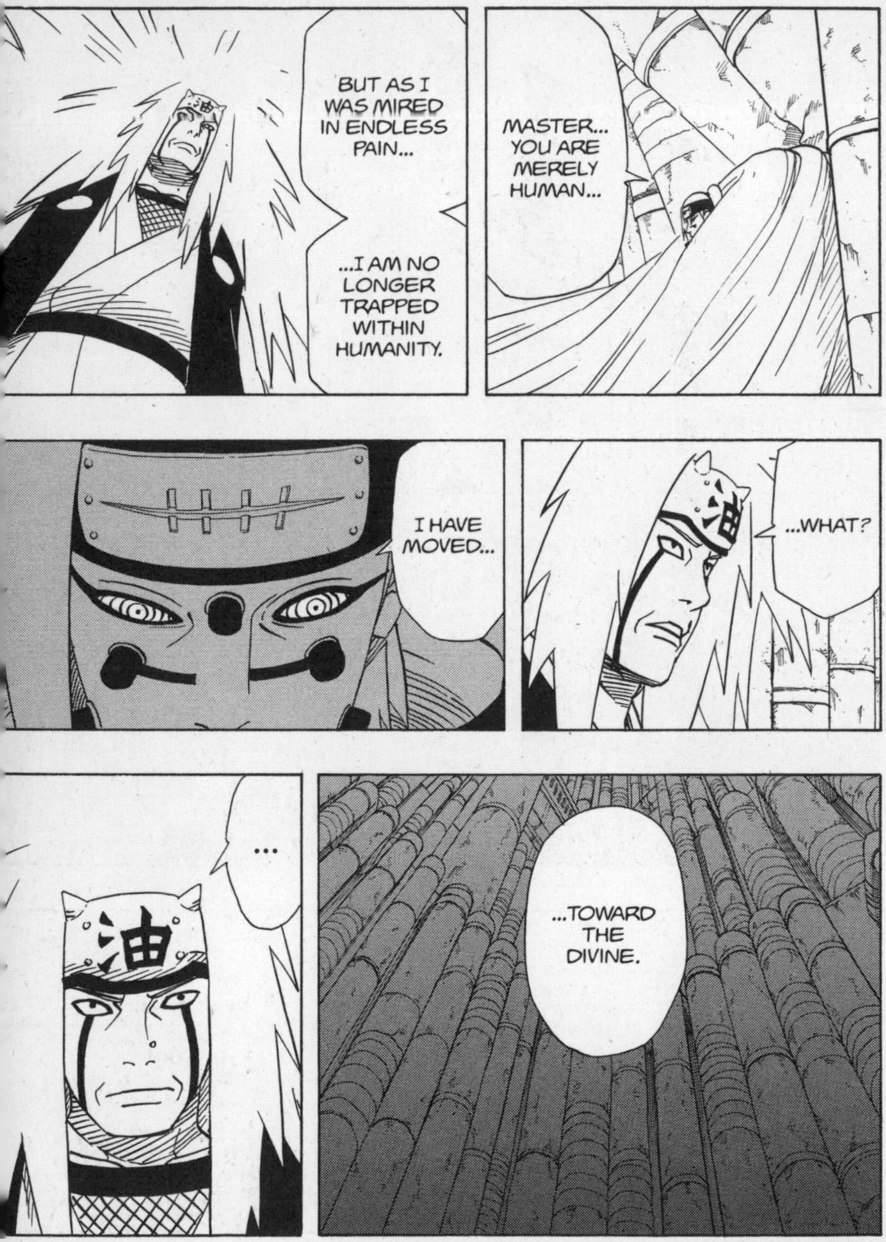
MASTER... YOU ARE MERELY HUMAN...
BUT AS I WAS MIRED IN ENDLESS PAIN...
...I AM NO LONGER TRAPPED WITHIN HUMANITY.
...WHAT?
I HAVE MOVED...
...TOWARD THE DIVINE.
...

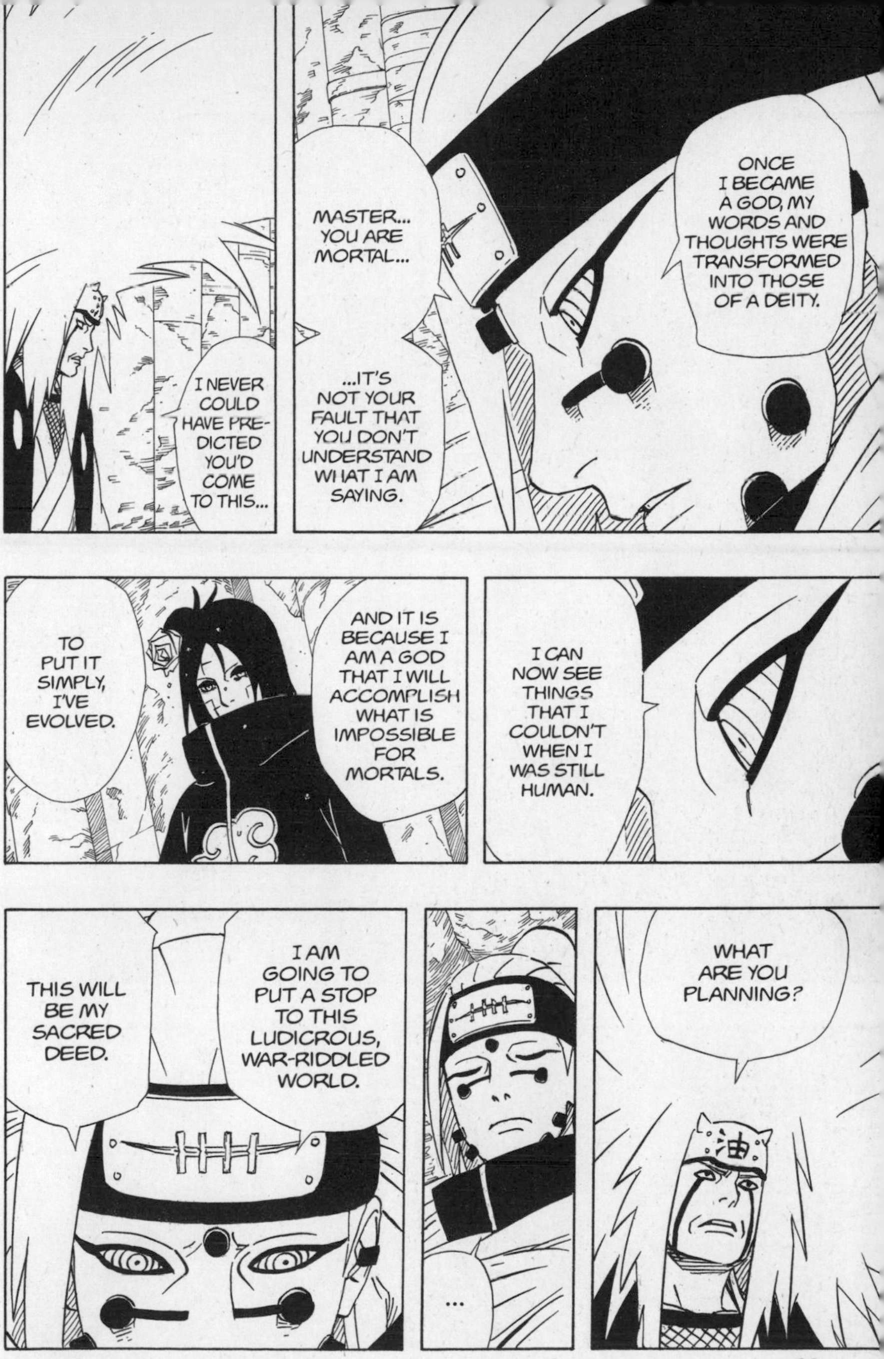
ONCE I BECAME A GOD, MY WORDS AND THOUGHTS WERE TRANSFORMED INTO THOSE OF A DEITY.
MASTER... YOU ARE MORTAL...
...IT'S NOT YOUR FAULT THAT YOU DON'T UNDERSTAND WHAT I AM SAYING.
I NEVER COULD HAVE PRE-DICTED YOU'D COME TO THIS...
I CAN NOW SEE THINGS THAT I COULDN'T WHEN I WAS STILL HUMAN.
AND IT IS BECAUSE I AM A GOD THAT I WILL ACCOMPLISH WHAT IS IMPOSSIBLE FOR MORTALS.
TO PUT IT SIMPLY, I'VE EVOLVED.
WHAT ARE YOU PLANNING?
...
I AM GOING TO PUT A STOP TO THIS LUDICROUS, WAR-RIDDLED WORLD.
THIS WILL BE MY SACRED DEED.

READ THIS WAY

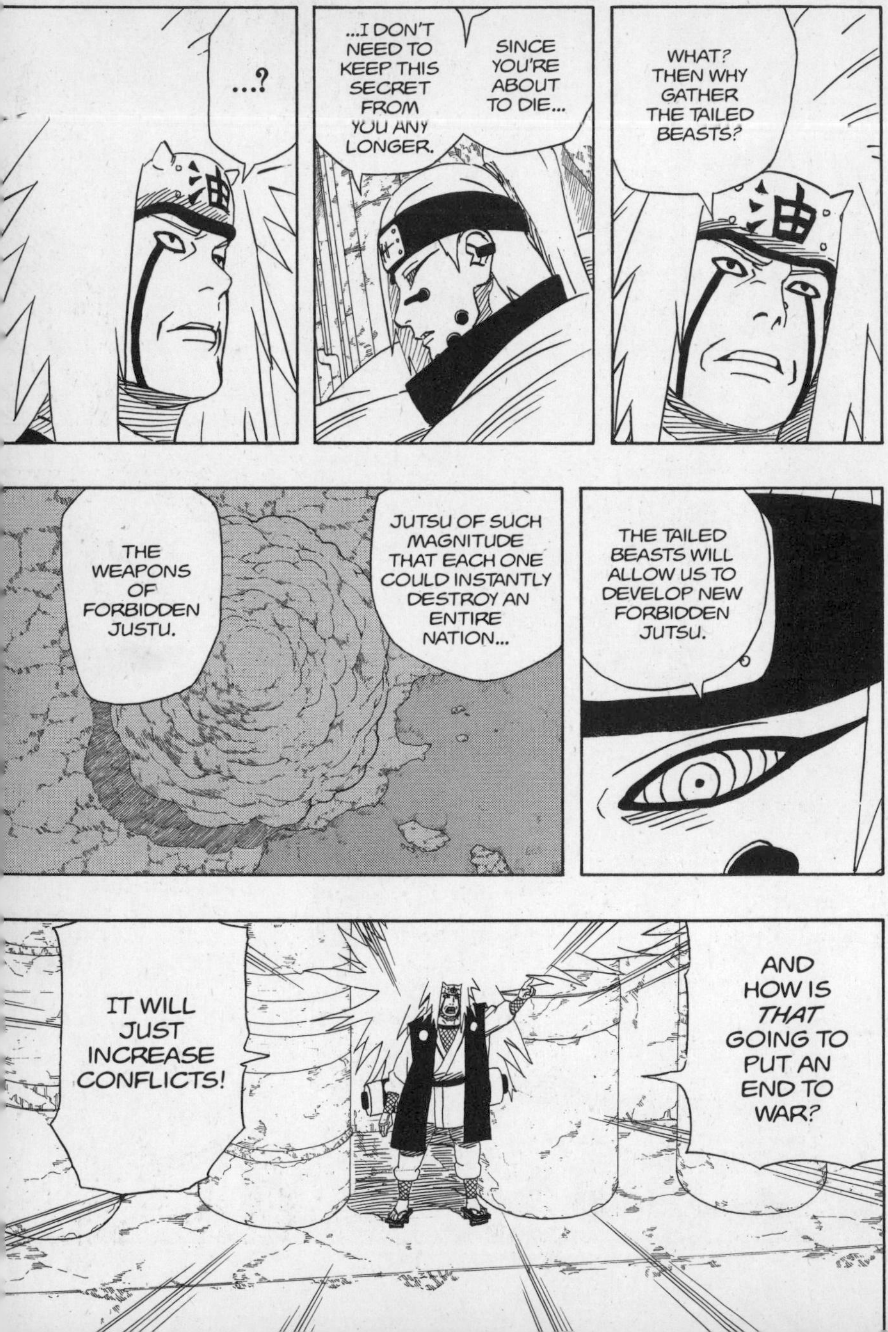
WHAT? THEN WHY GATHER THE TAILED BEASTS?
SINCE YOU'RE ABOUT TO DIE...
...I DON'T NEED TO KEEP THIS SECRET FROM YOU ANY LONGER.
...?
THE TAILED BEASTS WILL ALLOW US TO DEVELOP NEW FORBIDDEN JUTSU.
JUTSU OF SUCH MAGNITUDE THAT EACH ONE COULD INSTANTLY DESTROY AN ENTIRE NATION...
THE WEAPONS OF FORBIDDEN JUSTU.
AND HOW IS *THAT* GOING TO PUT AN END TO WAR?
IT WILL JUST INCREASE CONFLICTS!

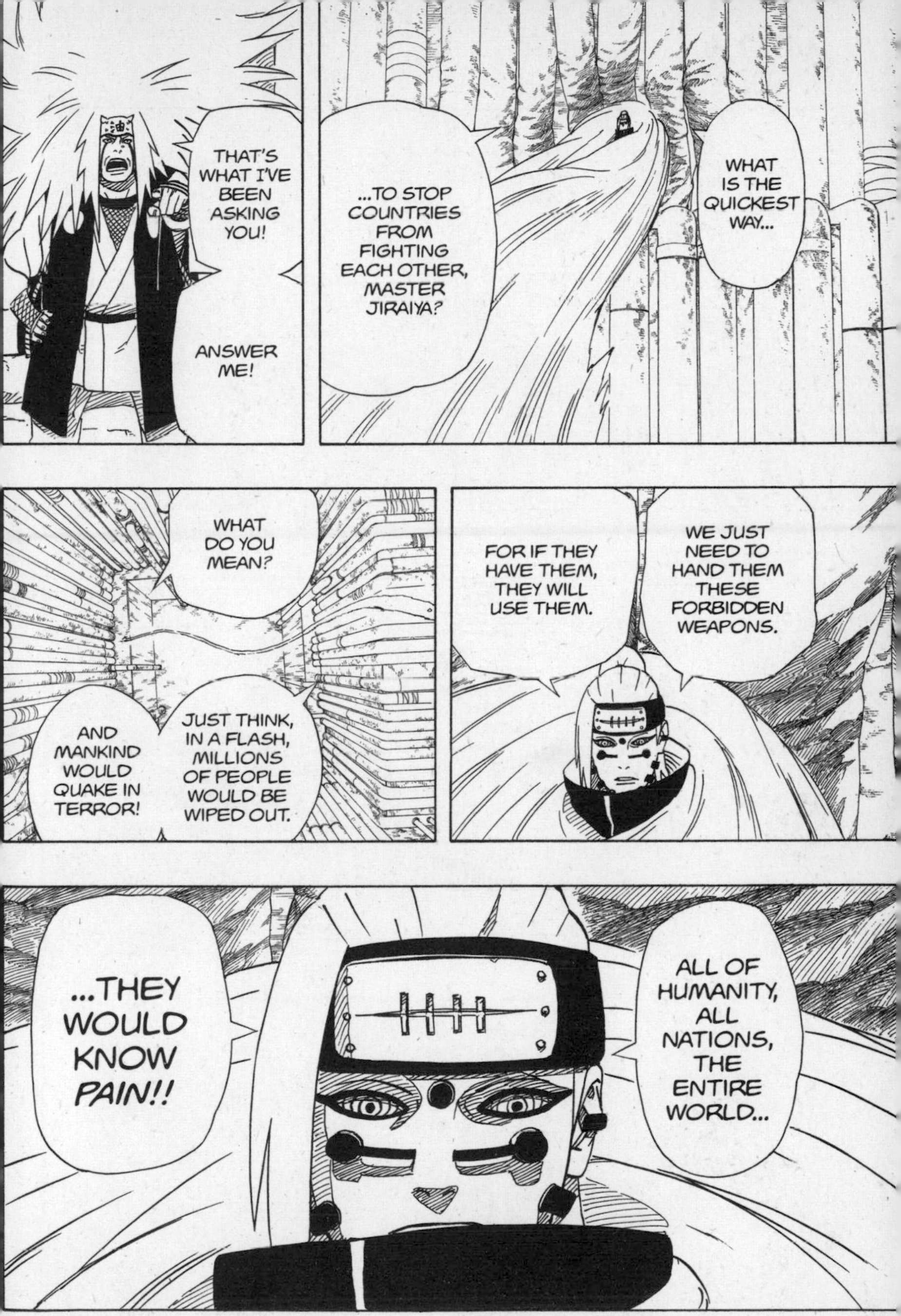
WHAT IS THE QUICKEST WAY...
...TO STOP COUNTRIES FROM FIGHTING EACH OTHER, MASTER JIRAIYA?
THAT'S WHAT I'VE BEEN ASKING YOU!
ANSWER ME!
WE JUST NEED TO HAND THEM THESE FORBIDDEN WEAPONS.
FOR IF THEY HAVE THEM, THEY WILL USE THEM.
WHAT DO YOU MEAN?
JUST THINK, IN A FLASH, MILLIONS OF PEOPLE WOULD BE WIPED OUT.
AND MANKIND WOULD QUAKE IN TERROR!
ALL OF HUMANITY, ALL NATIONS, THE ENTIRE WORLD...
...THEY WOULD KNOW PAIN!!

READ THIS WAY

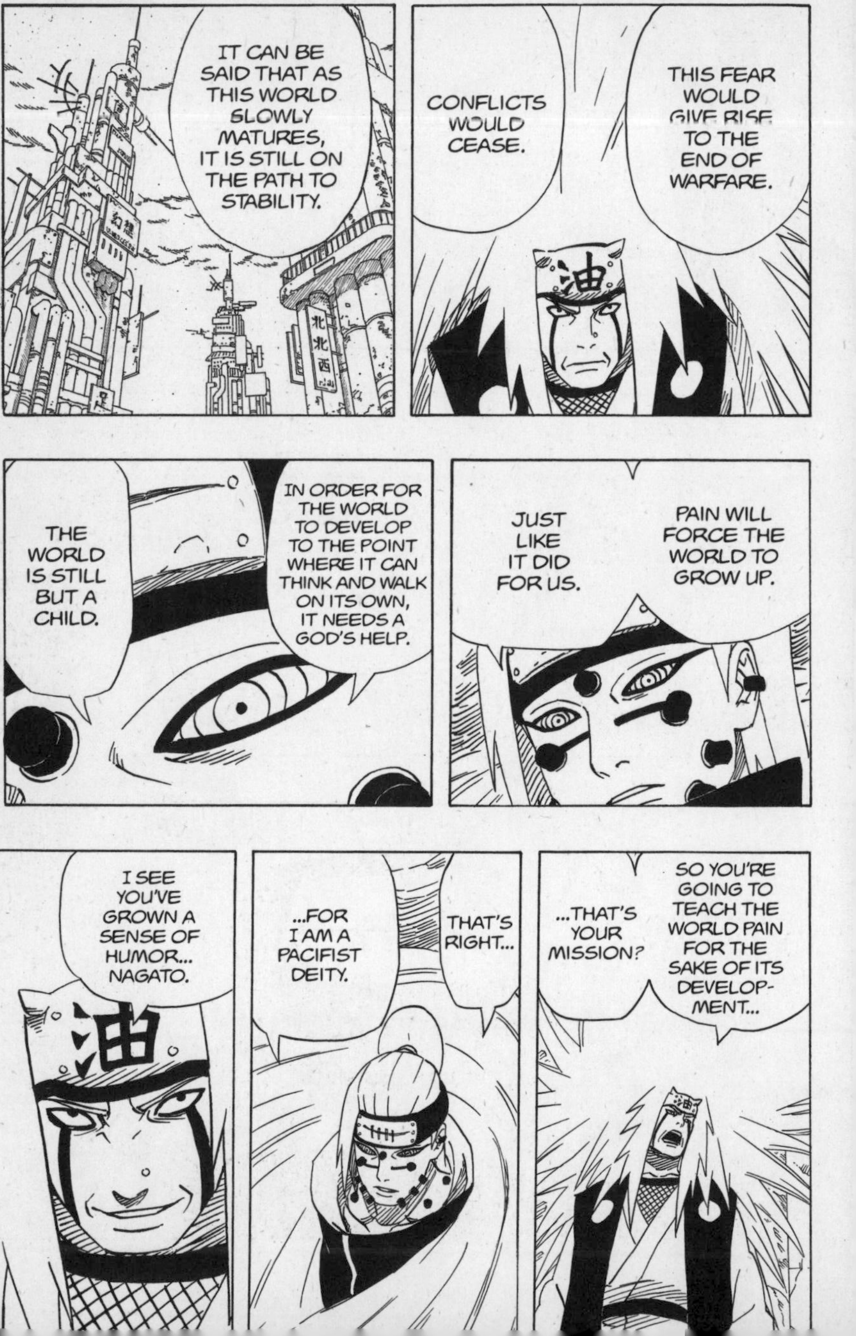
THIS FEAR WOULD GIVE RISE TO THE END OF WARFARE.
CONFLICTS WOULD CEASE.
IT CAN BE SAID THAT AS THIS WORLD SLOWLY MATURES, IT IS STILL ON THE PATH TO STABILITY.
PAIN WILL FORCE THE WORLD TO GROW UP.
JUST LIKE IT DID FOR US.
IN ORDER FOR THE WORLD TO DEVELOP TO THE POINT WHERE IT CAN THINK AND WALK ON ITS OWN, IT NEEDS A GOD'S HELP.
THE WORLD IS STILL BUT A CHILD.
SO YOU'RE GOING TO TEACH THE WORLD PAIN FOR THE SAKE OF ITS DEVELOPMENT...
...THAT'S YOUR MISSION?
THAT'S RIGHT...
...FOR I AM A PACIFIST DEITY.
I SEE YOU'VE GROWN A SENSE OF HUMOR... NAGATO.

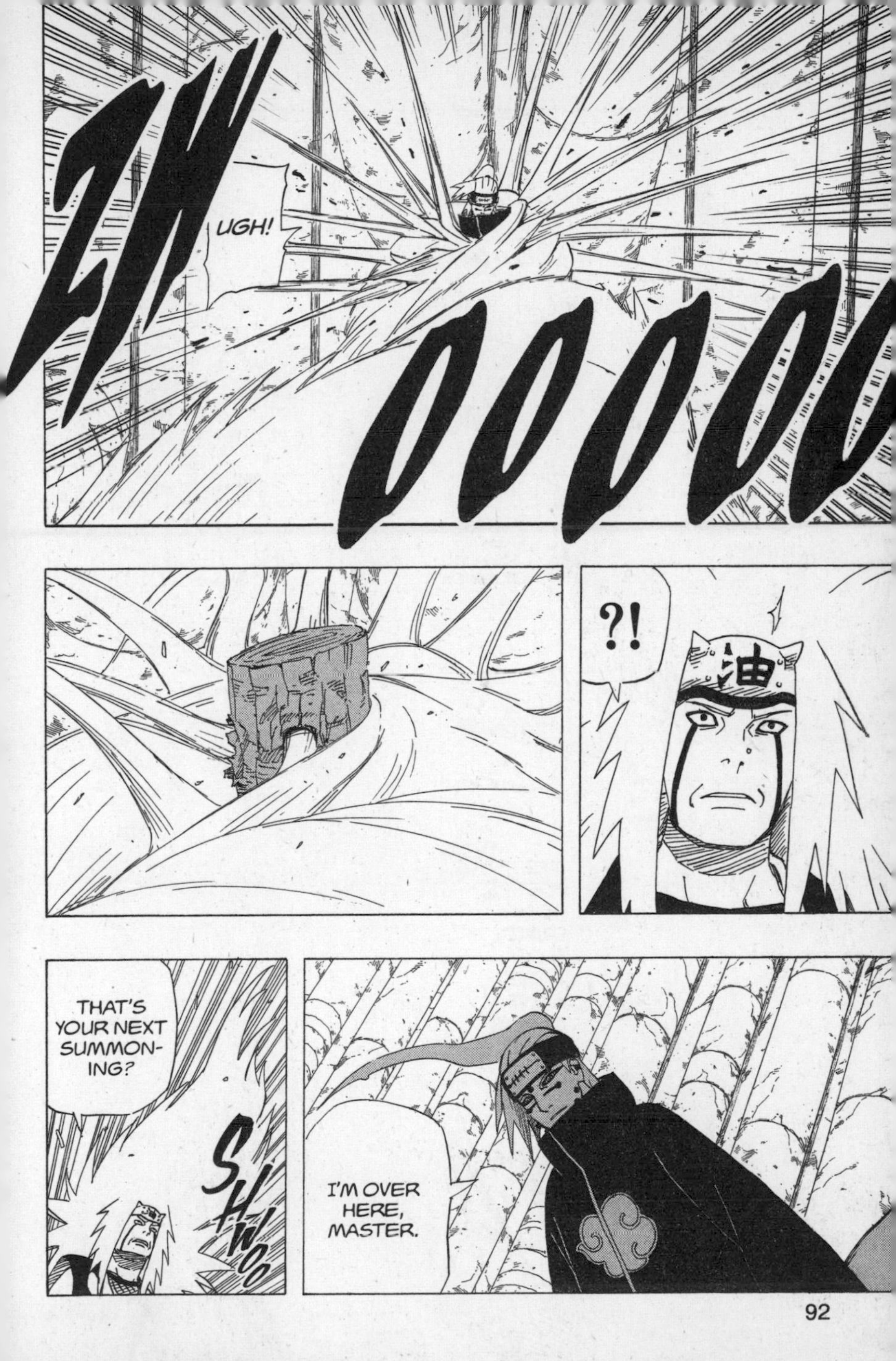
ZWOOOOOO
UGH!
?!
I'M OVER HERE, MASTER.
THAT'S YOUR NEXT SUMMONING?
SHWOO

READ THIS WAY

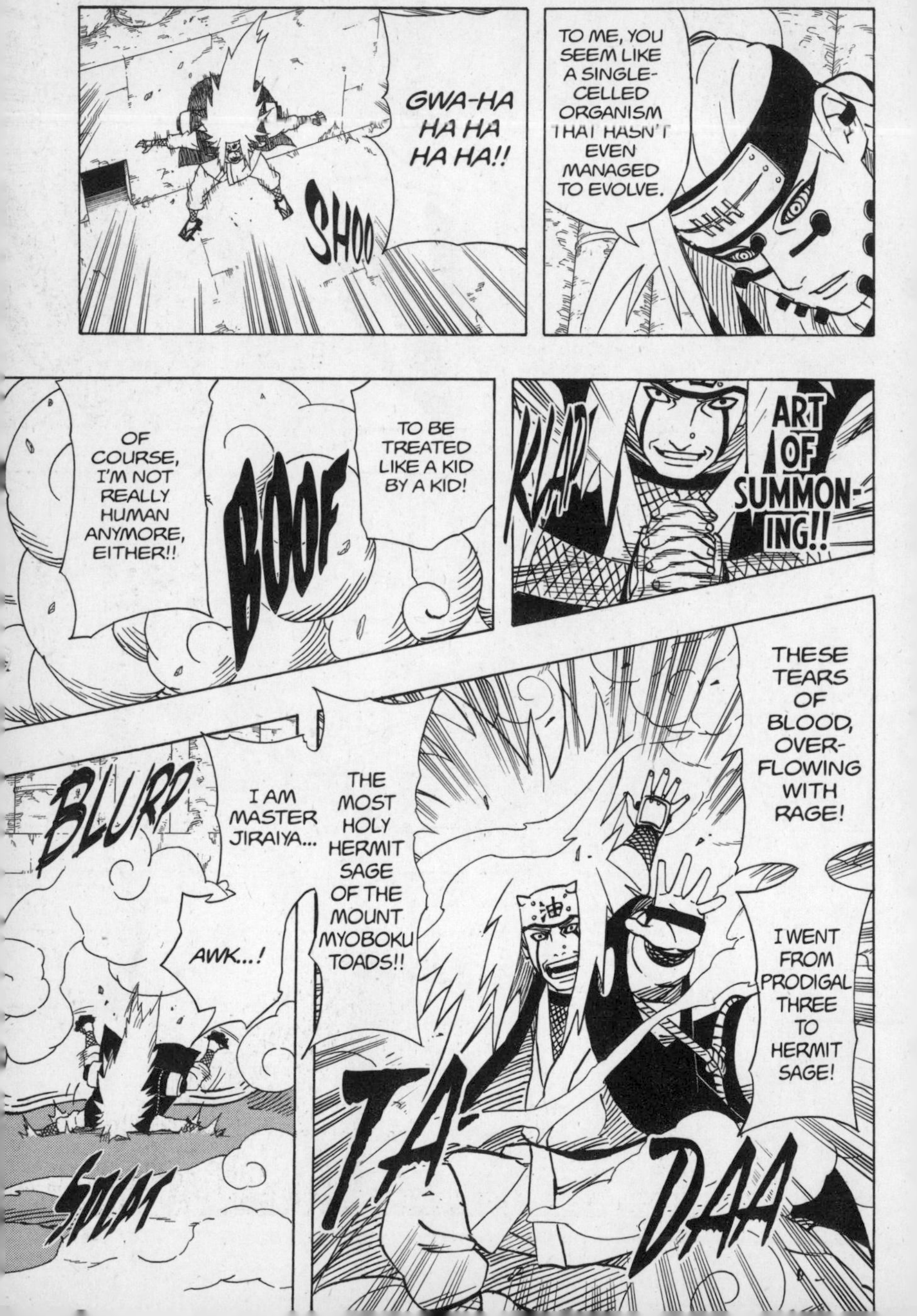
TO ME, YOU SEEM LIKE A SINGLE-CELLED ORGANISM THAT HASN'T EVEN MANAGED TO EVOLVE.
GWA-HA HA HA HA HA!!
SHOO
KLAP
ART OF SUMMON-ING!!
TO BE TREATED LIKE A KID BY A KID!
BOOF
OF COURSE, I'M NOT REALLY HUMAN ANYMORE, EITHER!!
THESE TEARS OF BLOOD, OVER-FLOWING WITH RAGE!
I WENT FROM PRODIGAL THREE TO HERMIT SAGE!
I AM MASTER JIRAIYA...
THE MOST HOLY HERMIT SAGE OF THE MOUNT MYOBOKU TOADS!!
TA-DAA
BLURP
AWK...!
SPLAT

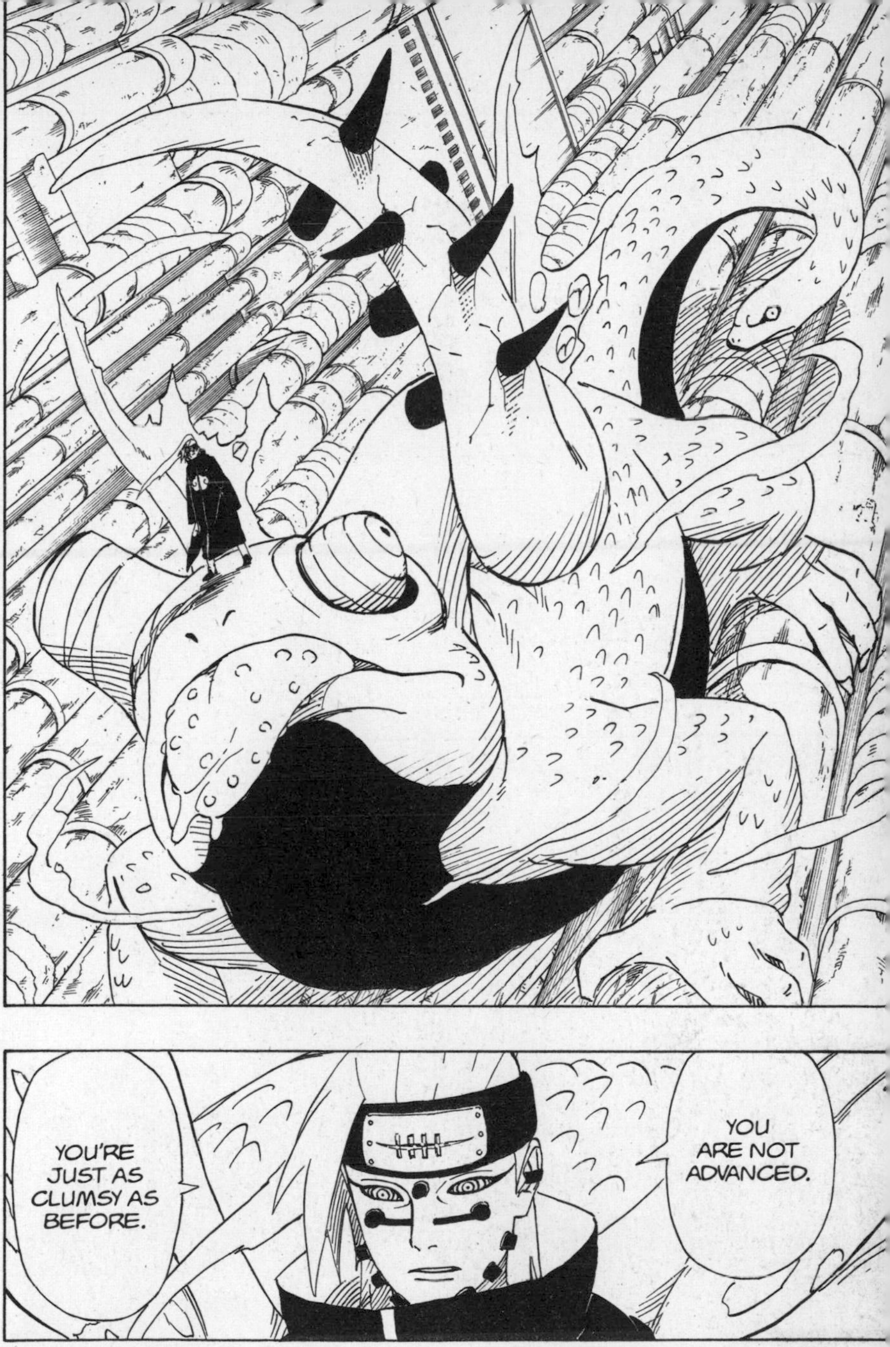
YOU ARE NOT ADVANCED.
YOU'RE JUST AS CLUMSY AS BEFORE.

READ THIS WAY

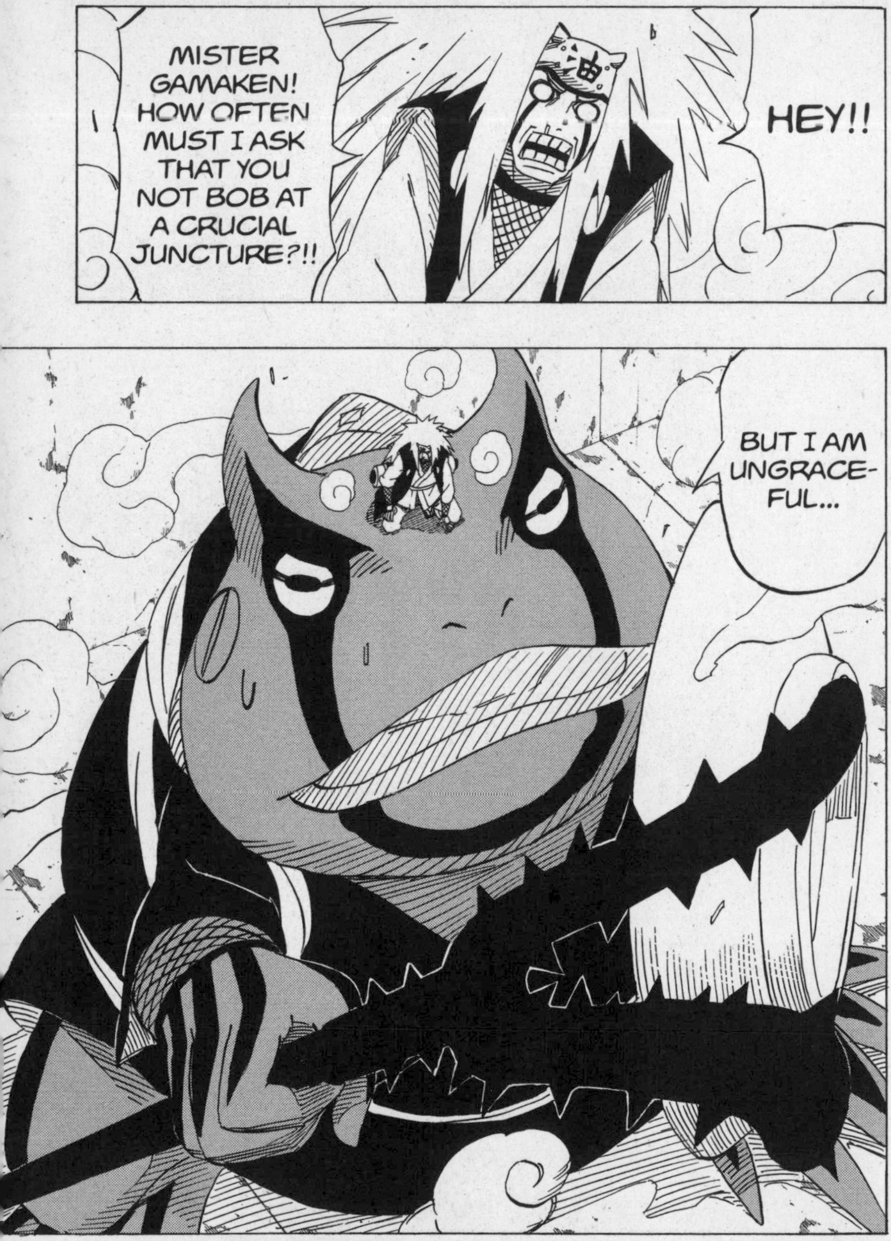
HEY!!
MISTER GAMAKEN! HOW OFTEN MUST I ASK THAT YOU NOT BOB AT A CRUCIAL JUNCTURE?!!
BUT I AM UNGRACE-FUL...

NARUTO

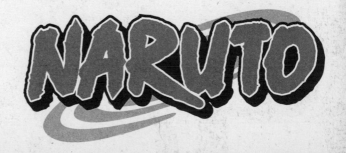

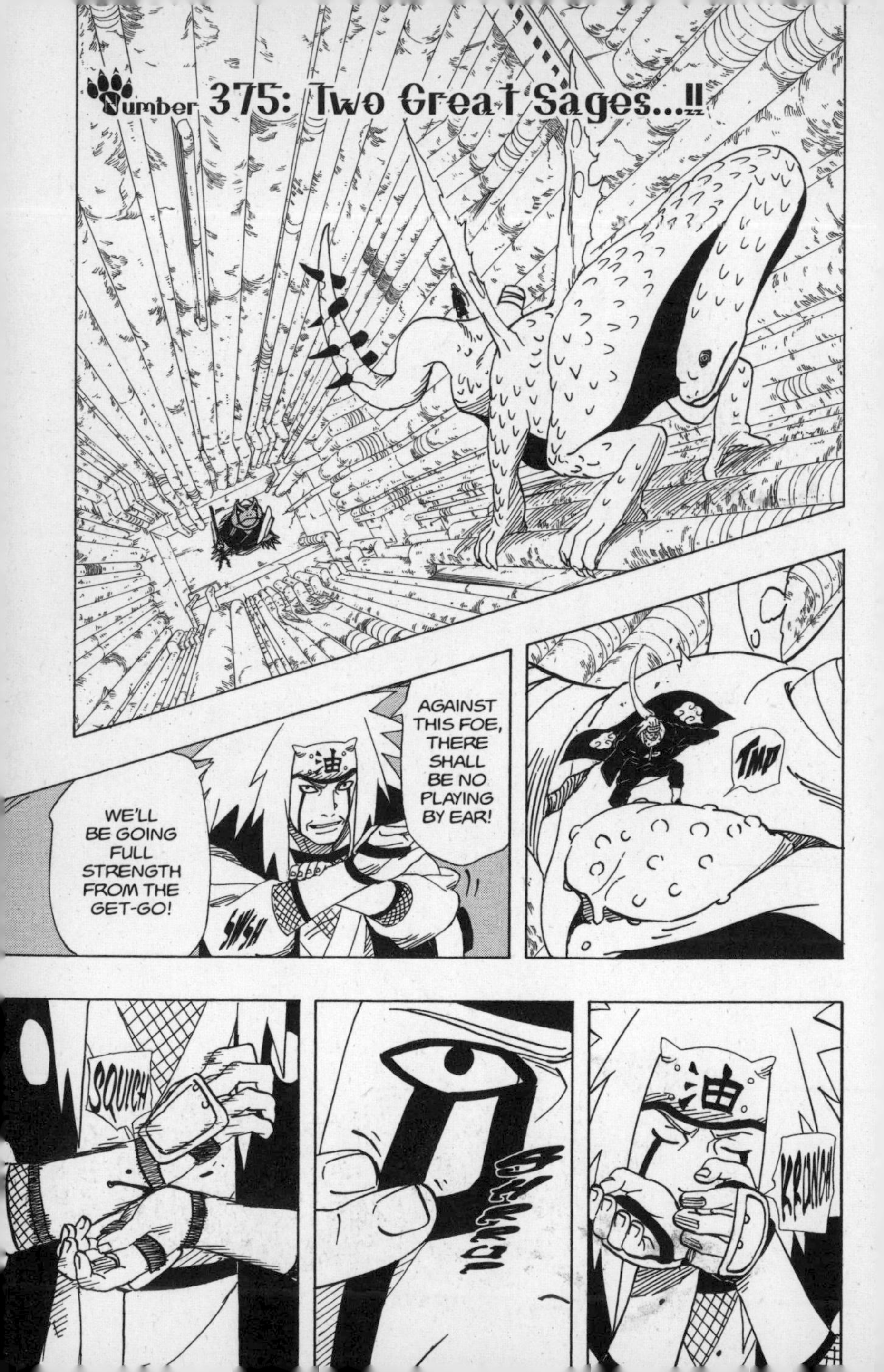
Number 375: Two Great Sages...!!
TMP
AGAINST THIS FOE, THERE SHALL BE NO PLAYING BY EAR!
WE'LL BE GOING FULL STRENGTH FROM THE GET-GO!
SWSH
KRUNCH
SQUICH

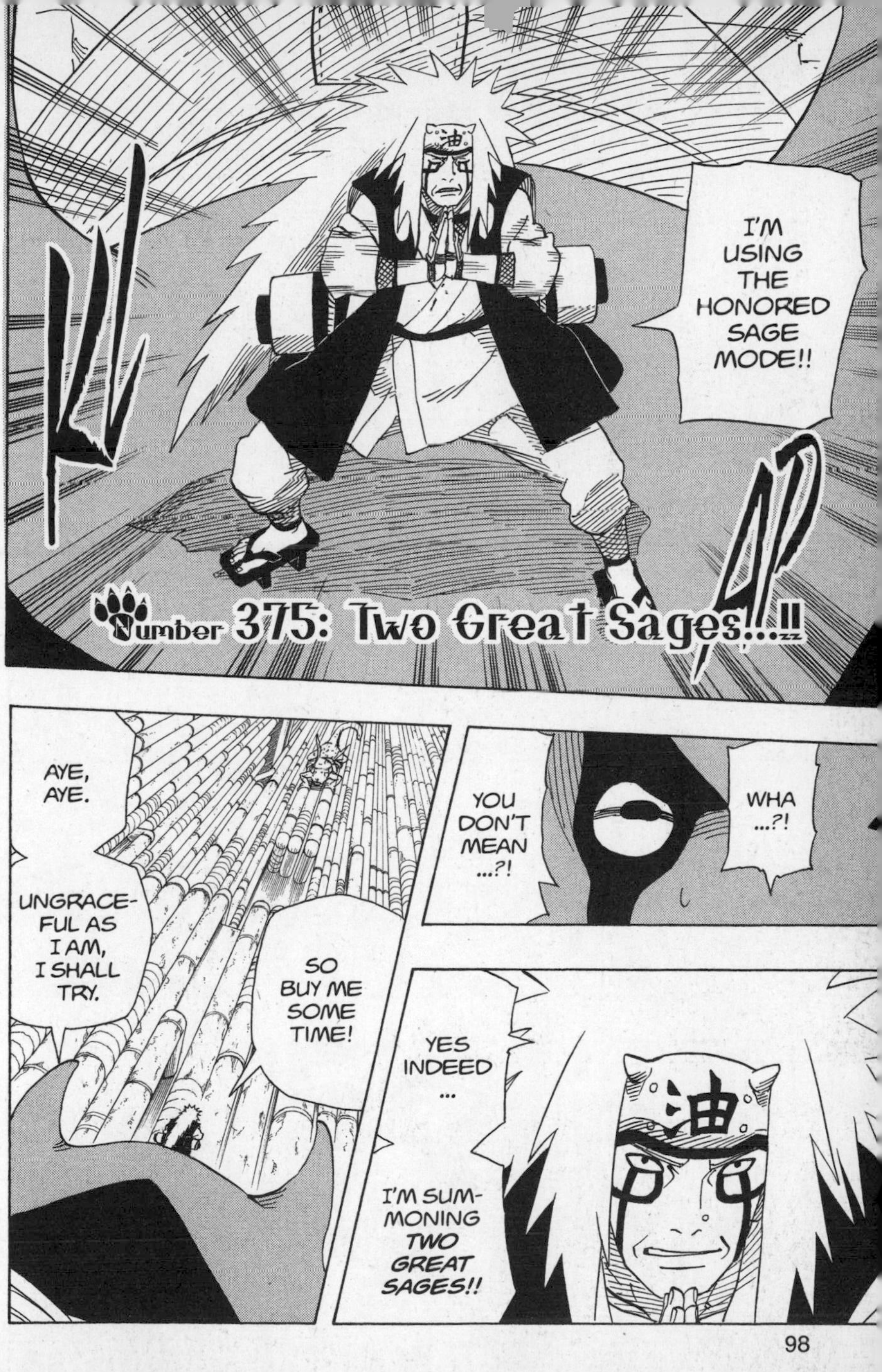
I'M USING THE HONORED SAGE MODE!!
Number 375: Two Great Sages...!!
WHA...?!
YOU DON'T MEAN...?!
YES INDEED...
I'M SUMMONING TWO GREAT SAGES!!
SO BUY ME SOME TIME!
AYE, AYE.
UNGRACEFUL AS I AM, I SHALL TRY.

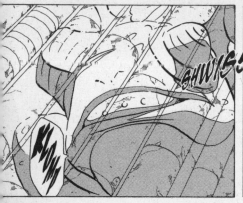

SHWISST

KHOMM

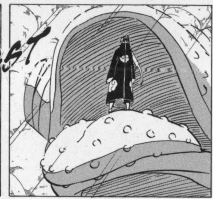

WHAT A BOTHER... WHERE IN THE WORLD DID HE FIND SUCH A CREATURE...?

HE VANISHED...!

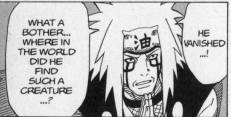

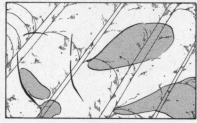

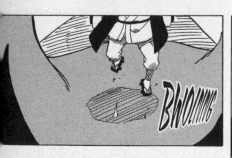

BWOING

NOW THAT HE'S MADE HIMSELF INVISIBLE, WE'VE GOT TO USE BARRIER BATTLE ARTS.

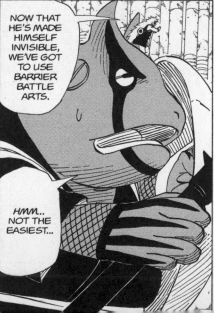

HMM... NOT THE EASIEST...

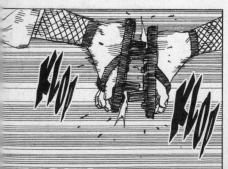

KLOT

KLOT

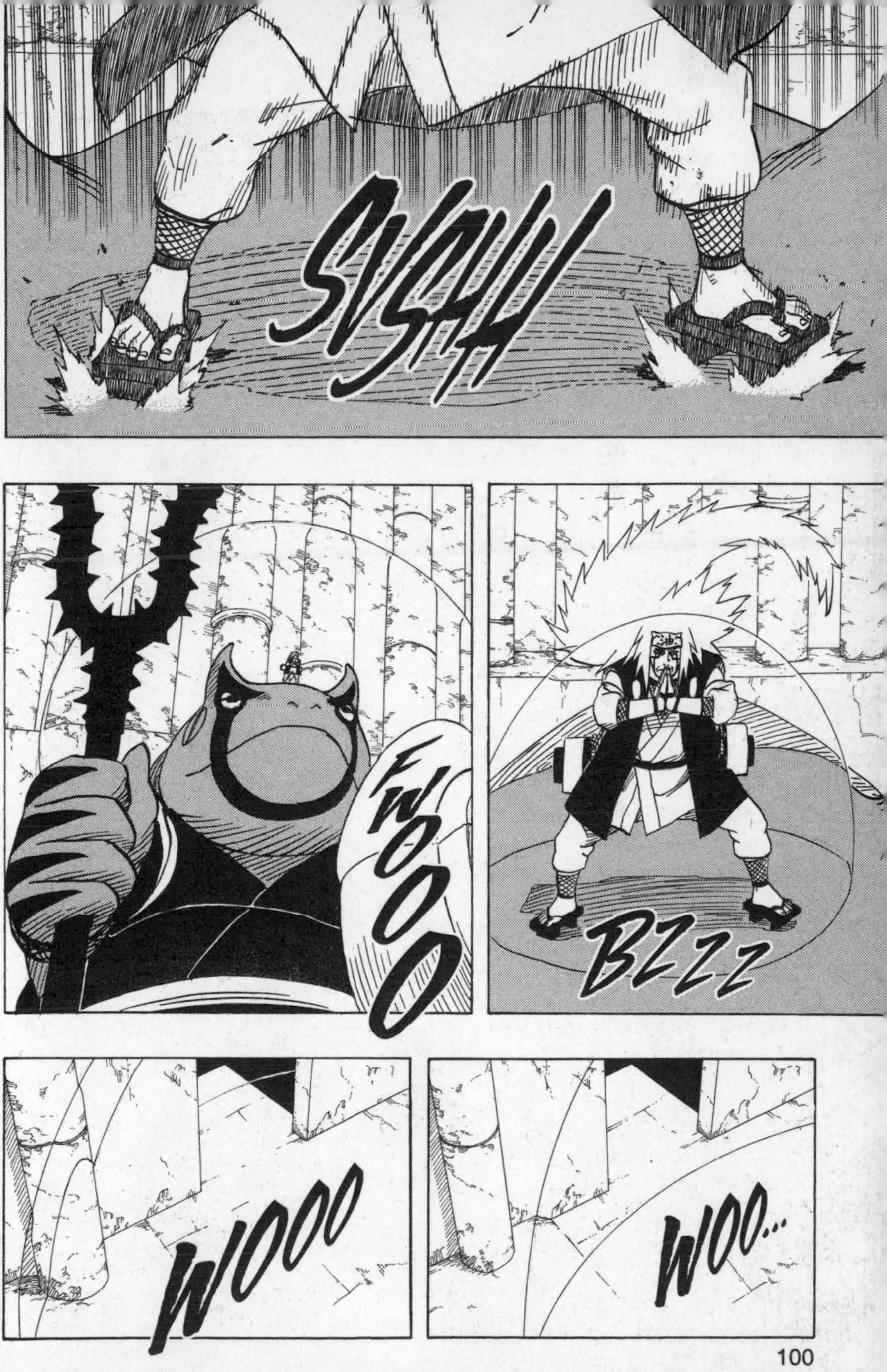
SVSHH
BZZZ
FWOOOO
WOO...
WOOO

READ THIS WAY

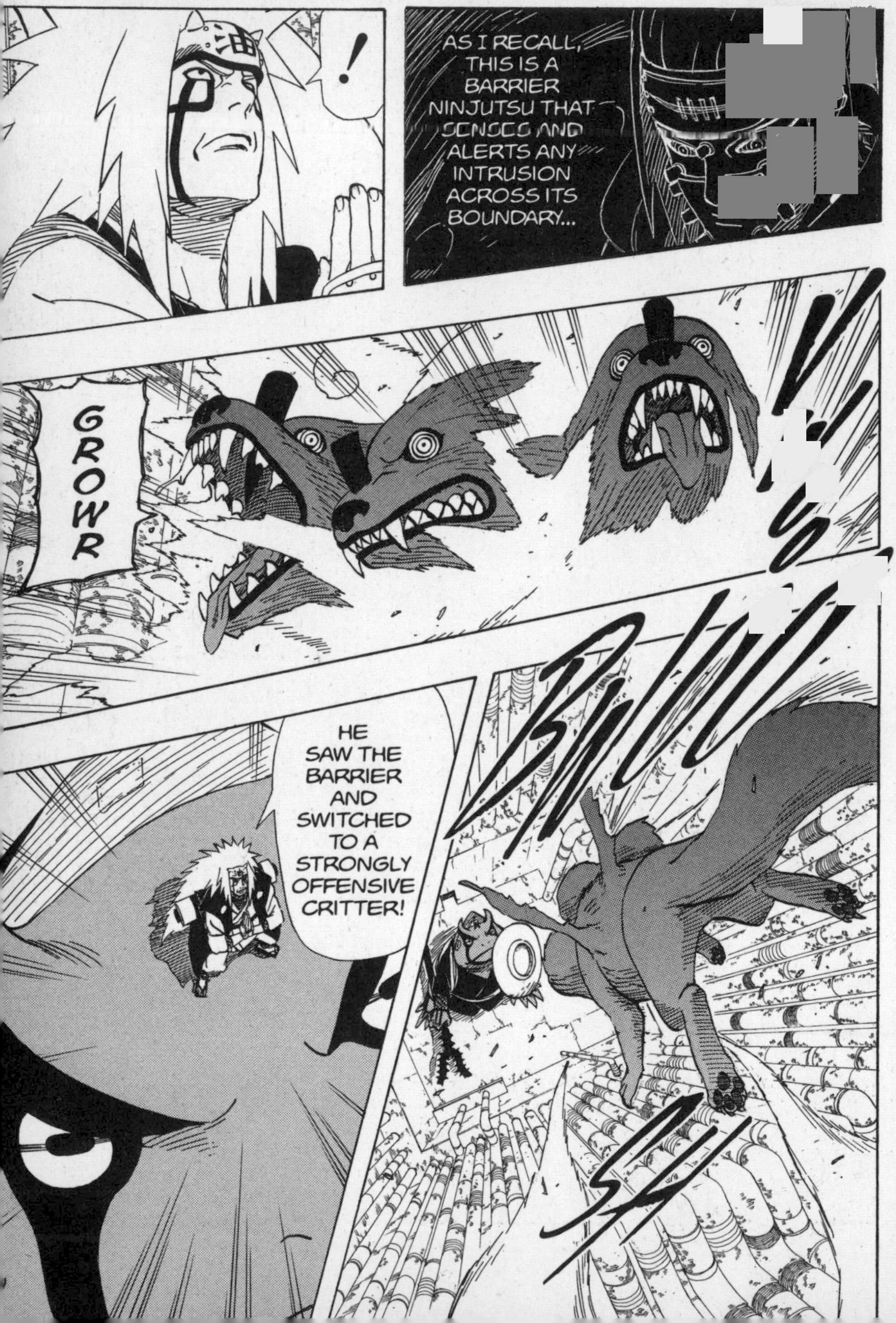
AS I RECALL, THIS IS A BARRIER NINJUTSU THAT SENSES AND ALERTS ANY INTRUSION ACROSS ITS BOUNDARY...
!
GROWR
HE SAW THE BARRIER AND SWITCHED TO A STRONGLY OFFENSIVE CRITTER!

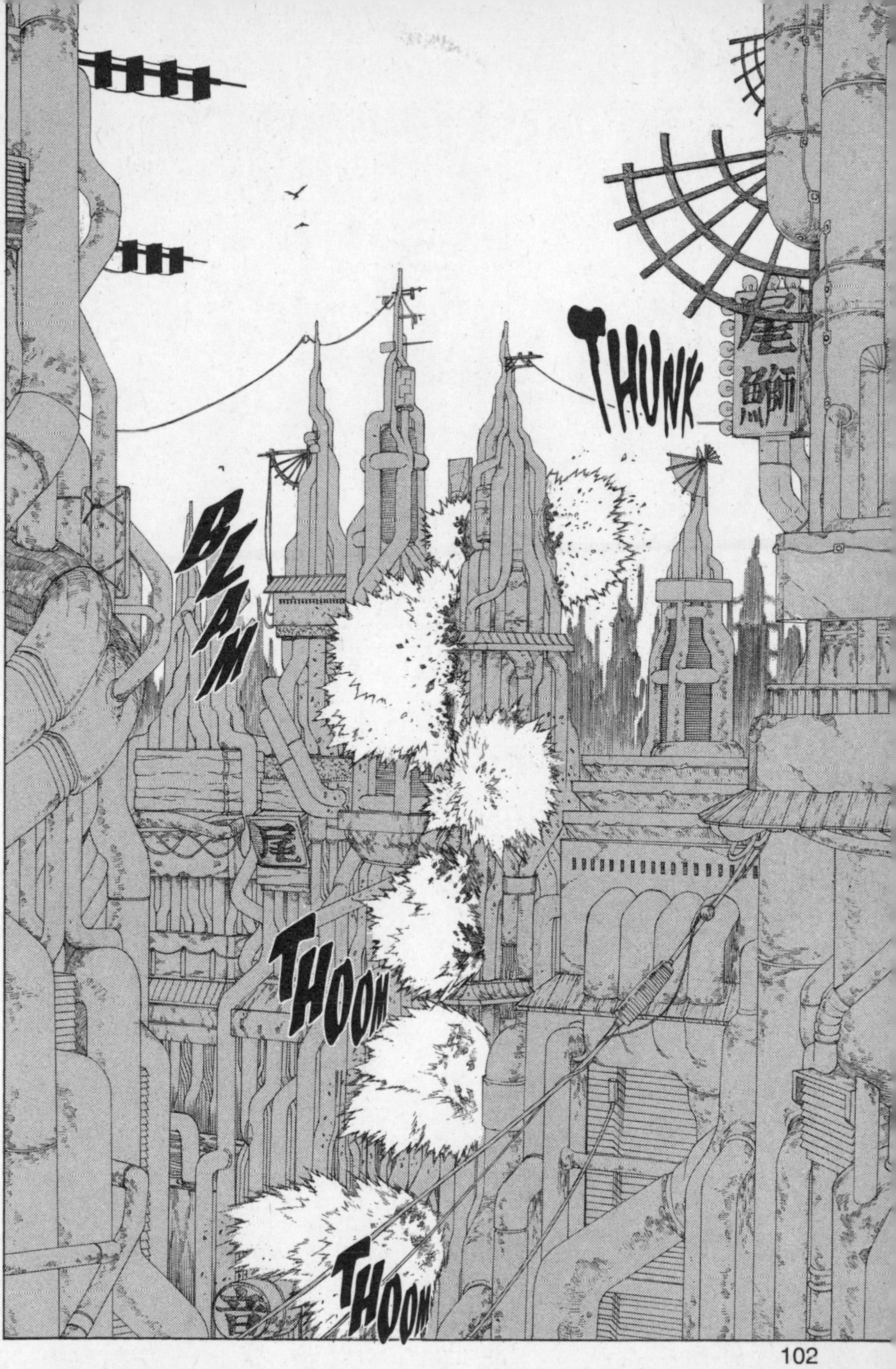
THUNK
BLAM
尾
THOOM
THOOM

READ THIS WAY

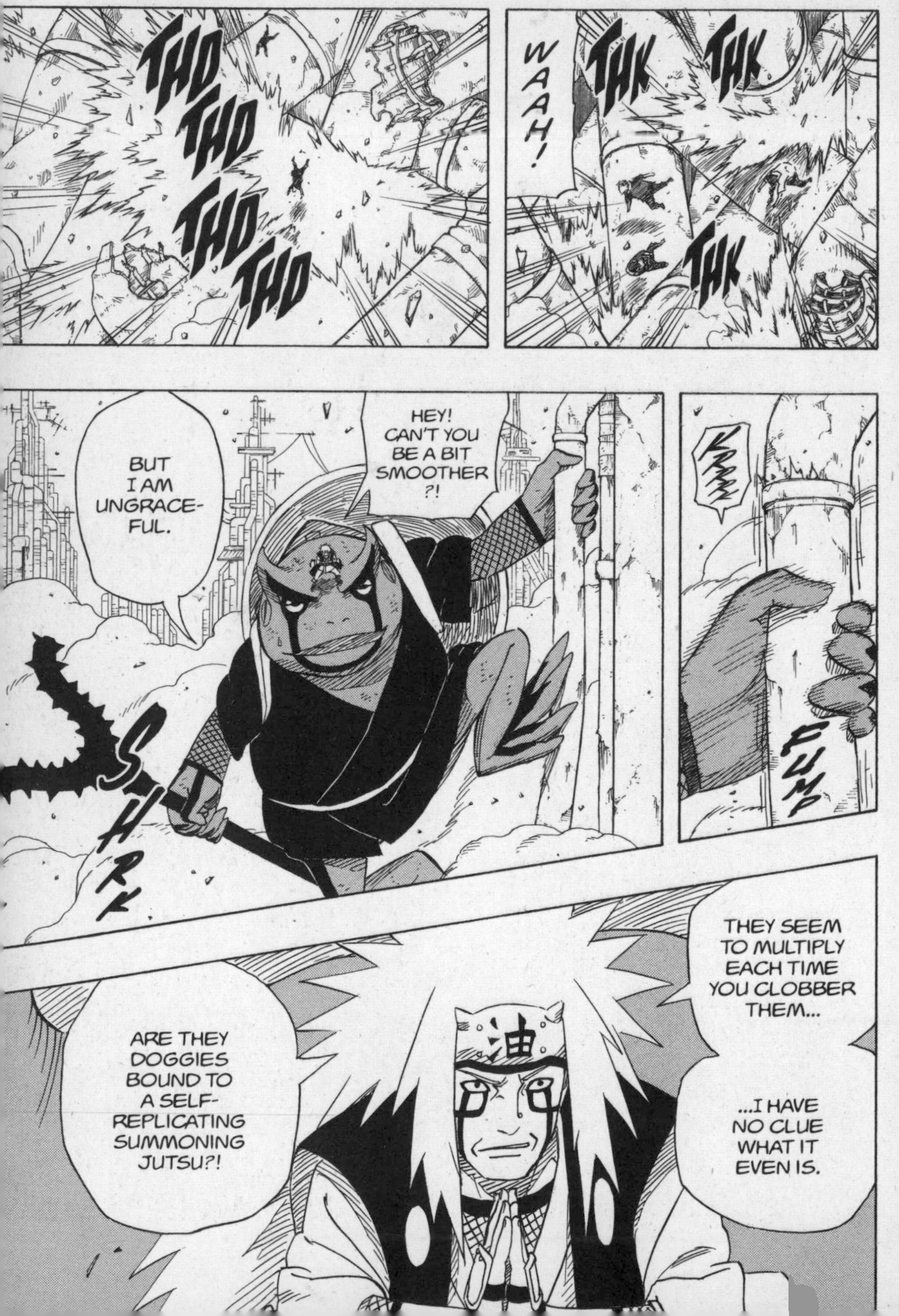
WAAAH!
THK THK THK
THD THD THD THD
FUMP
HEY! CAN'T YOU BE A BIT SMOOTHER?!
BUT I AM UNGRACEFUL.
SHRK
THEY SEEM TO MULTIPLY EACH TIME YOU CLOBBER THEM...
...I HAVE NO CLUE WHAT IT EVEN IS.
ARE THEY DOGGIES BOUND TO A SELF-REPLICATING SUMMONING JUTSU?!

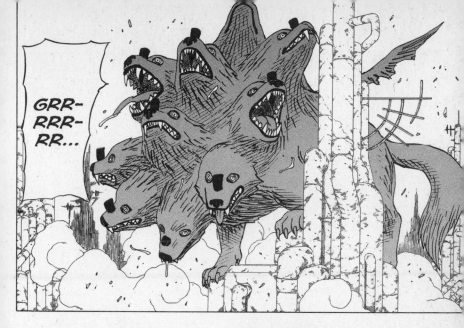

GRR-
RRR-
RR...

INCOMING!
AND
THEY'RE
GOING TO
SPLIT UP
AGAIN!!

TOP

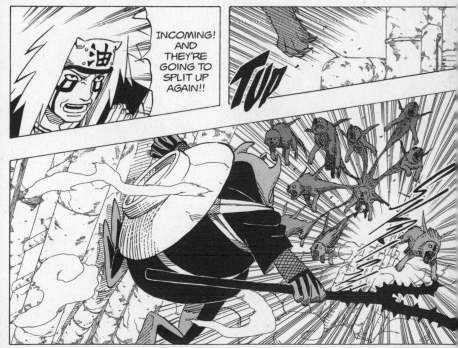

READ THIS WAY

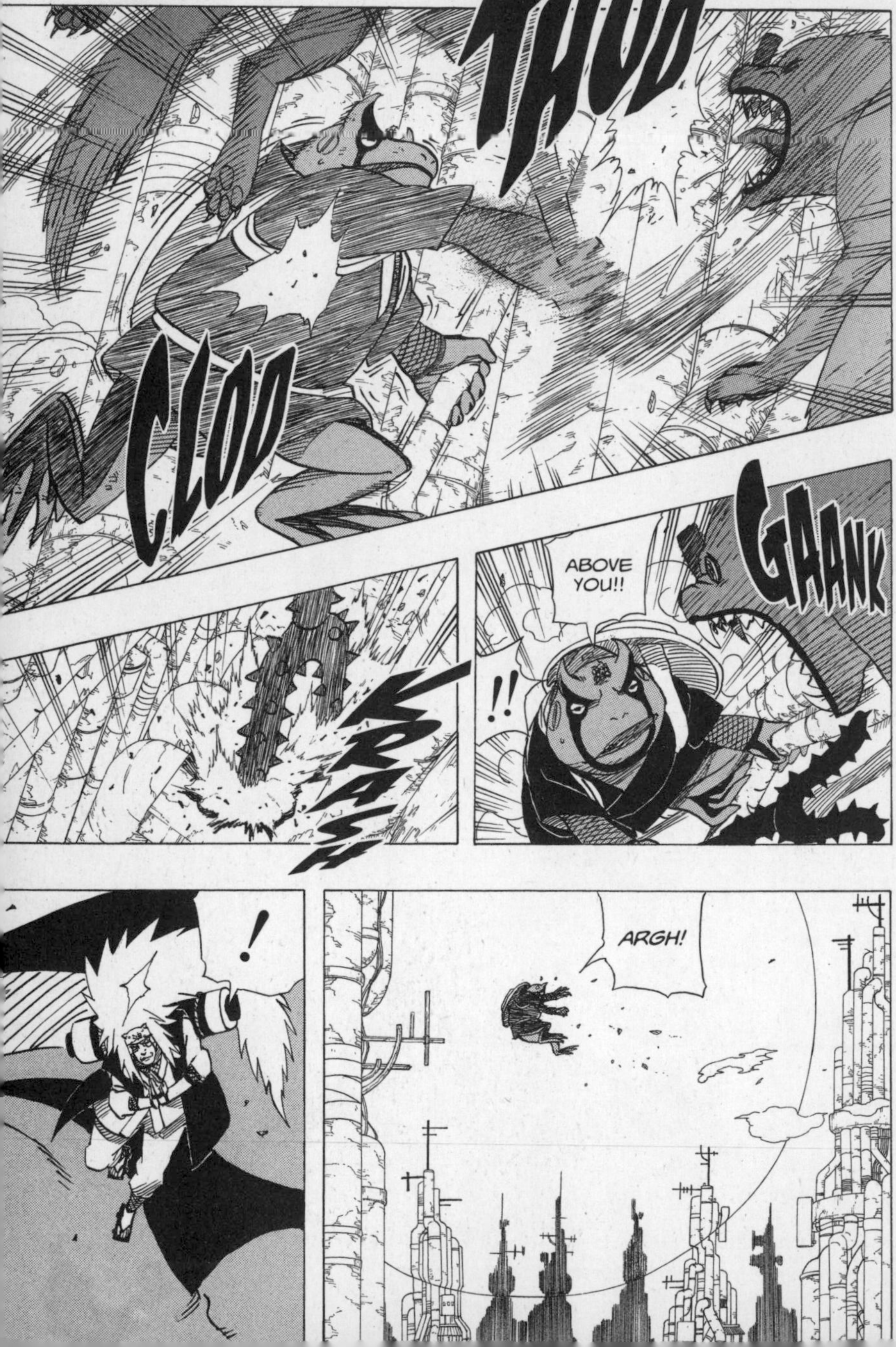
THUD
CLOD
GAANK
ABOVE YOU!!
!!
VRASH
ARGH!
!

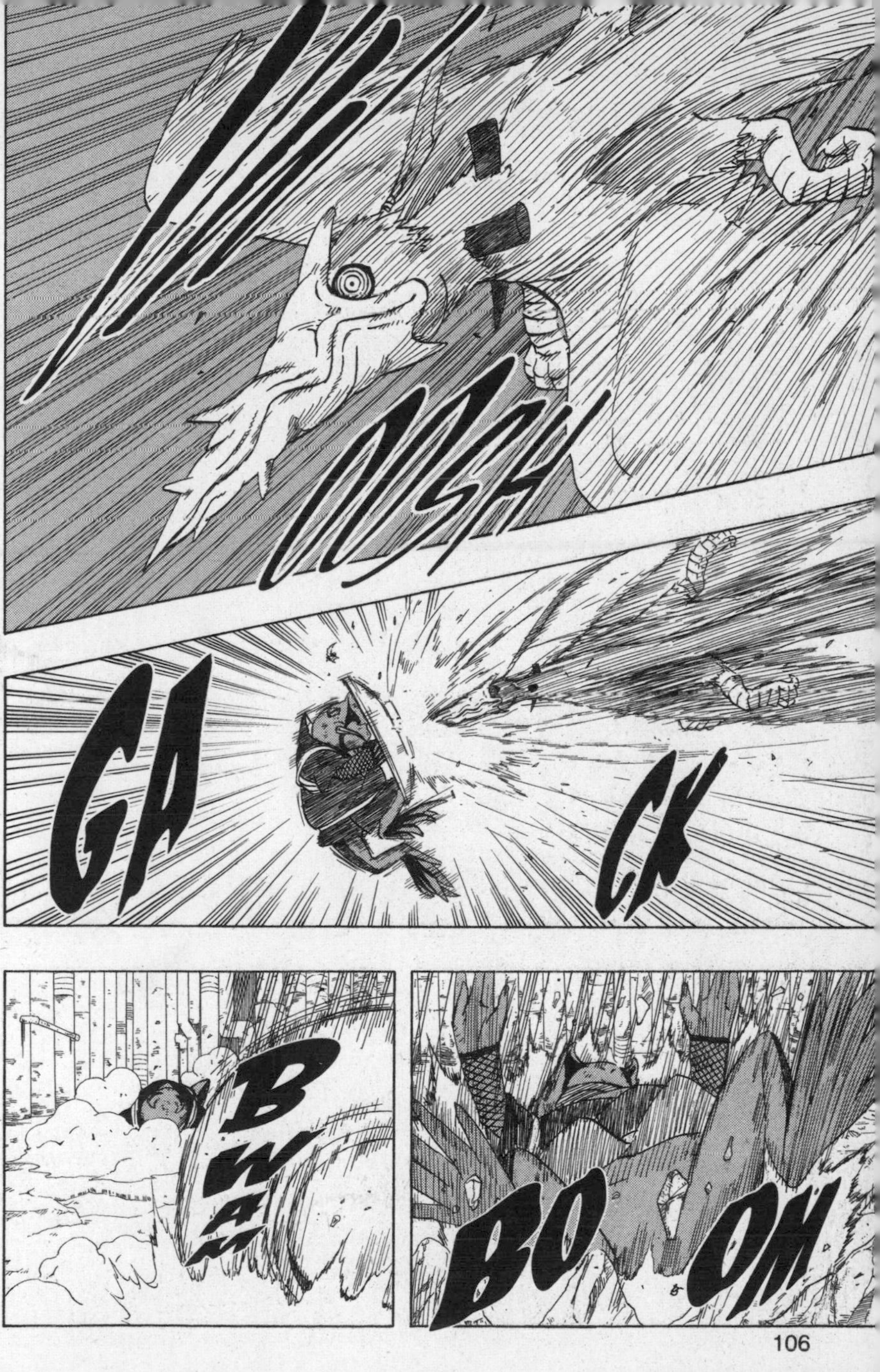
WHOOSH
GACK
BOOM
BWAA

READ THIS WAY

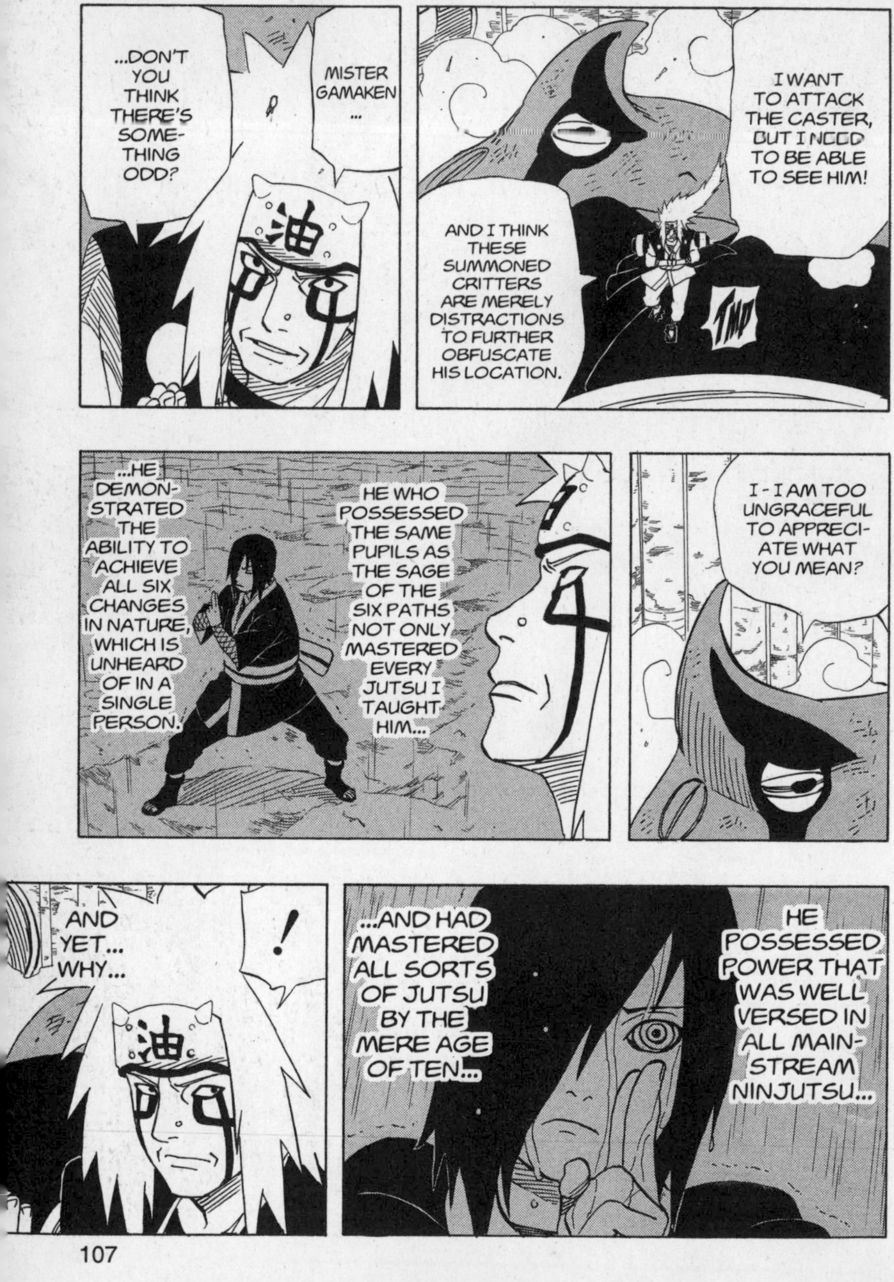
I WANT TO ATTACK THE CASTER, BUT I NEED TO BE ABLE TO SEE HIM!
AND I THINK THESE SUMMONED CRITTERS ARE MERELY DISTRACTIONS TO FURTHER OBFUSCATE HIS LOCATION.
TMP
MISTER GAMAKEN...
...DON'T YOU THINK THERE'S SOME-THING ODD?
I-I AM TOO UNGRACEFUL TO APPRECI-ATE WHAT YOU MEAN?
HE WHO POSSESSED THE SAME PUPILS AS THE SAGE OF THE SIX PATHS NOT ONLY MASTERED EVERY JUTSU I TAUGHT HIM...
...HE DEMON-STRATED THE ABILITY TO ACHIEVE ALL SIX CHANGES IN NATURE, WHICH IS UNHEARD OF IN A SINGLE PERSON.
HE POSSESSED POWER THAT WAS WELL VERSED IN ALL MAIN-STREAM NINJUTSU...
...AND HAD MASTERED ALL SORTS OF JUTSU BY THE MERE AGE OF TEN...
!
AND YET... WHY...

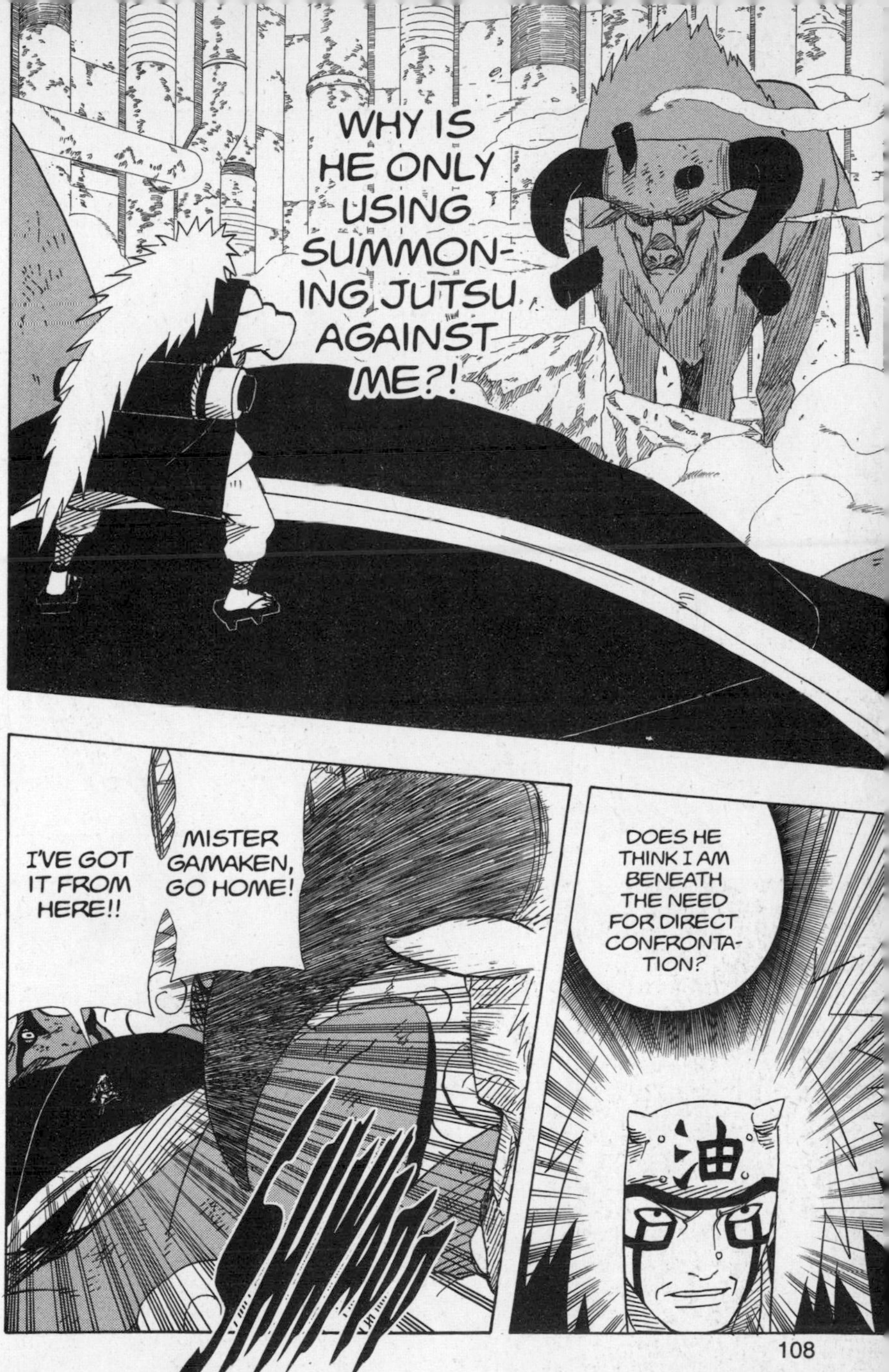
WHY IS HE ONLY USING SUMMONING JUTSU AGAINST ME?!
DOES HE THINK I AM BENEATH THE NEED FOR DIRECT CONFRONTATION?
油
MISTER GAMAKEN, GO HOME!
I'VE GOT IT FROM HERE!!

READ THIS WAY

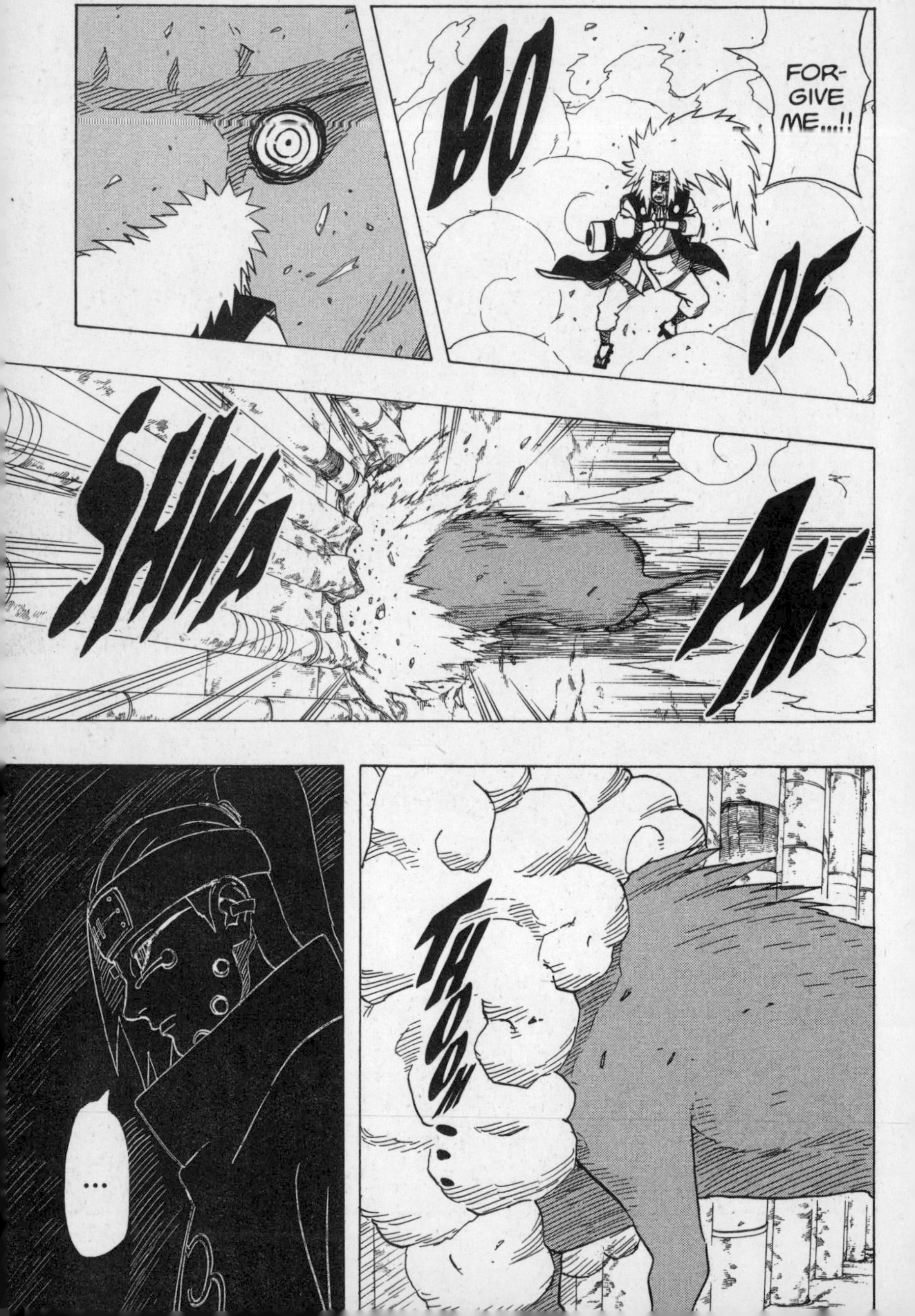
BO
OF
FOR-GIVE ME...!!
SHWA
AM
THOOM
...

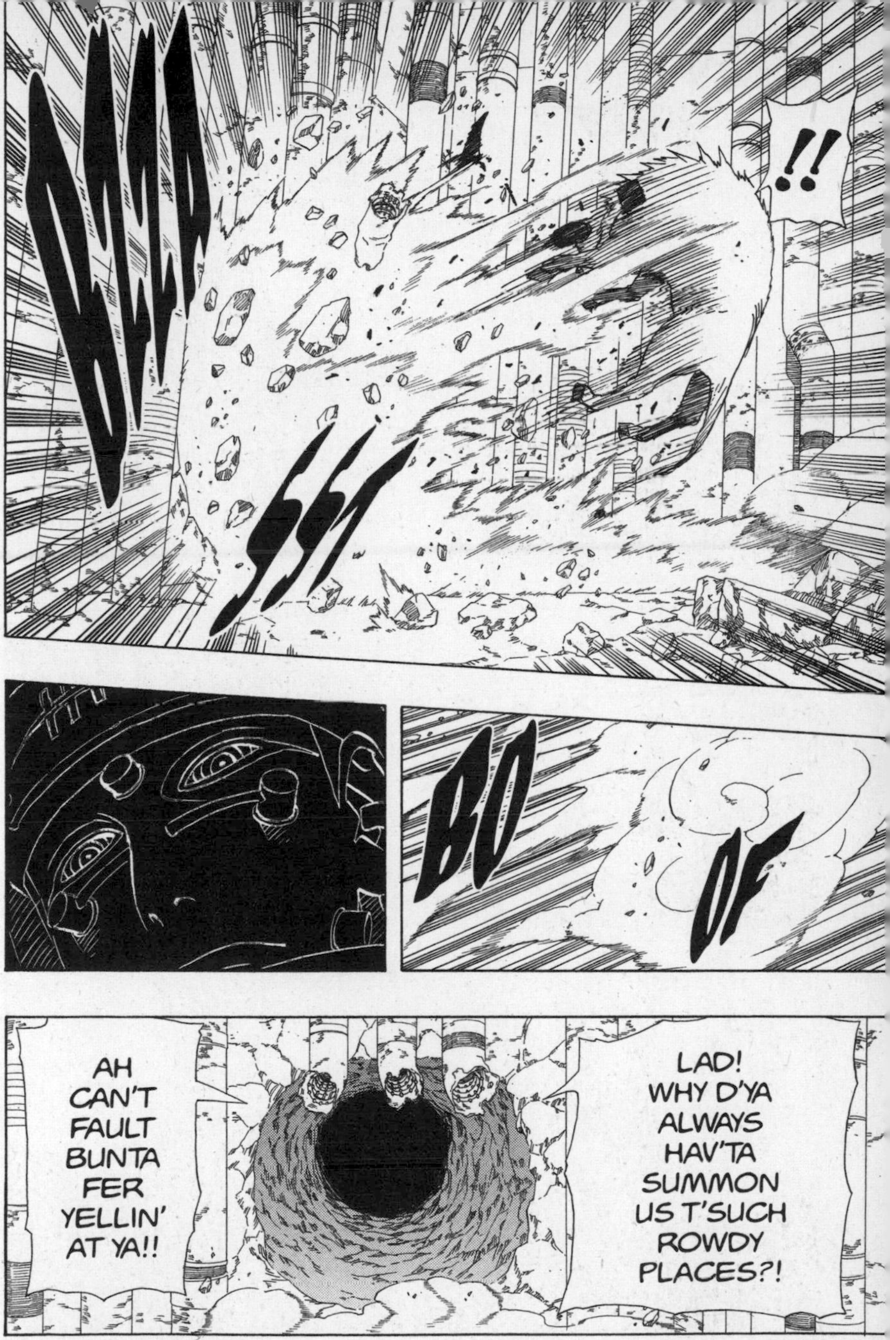
!!
BOOF
LAD! WHY D'YA ALWAYS HAV'TA SUMMON US T'SUCH ROWDY PLACES?!
AH CAN'T FAULT BUNTA FER YELLIN' AT YA!!

READ THIS WAY

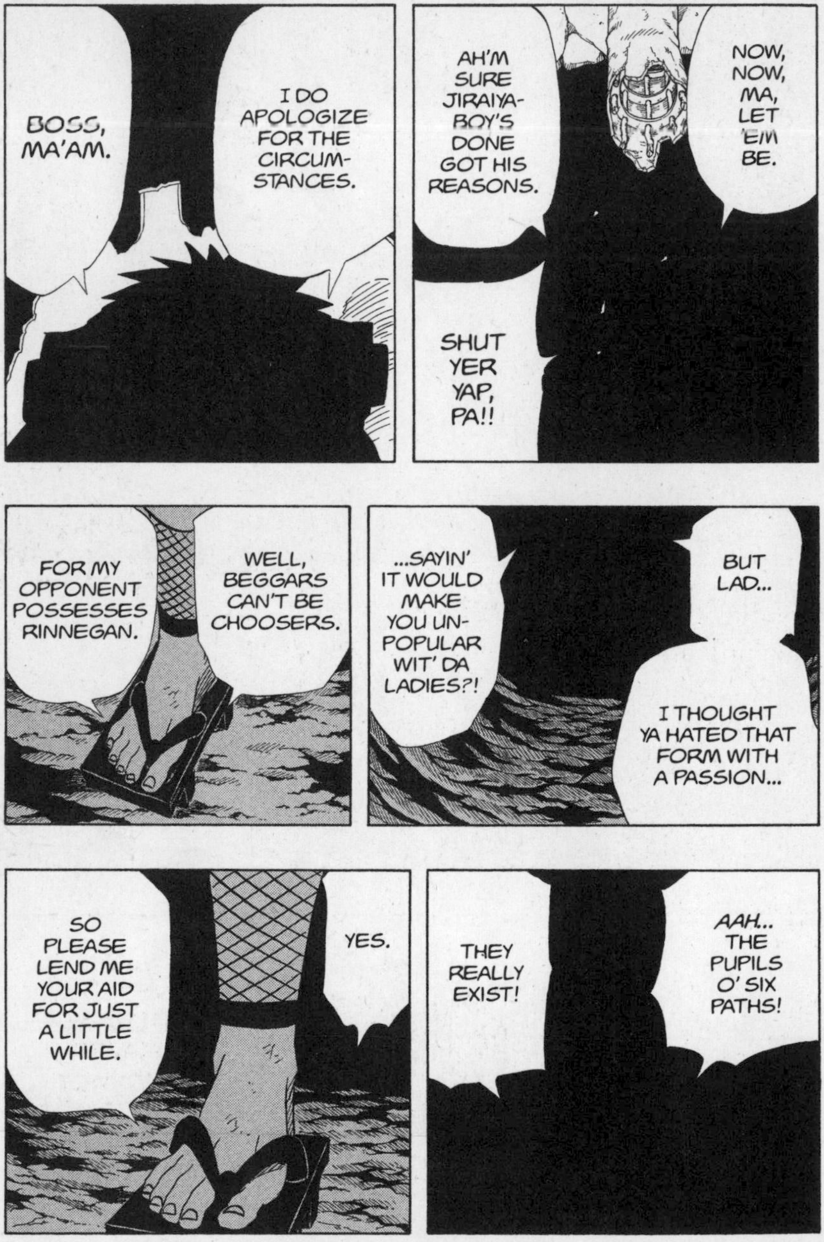
NOW, NOW, MA, LET 'EM BE.
AH'M SURE JIRAIYA-BOY'S DONE GOT HIS REASONS.
SHUT YER YAP, PA!!
I DO APOLOGIZE FOR THE CIRCUM-STANCES.
BOSS, MA'AM.
BUT LAD...
I THOUGHT YA HATED THAT FORM WITH A PASSION...
...SAYIN' IT WOULD MAKE YOU UN-POPULAR WIT' DA LADIES?!
WELL, BEGGARS CAN'T BE CHOOSERS.
FOR MY OPPONENT POSSESSES RINNEGAN.
AAH... THE PUPILS O' SIX PATHS!
THEY REALLY EXIST!
YES.
SO PLEASE LEND ME YOUR AID FOR JUST A LITTLE WHILE.

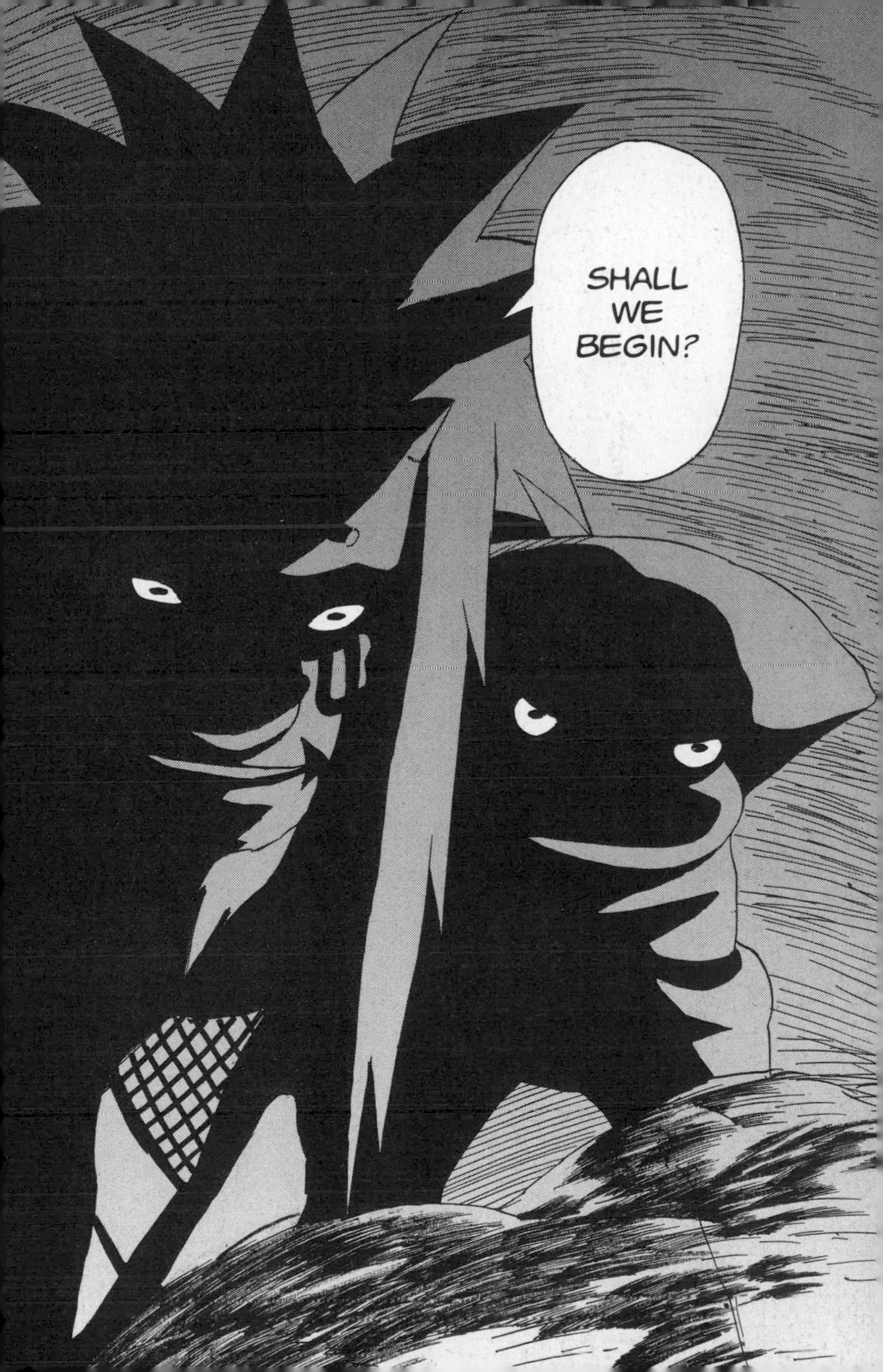
SHALL WE BEGIN?

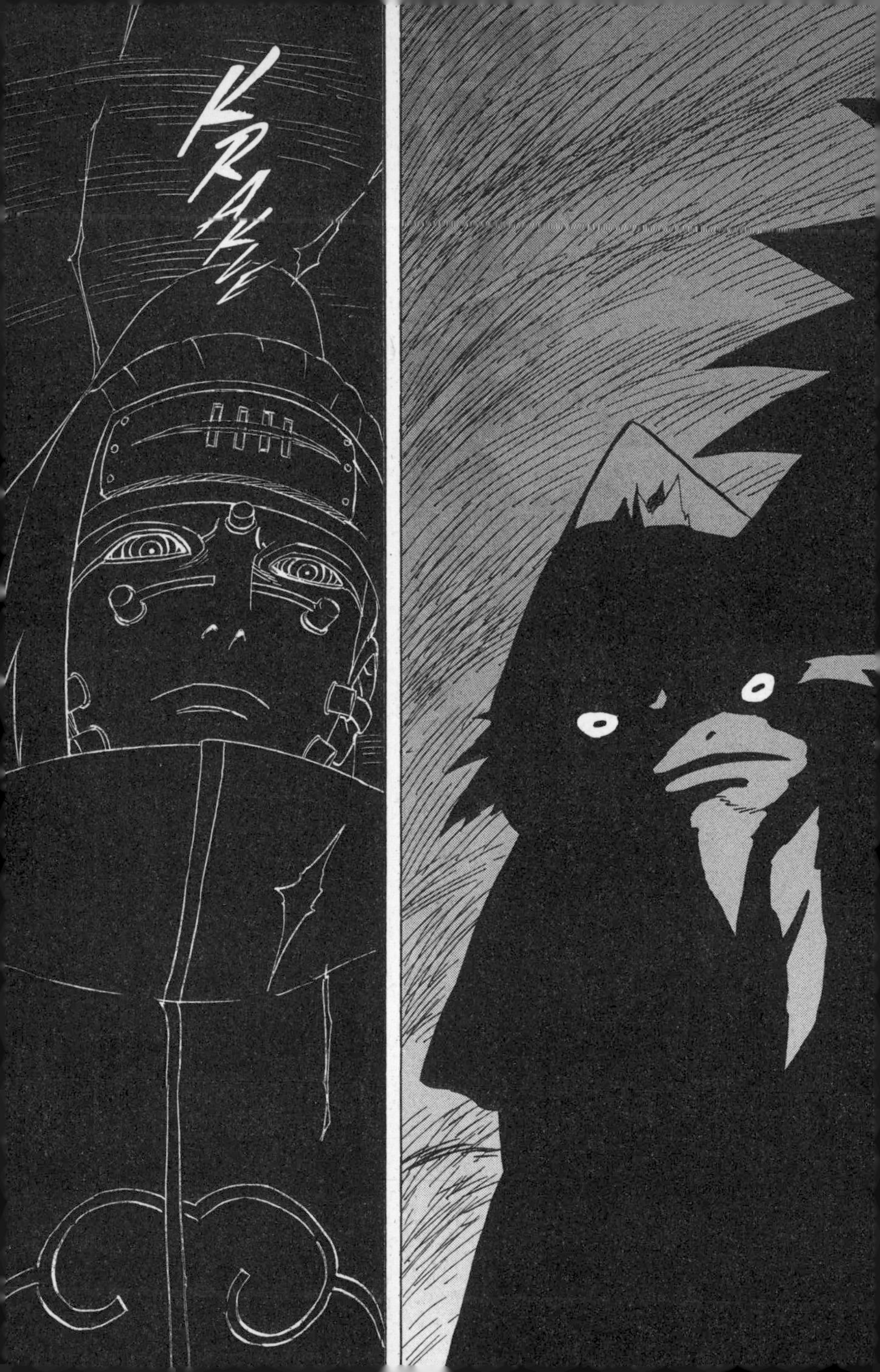
KRAKK

NARUTO

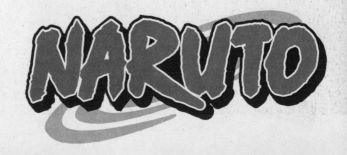

Number 376: Child of Prophecy!!

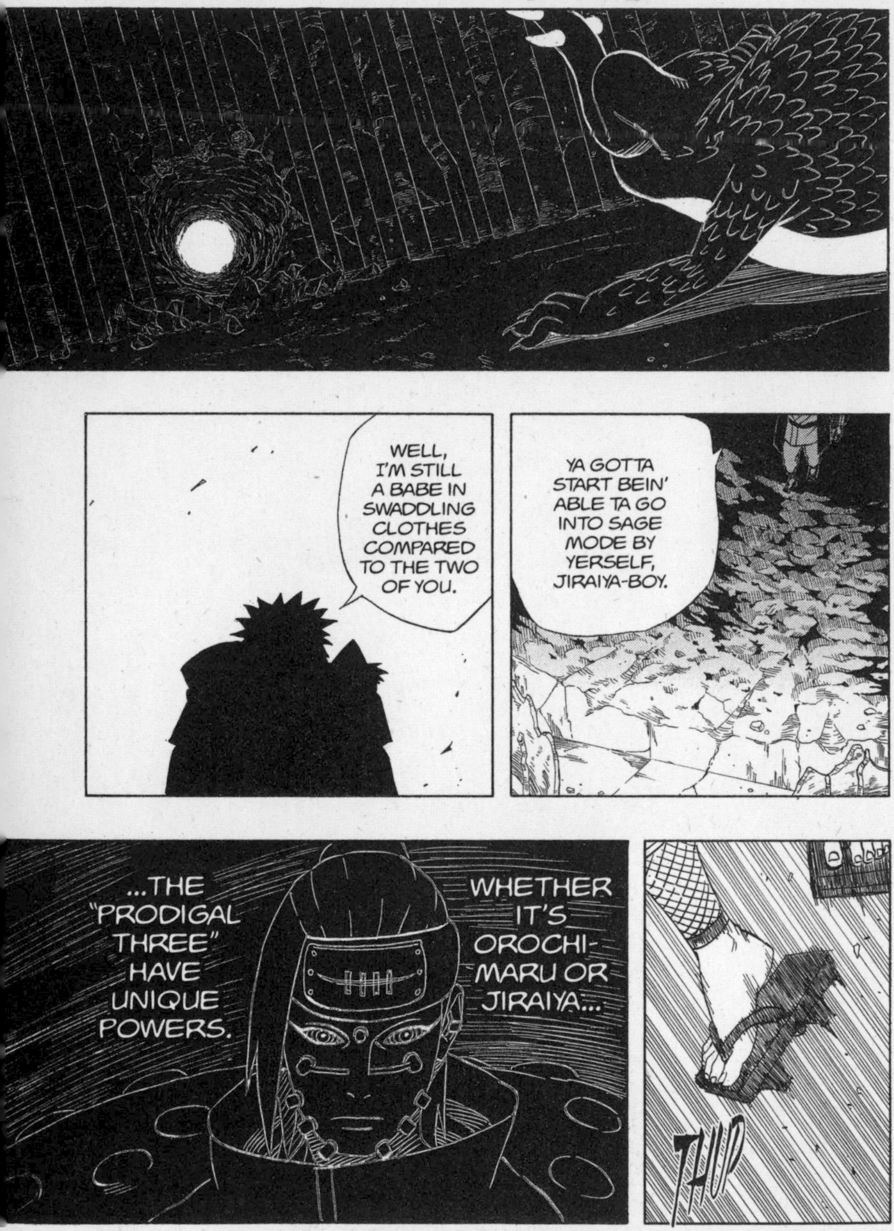
YA GOTTA START BEIN' ABLE TA GO INTO SAGE MODE BY YERSELF, JIRAIYA-BOY.
WELL, I'M STILL A BABE IN SWADDLING CLOTHES COMPARED TO THE TWO OF YOU.
THUP
WHETHER IT'S OROCHIMARU OR JIRAIYA...
...THE "PRODIGAL THREE" HAVE UNIQUE POWERS.

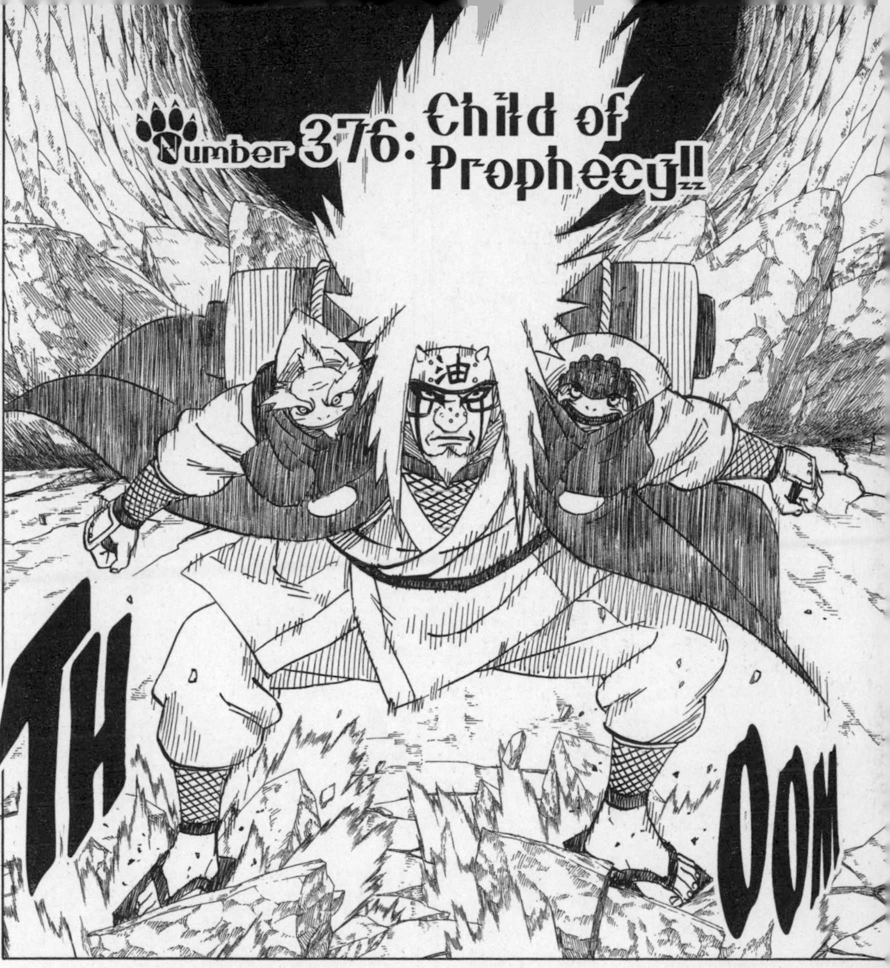
Number 376: Child of Prophecy!!
TH
OOM

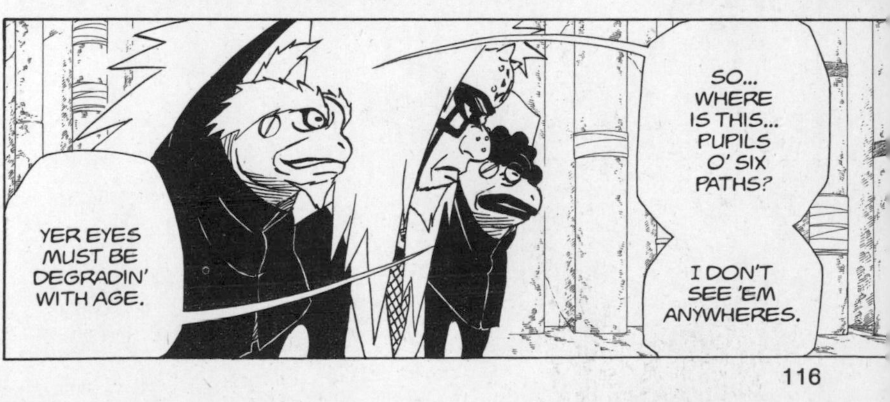
SO... WHERE IS THIS... PUPILS O' SIX PATHS?
I DON'T SEE 'EM ANYWHERES.
YER EYES MUST BE DEGRADIN' WITH AGE.

READ THIS WAY

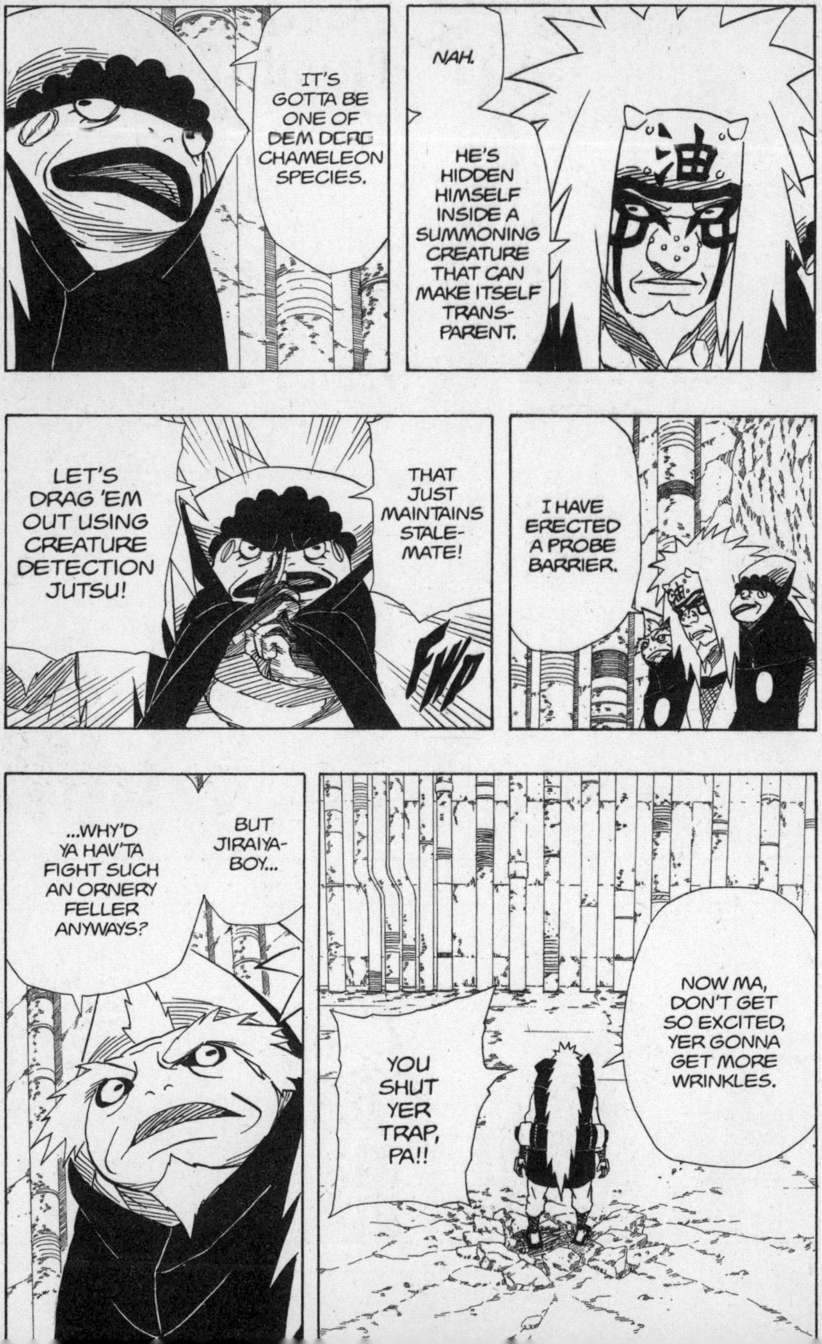
NAH.
HE'S HIDDEN HIMSELF INSIDE A SUMMONING CREATURE THAT CAN MAKE ITSELF TRANS-PARENT.
IT'S GOTTA BE ONE OF DEM DERE CHAMELEON SPECIES.
I HAVE ERECTED A PROBE BARRIER.
THAT JUST MAINTAINS STALE-MATE!
LET'S DRAG 'EM OUT USING CREATURE DETECTION JUTSU!
NOW MA, DON'T GET SO EXCITED, YER GONNA GET MORE WRINKLES.
YOU SHUT YER TRAP, PA!!
BUT JIRAIYA-BOY...
...WHY'D YA HAV'TA FIGHT SUCH AN ORNERY FELLER ANYWAYS?

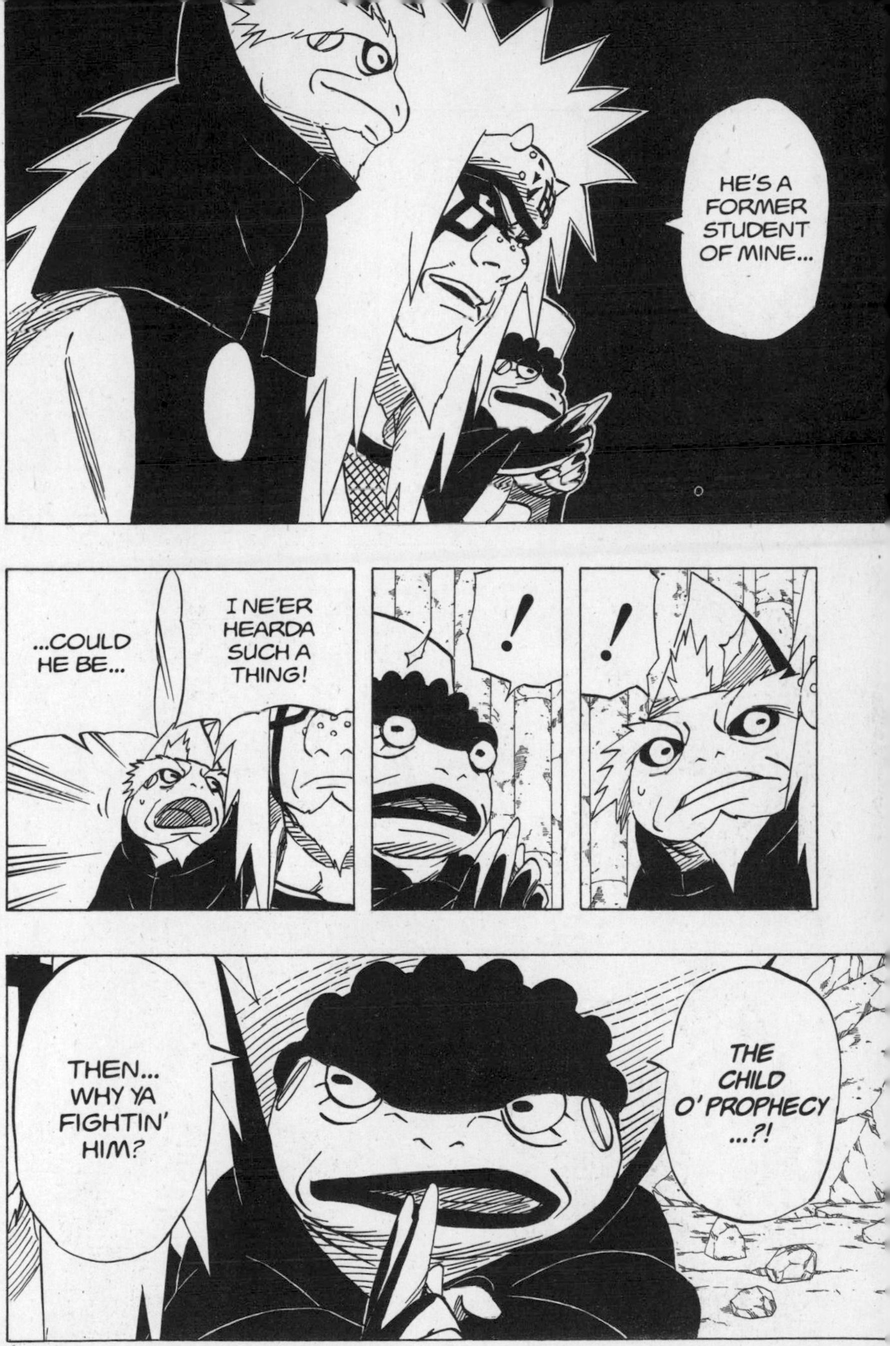
HE'S A FORMER STUDENT OF MINE...
!
!
I NE'ER HEARDA SUCH A THING!
...COULD HE BE...
THE CHILD O' PROPHECY ...?!
THEN... WHY YA FIGHTIN' HIM?

READ THIS WAY

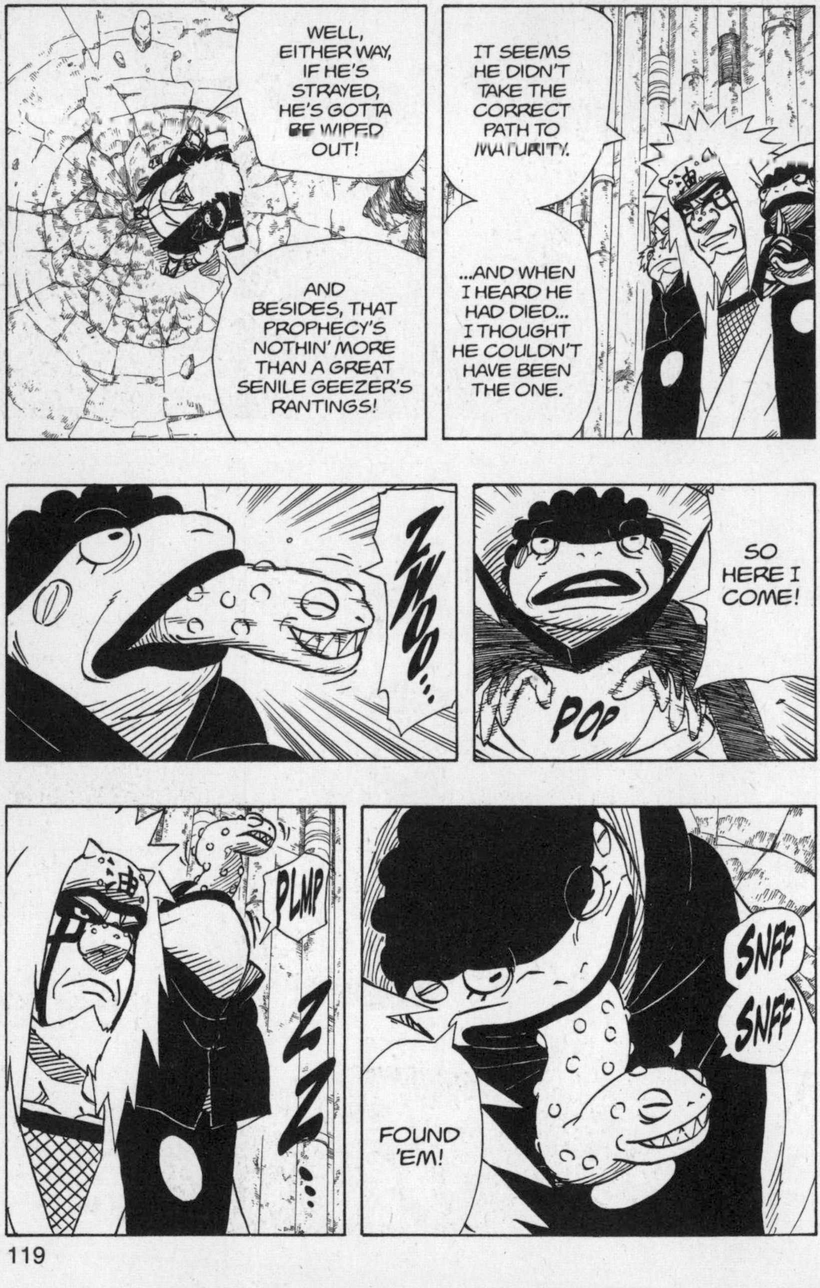
IT SEEMS HE DIDN'T TAKE THE CORRECT PATH TO MATURITY.
...AND WHEN I HEARD HE HAD DIED... I THOUGHT HE COULDN'T HAVE BEEN THE ONE.
WELL, EITHER WAY, IF HE'S STRAYED, HE'S GOTTA BE WIPED OUT!
AND BESIDES, THAT PROPHECY'S NOTHIN' MORE THAN A GREAT SENILE GEEZER'S RANTINGS!
SO HERE I COME!
POP
ZWOO...
SNFF SNFF
FOUND 'EM!
PLMP
ZZZ...

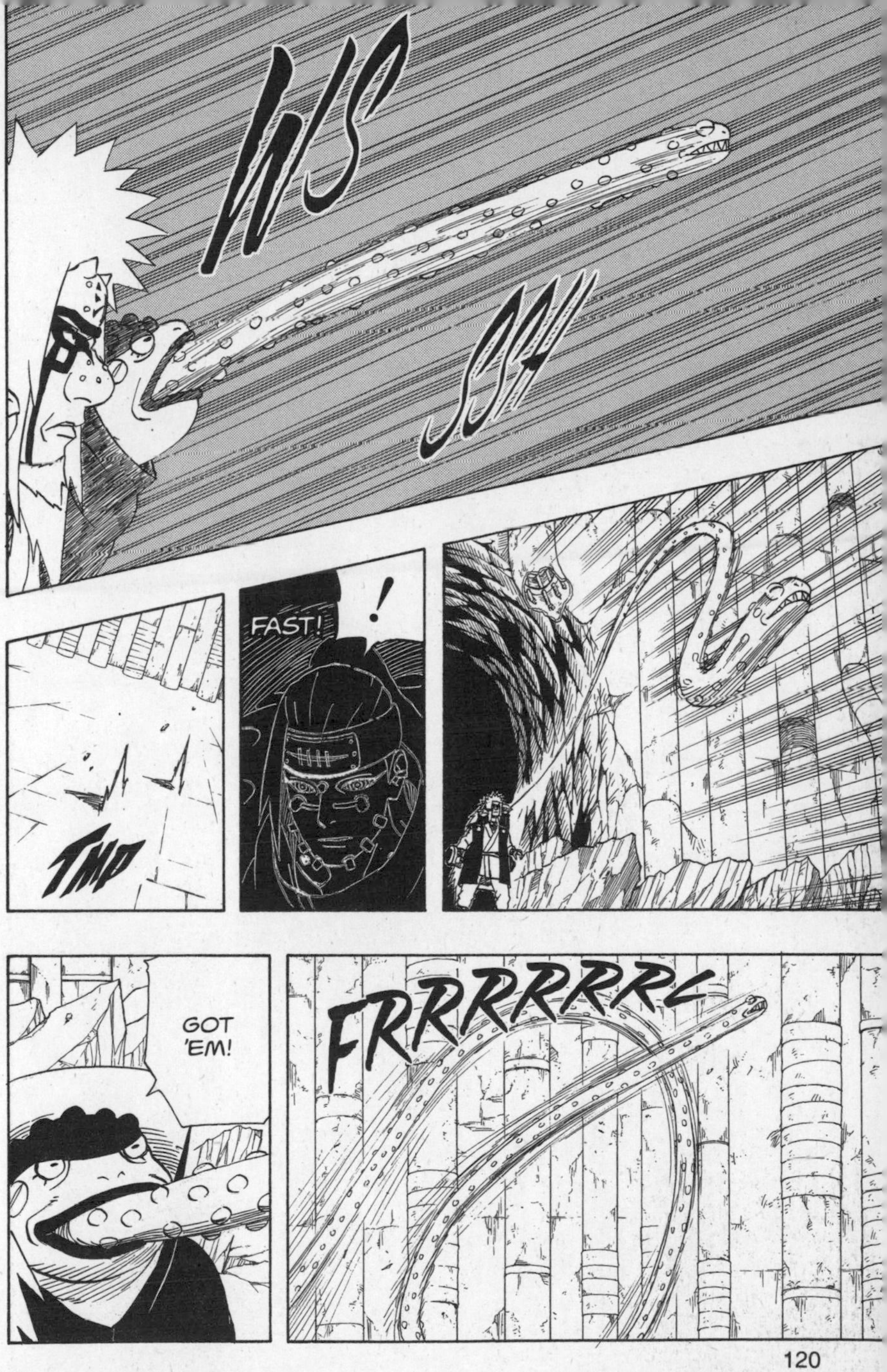
WHS
SSH
!
FAST!
TMP
FRRRRRRC
GOT 'EM!

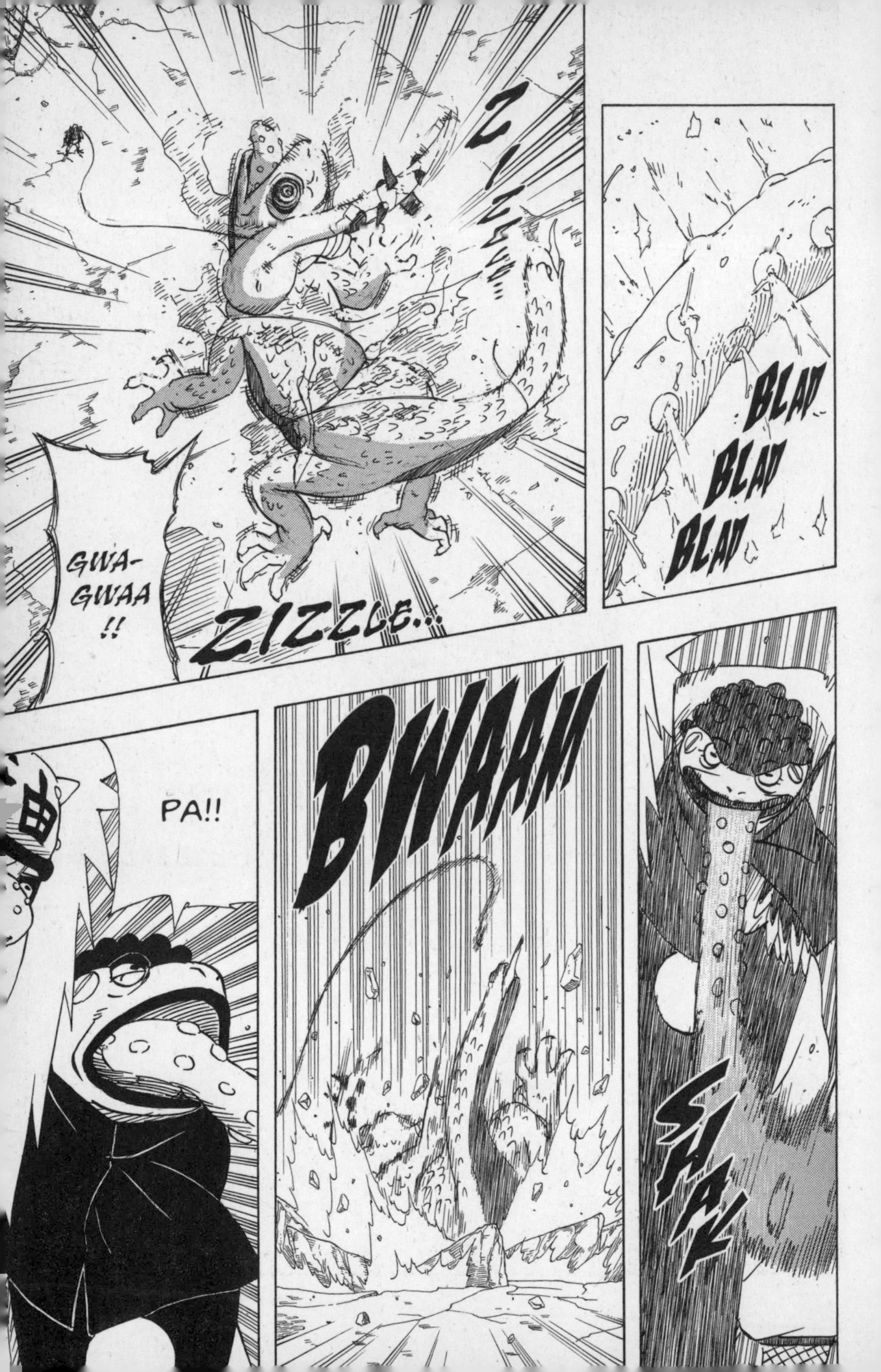
BLAD
BLAD
BLAD
BLAD
GWA-GWAA!!
ZIZZLE...
SHAK
BWAAM
PA!!

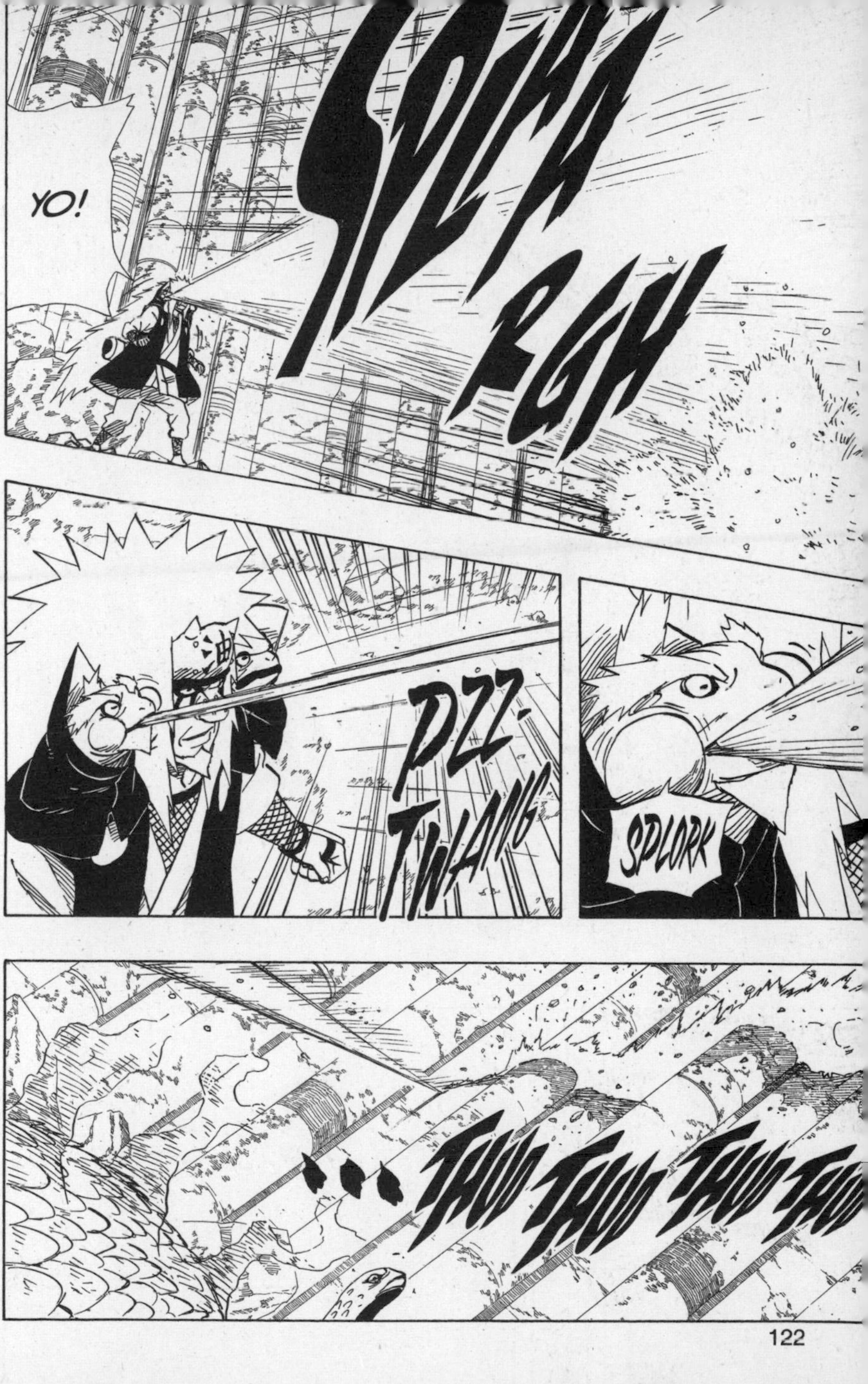
YO!
SPLORK
DZZ-TWANG
THUD THUD THUD

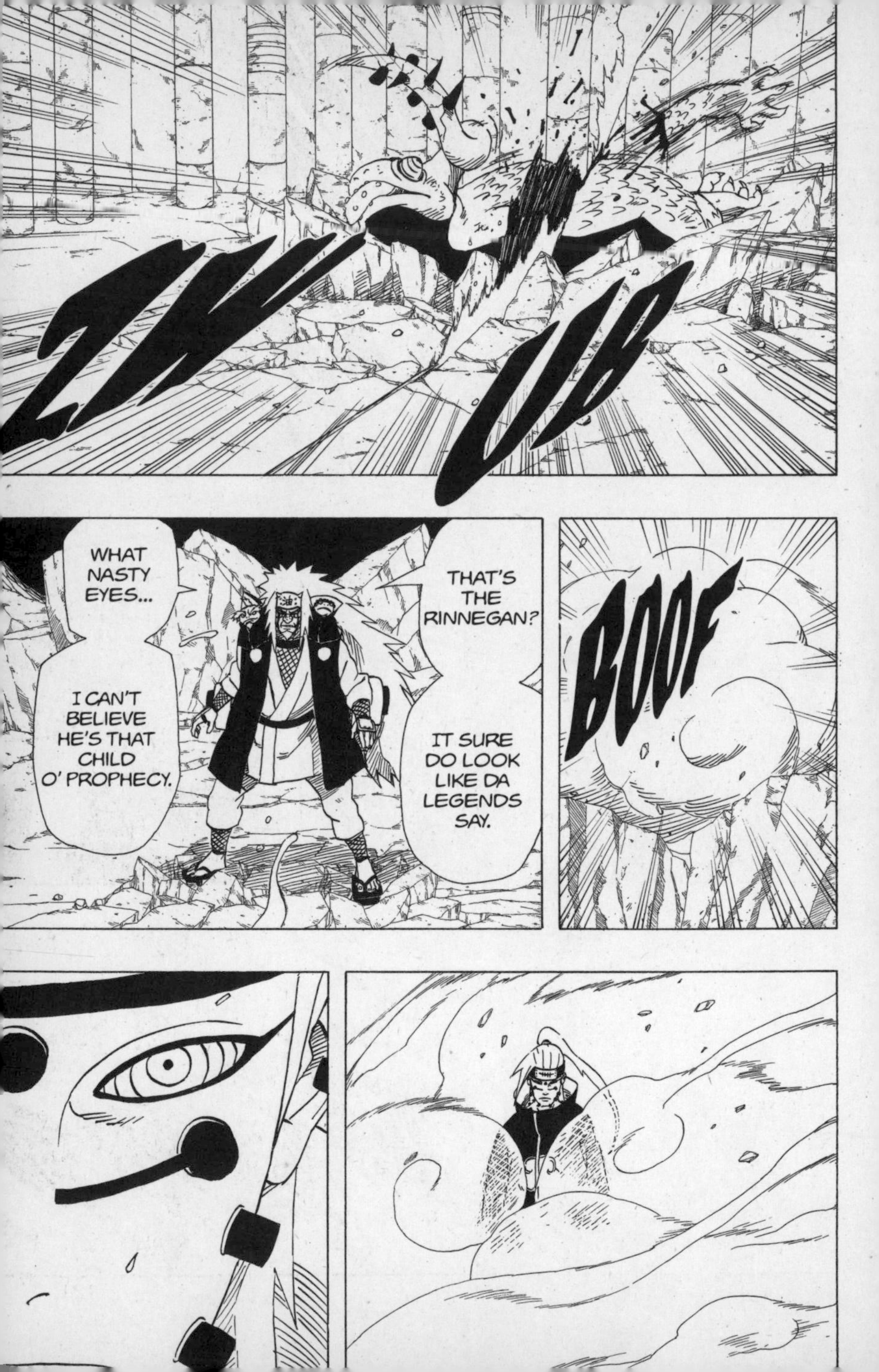
ZWUB
BOOF
THAT'S THE RINNEGAN?
IT SURE DO LOOK LIKE DA LEGENDS SAY.
WHAT NASTY EYES...
I CAN'T BELIEVE HE'S THAT CHILD O' PROPHECY.

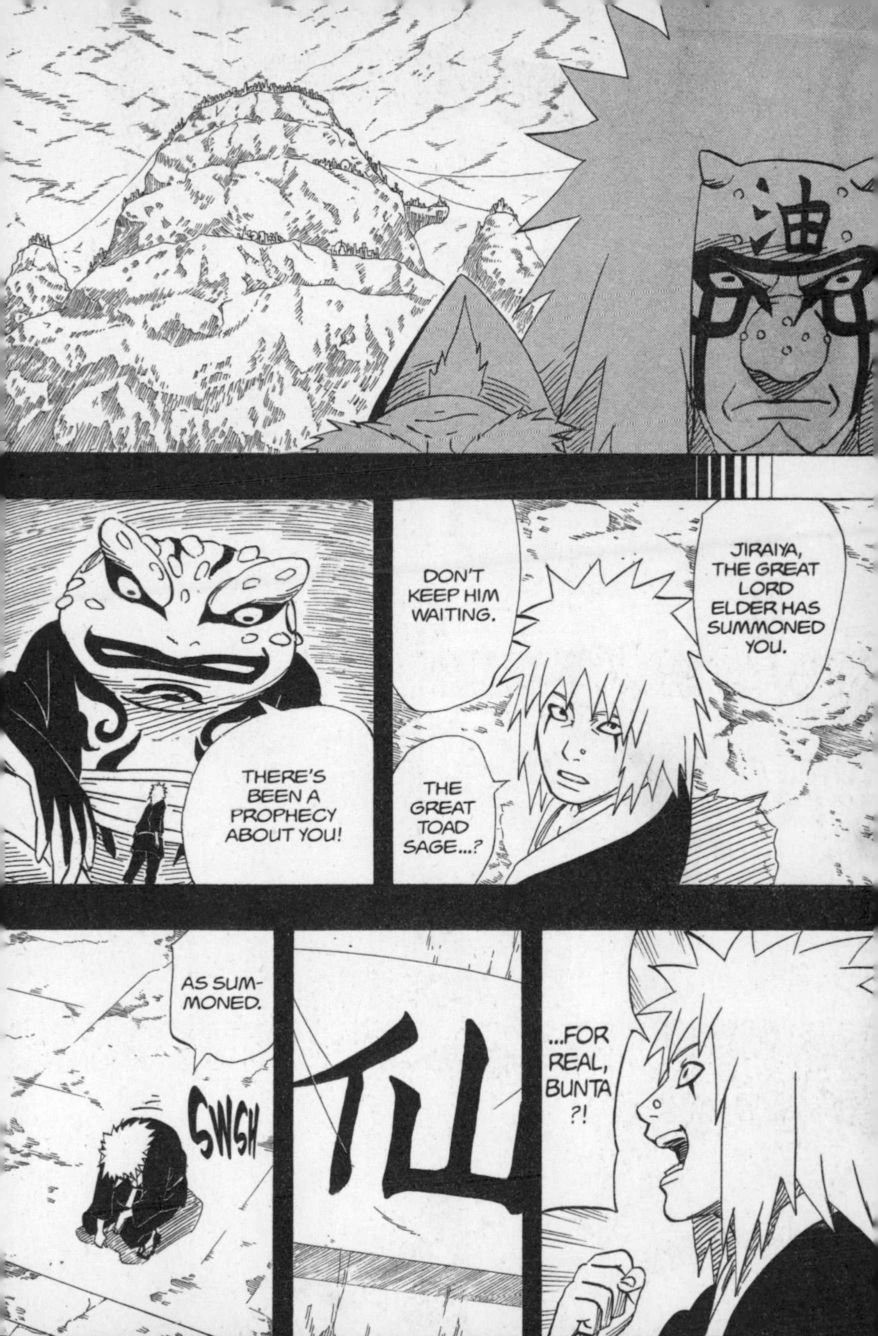
JIRAIYA, THE GREAT LORD ELDER HAS SUMMONED YOU.
DON'T KEEP HIM WAITING.
THE GREAT TOAD SAGE...?
THERE'S BEEN A PROPHECY ABOUT YOU!
...FOR REAL, BUNTA?!
仙
AS SUM-MONED.
SWSH

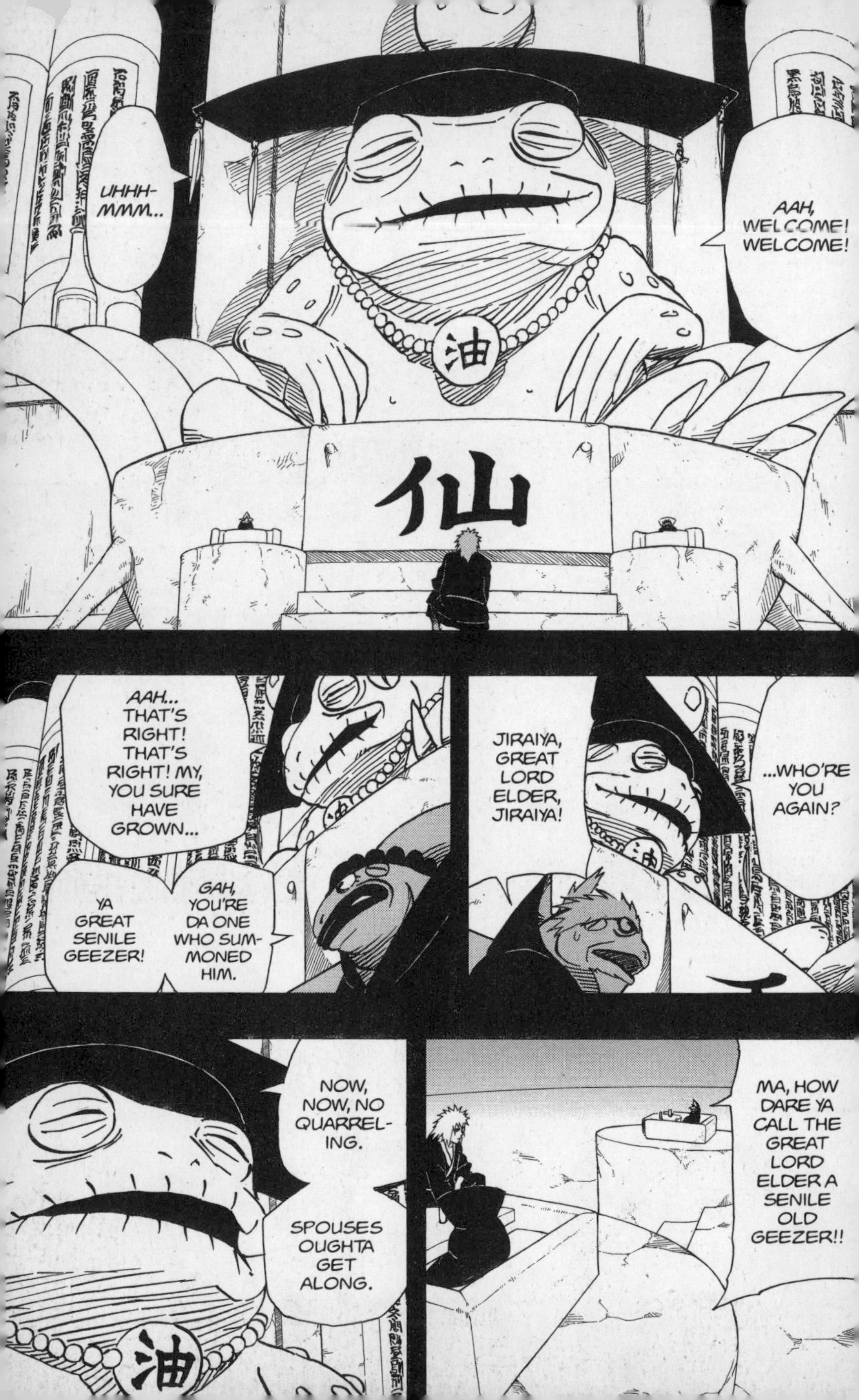
AAH, WELCOME! WELCOME!
UHHH-MMM...
油
仙
...WHO'RE YOU AGAIN?
JIRAIYA, GREAT LORD ELDER, JIRAIYA!
AAH... THAT'S RIGHT! THAT'S RIGHT! MY, YOU SURE HAVE GROWN...
GAH, YOU'RE DA ONE WHO SUMMONED HIM.
YA GREAT SENILE GEEZER!
MA, HOW DARE YA CALL THE GREAT LORD ELDER A SENILE OLD GEEZER!!
NOW, NOW, NO QUARRELING.
SPOUSES OUGHTA GET ALONG.

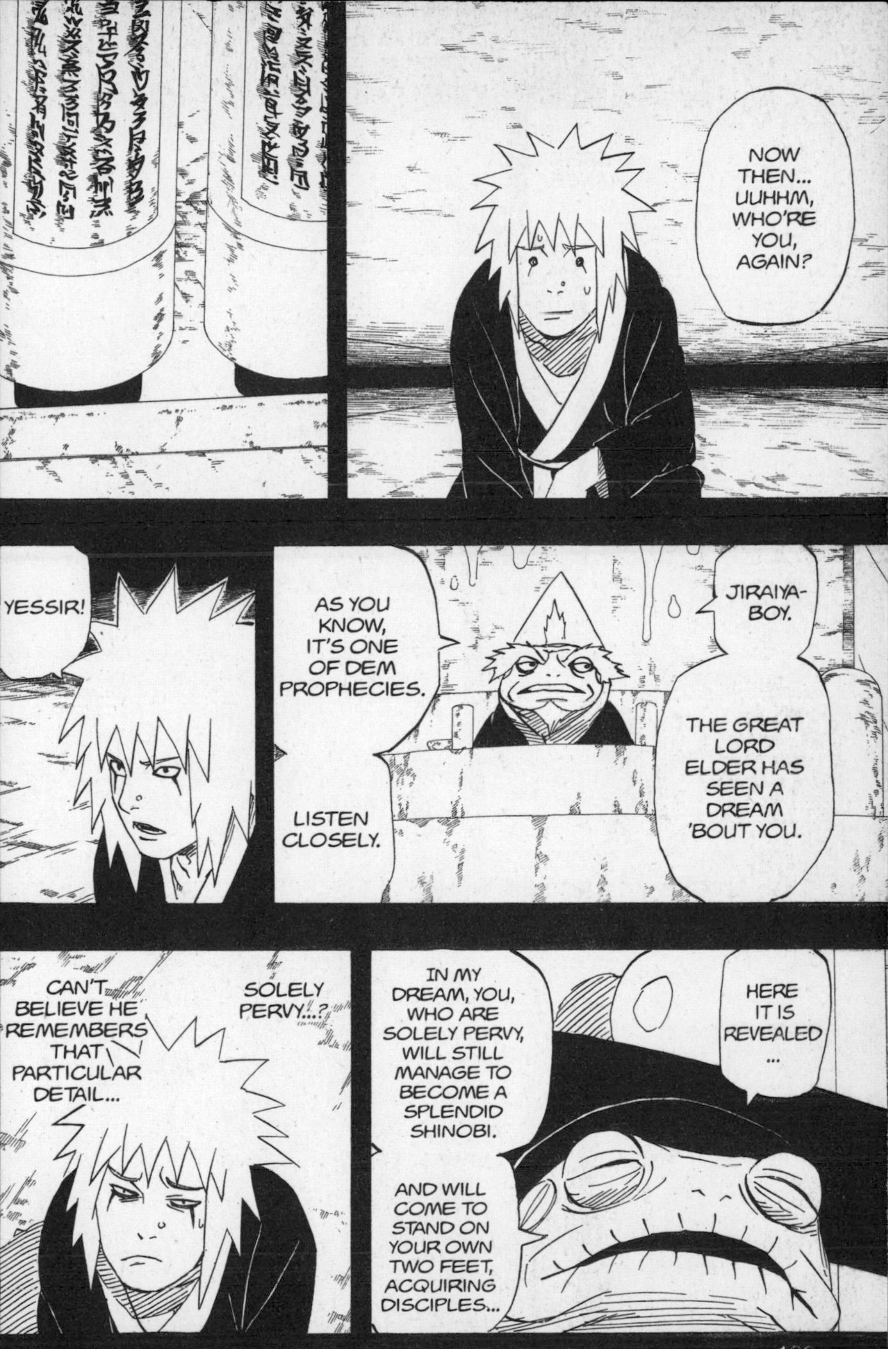
NOW THEN... UUHHM, WHO'RE YOU, AGAIN?
JIRAIYA-BOY.
THE GREAT LORD ELDER HAS SEEN A DREAM 'BOUT YOU.
AS YOU KNOW, IT'S ONE OF DEM PROPHECIES.
LISTEN CLOSELY.
YESSIR!
HERE IT IS REVEALED ...
IN MY DREAM, YOU, WHO ARE SOLELY PERVY, WILL STILL MANAGE TO BECOME A SPLENDID SHINOBI.
AND WILL COME TO STAND ON YOUR OWN TWO FEET, ACQUIRING DISCIPLES...
SOLELY PERVY...?
CAN'T BELIEVE HE REMEMBERS THAT PARTICULAR DETAIL...

READ THIS WAY

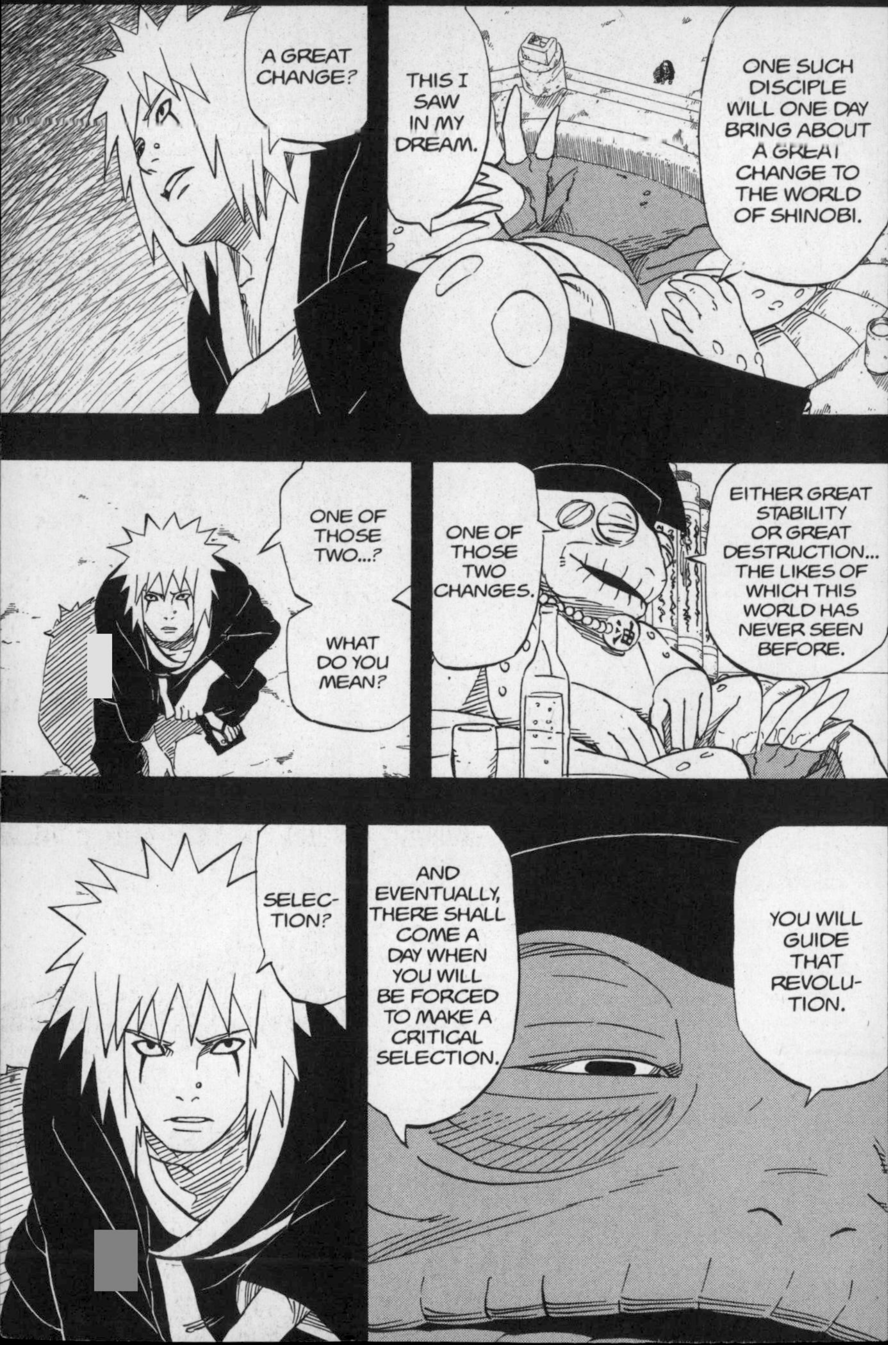

ONE SUCH DISCIPLE WILL ONE DAY BRING ABOUT A GREAT CHANGE TO THE WORLD OF SHINOBI.
THIS I SAW IN MY DREAM.
A GREAT CHANGE?
EITHER GREAT STABILITY OR GREAT DESTRUCTION... THE LIKES OF WHICH THIS WORLD HAS NEVER SEEN BEFORE.
ONE OF THOSE TWO CHANGES.
ONE OF THOSE TWO...?
WHAT DO YOU MEAN?
YOU WILL GUIDE THAT REVOLUTION.
AND EVENTUALLY, THERE SHALL COME A DAY WHEN YOU WILL BE FORCED TO MAKE A CRITICAL SELECTION.
SELECTION?

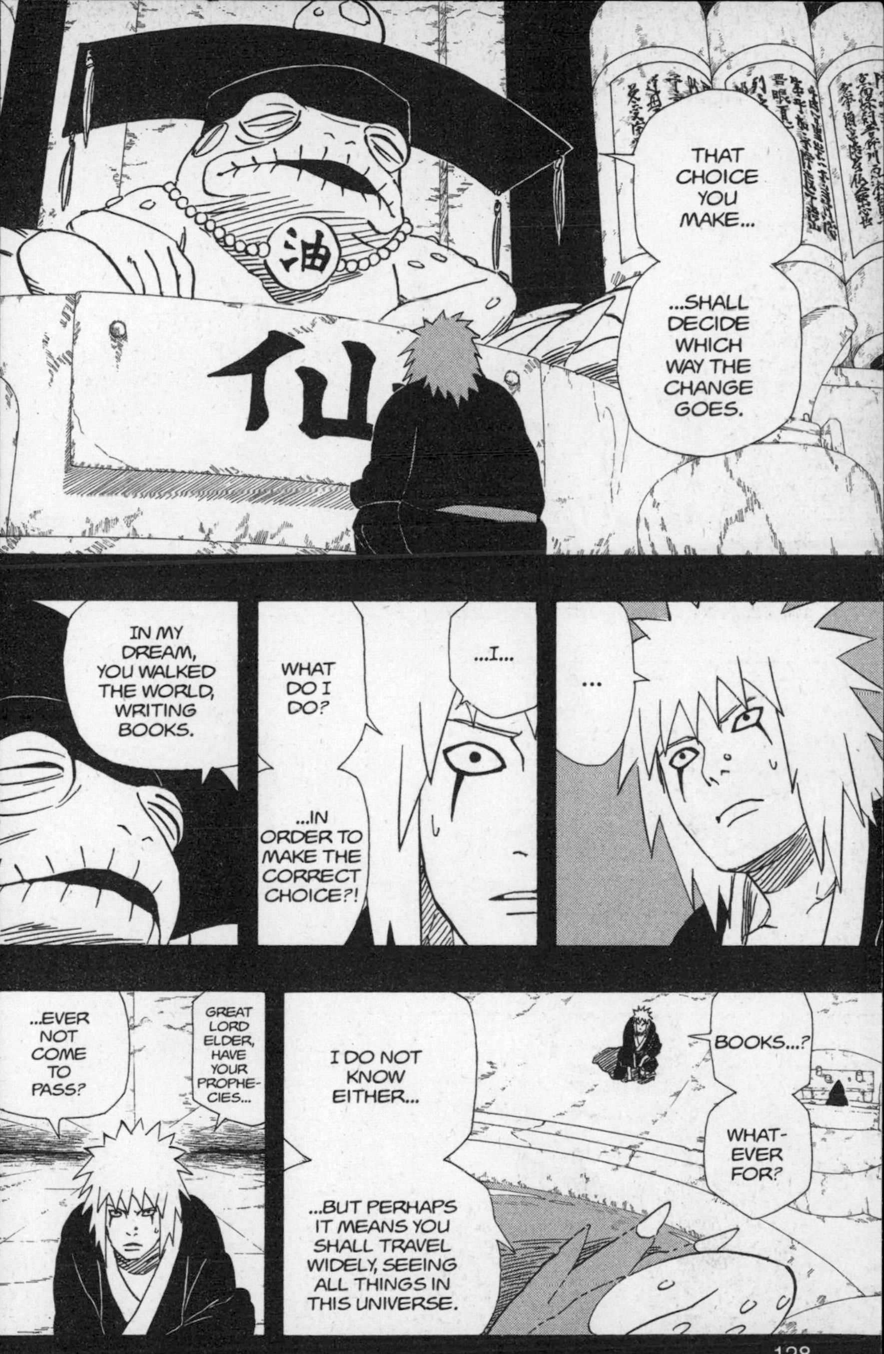
THAT CHOICE YOU MAKE...
...SHALL DECIDE WHICH WAY THE CHANGE GOES.
...
...I...
WHAT DO I DO?
...IN ORDER TO MAKE THE CORRECT CHOICE?!
IN MY DREAM, YOU WALKED THE WORLD, WRITING BOOKS.
BOOKS...?
WHAT-EVER FOR?
I DO NOT KNOW EITHER...
...BUT PERHAPS IT MEANS YOU SHALL TRAVEL WIDELY, SEEING ALL THINGS IN THIS UNIVERSE.
GREAT LORD ELDER, HAVE YOUR PROPHE-CIES...
...EVER NOT COME TO PASS?

READ THIS WAY

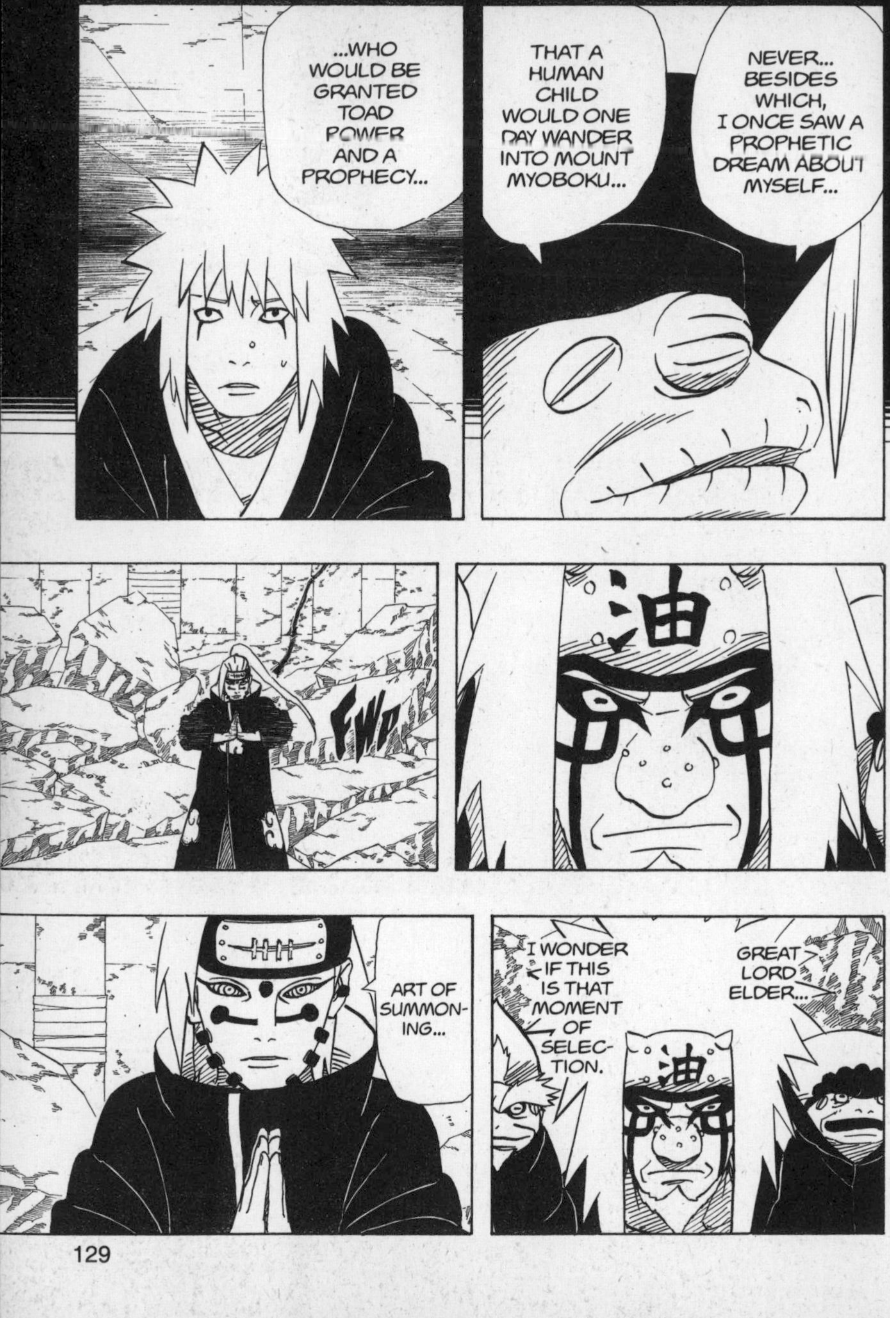
NEVER... BESIDES WHICH, I ONCE SAW A PROPHETIC DREAM ABOUT MYSELF...
THAT A HUMAN CHILD WOULD ONE DAY WANDER INTO MOUNT MYOBOKU...
...WHO WOULD BE GRANTED TOAD POWER AND A PROPHECY...
FWD
GREAT LORD ELDER...
I WONDER IF THIS IS THAT MOMENT OF SELECTION.
ART OF SUMMONING...

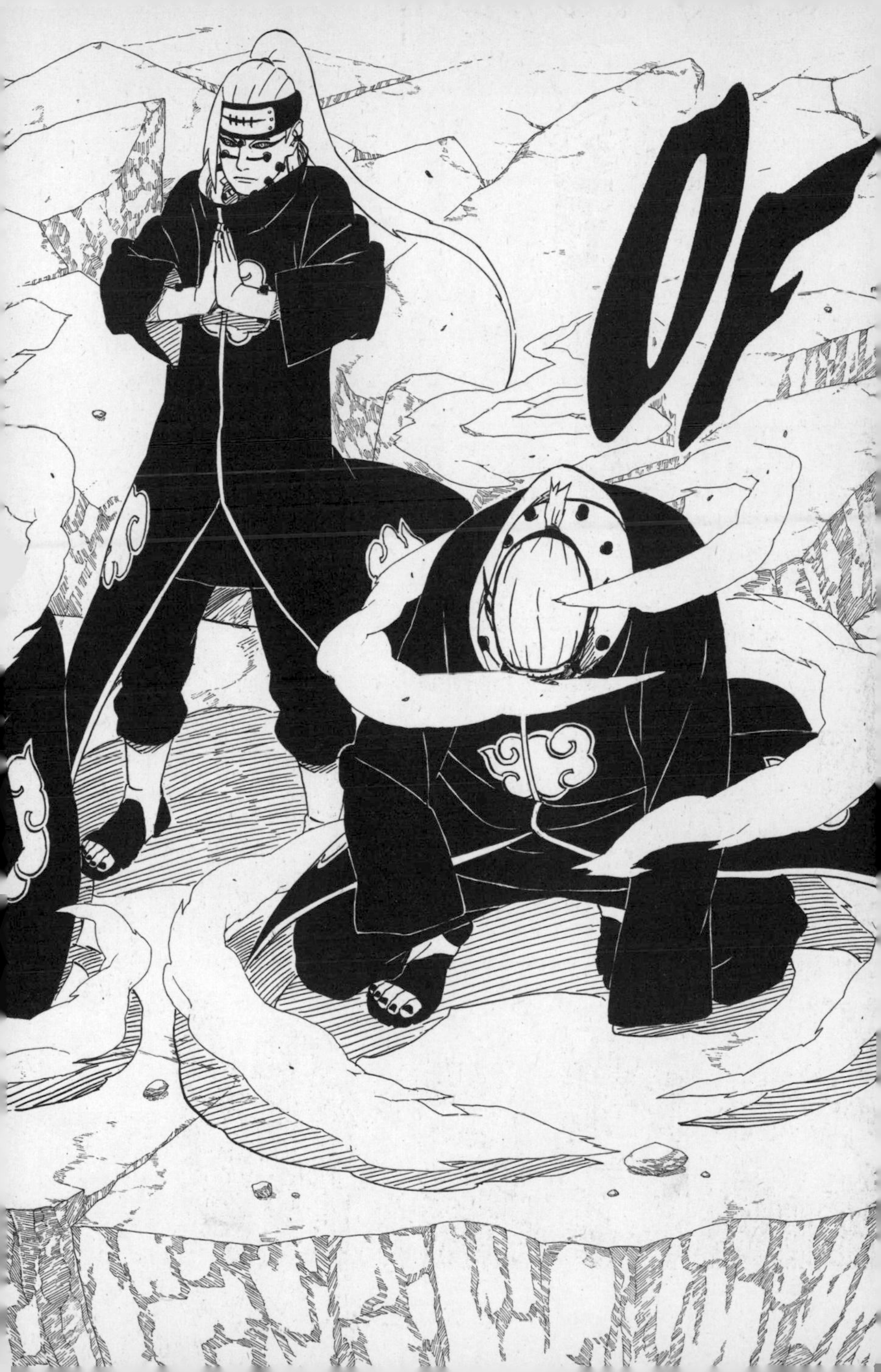
OF

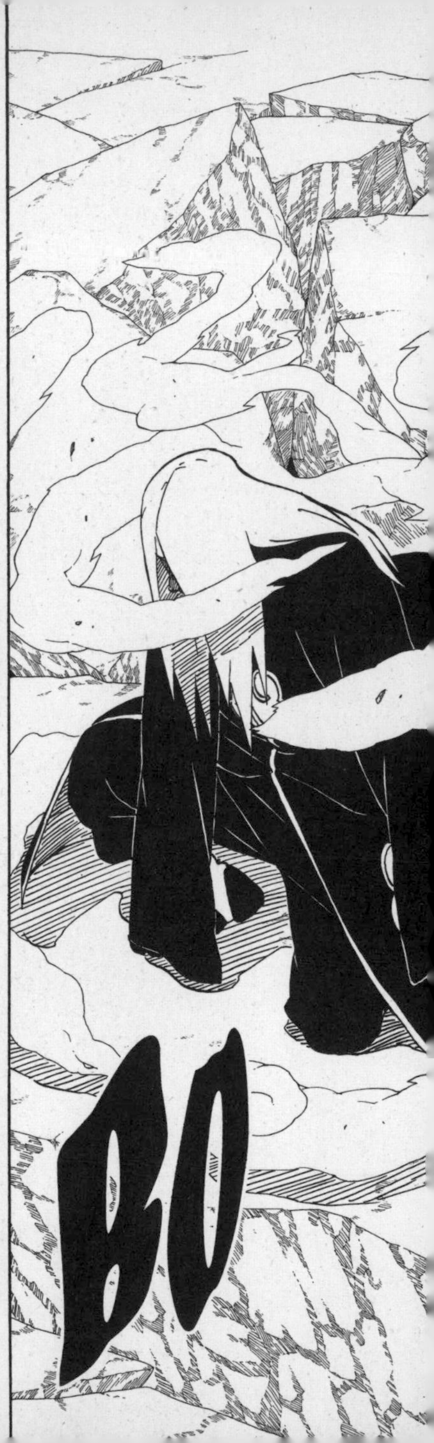
BO

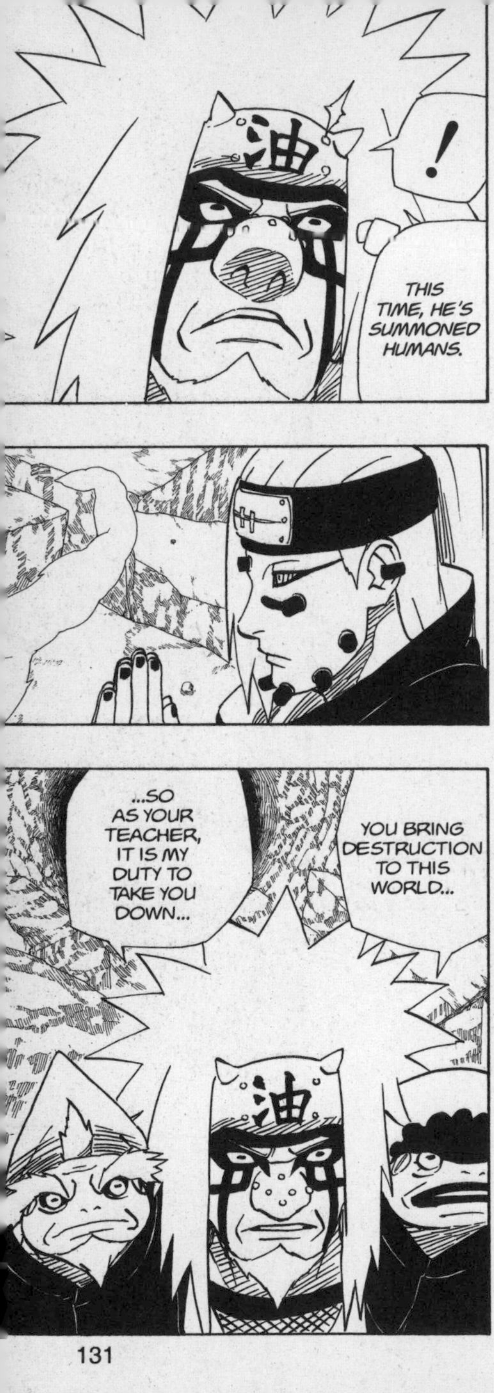
!
THIS TIME, HE'S SUMMONED HUMANS.
YOU BRING DESTRUCTION TO THIS WORLD...
...SO AS YOUR TEACHER, IT IS MY DUTY TO TAKE YOU DOWN...

NARUTO

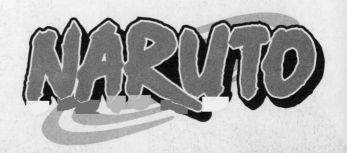

Number 377: Honored Sage Mode!!

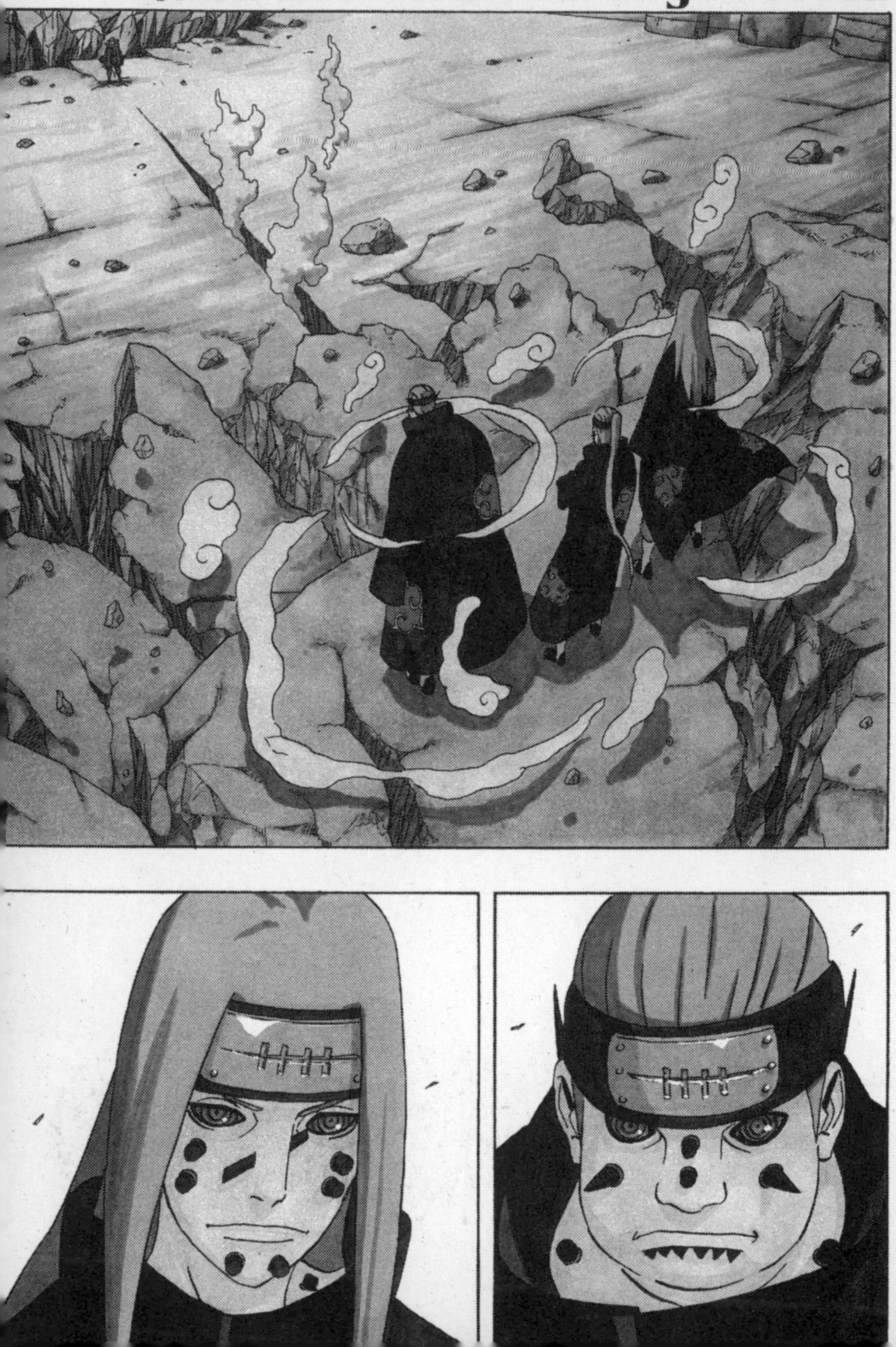

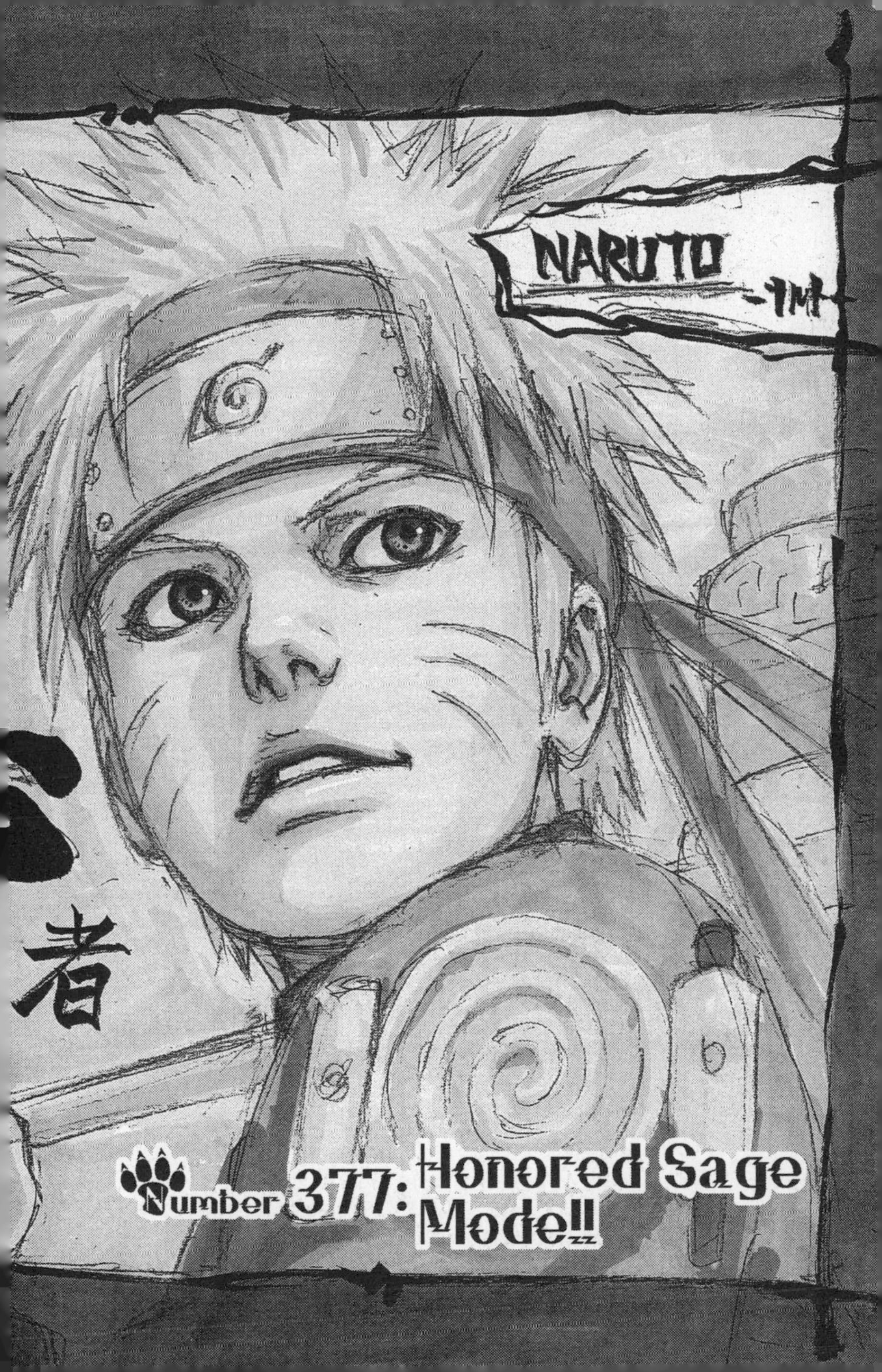
NARUTO
者
Number 377: Honored Sage Mode!!

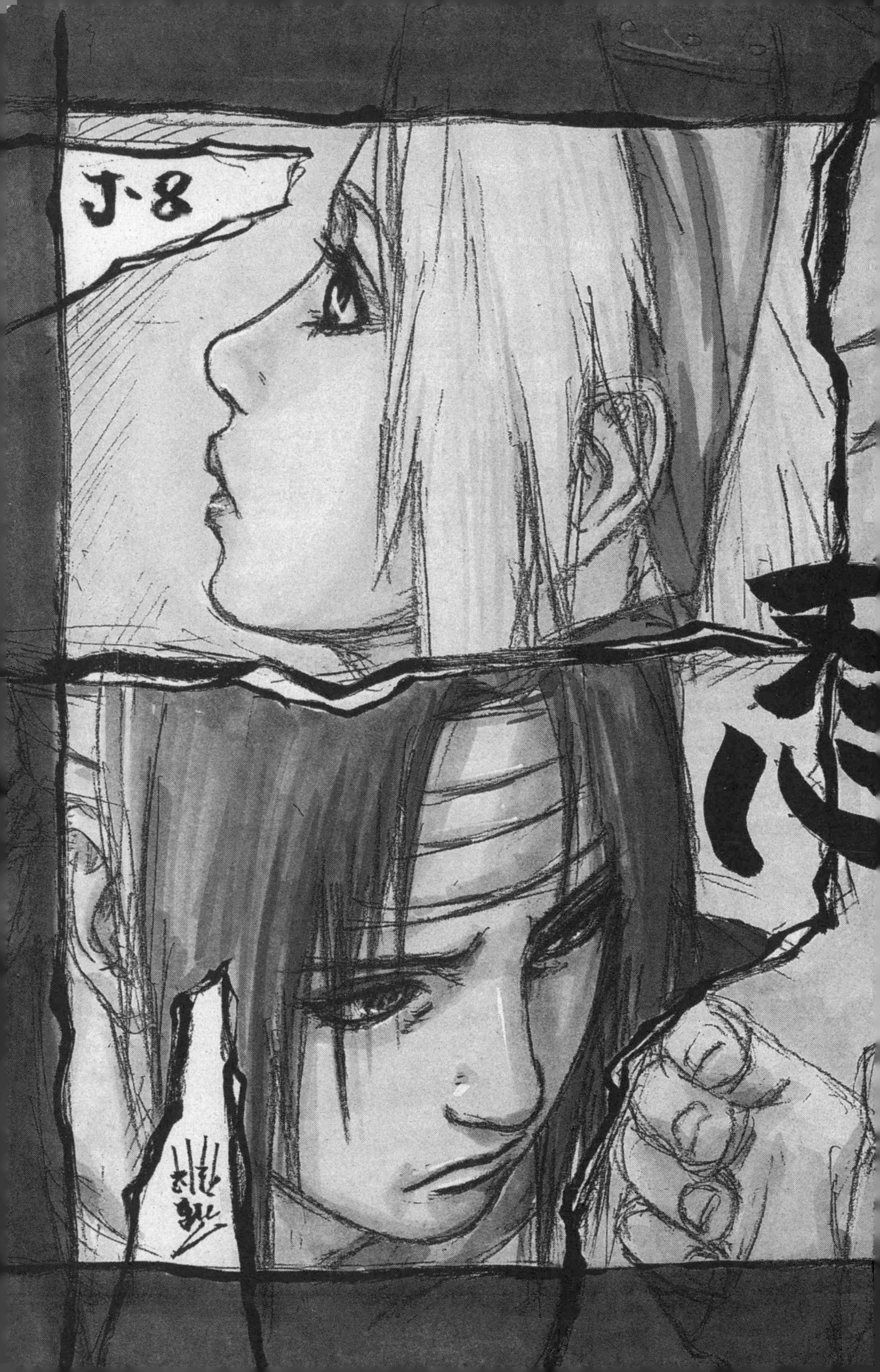
J-8

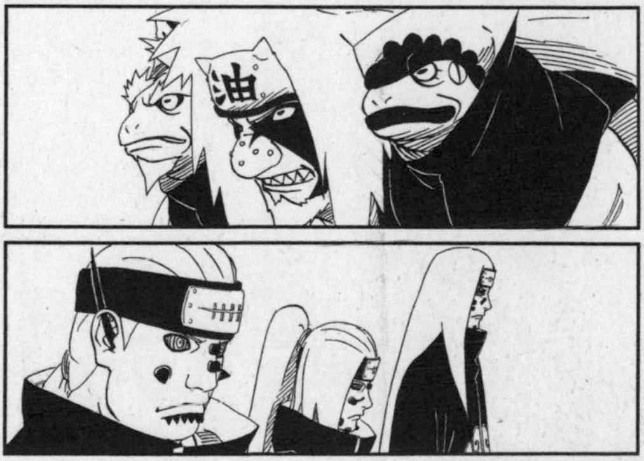
油

READ THIS WAY

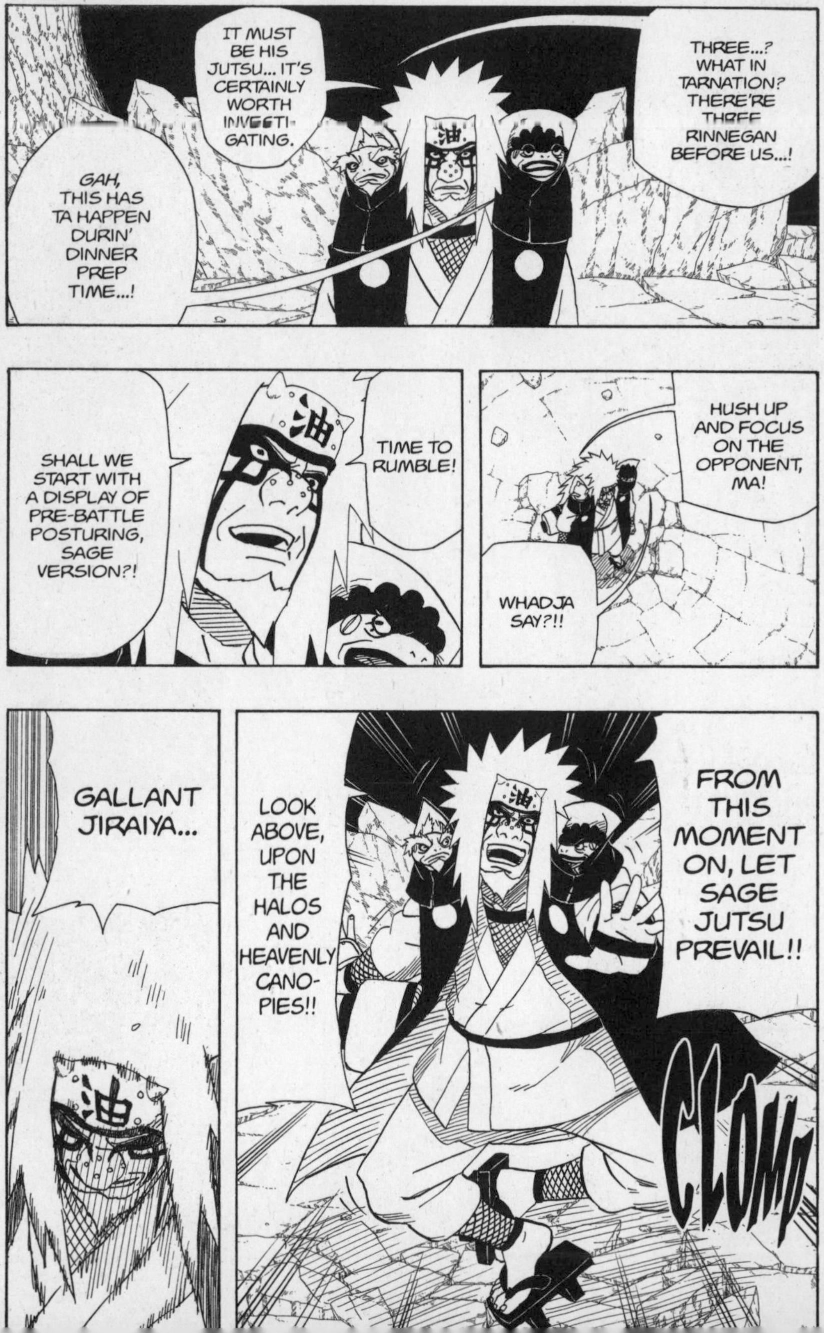
THREE...? WHAT IN TARNATION? THERE'RE THREE RINNEGAN BEFORE US...!
IT MUST BE HIS JUTSU... IT'S CERTAINLY WORTH INVESTI-GATING.
GAH, THIS HAS TA HAPPEN DURIN' DINNER PREP TIME...!
HUSH UP AND FOCUS ON THE OPPONENT, MA!
WHADJA SAY?!!
TIME TO RUMBLE!
SHALL WE START WITH A DISPLAY OF PRE-BATTLE POSTURING, SAGE VERSION?!
FROM THIS MOMENT ON, LET SAGE JUTSU PREVAIL!!
LOOK ABOVE, UPON THE HALOS AND HEAVENLY CANO-PIES!!
CLOMP
GALLANT JIRAIYA...

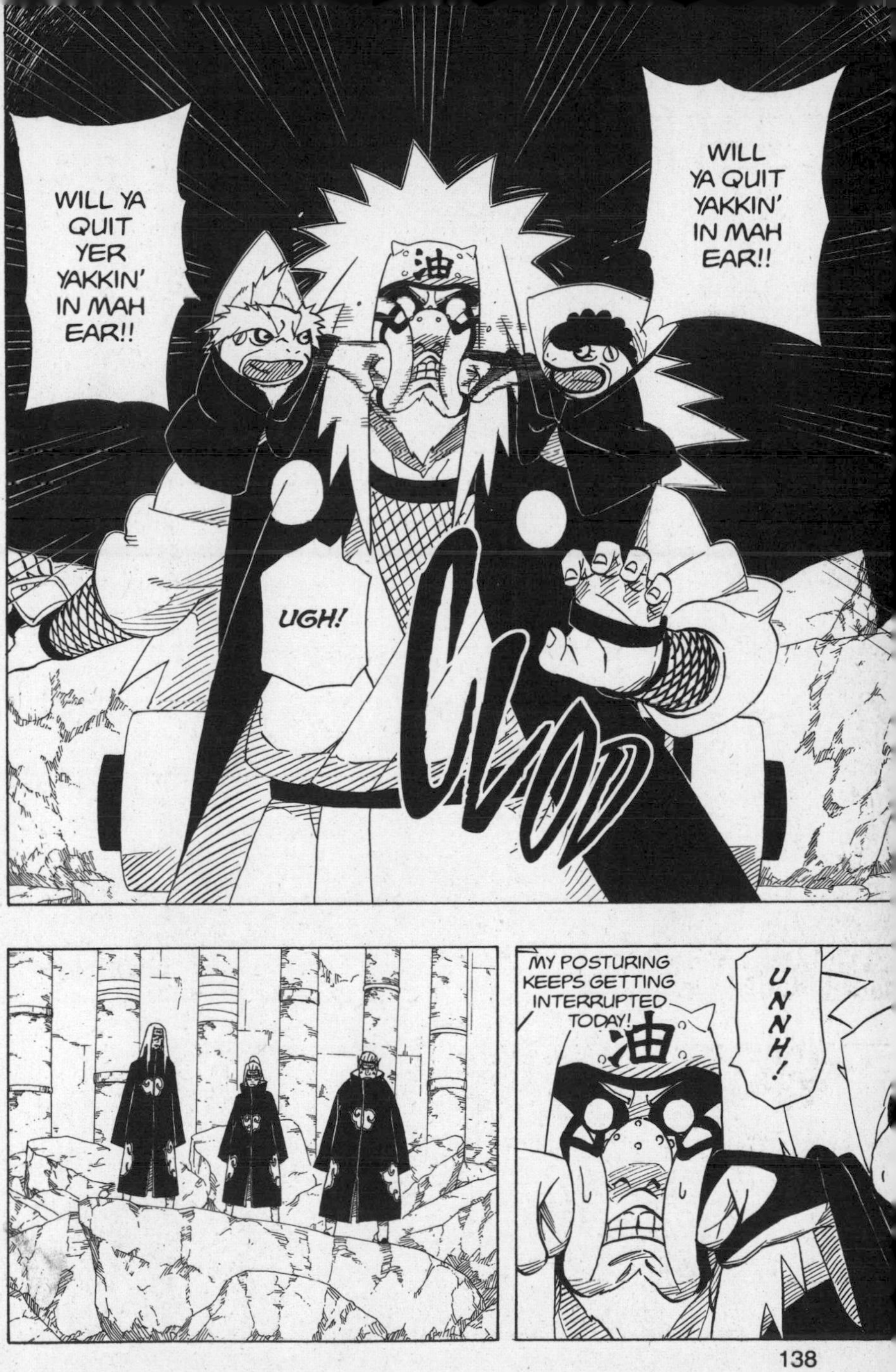
WILL YA QUIT YAKKIN' IN MAH EAR!!
WILL YA QUIT YER YAKKIN' IN MAH EAR!!
UGH!
UNNH!
MY POSTURING KEEPS GETTING INTERRUPTED TODAY!

READ THIS WAY

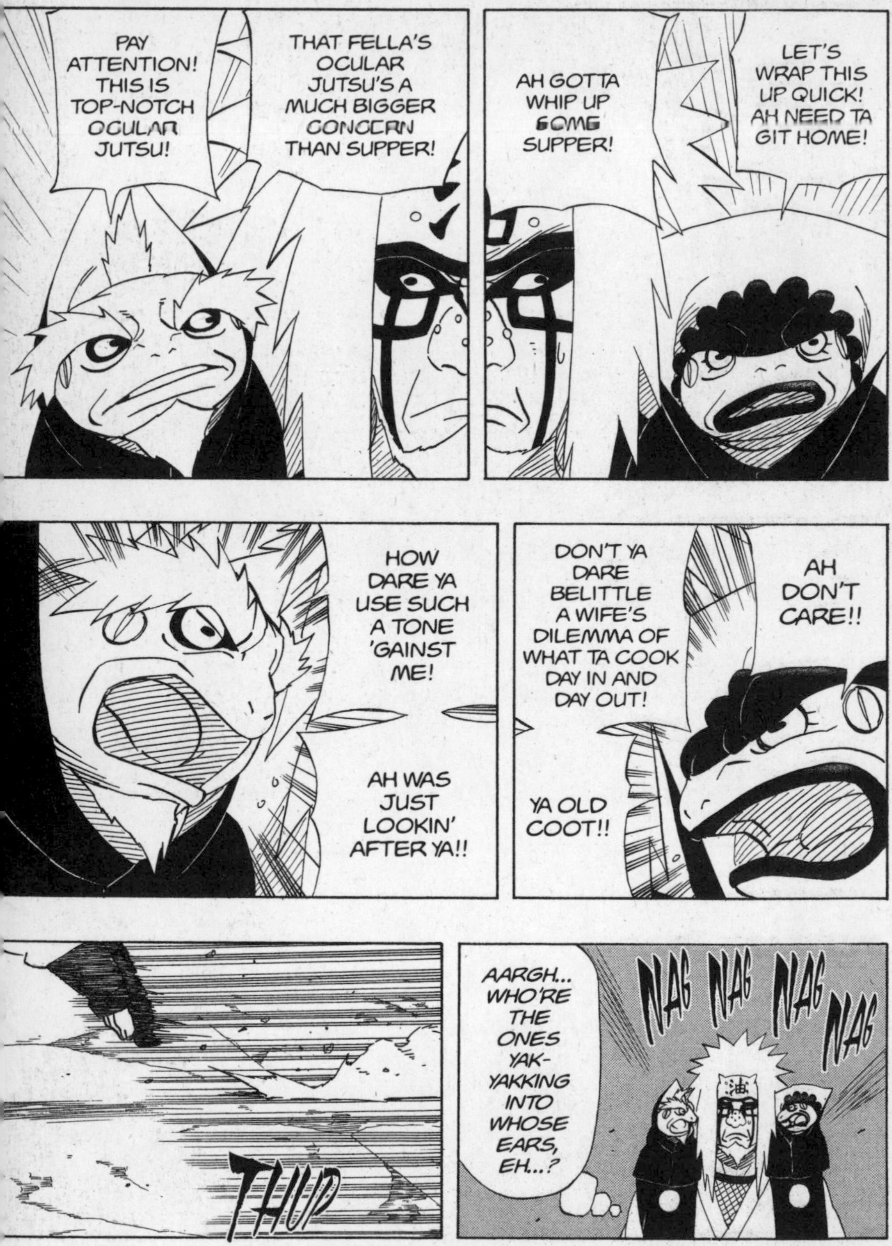
LET'S WRAP THIS UP QUICK! AH NEED TA GIT HOME!
AH GOTTA WHIP UP SOME SUPPER!
THAT FELLA'S OCULAR JUTSU'S A MUCH BIGGER CONCERN THAN SUPPER!
PAY ATTENTION! THIS IS TOP-NOTCH OCULAR JUTSU!
AH DON'T CARE!!
DON'T YA DARE BELITTLE A WIFE'S DILEMMA OF WHAT TA COOK DAY IN AND DAY OUT!
YA OLD COOT!!
HOW DARE YA USE SUCH A TONE 'GAINST ME!
AH WAS JUST LOOKIN' AFTER YA!!
NAG NAG NAG NAG
AARGH... WHO'RE THE ONES YAK-YAKKING INTO WHOSE EARS, EH...?
THUP

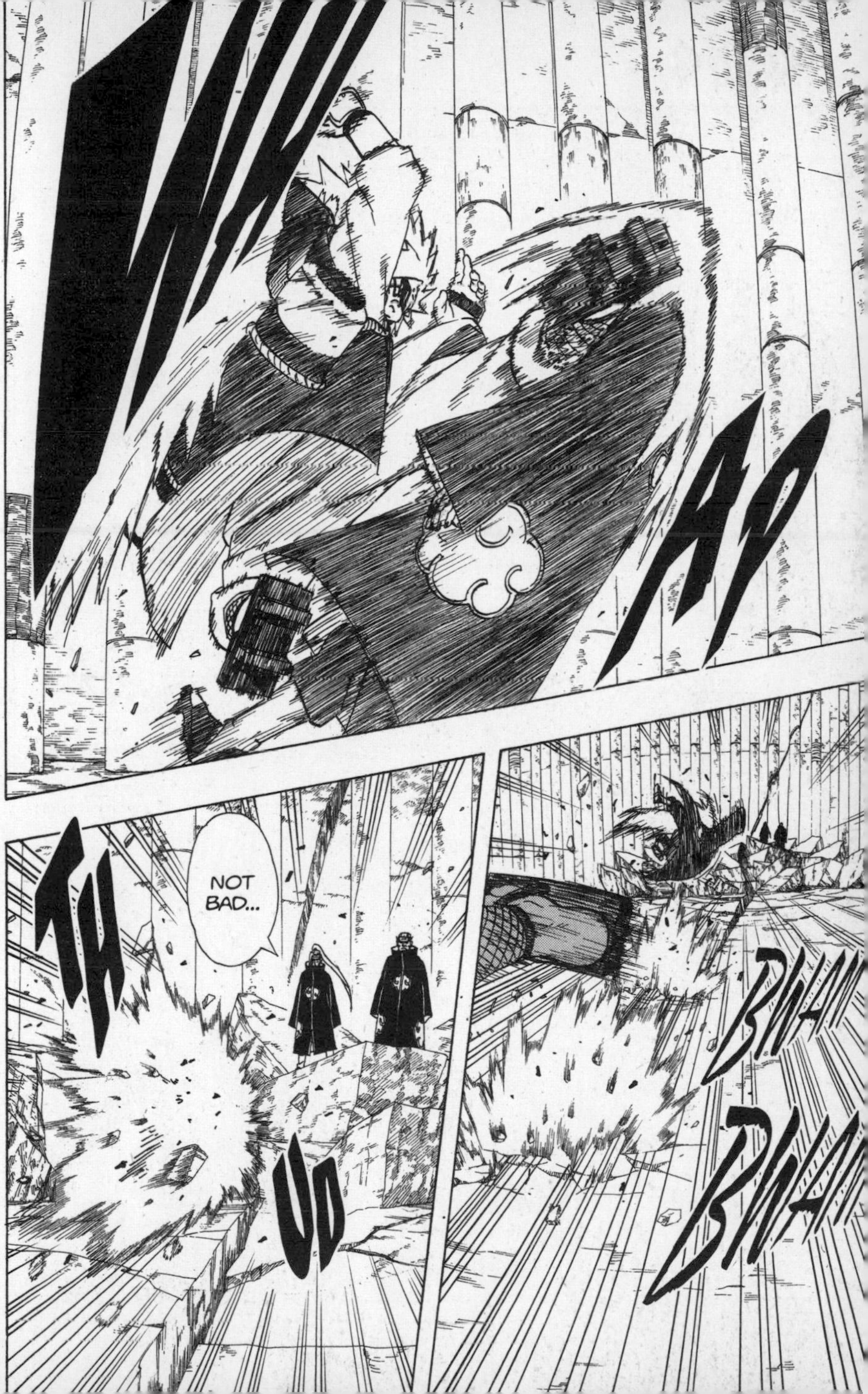
NOT BAD...
TH
UD

READ THIS WAY

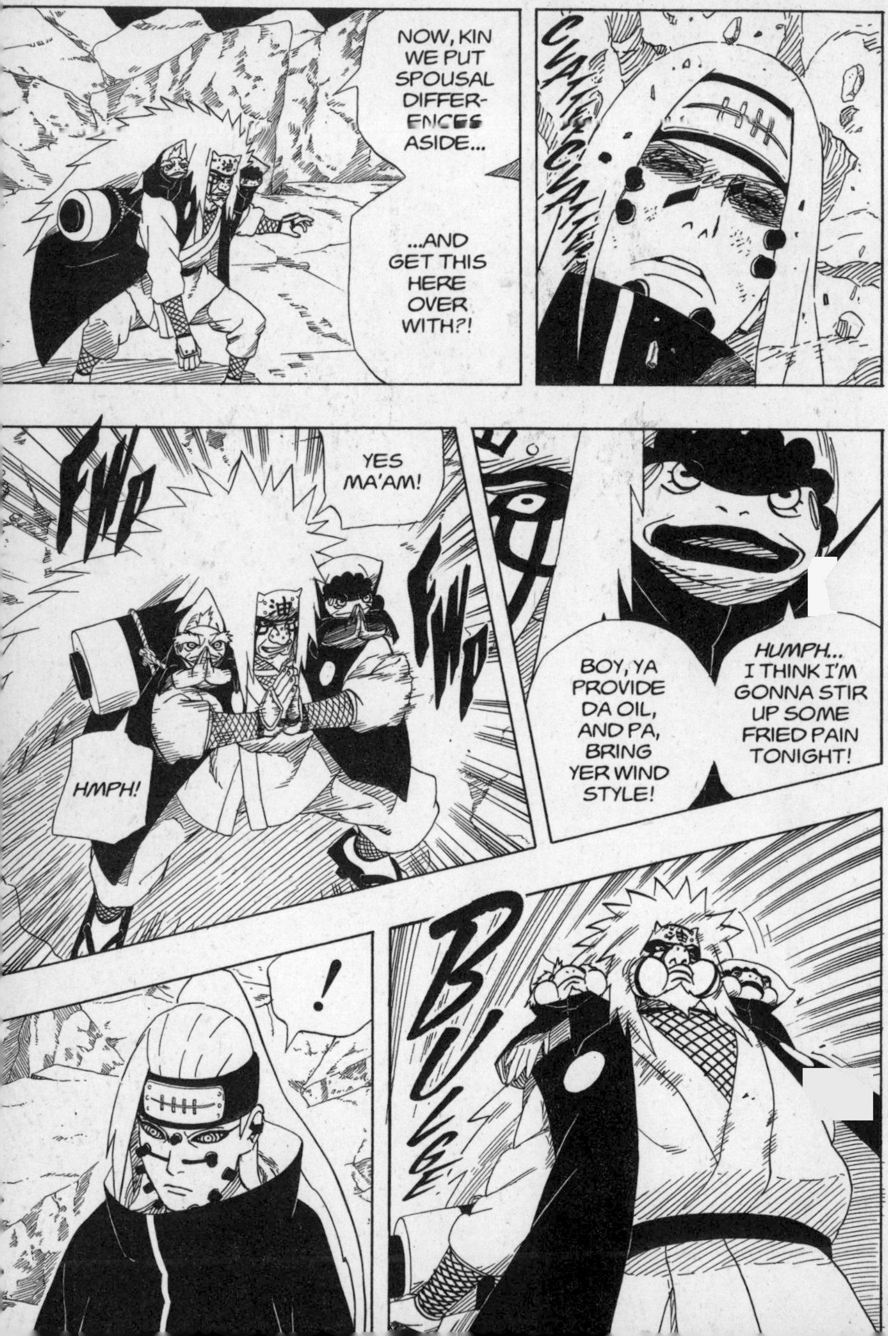
NOW, KIN WE PUT SPOUSAL DIFFER-ENCES ASIDE...
...AND GET THIS HERE OVER WITH?!
HUMPH... I THINK I'M GONNA STIR UP SOME FRIED PAIN TONIGHT!
BOY, YA PROVIDE DA OIL, AND PA, BRING YER WIND STYLE!
YES MA'AM!
FWP
HMPH!
FWP
BULGE
!

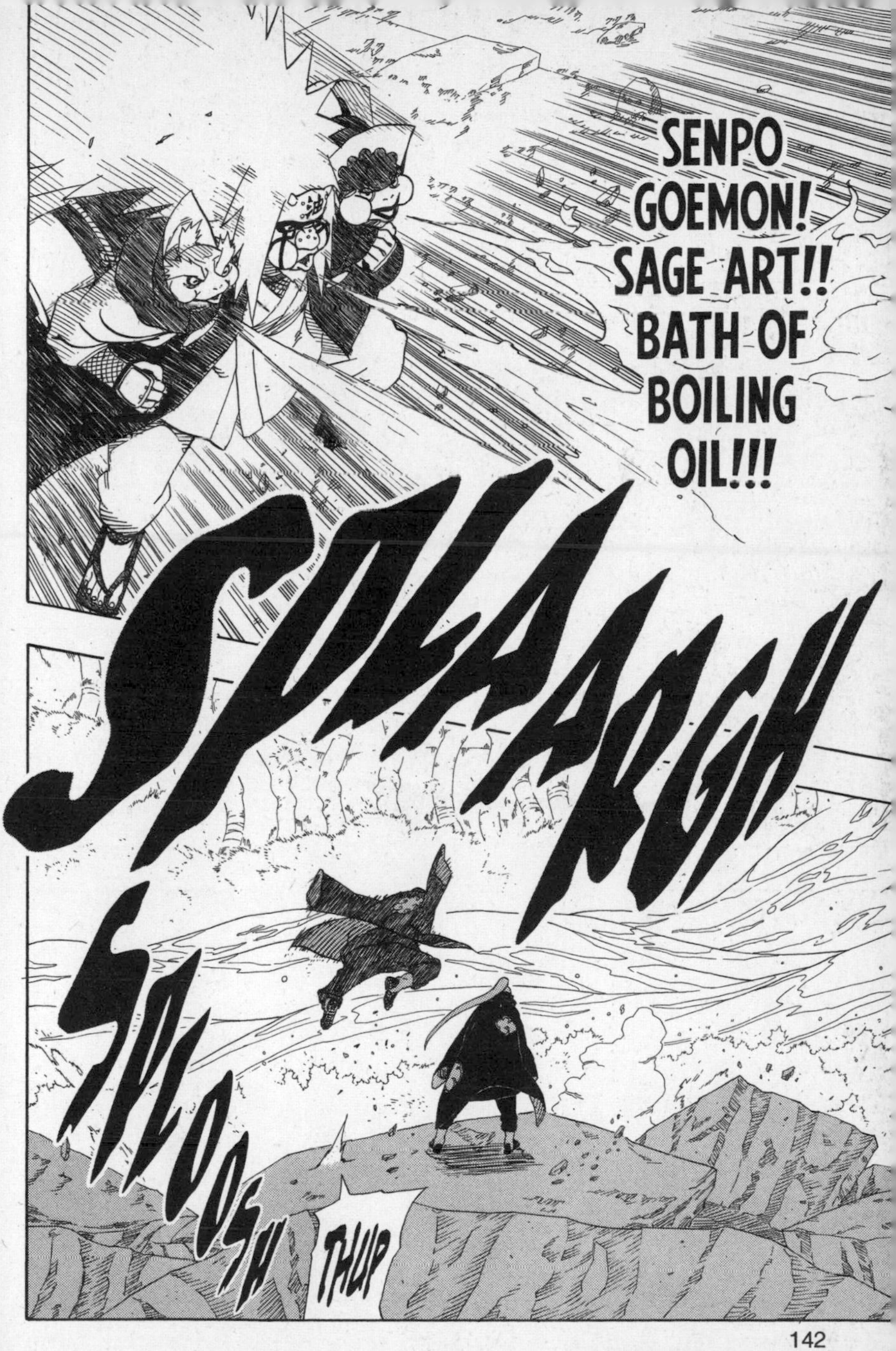
SENPO GOEMON! SAGE ART!! BATH OF BOILING OIL!!!
SPLAAAGH
SPLOOSH
THUP

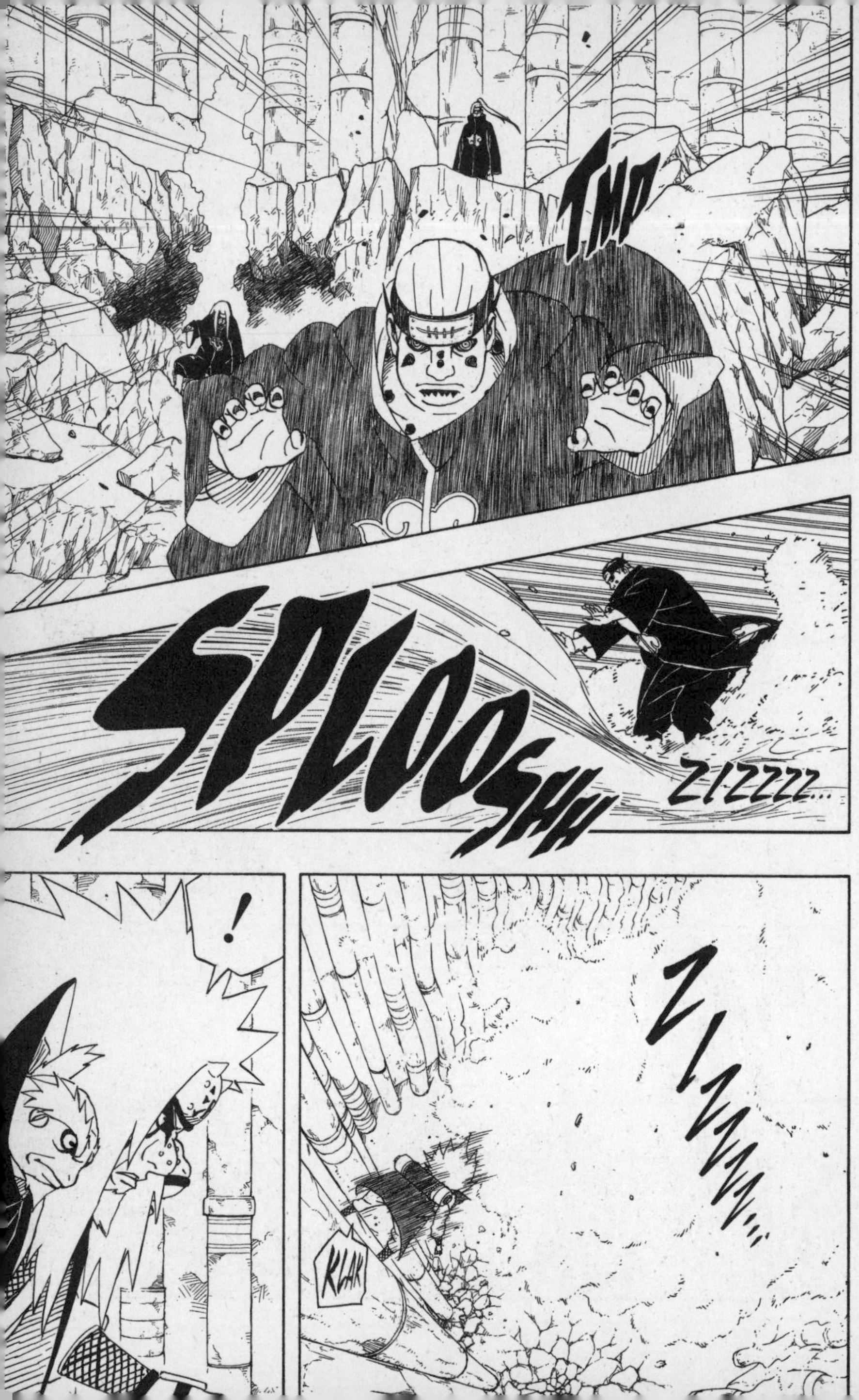
THP
!
SPLOOSHH
ZIZZZZ...
ZZZZZ...
KLAK
!

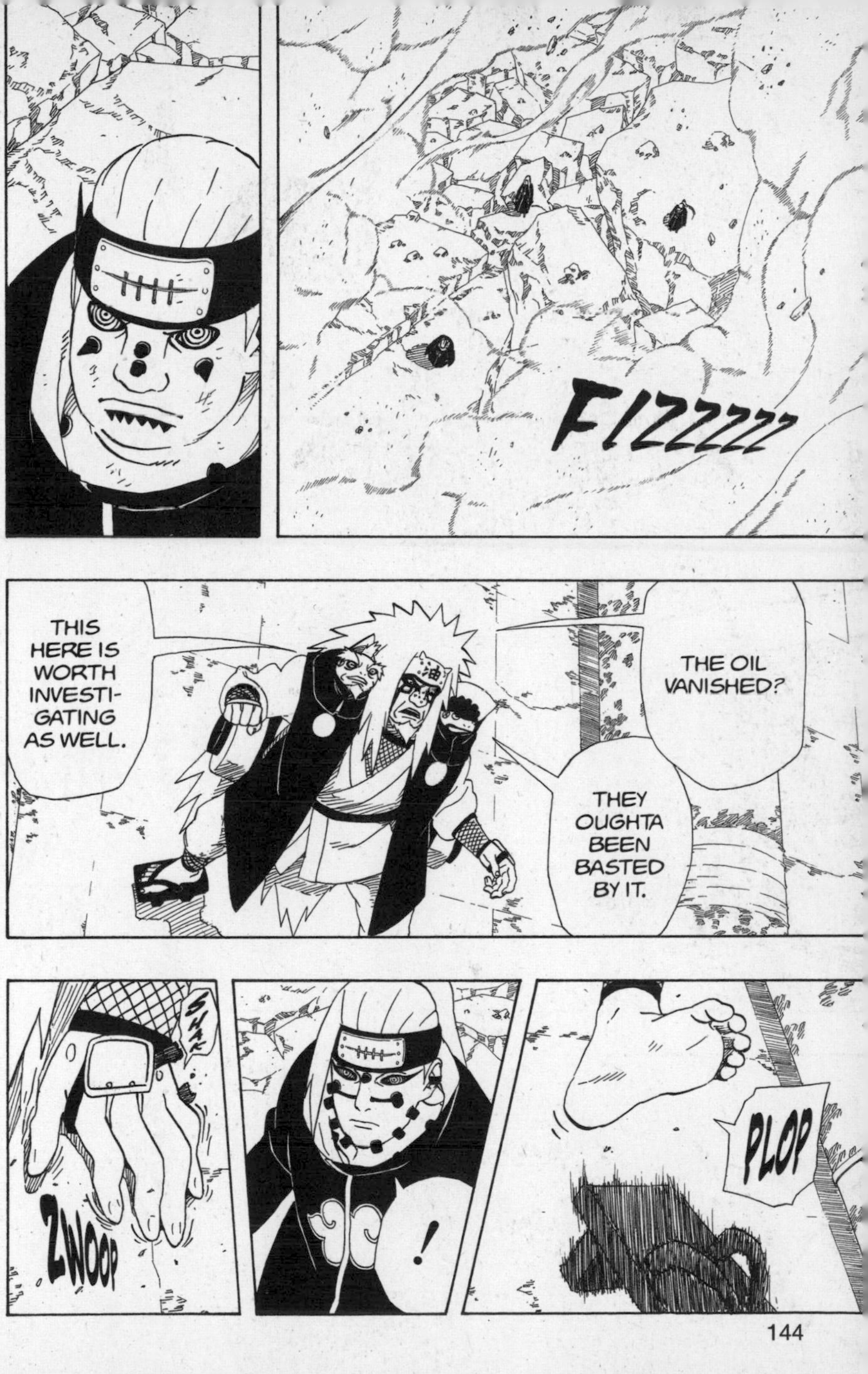
FIZZZZZ
THE OIL VANISHED?
THEY OUGHTA BEEN BASTED BY IT.
THIS HERE IS WORTH INVESTI-GATING AS WELL.
PLOP
!
SHAK
ZWOOP

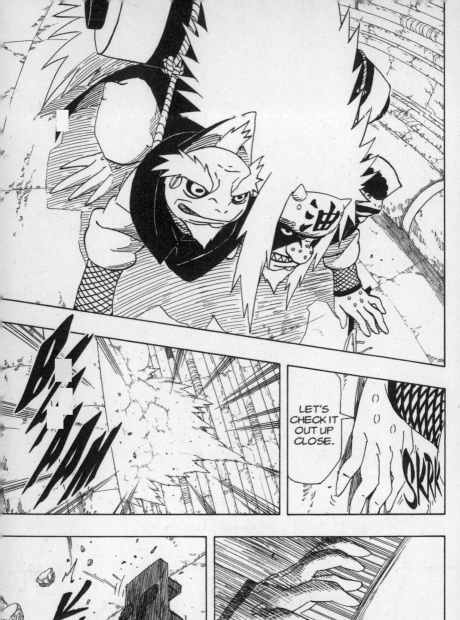

LET'S
CHECK IT
OUT UP
CLOSE.

SKRK

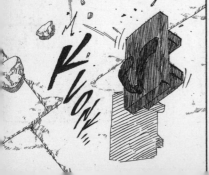

K-UON!!

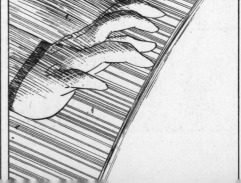

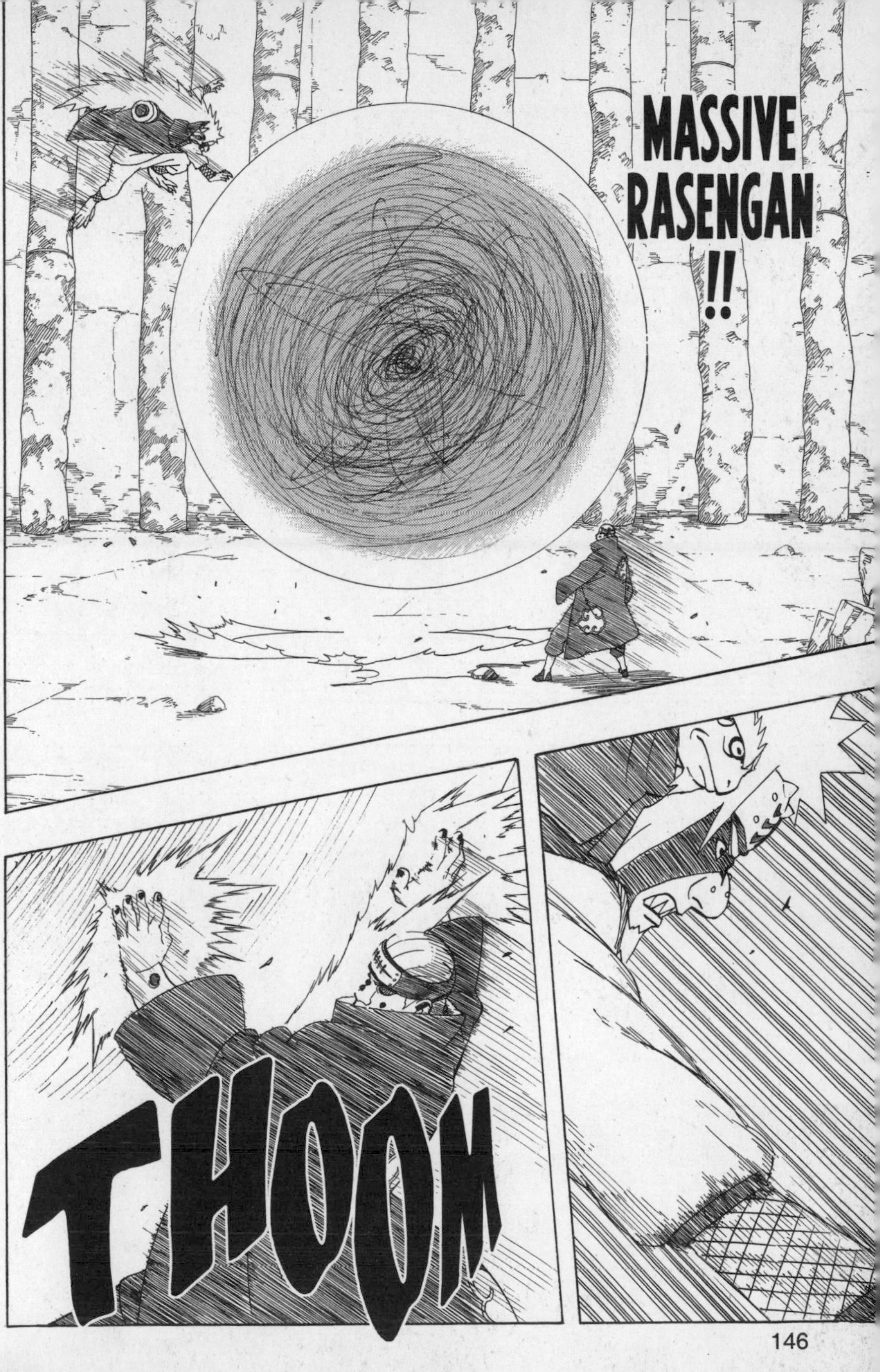
MASSIVE RASENGAN!!
THOOM

READ THIS WAY

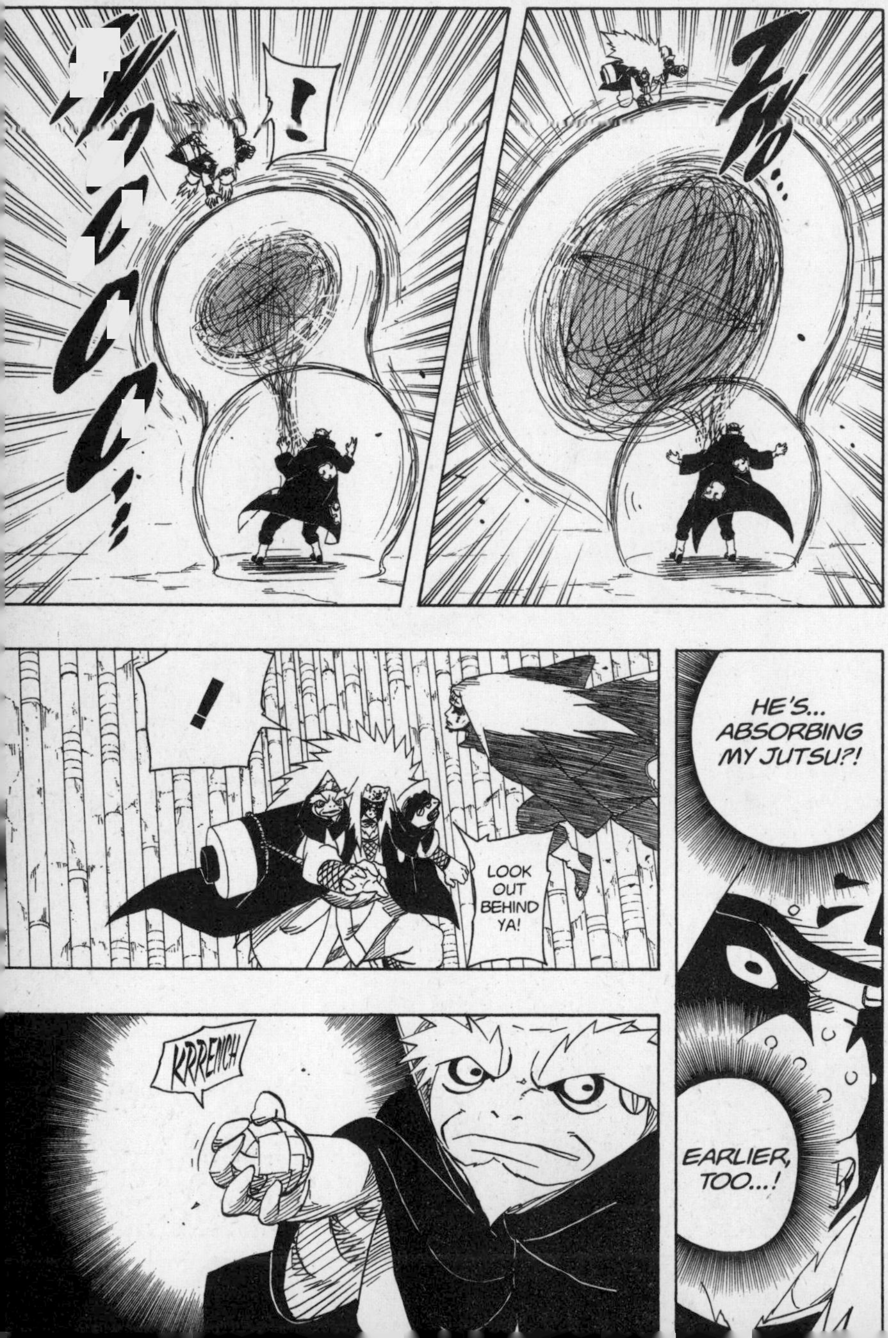
!
HE'S... ABSORBING MY JUTSU?!
EARLIER, TOO...!
!
LOOK OUT BEHIND YA!
KRRENCH

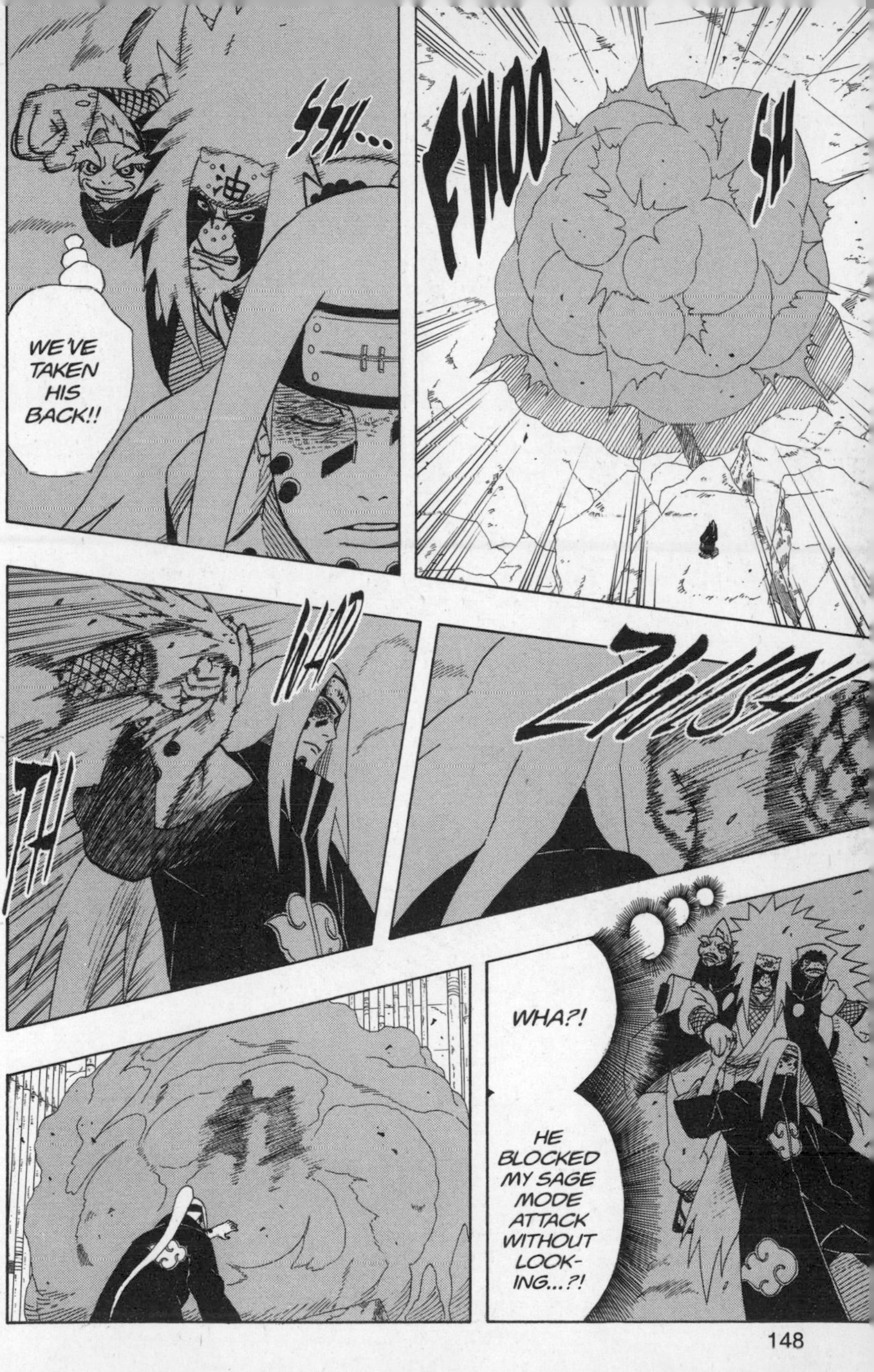
GWOO
SH
SSH...
WE'VE TAKEN HIS BACK!!
ZHUSH
WHAP
TH
WHA?!
HE BLOCKED MY SAGE MODE ATTACK WITHOUT LOOK-ING...?!

READ THIS WAY

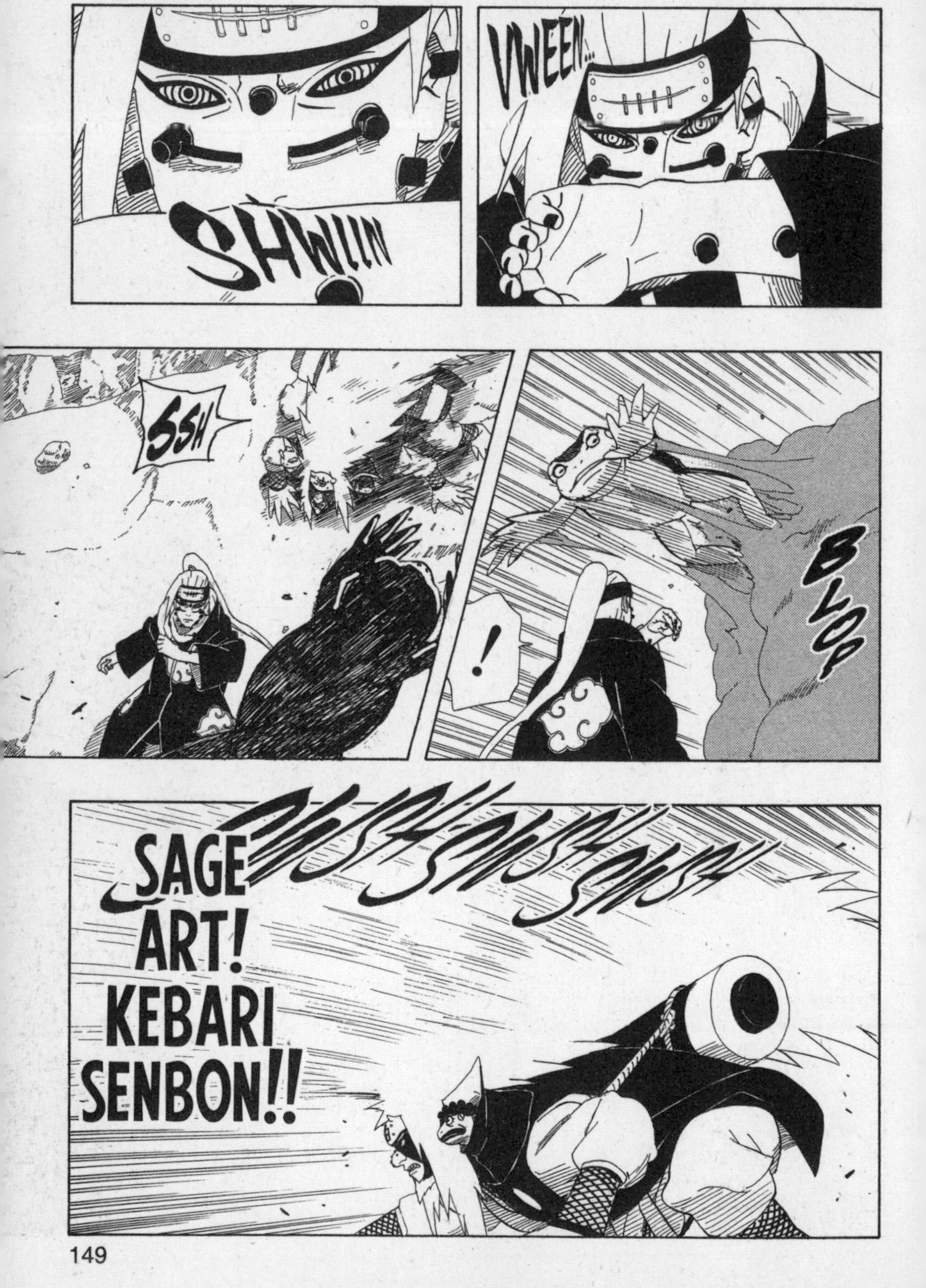
VWEEN...
SHWIIN
BLOP
!
SSH
SAGE ART! KEBARI SENBON!!

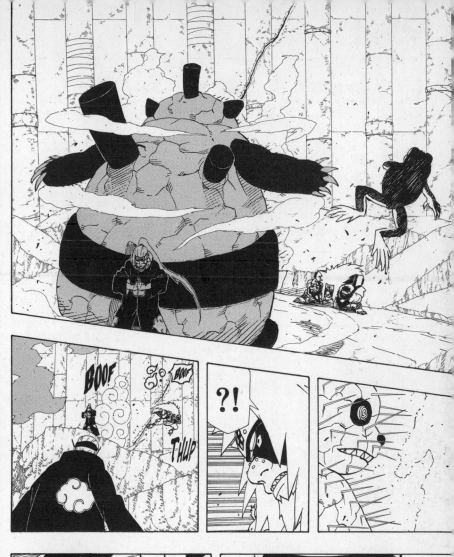

BOOF BOOF

THUP

?!

UWE EN

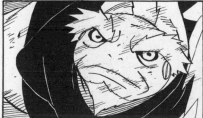

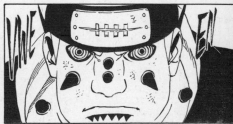

READ THIS WAY

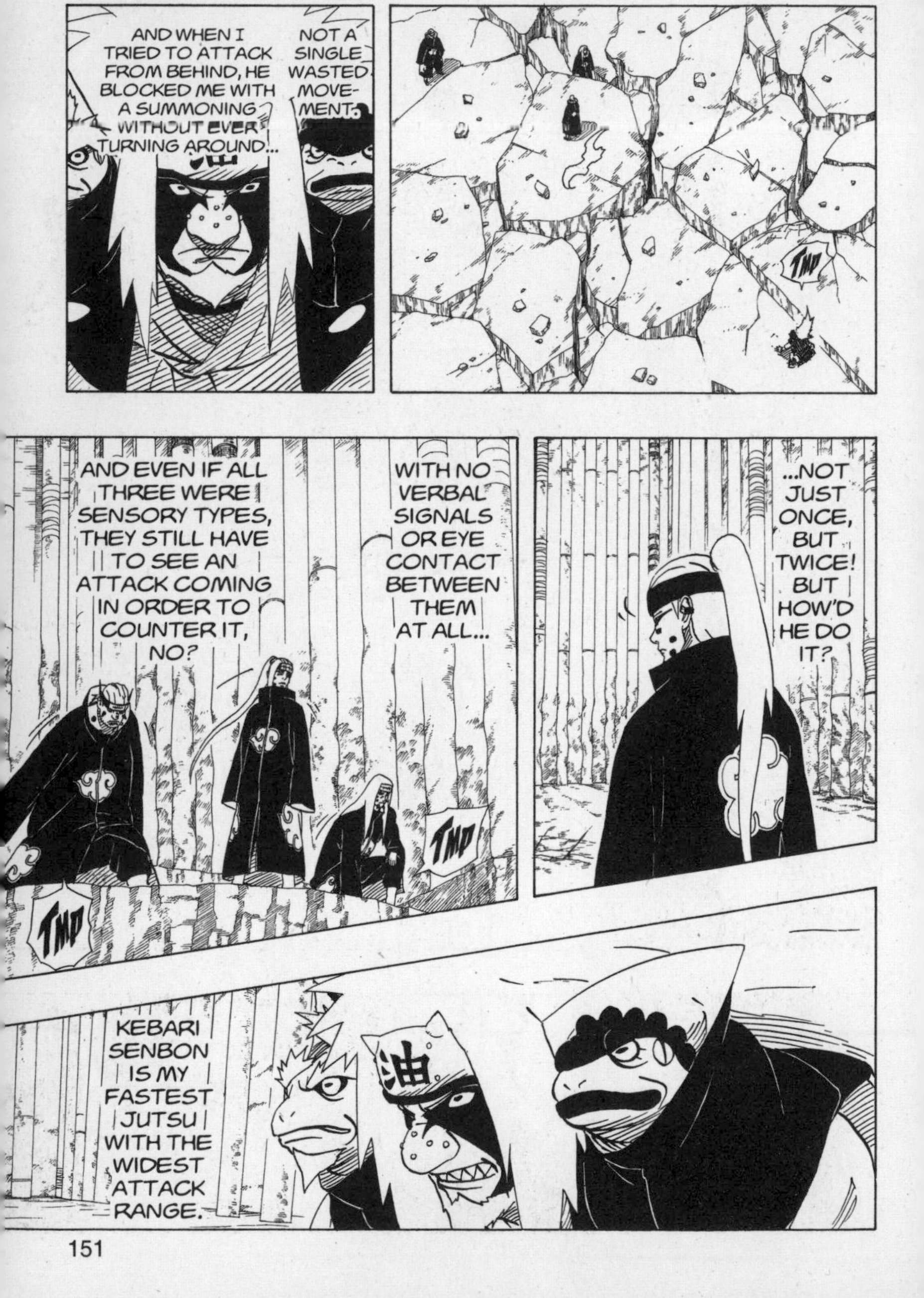
TMP
NOT A SINGLE WASTED MOVEMENT.
AND WHEN I TRIED TO ATTACK FROM BEHIND, HE BLOCKED ME WITH A SUMMONING WITHOUT EVER TURNING AROUND...
...NOT JUST ONCE, BUT TWICE! BUT HOW'D HE DO IT?
WITH NO VERBAL SIGNALS OR EYE CONTACT BETWEEN THEM AT ALL...
AND EVEN IF ALL THREE WERE SENSORY TYPES, THEY STILL HAVE TO SEE AN ATTACK COMING IN ORDER TO COUNTER IT, NO?
TMP
TMP
KEBARI SENBON IS MY FASTEST JUTSU WITH THE WIDEST ATTACK RANGE.

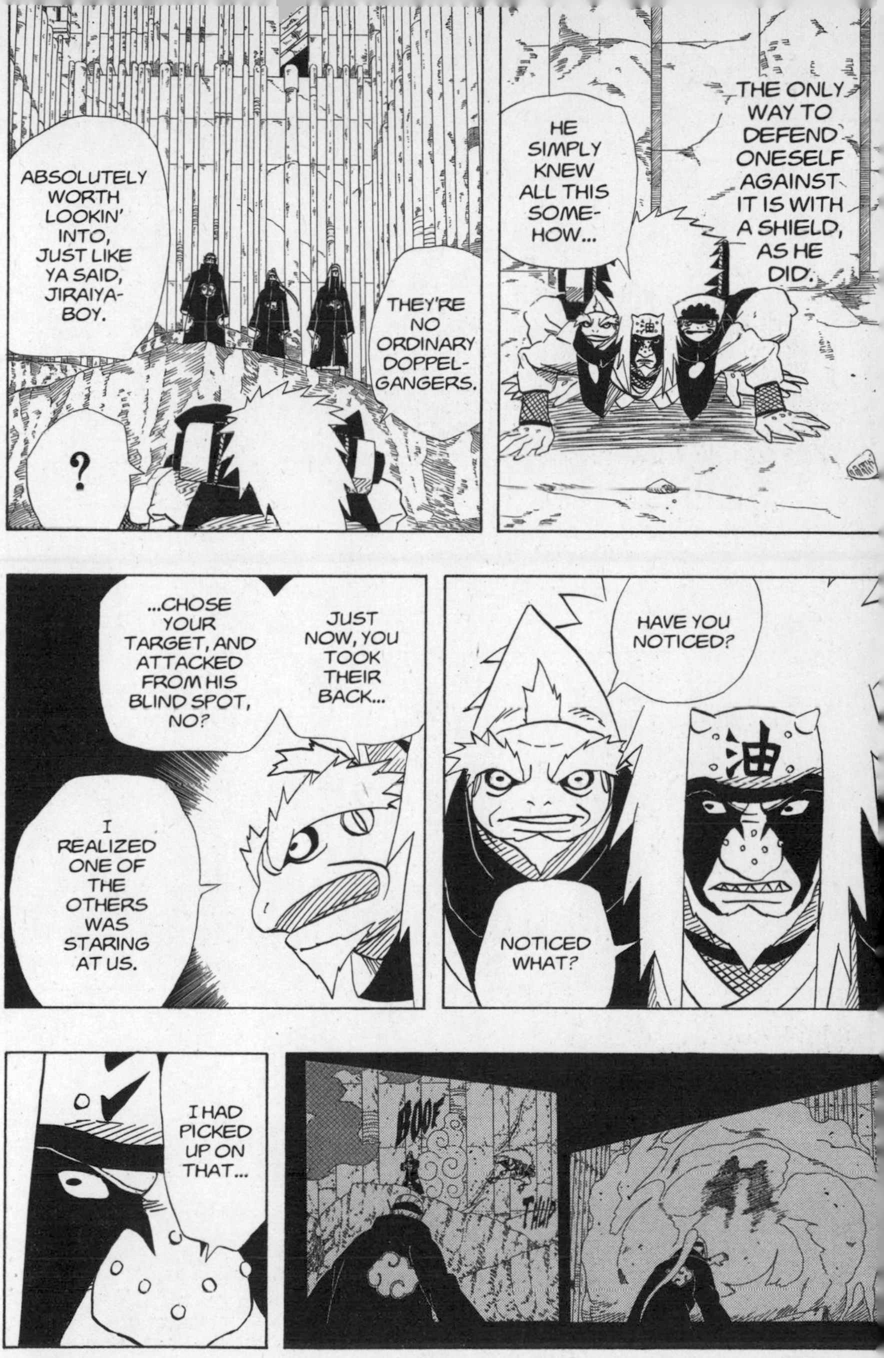
THE ONLY WAY TO DEFEND ONESELF AGAINST IT IS WITH A SHIELD, AS HE DID.
HE SIMPLY KNEW ALL THIS SOME-HOW...
THEY'RE NO ORDINARY DOPPEL-GANGERS.
ABSOLUTELY WORTH LOOKIN' INTO, JUST LIKE YA SAID, JIRAIYA-BOY.
?
HAVE YOU NOTICED?
NOTICED WHAT?
JUST NOW, YOU TOOK THEIR BACK...
...CHOSE YOUR TARGET, AND ATTACKED FROM HIS BLIND SPOT, NO?
I REALIZED ONE OF THE OTHERS WAS STARING AT US.
BOOF
THUP
I HAD PICKED UP ON THAT...

READ THIS WAY

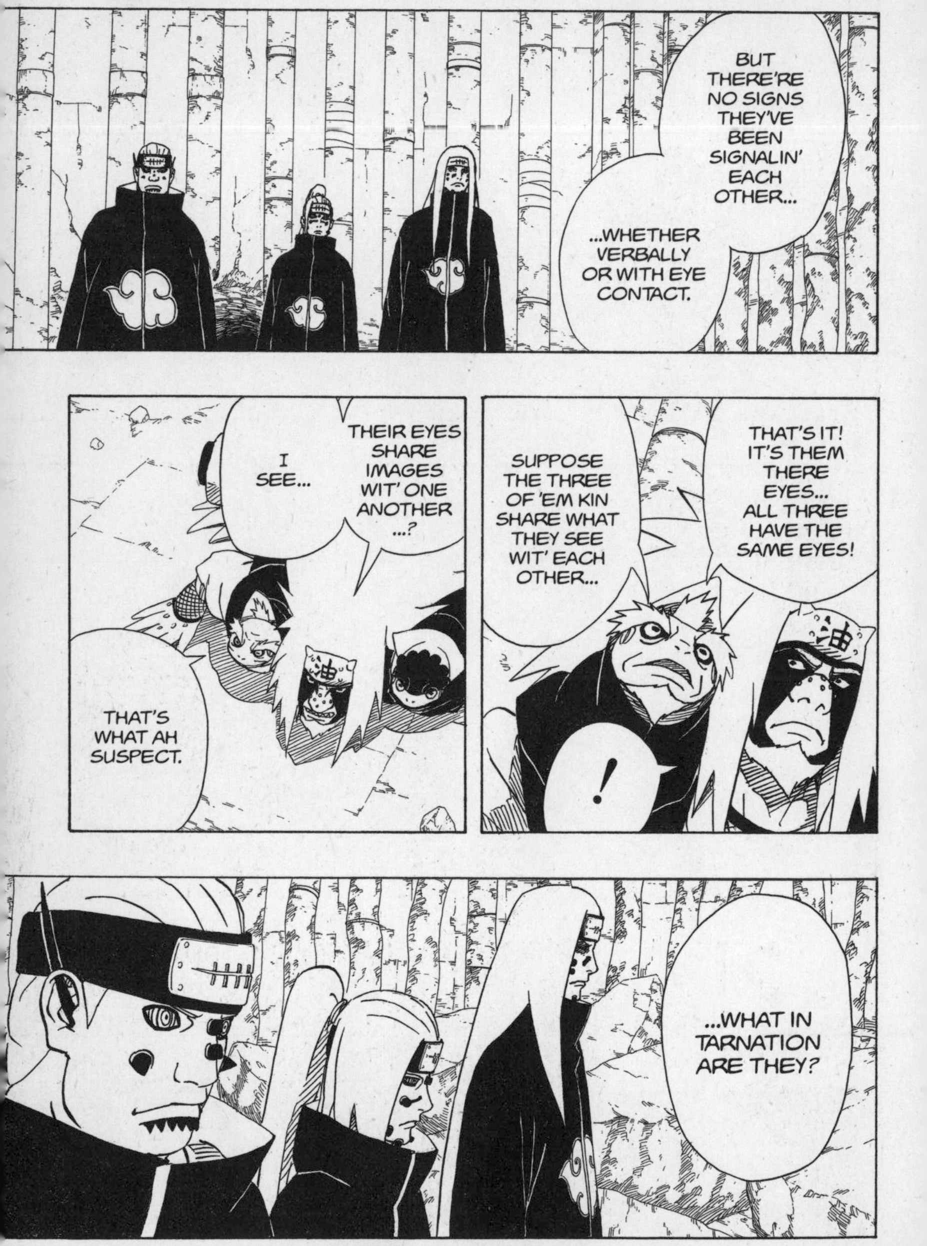
BUT THERE'RE NO SIGNS THEY'VE BEEN SIGNALIN' EACH OTHER...
...WHETHER VERBALLY OR WITH EYE CONTACT.
THAT'S IT! IT'S THEM THERE EYES... ALL THREE HAVE THE SAME EYES!
SUPPOSE THE THREE OF 'EM KIN SHARE WHAT THEY SEE WIT' EACH OTHER...
!
THEIR EYES SHARE IMAGES WIT' ONE ANOTHER ...?
I SEE...
THAT'S WHAT AH SUSPECT.
...WHAT IN TARNATION ARE THEY?

NARUTO

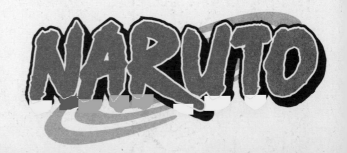

Number 378: One to One...!!

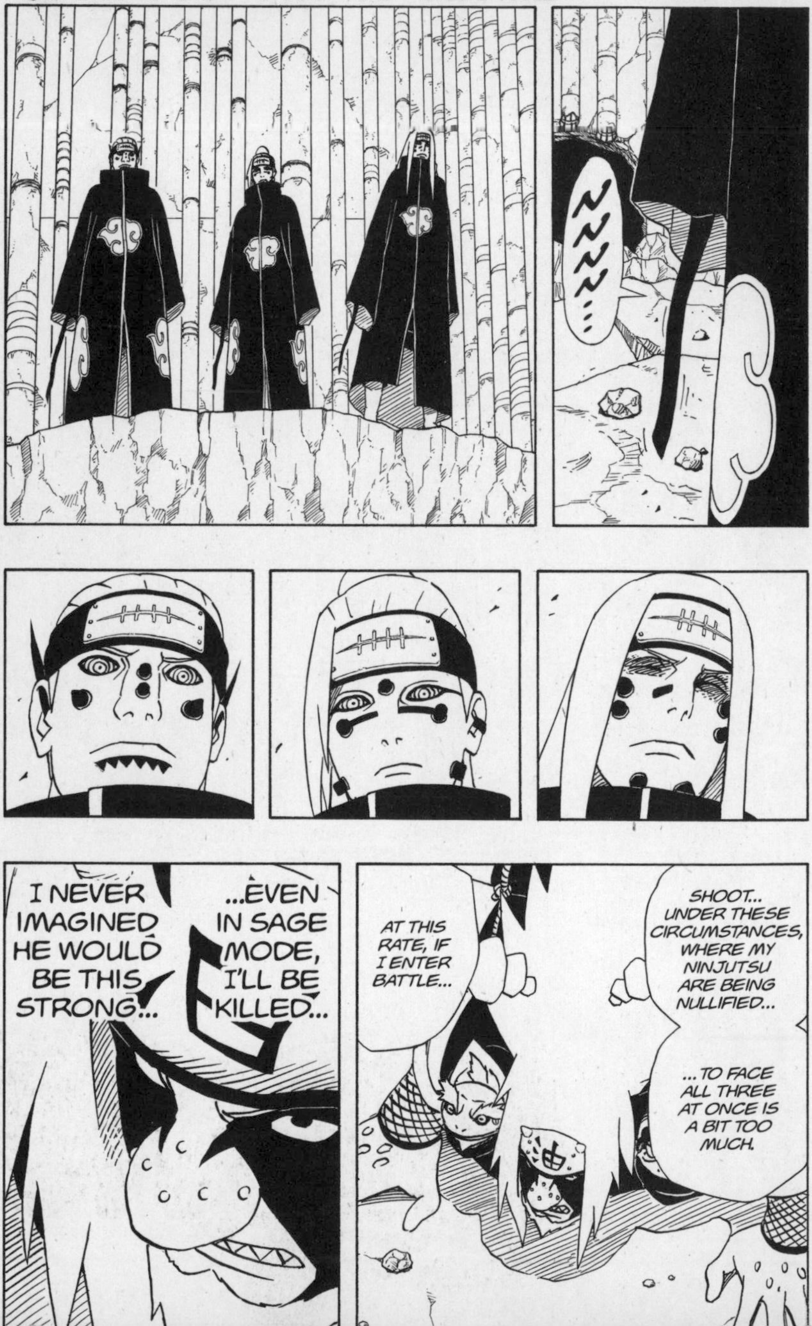
NNNN...
SHOOT... UNDER THESE CIRCUMSTANCES, WHERE MY NINJUTSU ARE BEING NULLIFIED...
...TO FACE ALL THREE AT ONCE IS A BIT TOO MUCH.
AT THIS RATE, IF I ENTER BATTLE...
...EVEN IN SAGE MODE, I'LL BE KILLED...
I NEVER IMAGINED HE WOULD BE THIS STRONG...

Number 378: One to One...!!

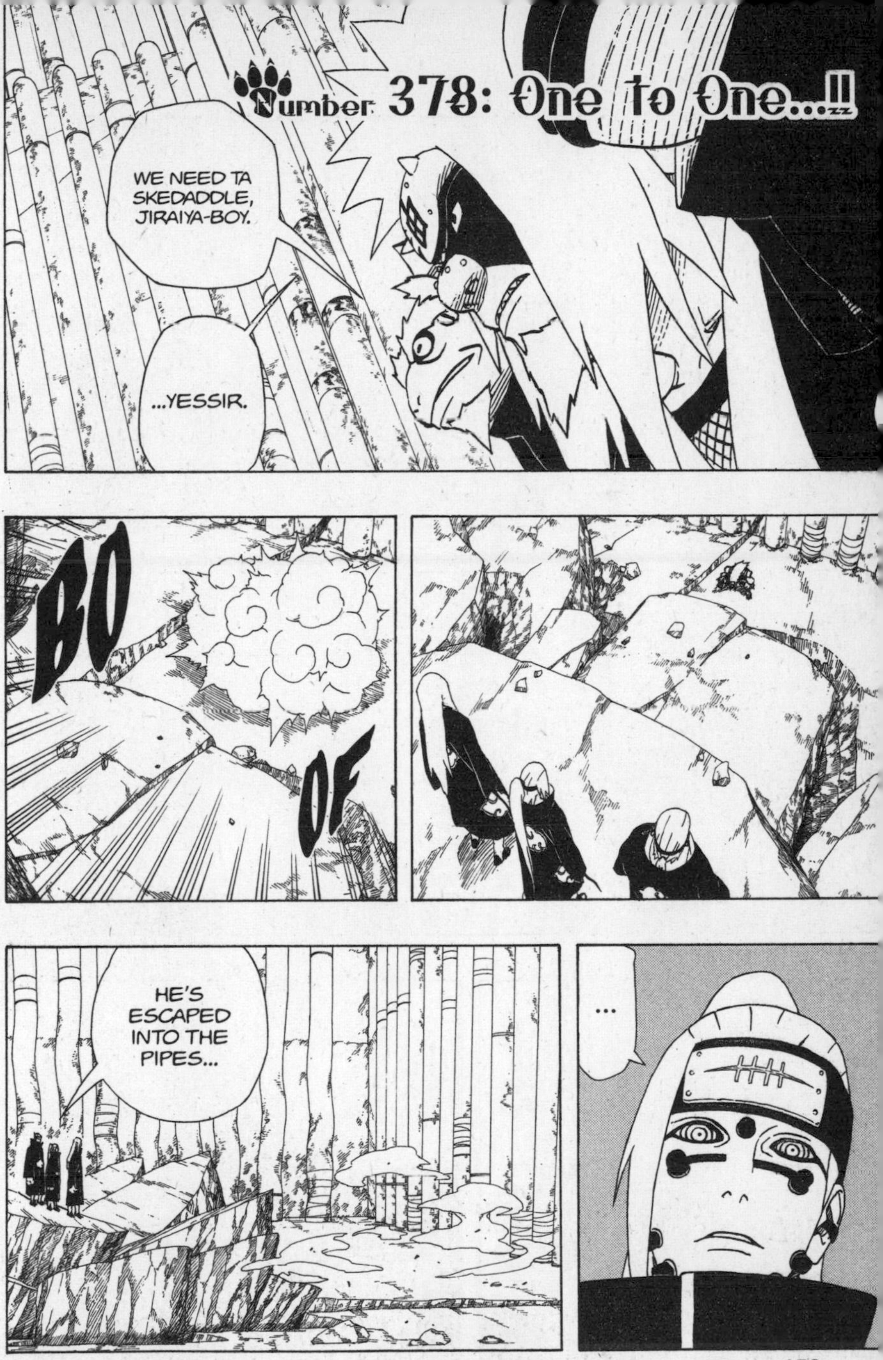
WE NEED TA SKEDADDLE, JIRAIYA-BOY.
...YESSIR.
BOOF
...
HE'S ESCAPED INTO THE PIPES...

READ THIS WAY

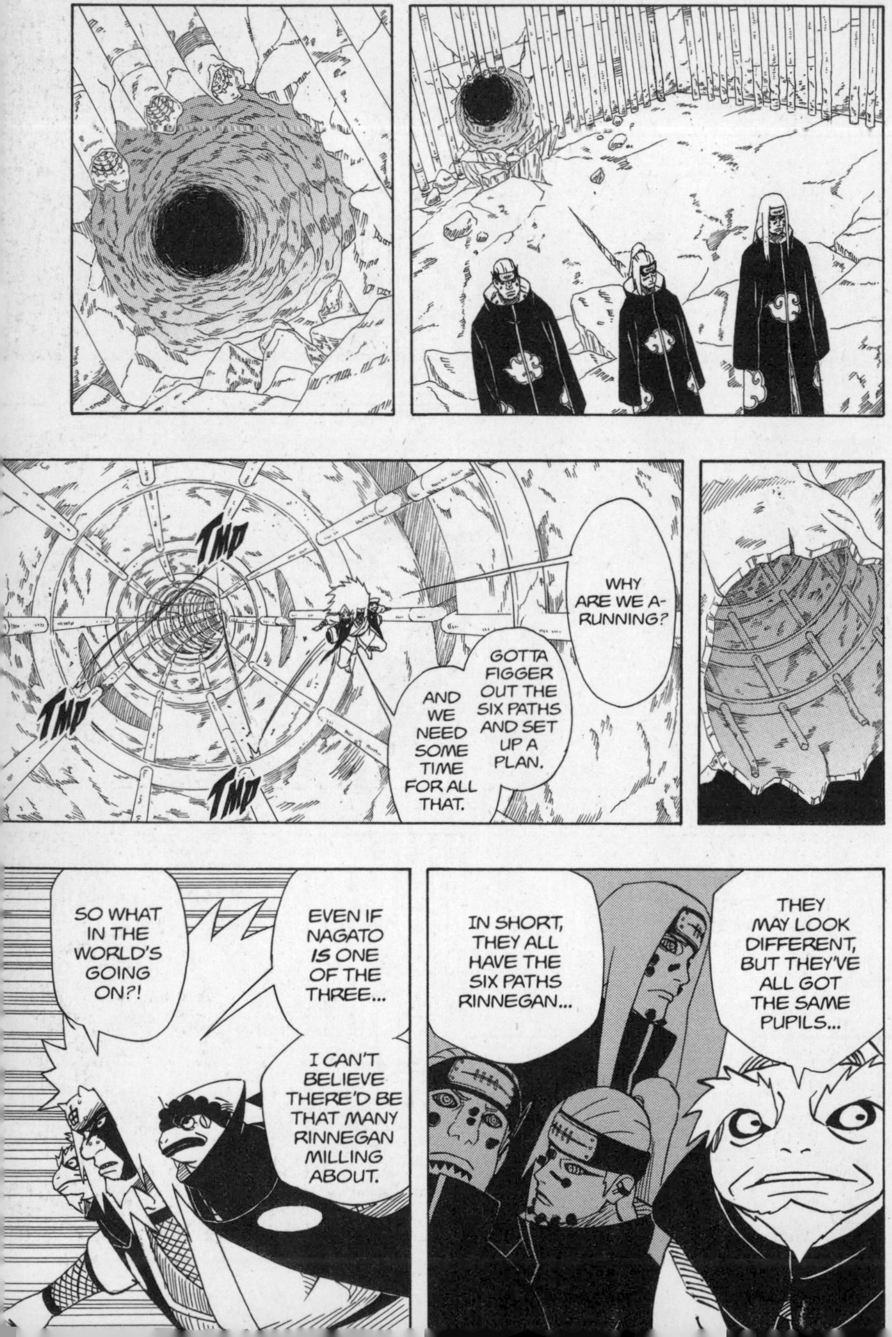
WHY ARE WE A-RUNNING?
GOTTA FIGGER OUT THE SIX PATHS AND SET UP A PLAN.
AND WE NEED SOME TIME FOR ALL THAT.
TMP
TMP
TMP
THEY MAY LOOK DIFFERENT, BUT THEY'VE ALL GOT THE SAME PUPILS...
IN SHORT, THEY ALL HAVE THE SIX PATHS RINNEGAN...
EVEN IF NAGATO *IS* ONE OF THE THREE...
I CAN'T BELIEVE THERE'D BE THAT MANY RINNEGAN MILLING ABOUT.
SO WHAT IN THE WORLD'S GOING ON?!

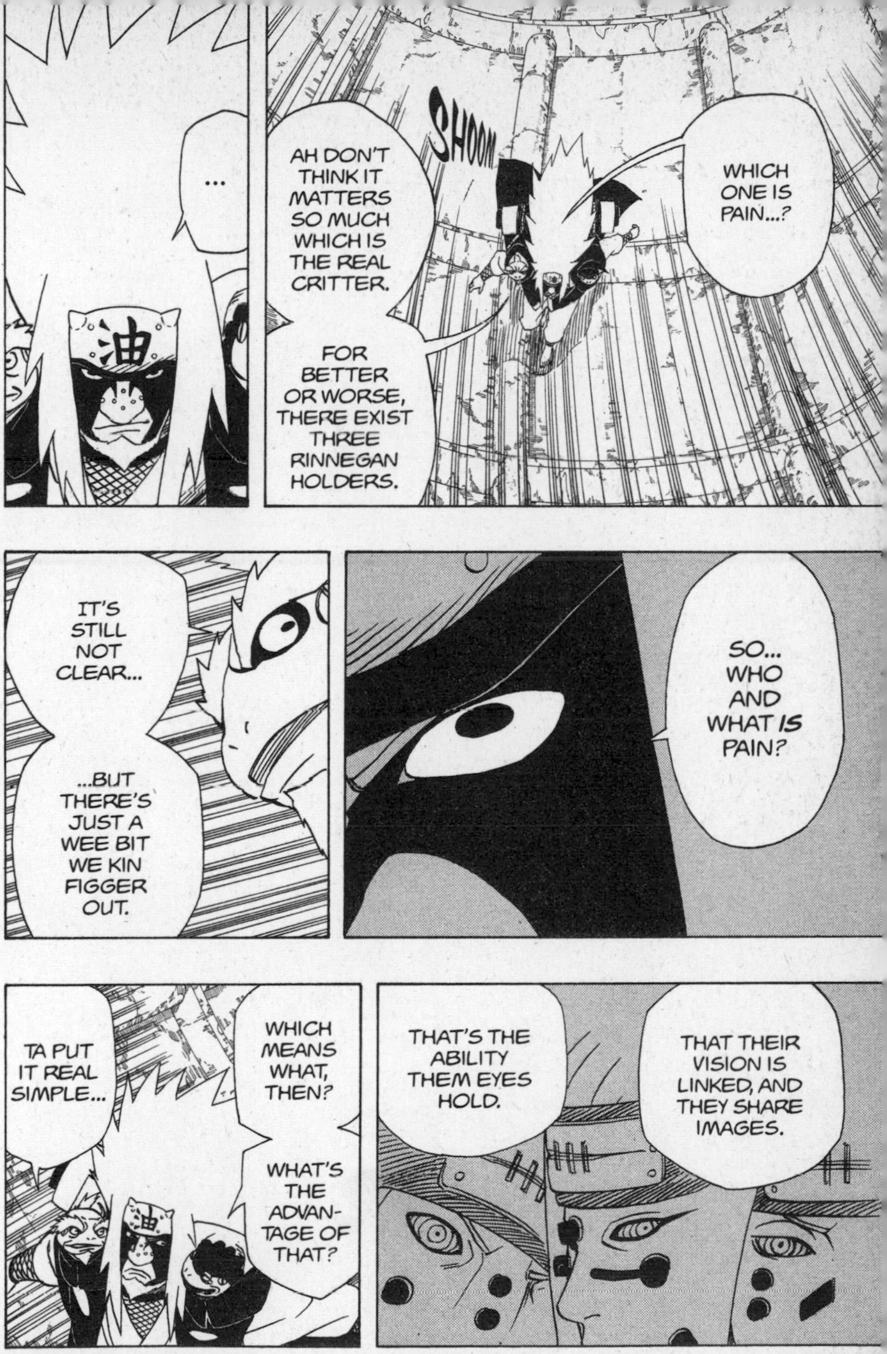
WHICH ONE IS PAIN...?
SHOOM
AH DON'T THINK IT MATTERS SO MUCH WHICH IS THE REAL CRITTER.
FOR BETTER OR WORSE, THERE EXIST THREE RINNEGAN HOLDERS.
...
SO... WHO AND WHAT *IS* PAIN?
IT'S STILL NOT CLEAR...
...BUT THERE'S JUST A WEE BIT WE KIN FIGGER OUT.
THAT THEIR VISION IS LINKED, AND THEY SHARE IMAGES.
THAT'S THE ABILITY THEM EYES HOLD.
WHICH MEANS WHAT, THEN?
WHAT'S THE ADVANTAGE OF THAT?
TA PUT IT REAL SIMPLE...

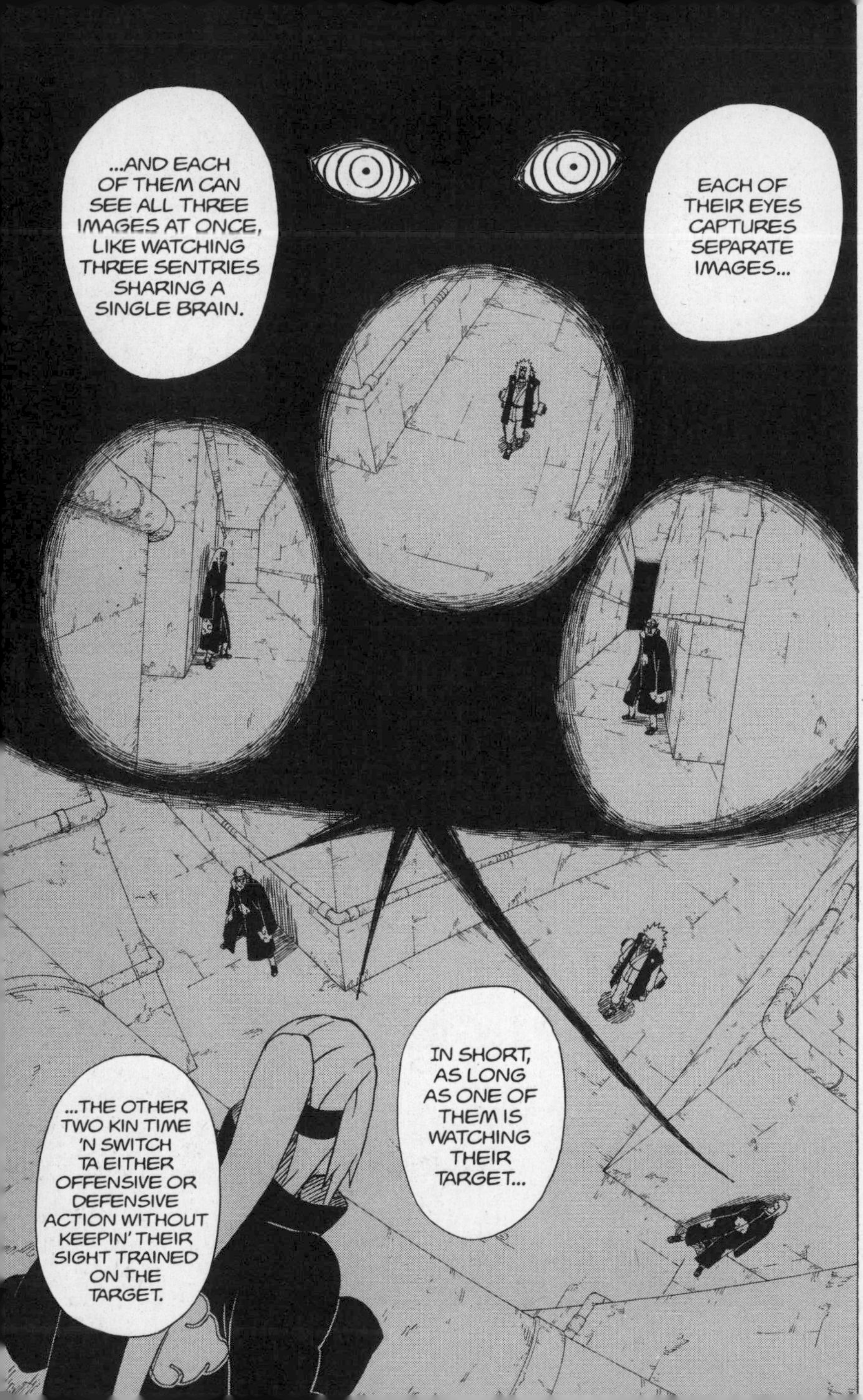
EACH OF THEIR EYES CAPTURES SEPARATE IMAGES...
...AND EACH OF THEM CAN SEE ALL THREE IMAGES AT ONCE, LIKE WATCHING THREE SENTRIES SHARING A SINGLE BRAIN.
IN SHORT, AS LONG AS ONE OF THEM IS WATCHING THEIR TARGET...
...THE OTHER TWO KIN TIME 'N SWITCH TA EITHER OFFENSIVE OR DEFENSIVE ACTION WITHOUT KEEPIN' THEIR SIGHT TRAINED ON THE TARGET.

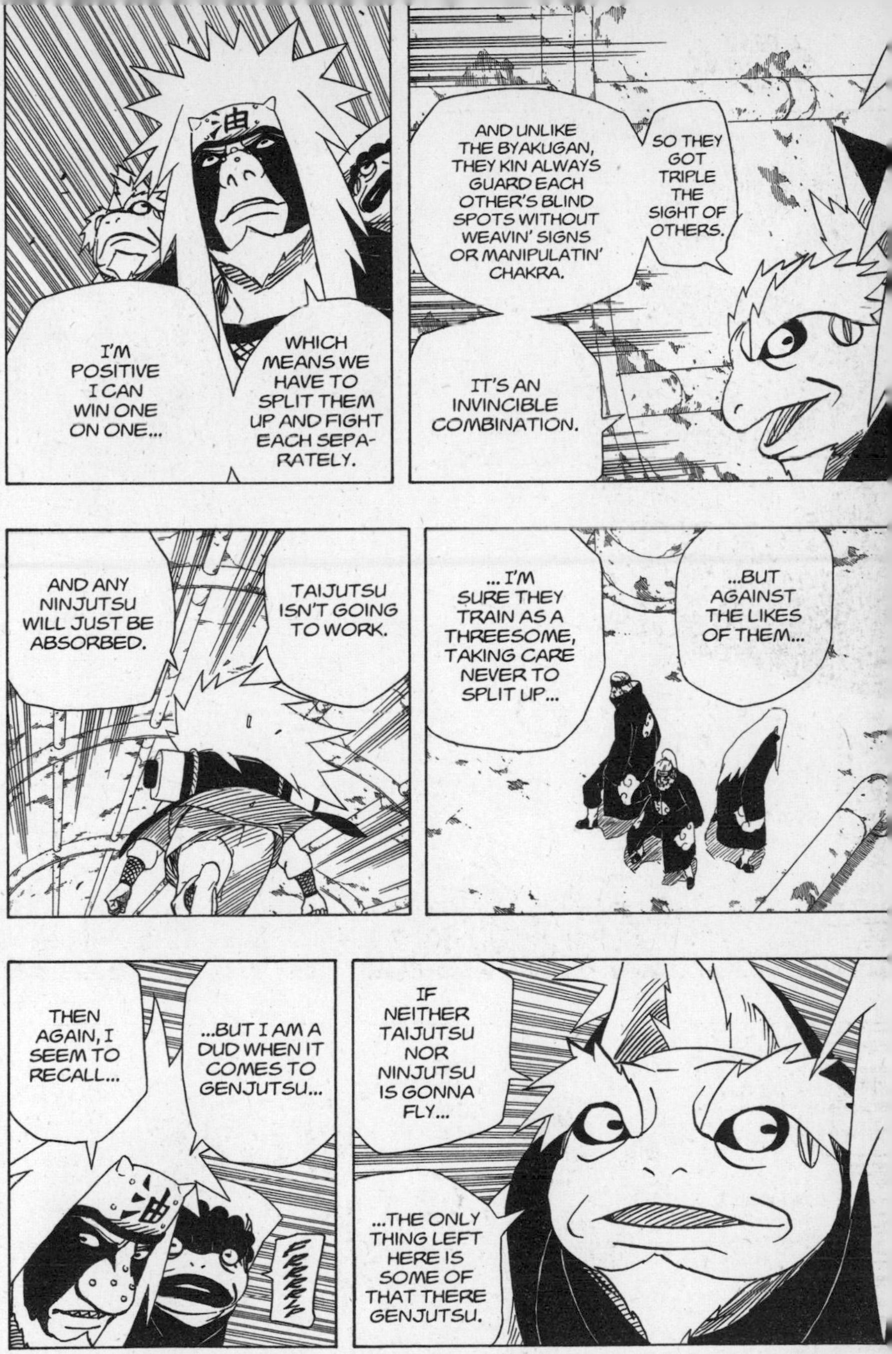
SO THEY GOT TRIPLE THE SIGHT OF OTHERS.
AND UNLIKE THE BYAKUGAN, THEY KIN ALWAYS GUARD EACH OTHER'S BLIND SPOTS WITHOUT WEAVIN' SIGNS OR MANIPULATIN' CHAKRA.
IT'S AN INVINCIBLE COMBINATION.
WHICH MEANS WE HAVE TO SPLIT THEM UP AND FIGHT EACH SEPA-RATELY.
I'M POSITIVE I CAN WIN ONE ON ONE...
...BUT AGAINST THE LIKES OF THEM...
... I'M SURE THEY TRAIN AS A THREESOME, TAKING CARE NEVER TO SPLIT UP...
TAIJUTSU ISN'T GOING TO WORK.
AND ANY NINJUTSU WILL JUST BE ABSORBED.
IF NEITHER TAIJUTSU NOR NINJUTSU IS GONNA FLY...
...THE ONLY THING LEFT HERE IS SOME OF THAT THERE GENJUTSU.
...BUT I AM A DUD WHEN IT COMES TO GENJUTSU...
THEN AGAIN, I SEEM TO RECALL...

READ THIS WAY

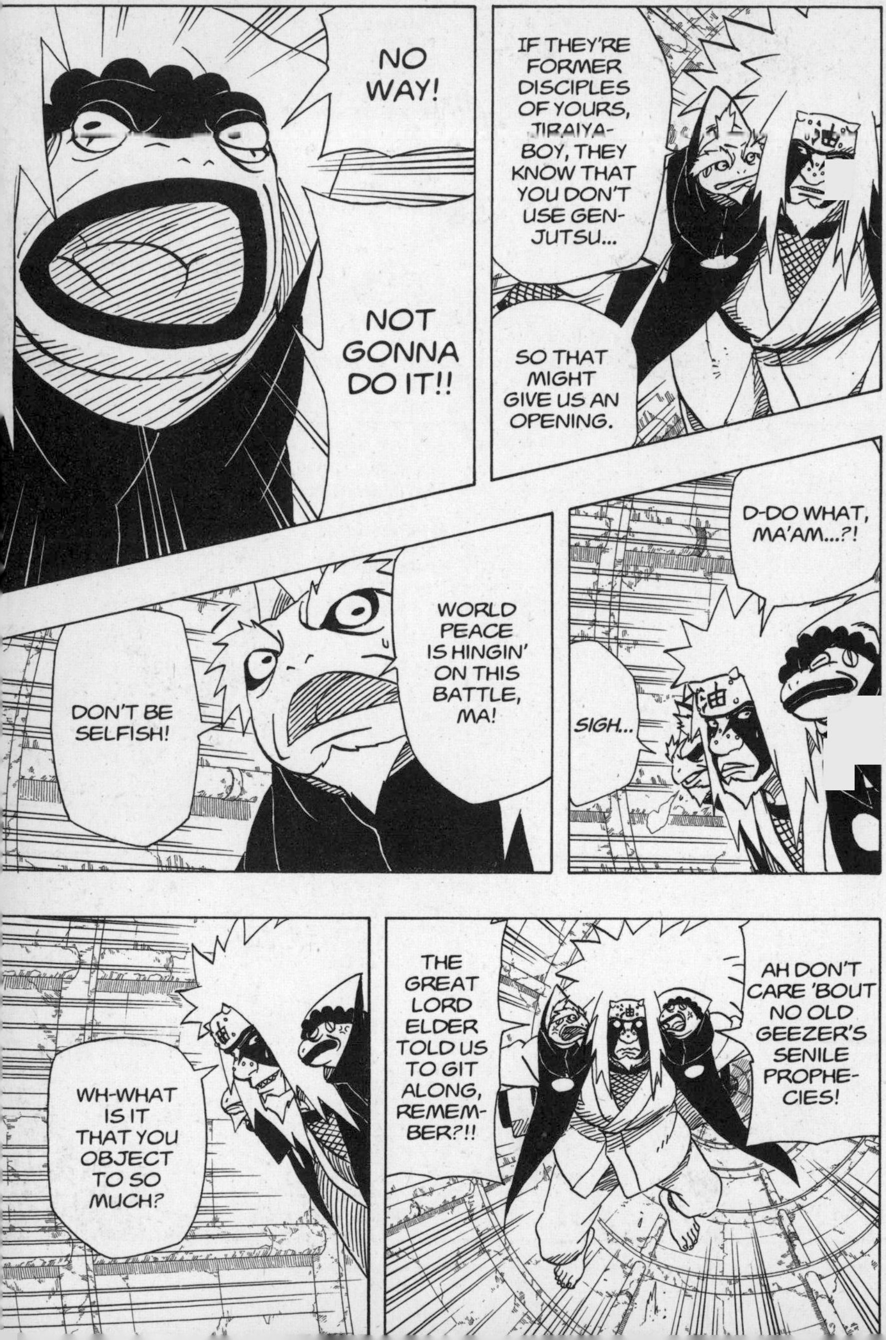

IF THEY'RE FORMER DISCIPLES OF YOURS, JIRAIYA-BOY, THEY KNOW THAT YOU DON'T USE GEN-JUTSU...
SO THAT MIGHT GIVE US AN OPENING.
NO WAY!
NOT GONNA DO IT!!
D-DO WHAT, MA'AM...?!
SIGH...
WORLD PEACE IS HINGIN' ON THIS BATTLE, MA!
DON'T BE SELFISH!
AH DON'T CARE 'BOUT NO OLD GEEZER'S SENILE PROPHE-CIES!
THE GREAT LORD ELDER TOLD US TO GIT ALONG, REMEM-BER?!!
WH-WHAT IS IT THAT YOU OBJECT TO SO MUCH?

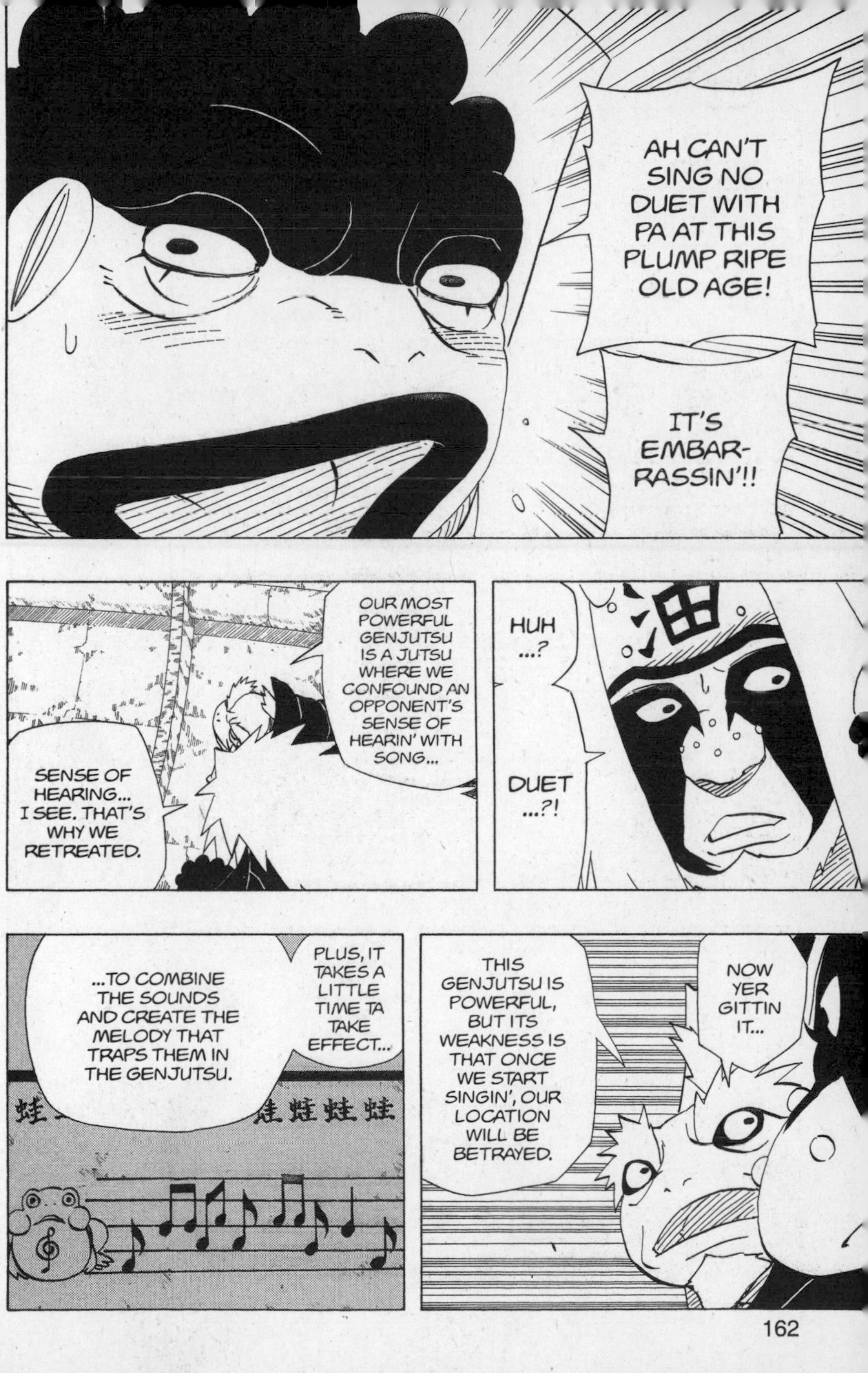
AH CAN'T SING NO DUET WITH PA AT THIS PLUMP RIPE OLD AGE!
IT'S EMBAR-RASSIN'!!
HUH ...?
DUET ...?!
OUR MOST POWERFUL GENJUTSU IS A JUTSU WHERE WE CONFOUND AN OPPONENT'S SENSE OF HEARIN' WITH SONG...
SENSE OF HEARING... I SEE. THAT'S WHY WE RETREATED.
NOW YER GITTIN IT...
THIS GENJUTSU IS POWERFUL, BUT ITS WEAKNESS IS THAT ONCE WE START SINGIN', OUR LOCATION WILL BE BETRAYED.
PLUS, IT TAKES A LITTLE TIME TA TAKE EFFECT...
...TO COMBINE THE SOUNDS AND CREATE THE MELODY THAT TRAPS THEM IN THE GENJUTSU.
蛙 蛙蛙蛙蛙

READ THIS WAY

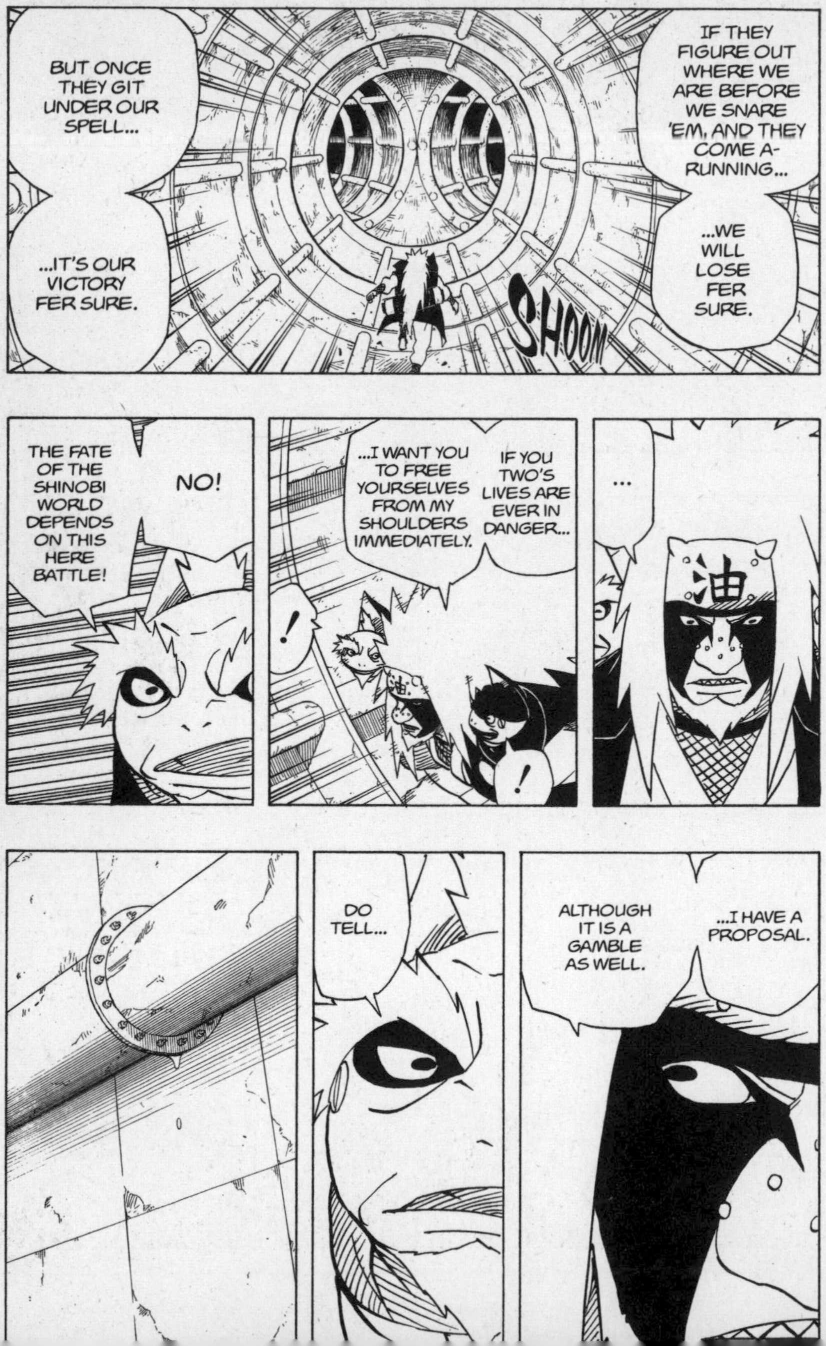
IF THEY FIGURE OUT WHERE WE ARE BEFORE WE SNARE 'EM, AND THEY COME A-RUNNING...
...WE WILL LOSE FER SURE.
BUT ONCE THEY GIT UNDER OUR SPELL...
...IT'S OUR VICTORY FER SURE.
SHOOM
...
IF YOU TWO'S LIVES ARE EVER IN DANGER...
...I WANT YOU TO FREE YOURSELVES FROM MY SHOULDERS IMMEDIATELY.
!
!
NO!
THE FATE OF THE SHINOBI WORLD DEPENDS ON THIS HERE BATTLE!
...I HAVE A PROPOSAL.
ALTHOUGH IT IS A GAMBLE AS WELL.
DO TELL...

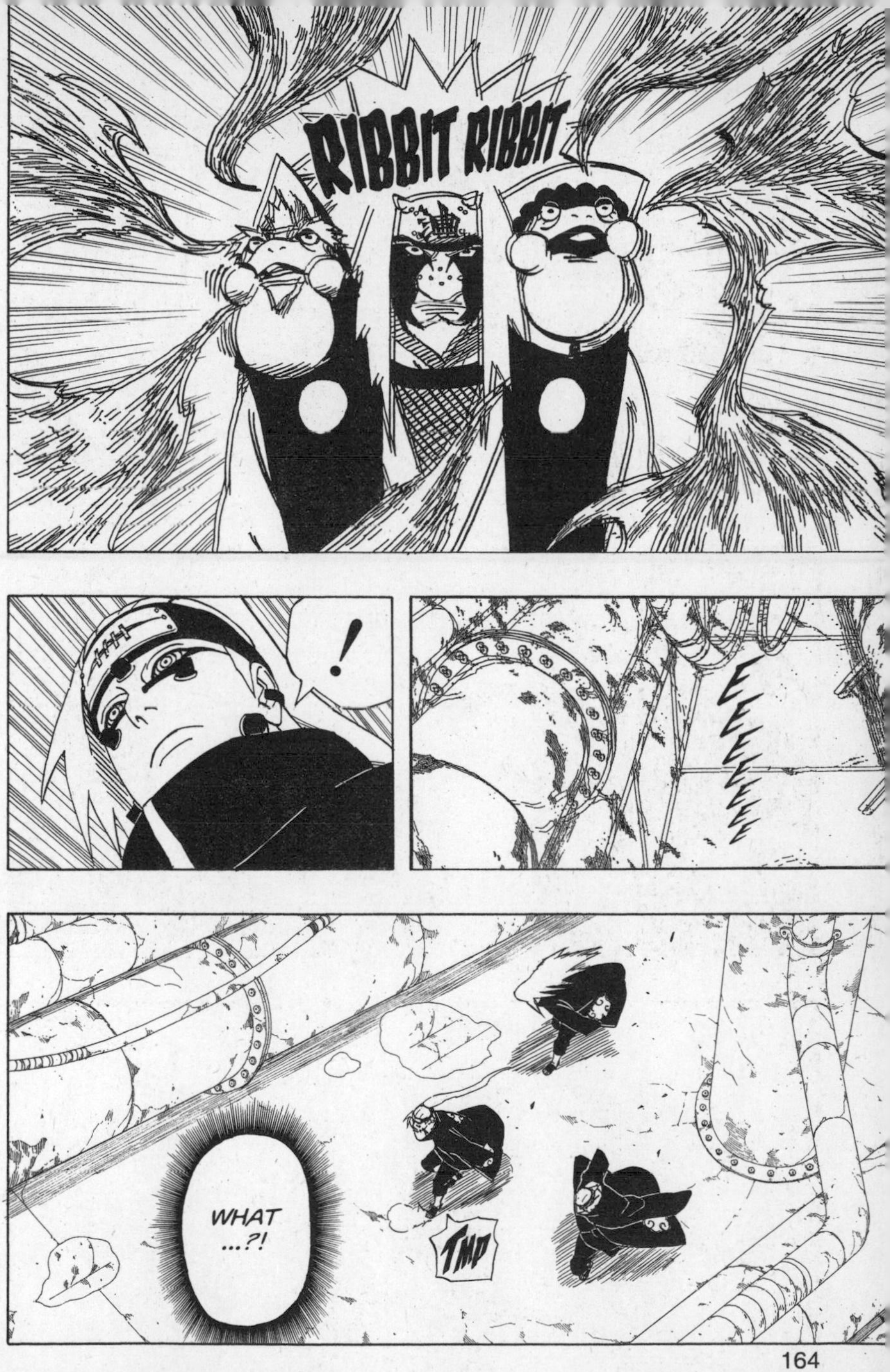
RIBBIT RIBBIT
!
TMP
WHAT …?!

READ THIS WAY

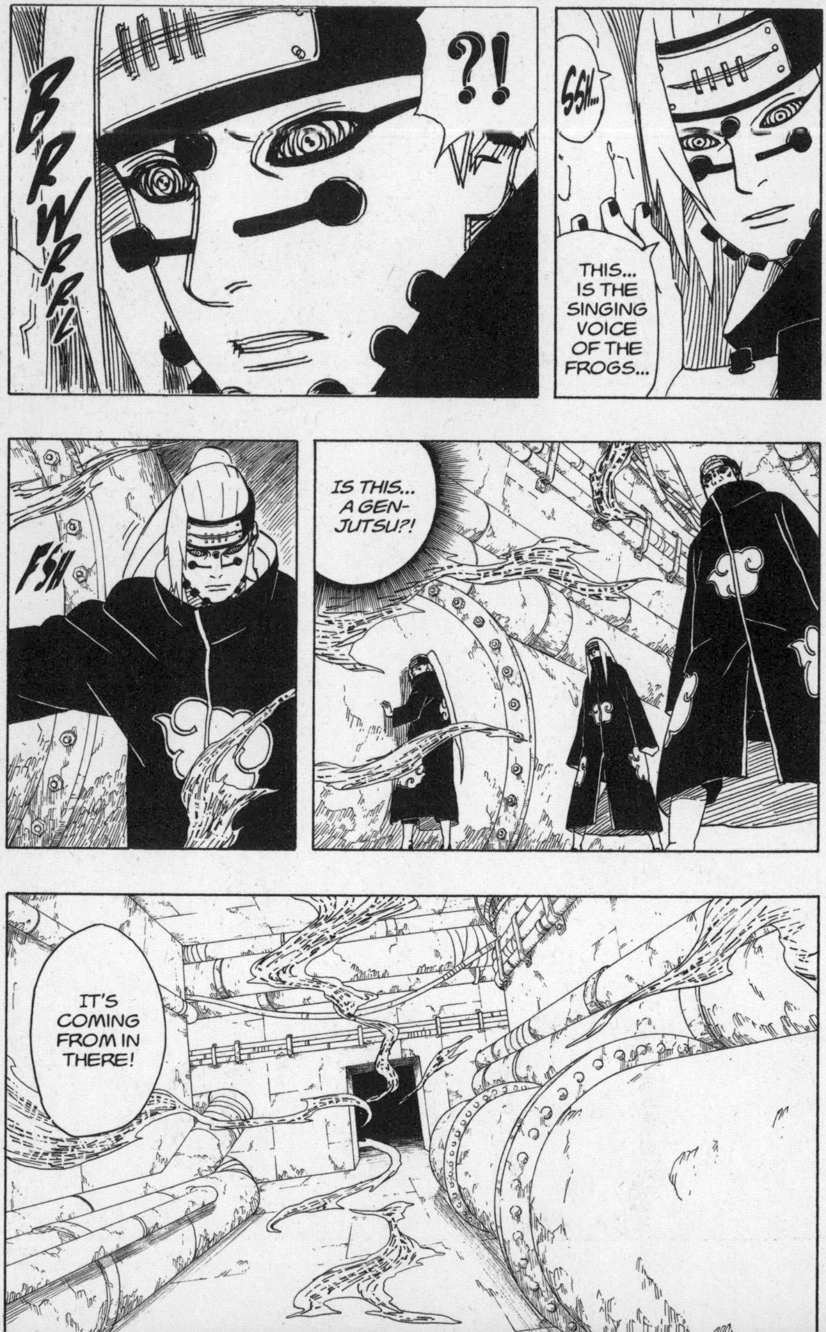
SSH...
THIS... IS THE SINGING VOICE OF THE FROGS...
?!
BRWRRL
IS THIS... A GEN-JUTSU?!
FSH
IT'S COMING FROM IN THERE!

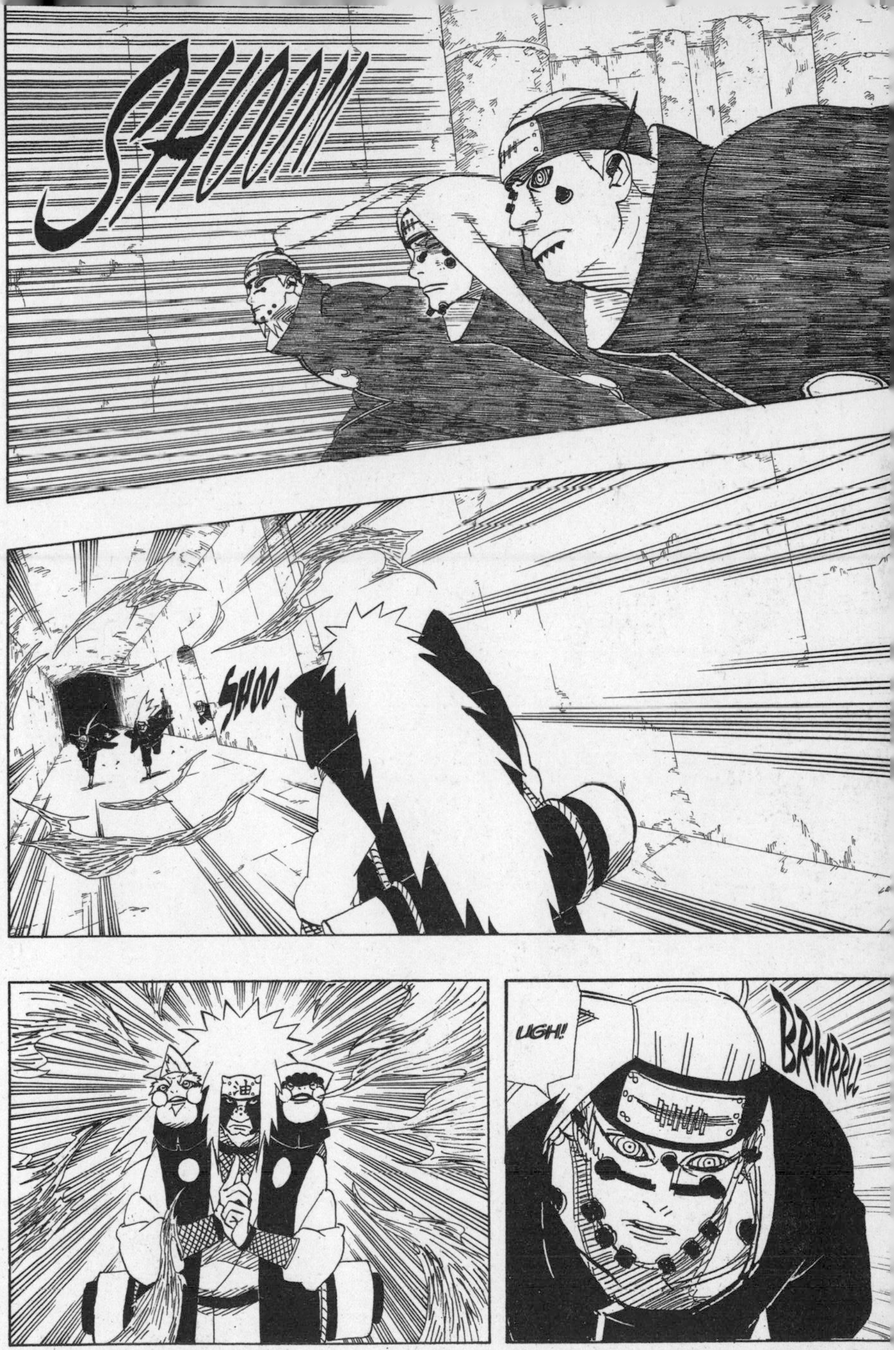
SHUOOM
SHOO
UGH!
BRWRRL

READ THIS WAY

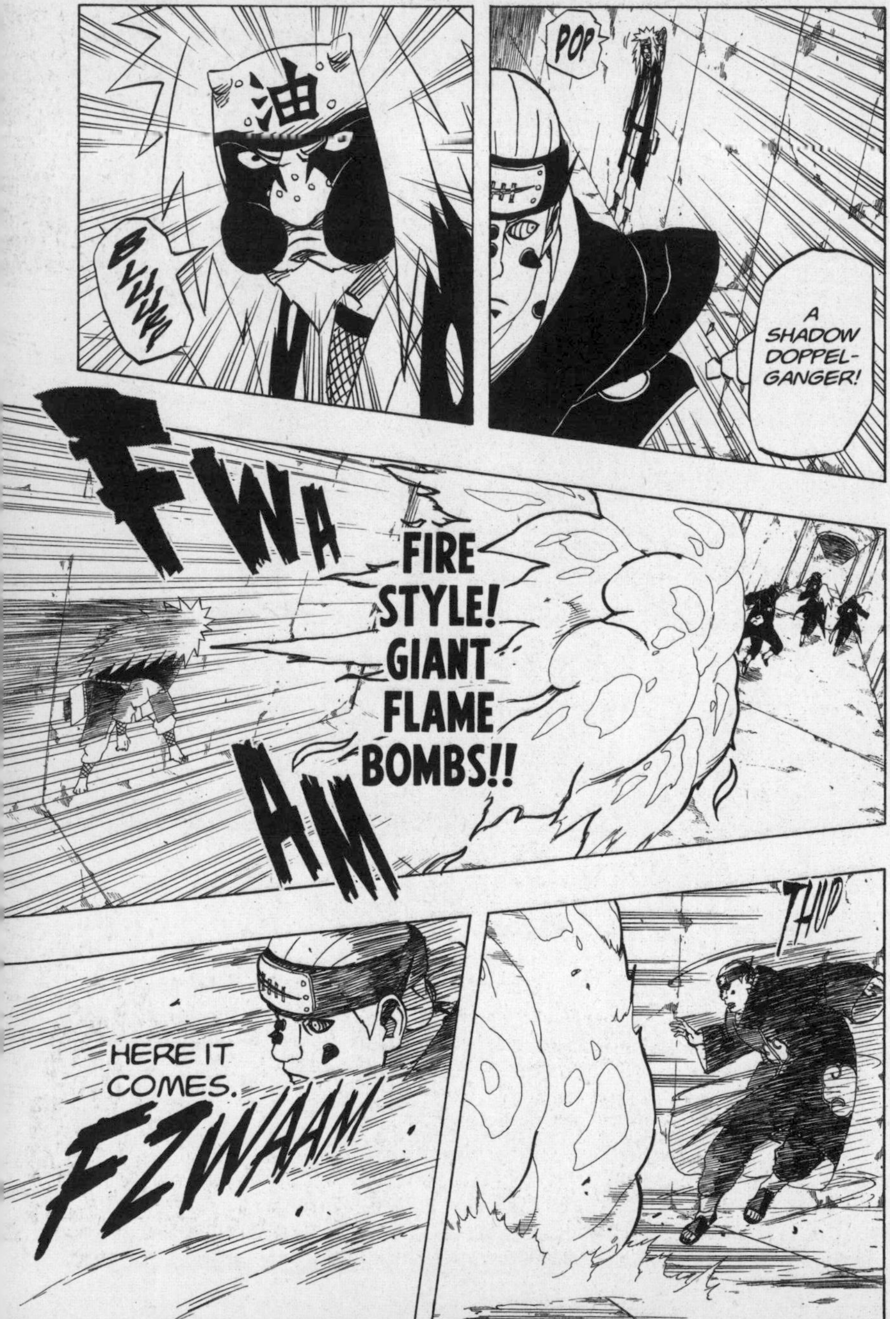
POP
A SHADOW DOPPEL-GANGER!
BLUUP
FWAAM
FIRE STYLE! GIANT FLAME BOMBS!!
THUP
HERE IT COMES.
FZWAAM

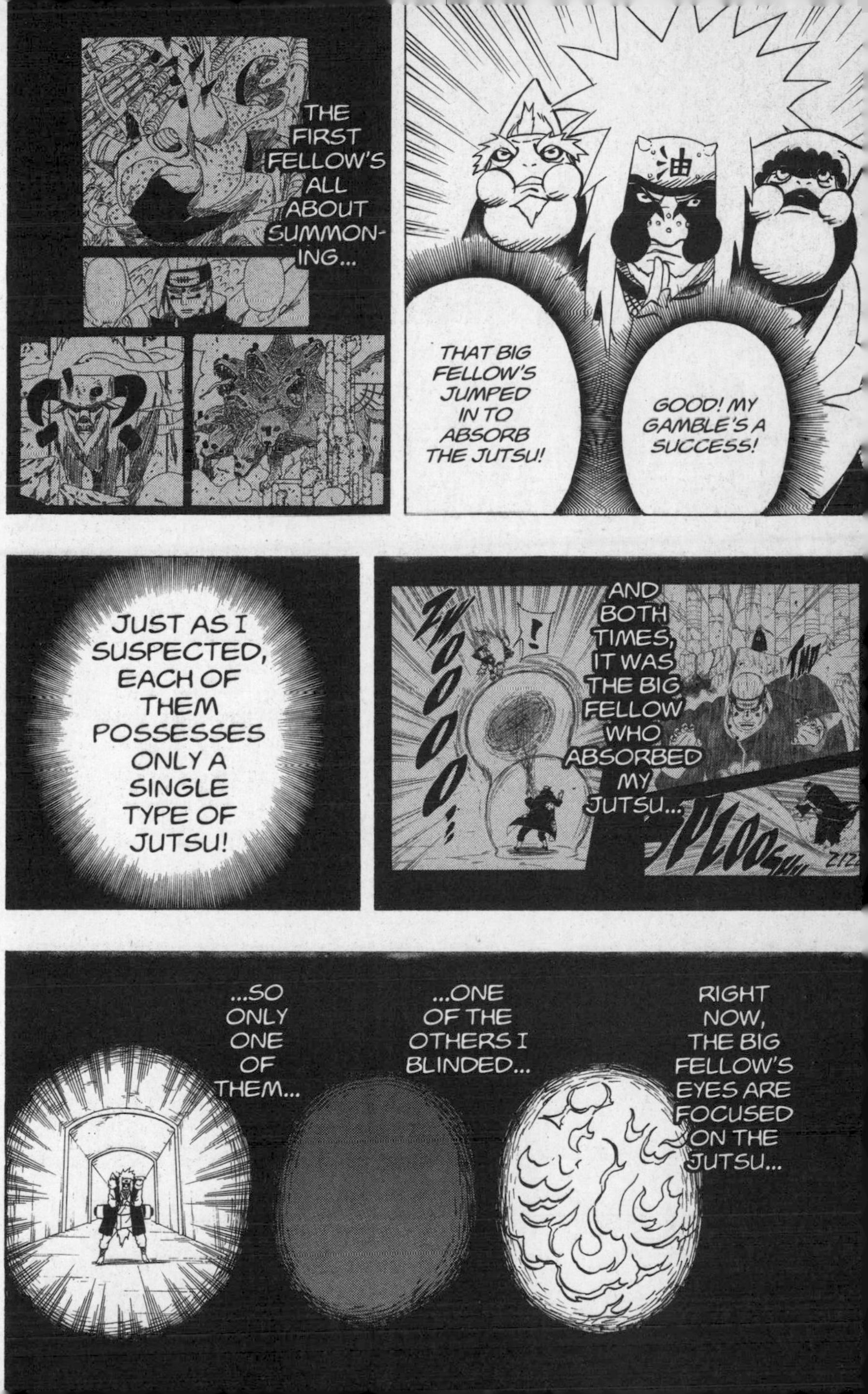
GOOD! MY GAMBLE'S A SUCCESS!
THAT BIG FELLOW'S JUMPED IN TO ABSORB THE JUTSU!
THE FIRST FELLOW'S ALL ABOUT SUMMONING...
AND BOTH TIMES, IT WAS THE BIG FELLOW WHO ABSORBED MY JUTSU...
!
JUST AS I SUSPECTED, EACH OF THEM POSSESSES ONLY A SINGLE TYPE OF JUTSU!
RIGHT NOW, THE BIG FELLOW'S EYES ARE FOCUSED ON THE JUTSU...
...ONE OF THE OTHERS I BLINDED...
...SO ONLY ONE OF THEM...

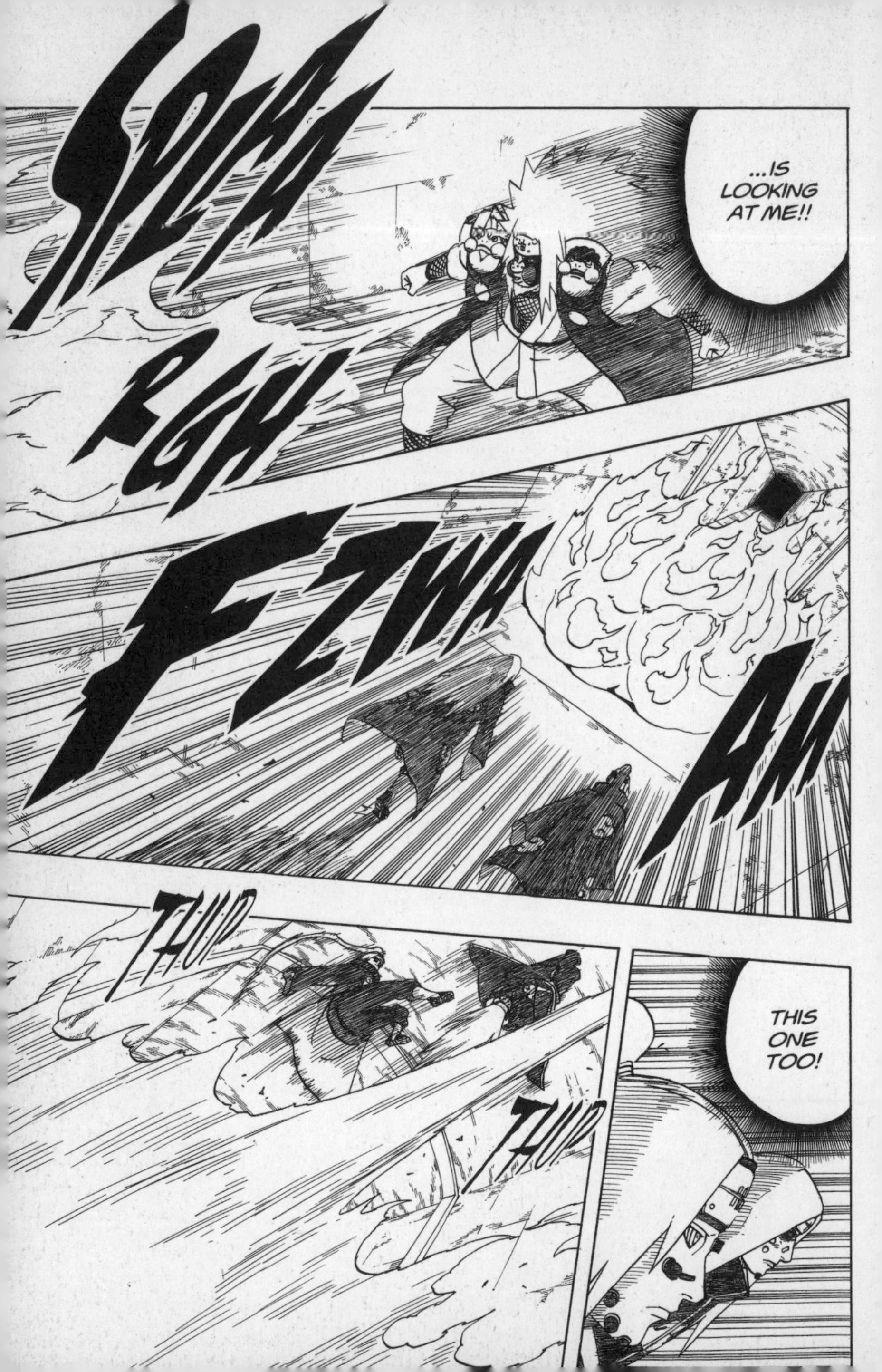
...IS LOOKING AT ME!!
SPLA
RGH
FZWA
AM
THIS ONE TOO!
THUD
THUD

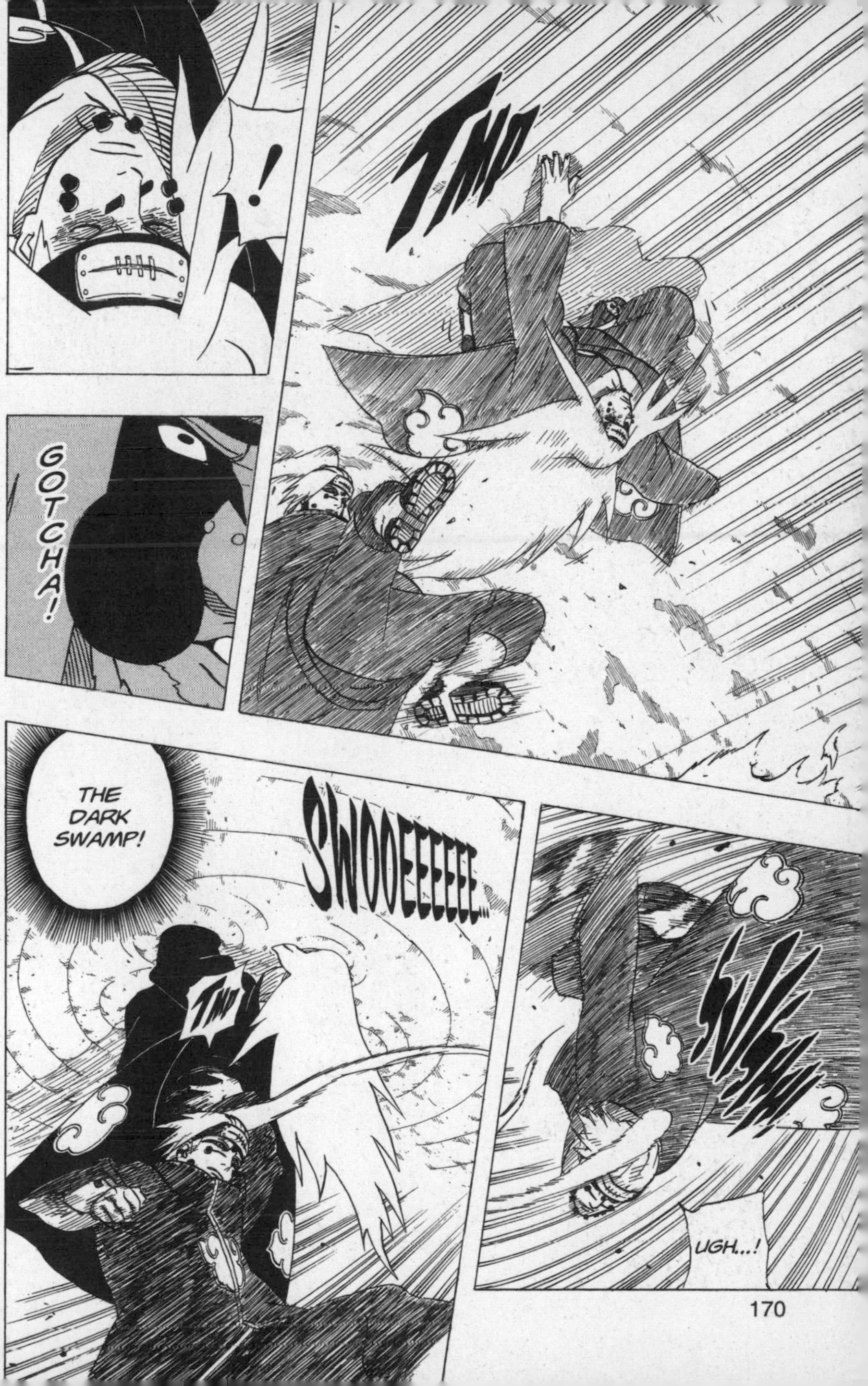
TMP
!
GOTCHA!
UGH...!
THE DARK SWAMP!
SWOOEEEEEE...
TMP

READ THIS WAY

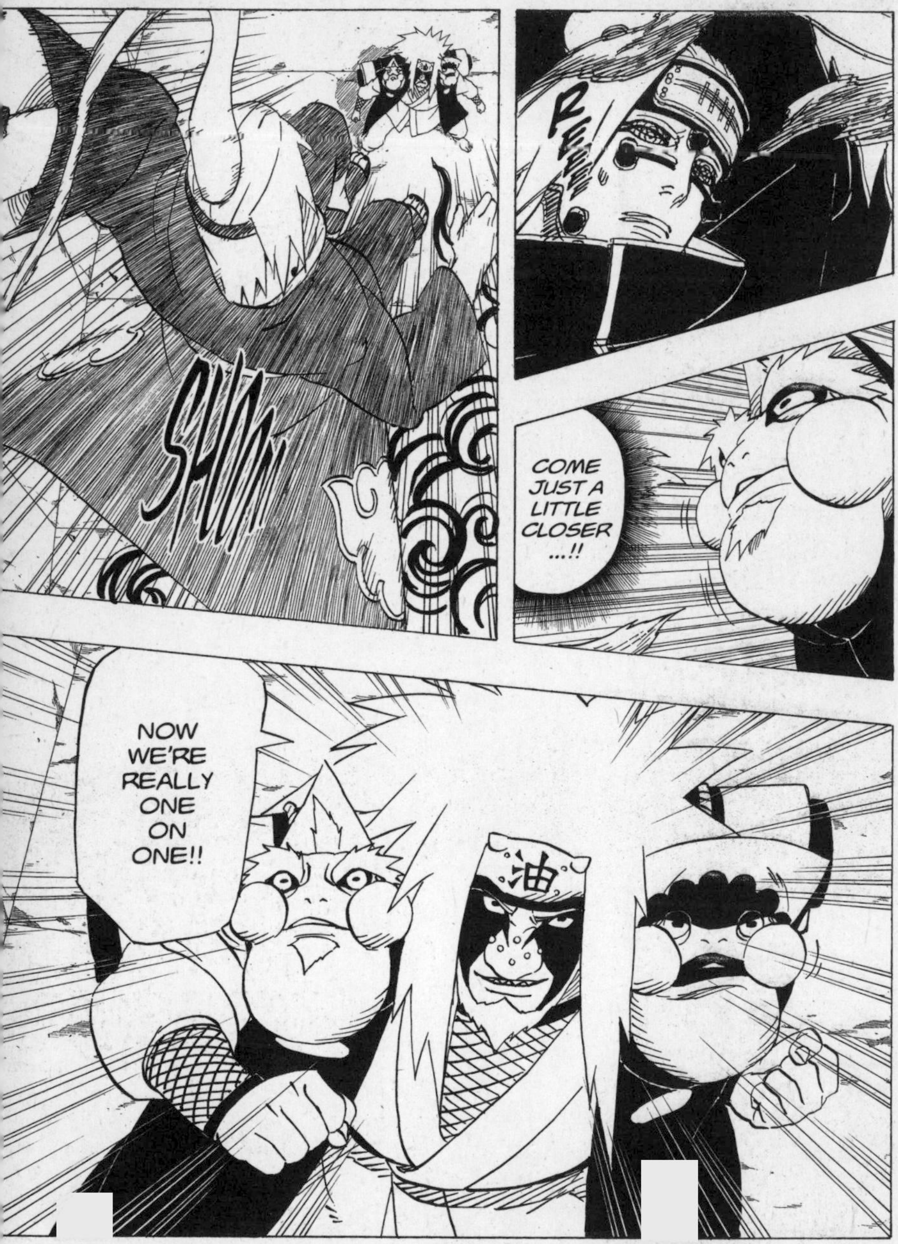
REEEE
COME JUST A LITTLE CLOSER ...!!
SHUNN
NOW WE'RE REALLY ONE ON ONE!!

NARUTO

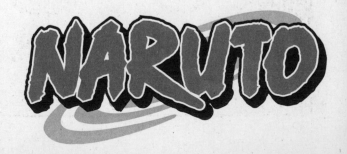

Number 379: Jiraiya's Decision!!

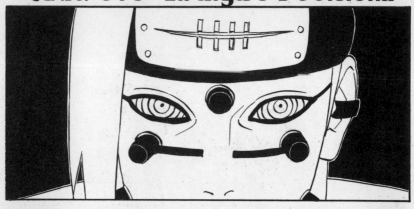

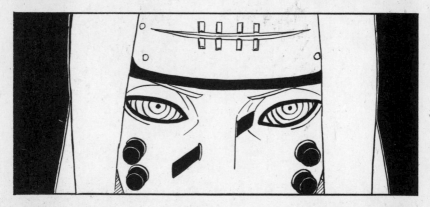

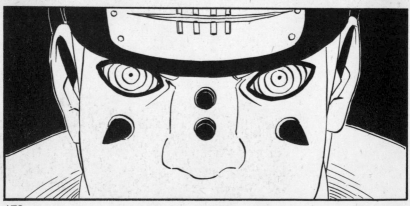

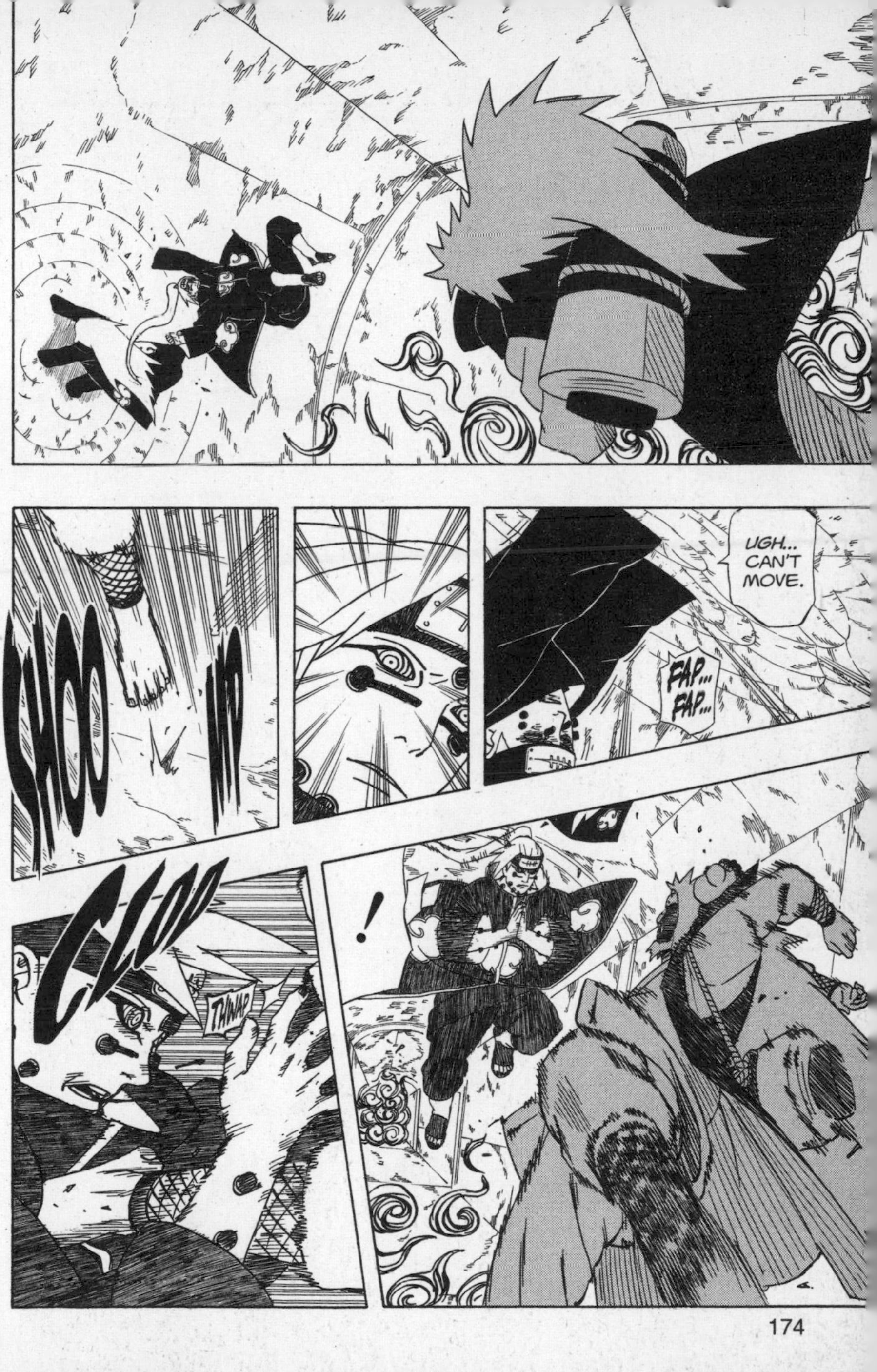
UGH... CAN'T MOVE.
FAP... FAP...
SHOO
WP
!
CLUD
THWAP

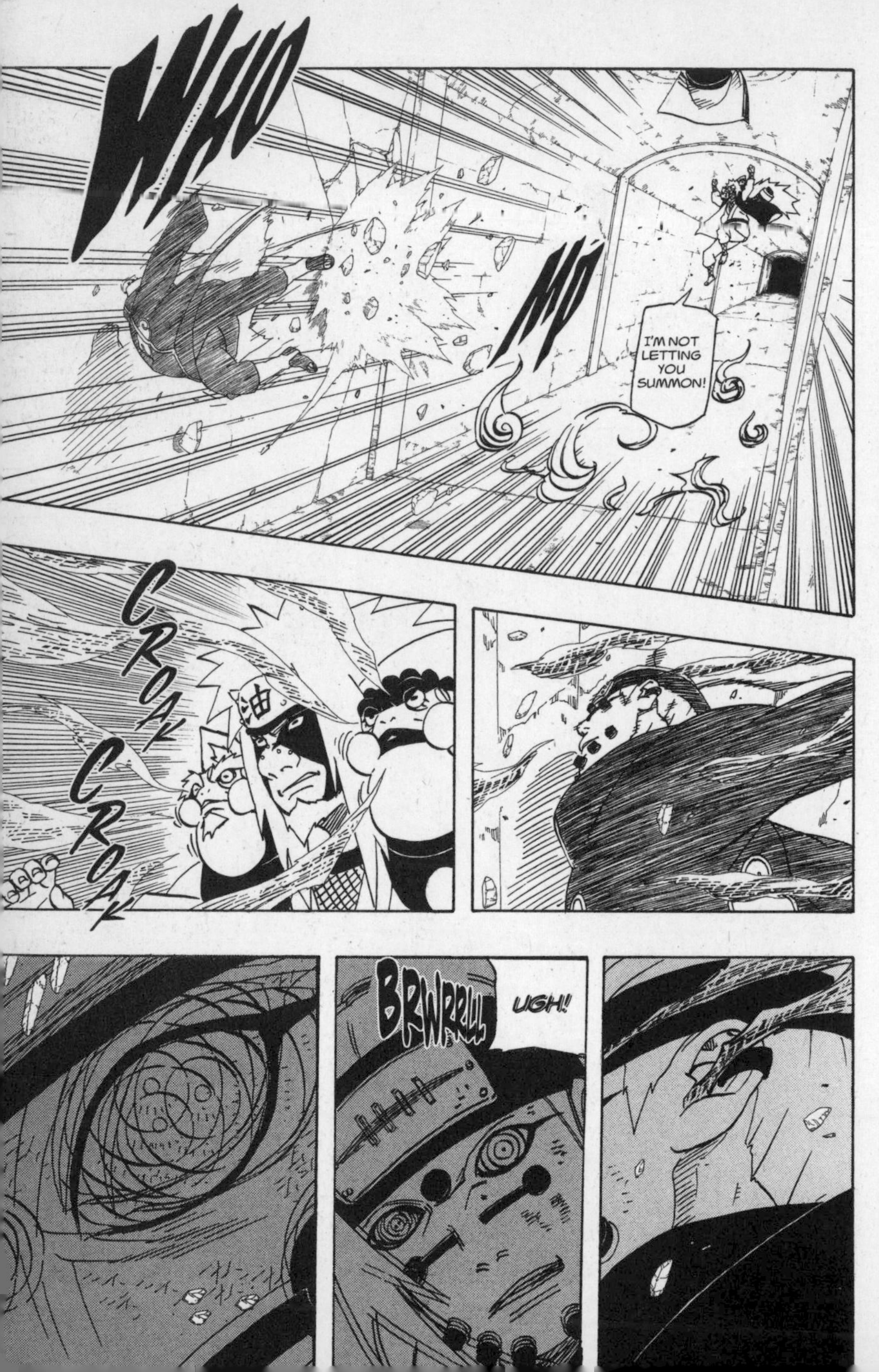
I'M NOT LETTING YOU SUMMON!
CROAK
CROAK
UGH!
BRWRRLL

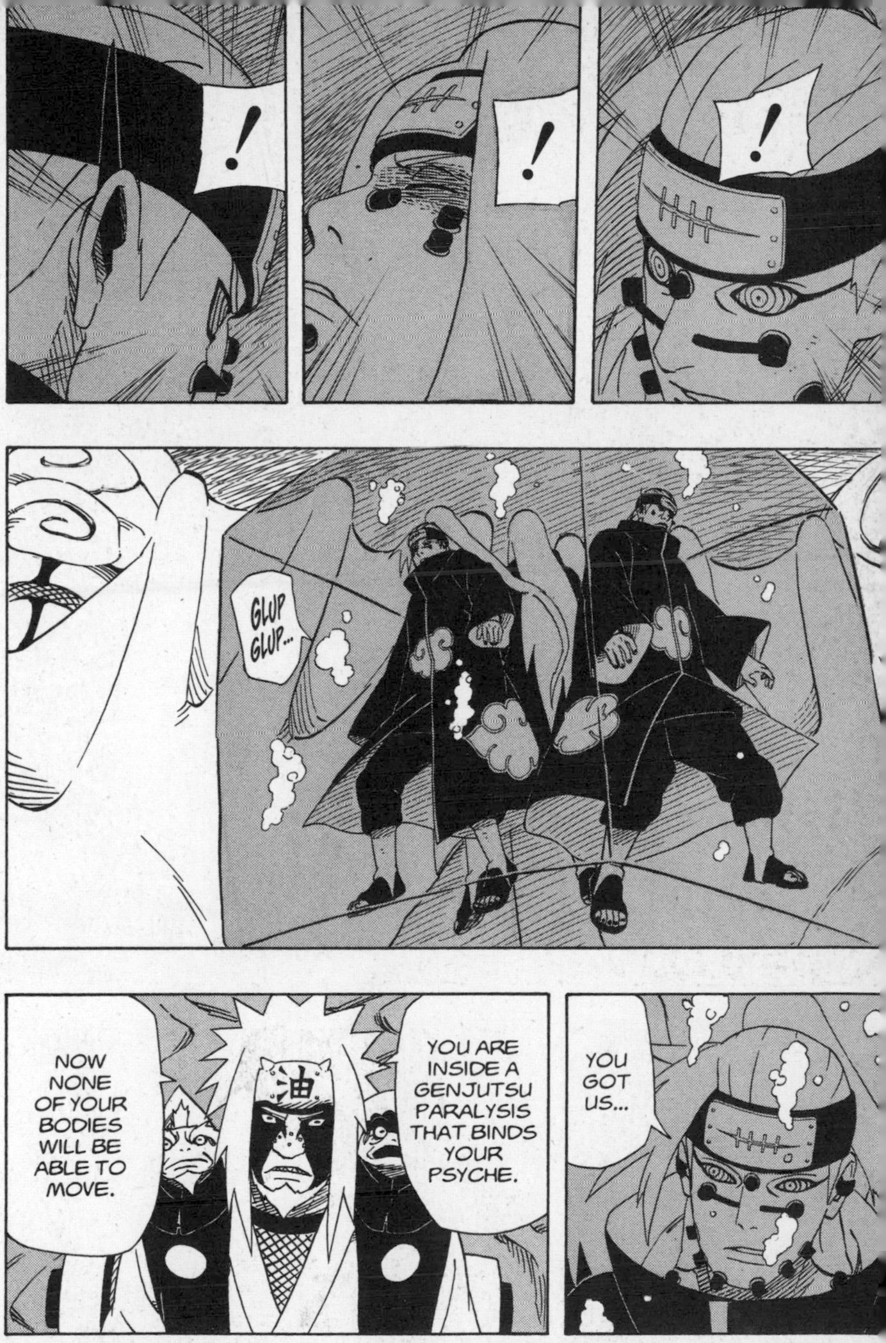
!
!
!
GLUP GLUP...
YOU GOT US...
YOU ARE INSIDE A GENJUTSU PARALYSIS THAT BINDS YOUR PSYCHE.
NOW NONE OF YOUR BODIES WILL BE ABLE TO MOVE.

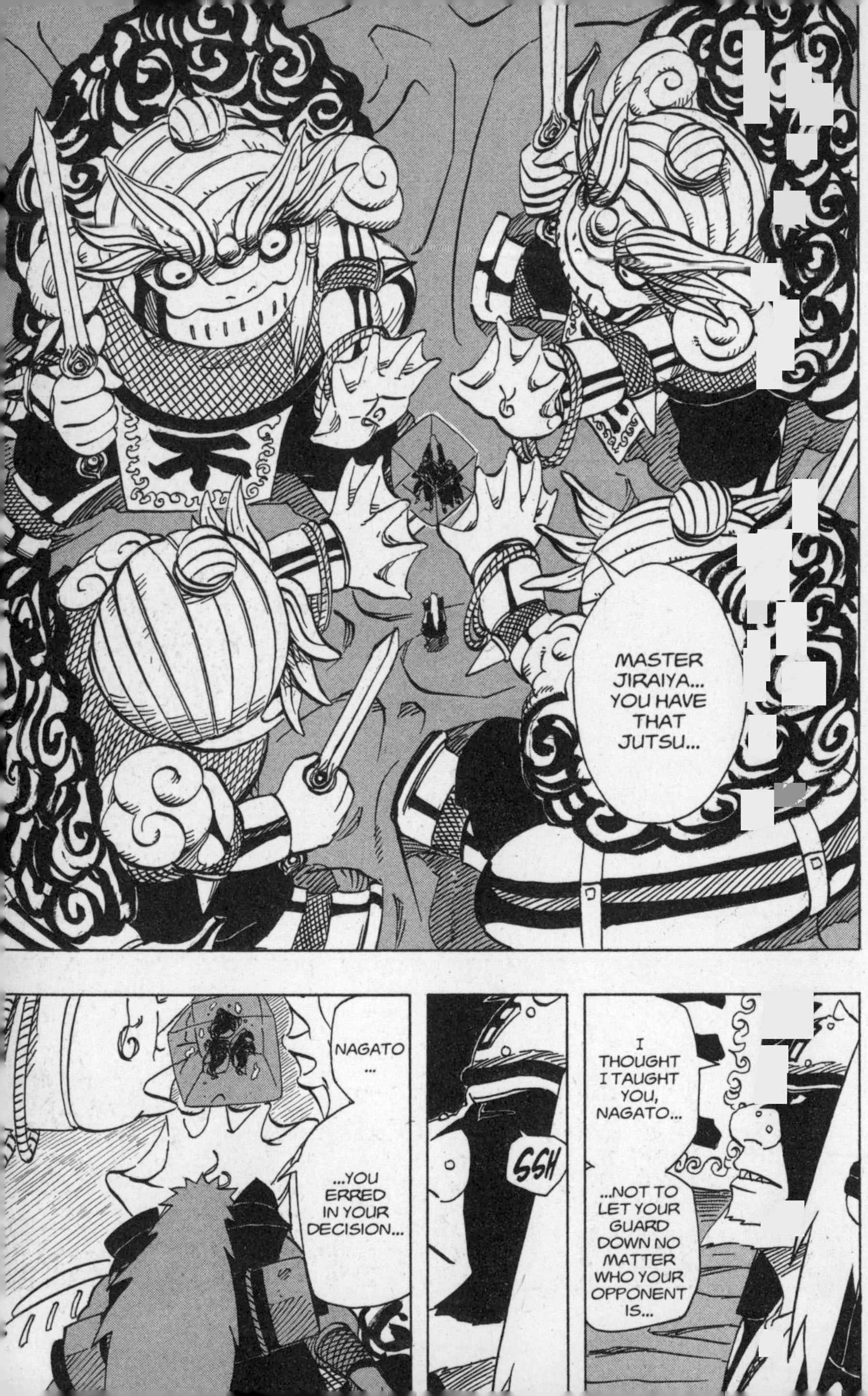
MASTER JIRAIYA... YOU HAVE THAT JUTSU...
I THOUGHT I TAUGHT YOU, NAGATO...
...NOT TO LET YOUR GUARD DOWN NO MATTER WHO YOUR OPPONENT IS...
SSH
NAGATO...
...YOU ERRED IN YOUR DECISION...

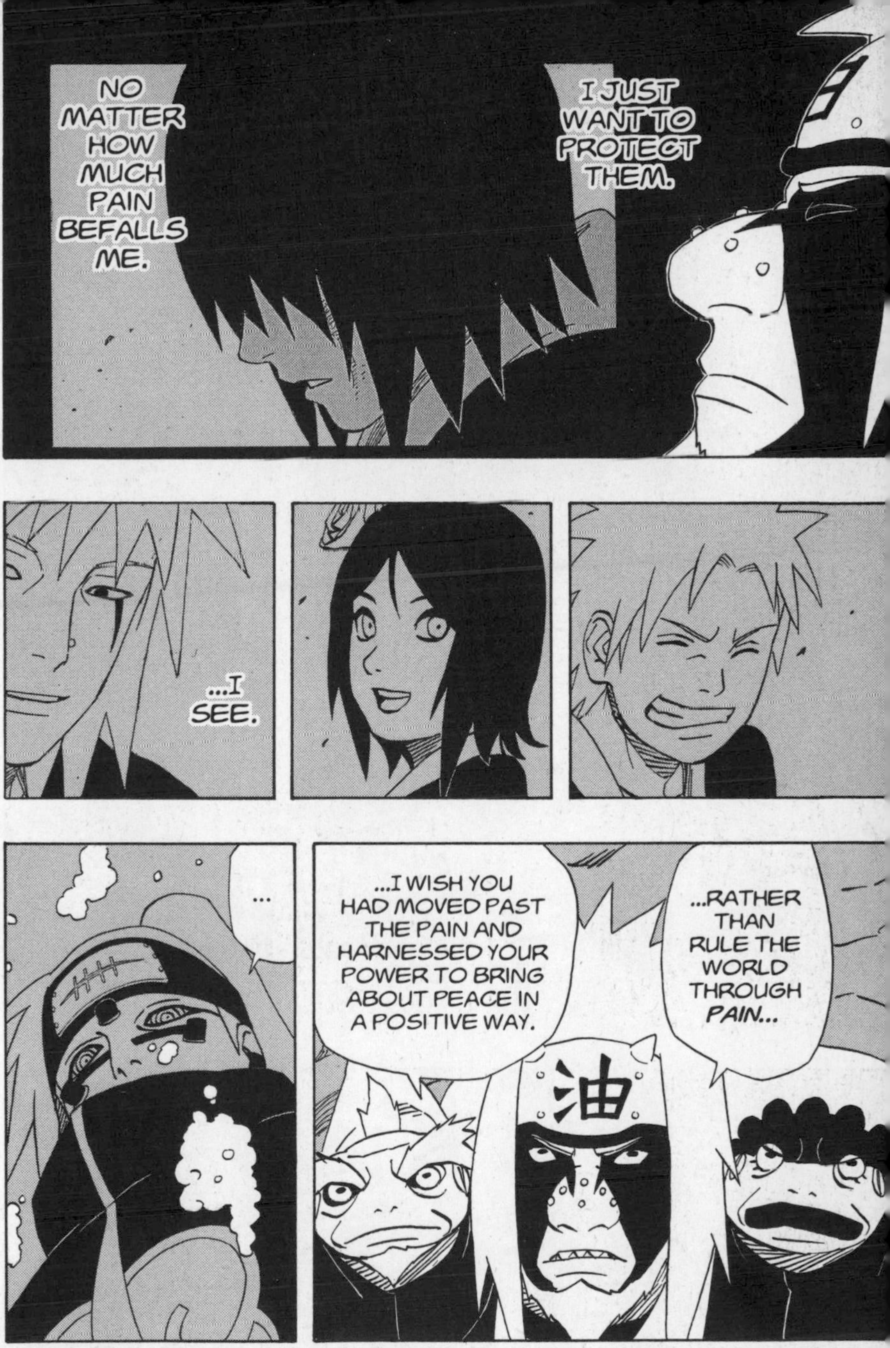
I JUST WANT TO PROTECT THEM.
NO MATTER HOW MUCH PAIN BEFALLS ME.
...I SEE.
...RATHER THAN RULE THE WORLD THROUGH *PAIN*...
...I WISH YOU HAD MOVED PAST THE PAIN AND HARNESSED YOUR POWER TO BRING ABOUT PEACE IN A POSITIVE WAY.
油
...

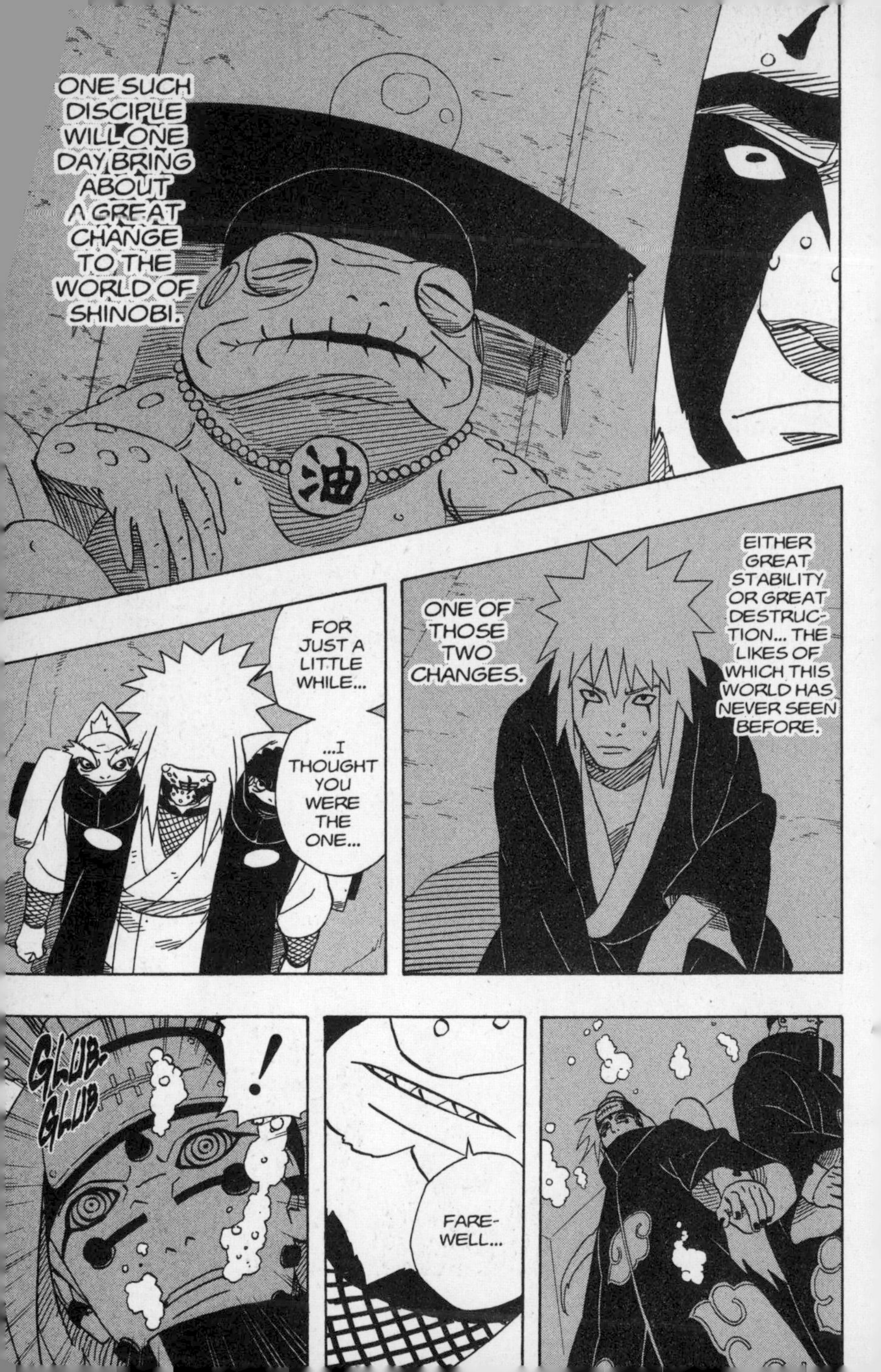

ONE SUCH DISCIPLE WILL ONE DAY BRING ABOUT A GREAT CHANGE TO THE WORLD OF SHINOBI.
EITHER GREAT STABILITY OR GREAT DESTRUC-TION... THE LIKES OF WHICH THIS WORLD HAS NEVER SEEN BEFORE.
ONE OF THOSE TWO CHANGES.
FOR JUST A LITTLE WHILE...
...I THOUGHT YOU WERE THE ONE...
FARE-WELL...
!
GLUB GLUB

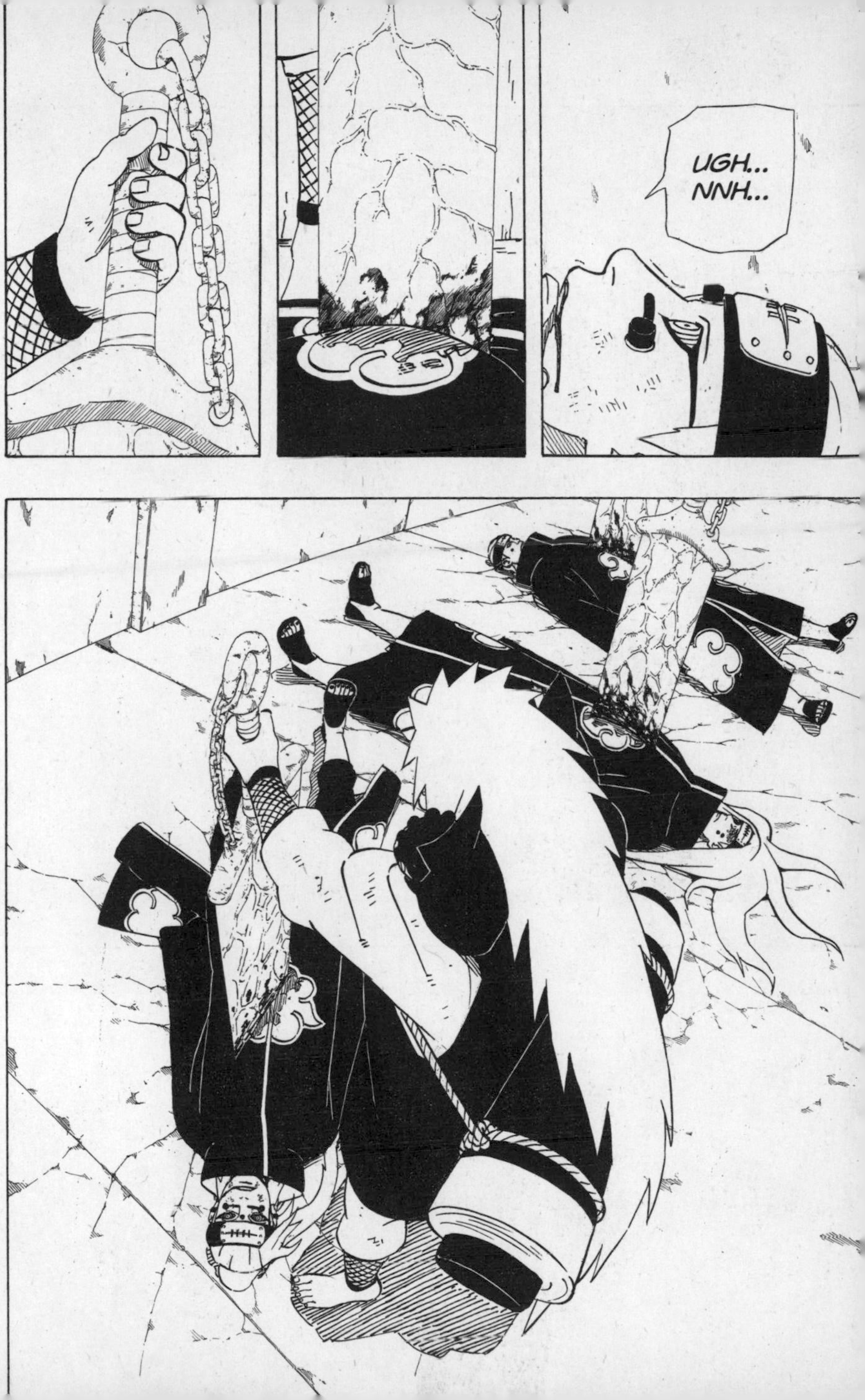
UGH...
NNH...

READ THIS WAY

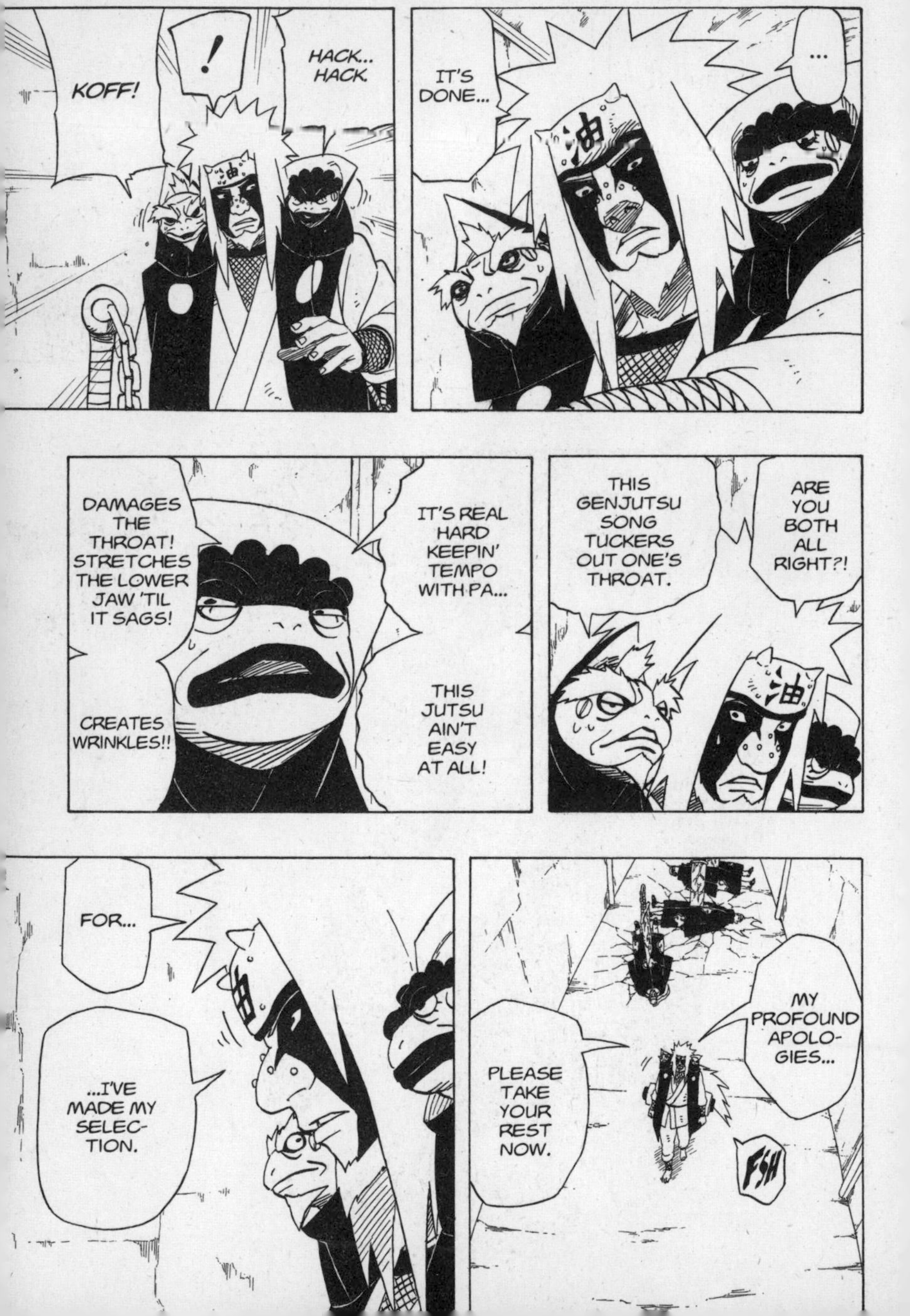
...
IT'S DONE...
HACK... HACK.
!
KOFF!
ARE YOU BOTH ALL RIGHT?!
THIS GENJUTSU SONG TUCKERS OUT ONE'S THROAT.
IT'S REAL HARD KEEPIN' TEMPO WITH PA...
THIS JUTSU AIN'T EASY AT ALL!
DAMAGES THE THROAT! STRETCHES THE LOWER JAW 'TIL IT SAGS!
CREATES WRINKLES!!
MY PROFOUND APOLOGIES...
PLEASE TAKE YOUR REST NOW.
FSH
FOR...
...I'VE MADE MY SELECTION.

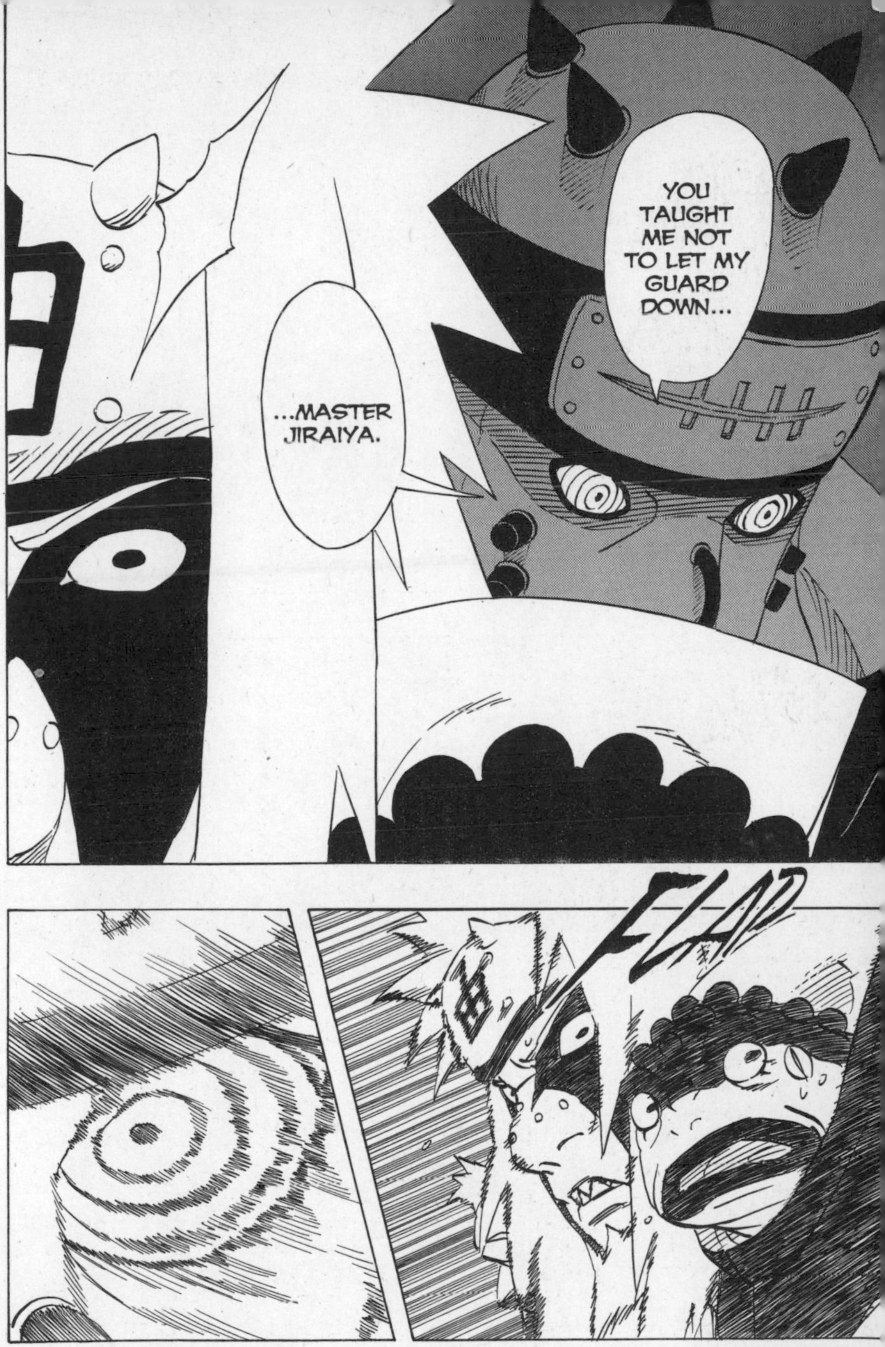
YOU TAUGHT ME NOT TO LET MY GUARD DOWN...
...MASTER JIRAIYA.
FLAP

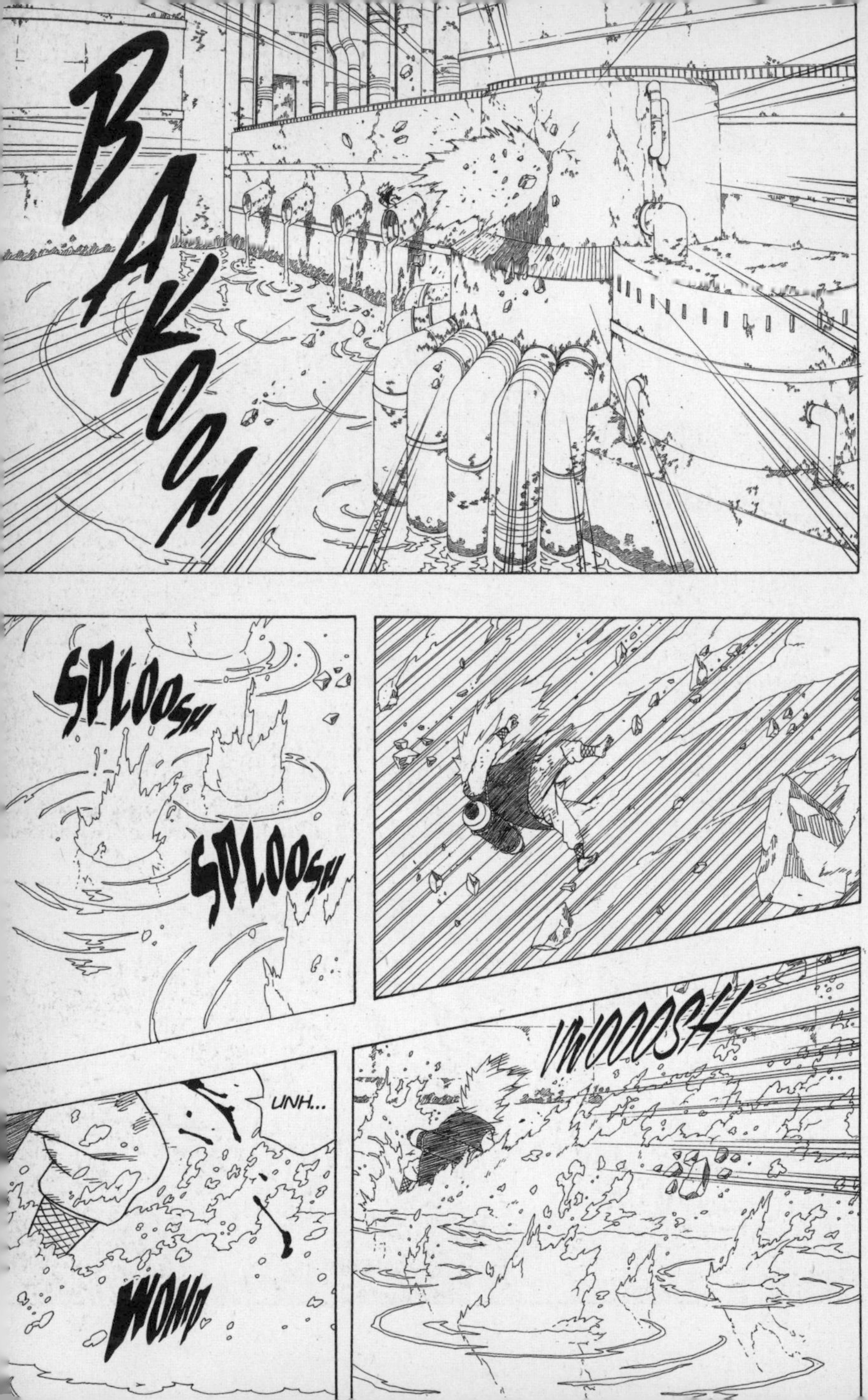
BAKOOM
SPLOOSH
SPLOOSH
WOOOSH
UNH...
WOMP

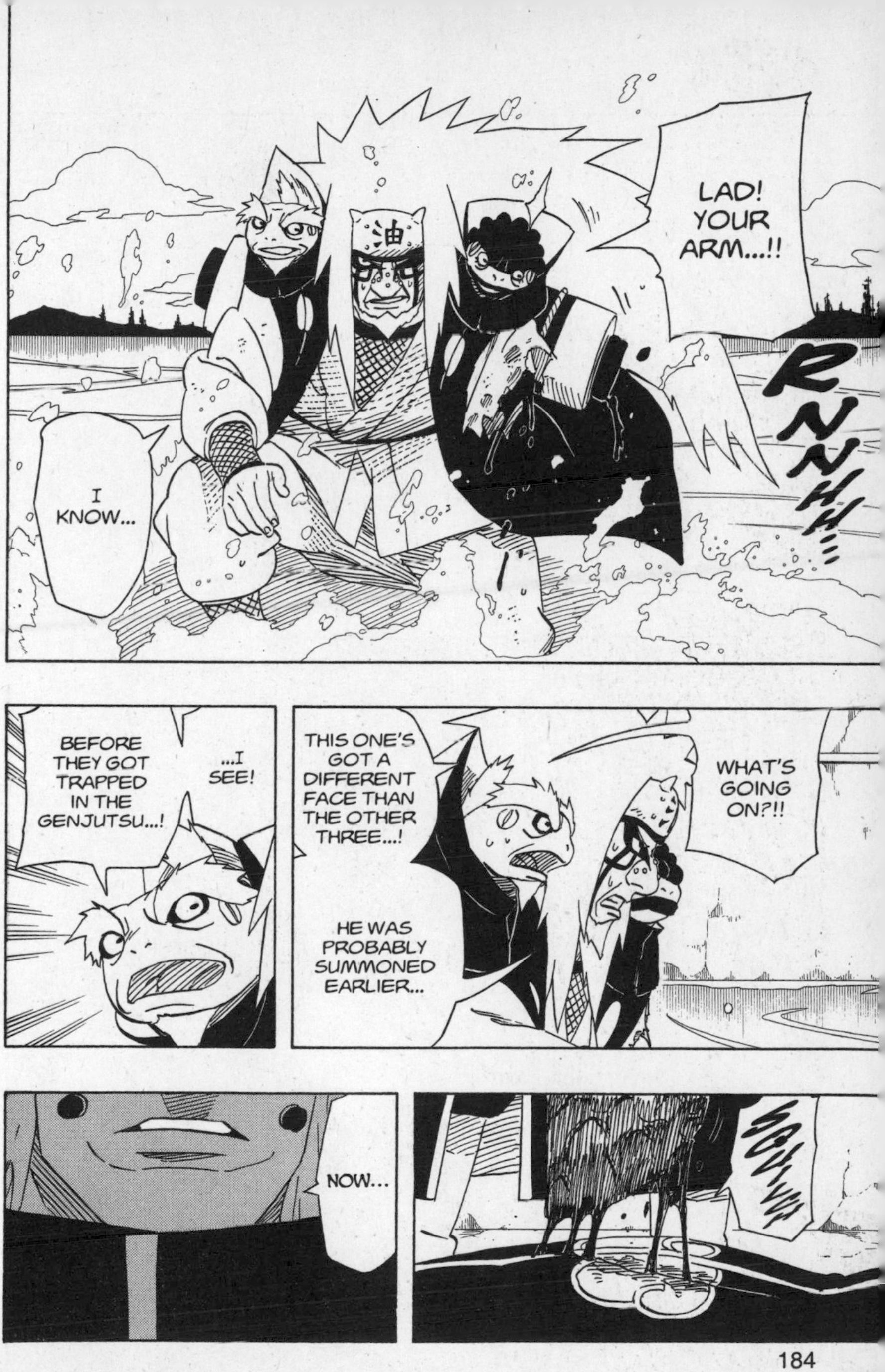
LAD! YOUR ARM...!!
RNNHH!!
I KNOW...
WHAT'S GOING ON?!!
THIS ONE'S GOT A DIFFERENT FACE THAN THE OTHER THREE...!
HE WAS PROBABLY SUMMONED EARLIER...
...I SEE!
BEFORE THEY GOT TRAPPED IN THE GENJUTSU...!
NOW...

READ THIS WAY

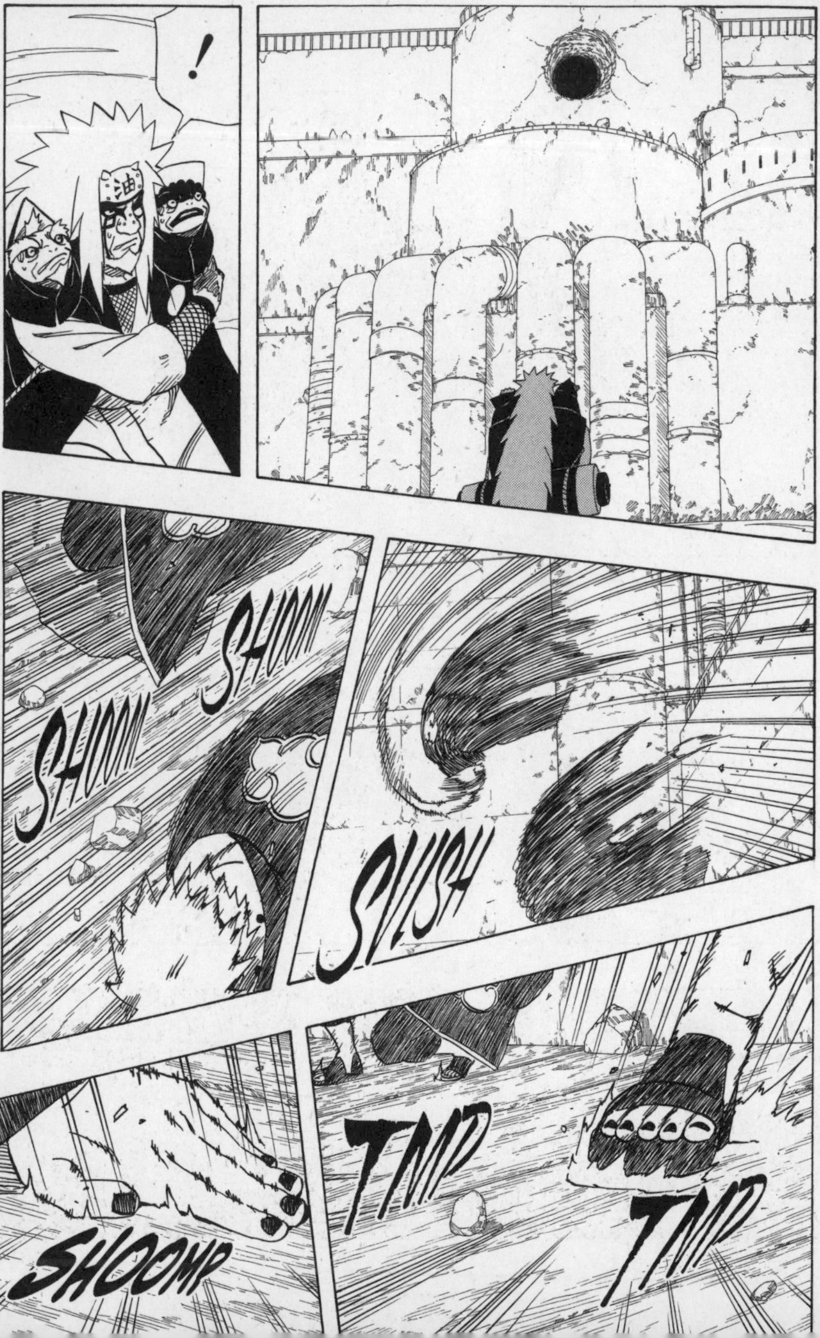
!
SWISH
SHOOM
SHOOM
TMP
TMP
SHOOMP

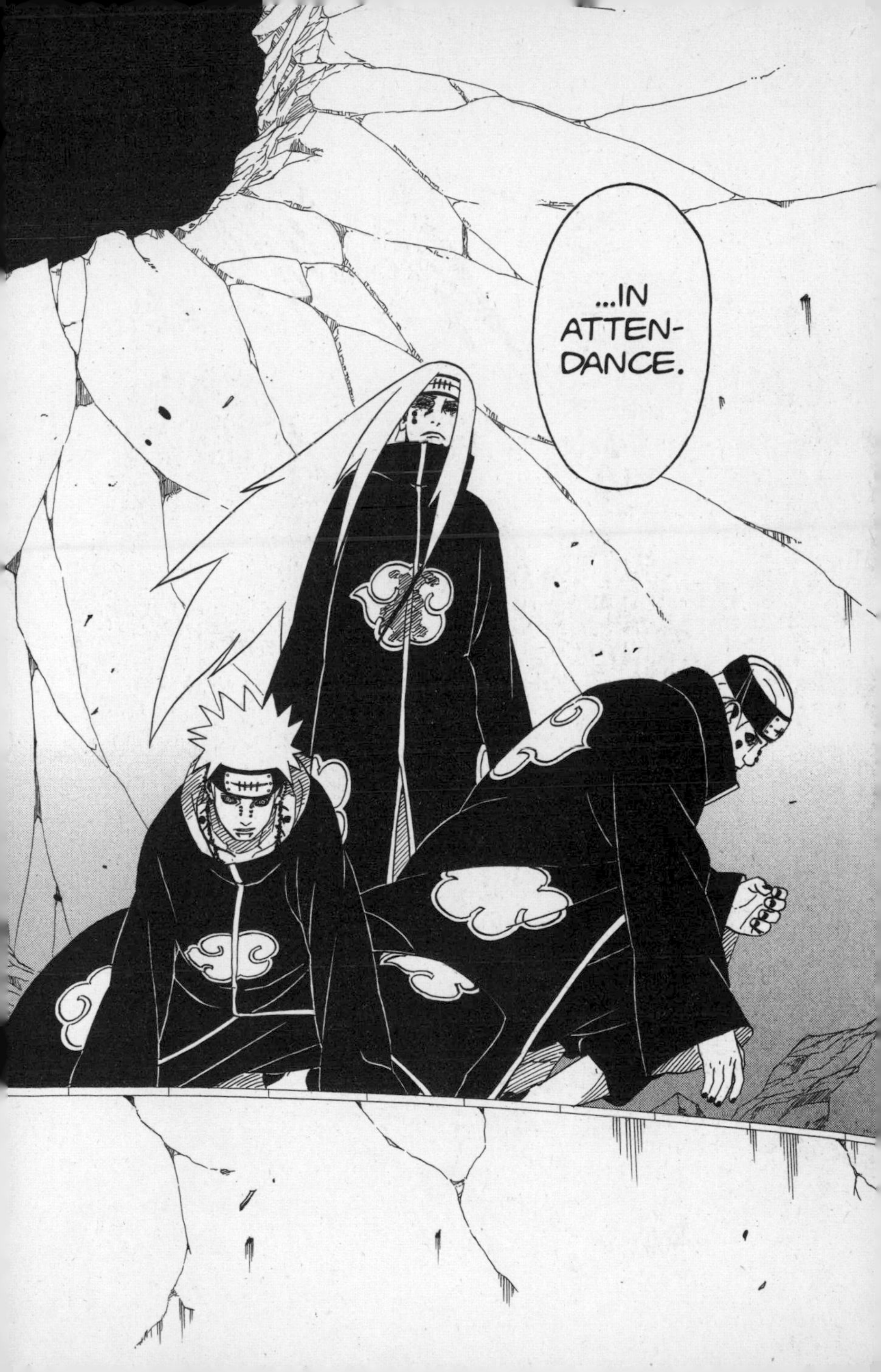
...IN ATTEN-DANCE.

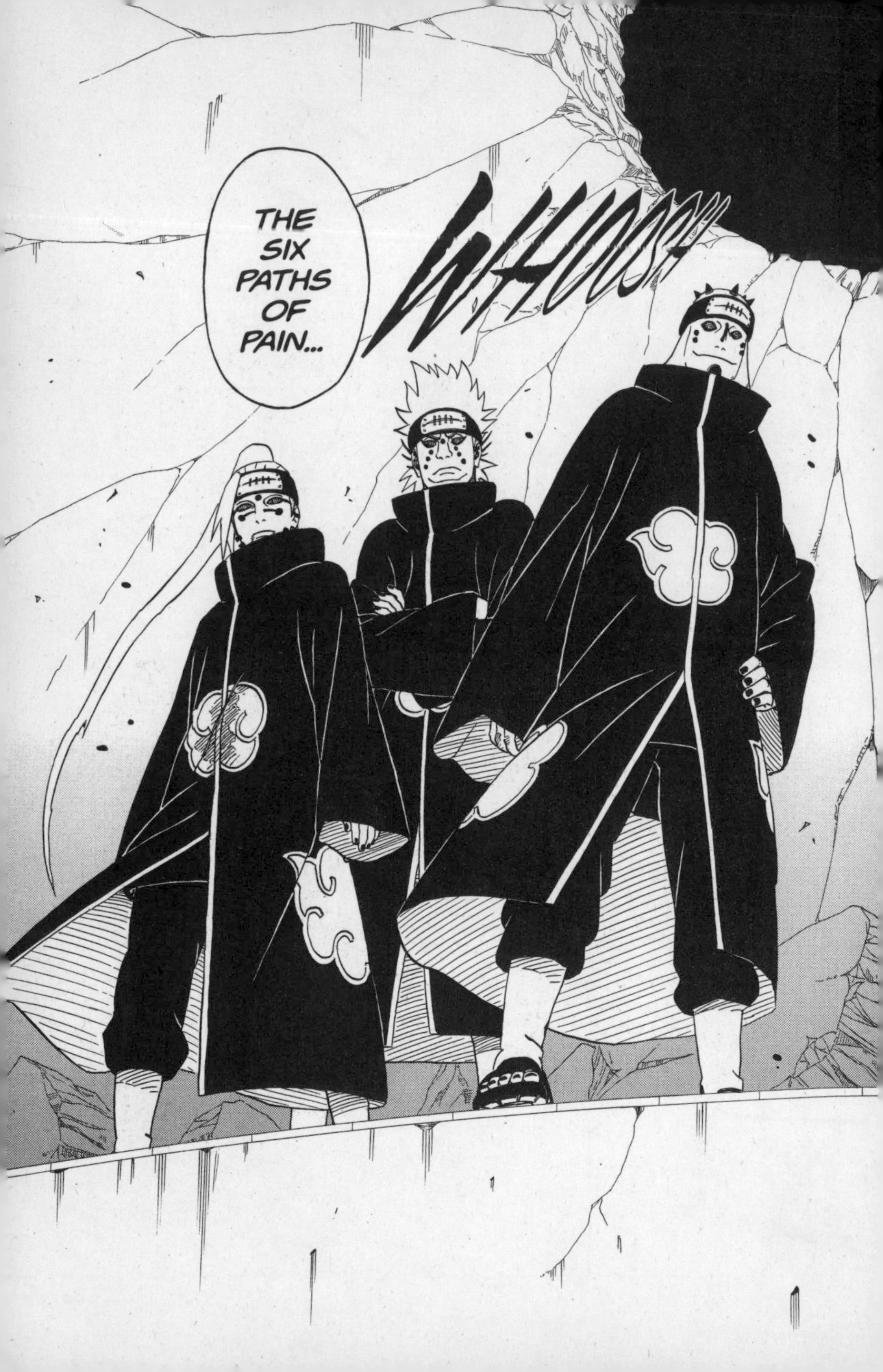
THE SIX PATHS OF PAIN...
WHOOSH

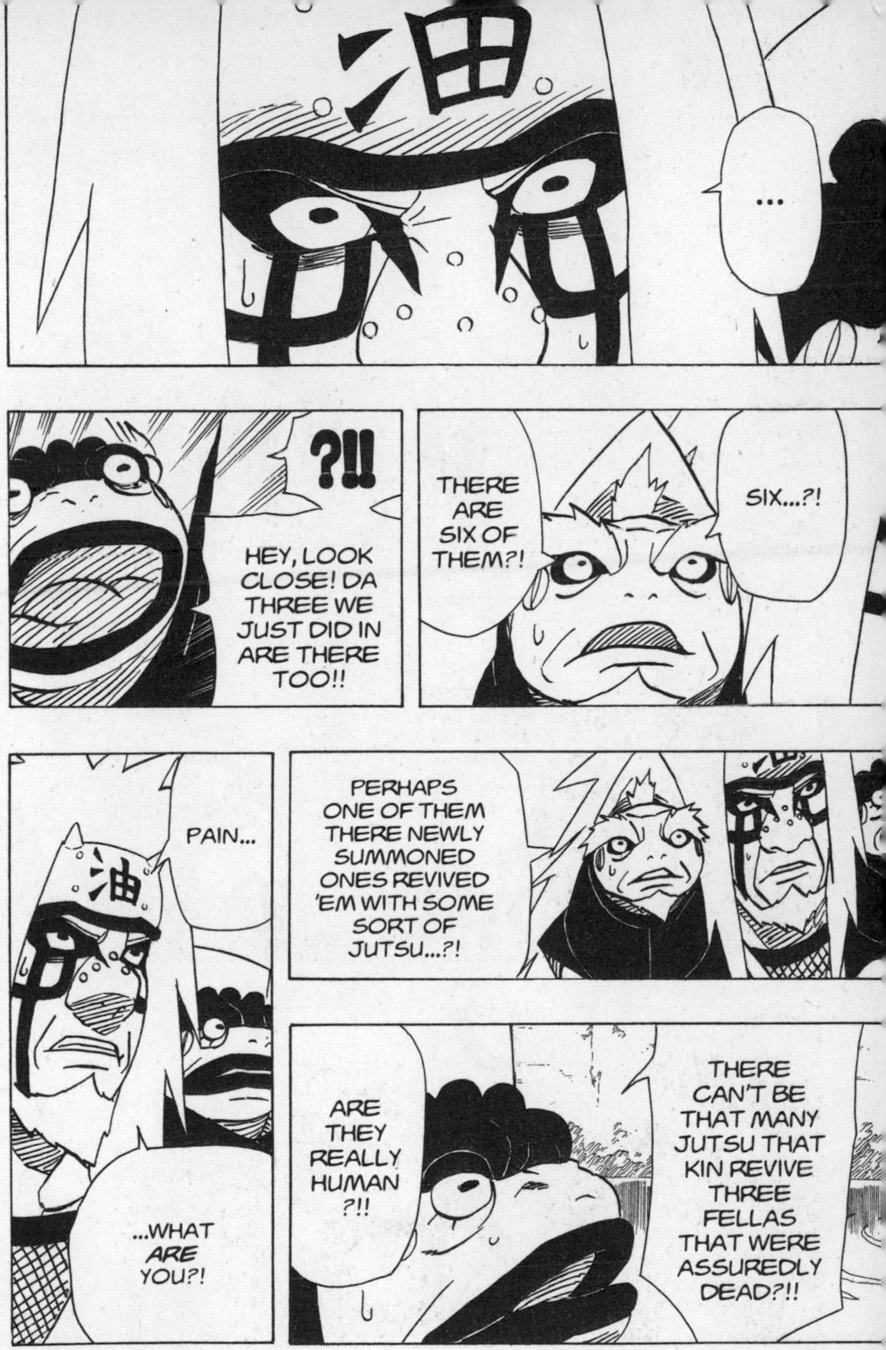
...
SIX...?!
THERE ARE SIX OF THEM?!
?!!
HEY, LOOK CLOSE! DA THREE WE JUST DID IN ARE THERE TOO!!
PERHAPS ONE OF THEM THERE NEWLY SUMMONED ONES REVIVED 'EM WITH SOME SORT OF JUTSU...?!
THERE CAN'T BE THAT MANY JUTSU THAT KIN REVIVE THREE FELLAS THAT WERE ASSUREDLY DEAD?!!
ARE THEY REALLY HUMAN ?!!
PAIN...
...WHAT *ARE* YOU?!

READ THIS WAY

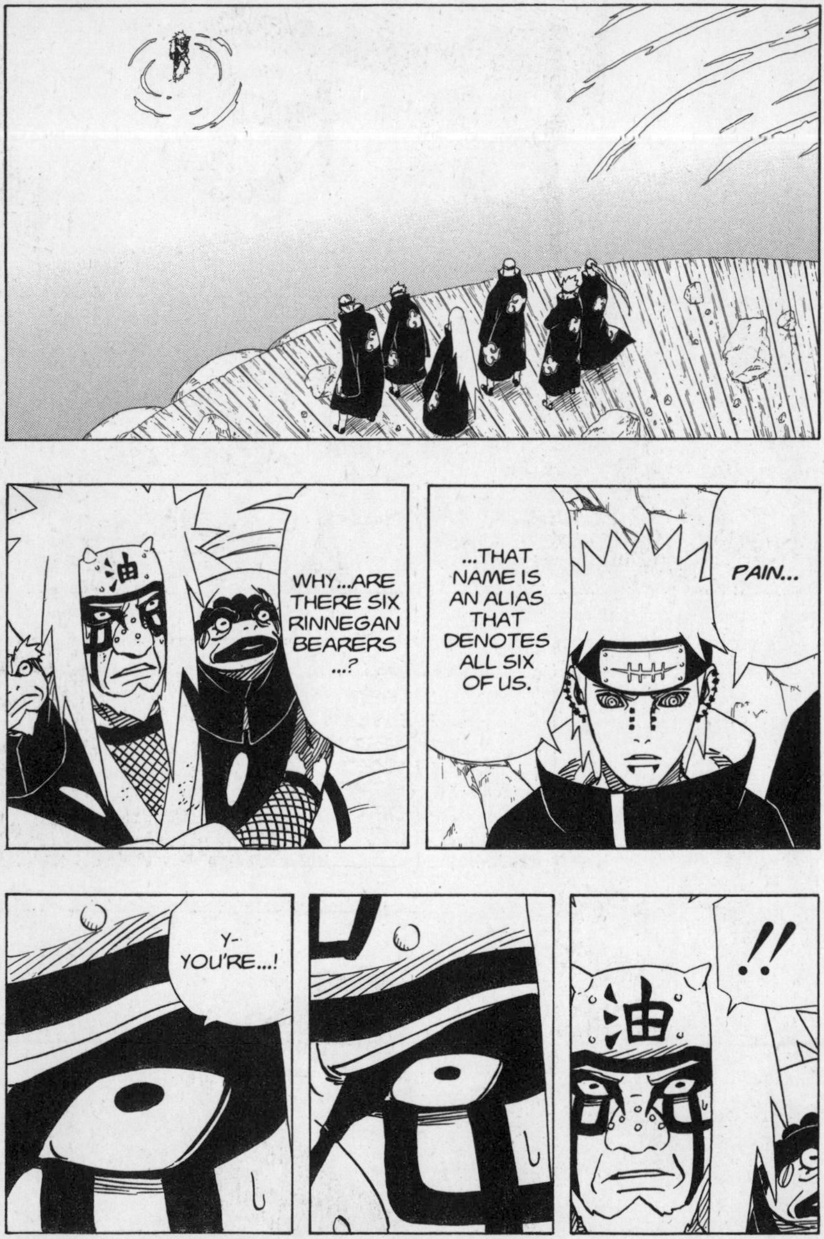
PAIN...
...THAT NAME IS AN ALIAS THAT DENOTES ALL SIX OF US.
WHY...ARE THERE SIX RINNEGAN BEARERS ...?
!!
Y- YOU'RE...!

 TO BE CONTINUED IN *NARUTO* VOLUME 42!

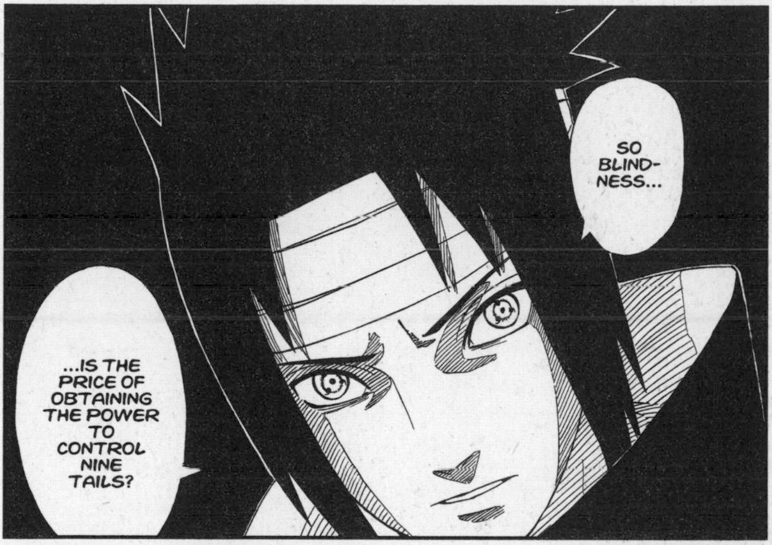
SO BLINDNESS...
...IS THE PRICE OF OBTAINING THE POWER TO CONTROL NINE TAILS?

IN THE NEXT VOLUME...

THE SECRET OF THE MANGEKYO

To truly end the reign of Pain of the Akatsuki, Jiraiya must delve deep into the past to uncover the secret of Pain's origin. At the same time, Sasuke moves toward the final battle of the Uchiha brothers when he closes in on the elusive Itachi!

AVAILABLE APRIL 2009!

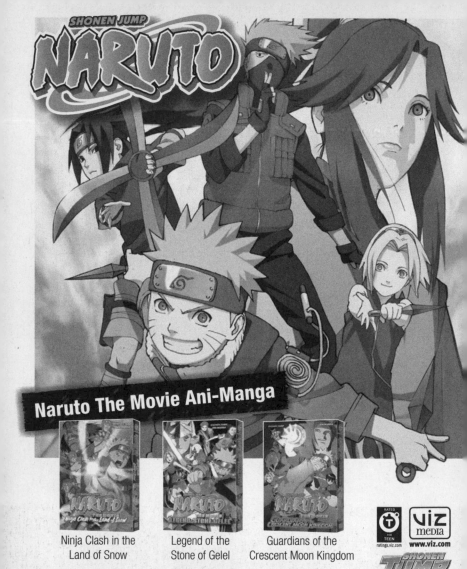

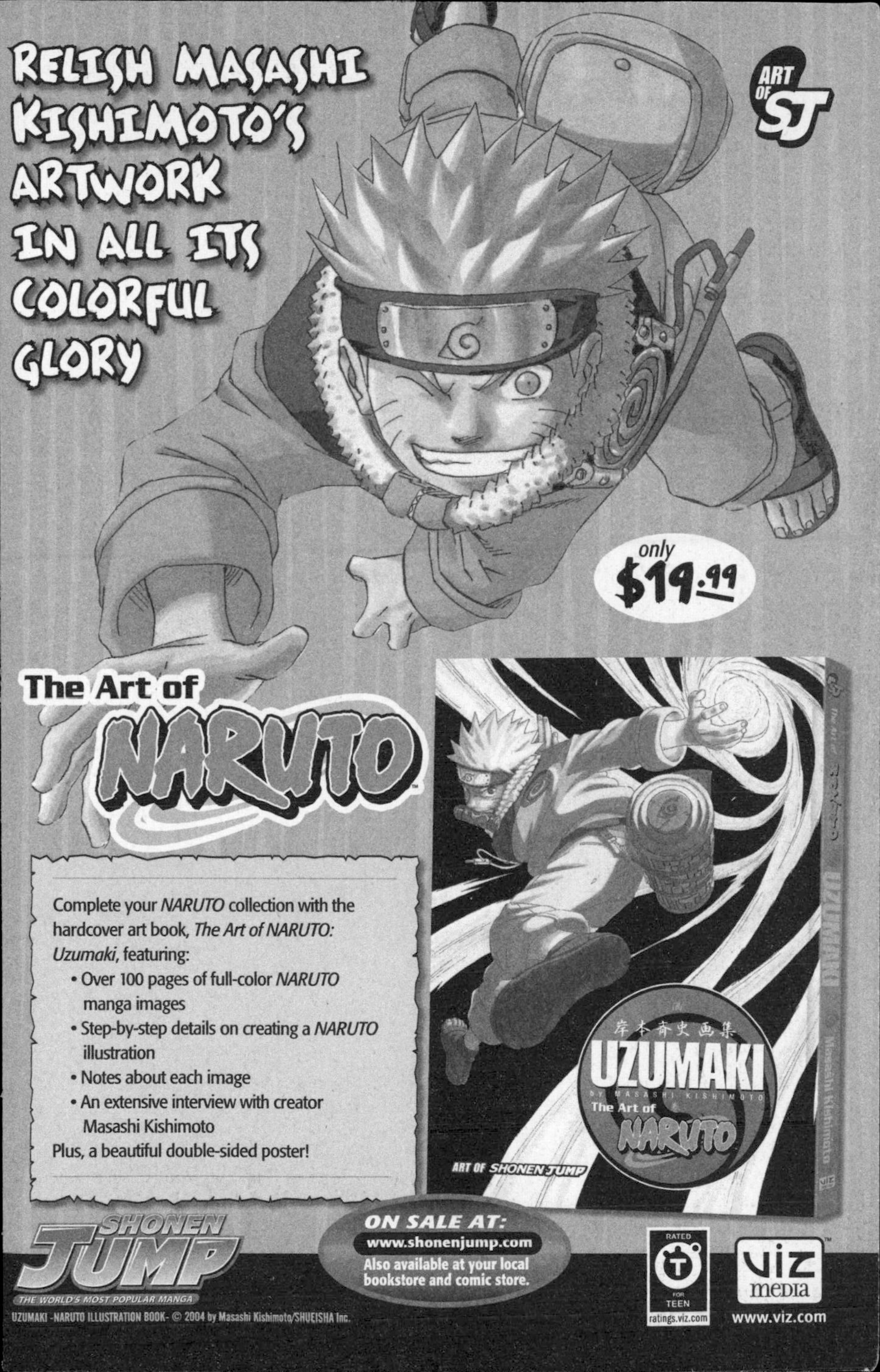
RELISH MASASHI KISHIMOTO'S ARTWORK IN ALL ITS COLORFUL GLORY
ART OF SJ
only $19.99
The Art of NARUTO
Complete your NARUTO collection with the hardcover art book, The Art of NARUTO: Uzumaki, featuring:
• Over 100 pages of full-color NARUTO manga images
• Step-by-step details on creating a NARUTO illustration
• Notes about each image
• An extensive interview with creator Masashi Kishimoto
Plus, a beautiful double-sided poster!
岸本斉史画集
UZUMAKI
BY MASASHI KISHIMOTO
The Art of NARUTO
ART OF SHONEN JUMP
SHONEN JUMP
THE WORLD'S MOST POPULAR MANGA
ON SALE AT:
www.shonenjump.com
Also available at your local bookstore and comic store.
RATED T FOR TEEN
ratings.viz.com
viz media
www.viz.com
UZUMAKI -NARUTO ILLUSTRATION BOOK- © 2004 by Masashi Kishimoto/SHUEISHA Inc.

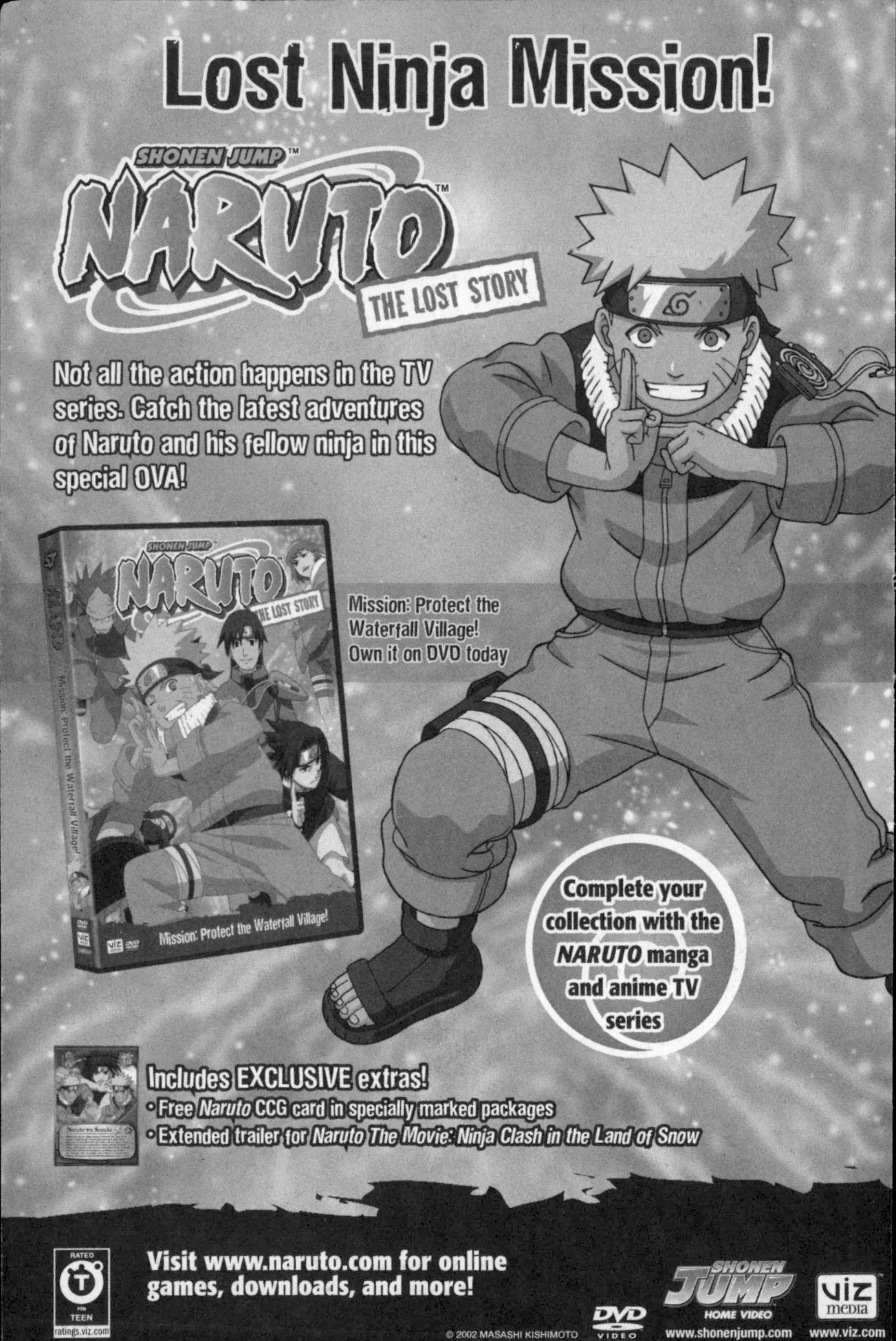
Lost Ninja Mission!
SHONEN JUMP™
NARUTO™
THE LOST STORY
Not all the action happens in the TV series. Catch the latest adventures of Naruto and his fellow ninja in this special OVA!
Mission: Protect the Waterfall Village! Own it on DVD today
Mission: Protect the Waterfall Village!
Complete your collection with the NARUTO manga and anime TV series
Includes EXCLUSIVE extras!
• Free Naruto CCG card in specially marked packages
• Extended trailer for Naruto The Movie: Ninja Clash in the Land of Snow
RATED T FOR TEEN
ratings.viz.com
Visit www.naruto.com for online games, downloads, and more!
© 2002 MASASHI KISHIMOTO
DVD VIDEO
SHONEN JUMP HOME VIDEO
www.shonenjump.com
viz media
www.viz.com

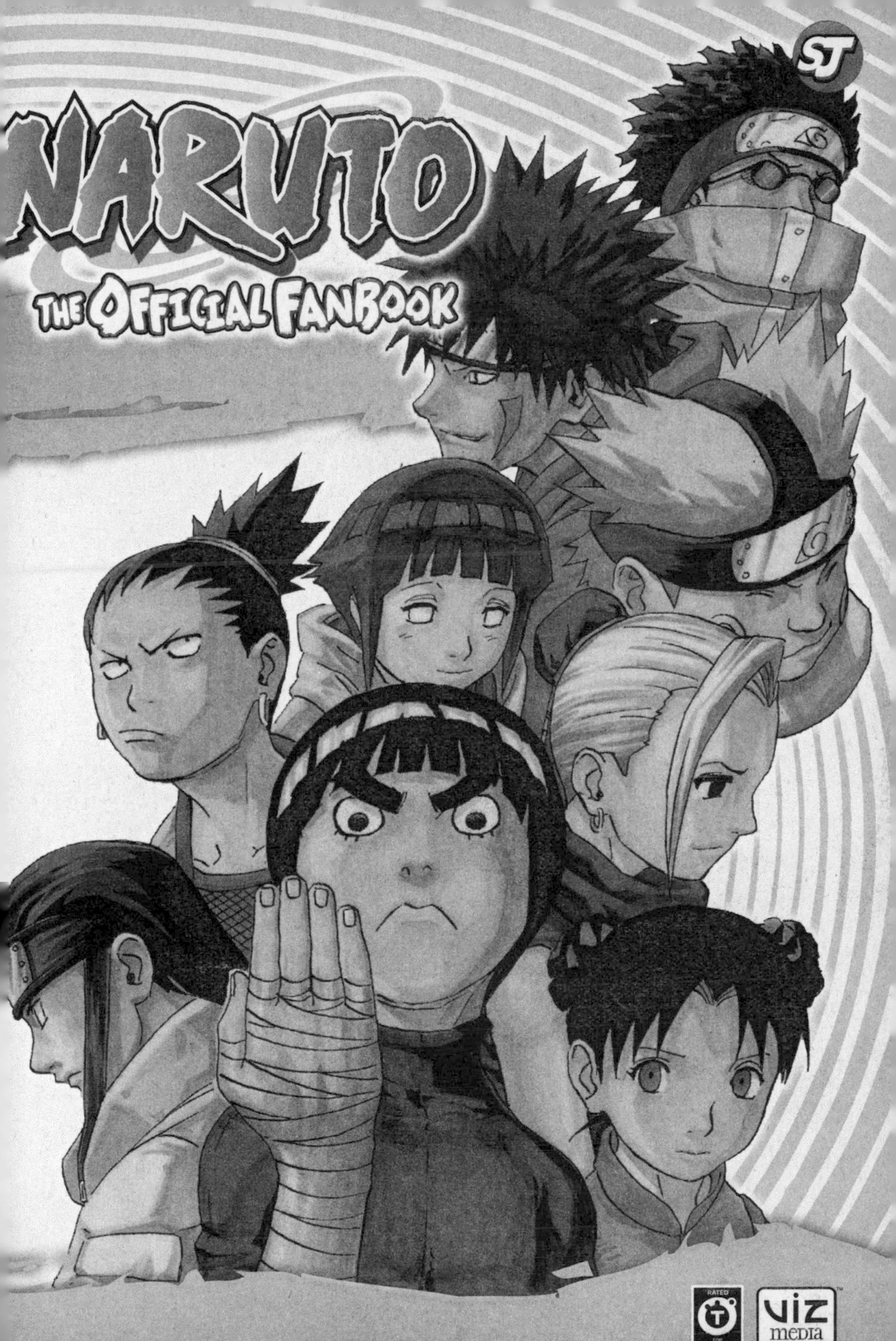
SJ
NARUTO
THE OFFICIAL FANBOOK
RATED T FOR TEEN
ratings.viz.com
viz media
www.viz.com

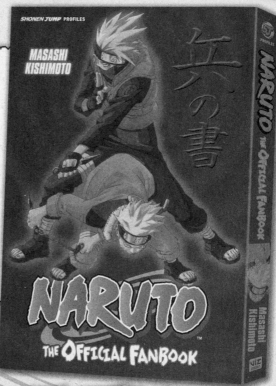
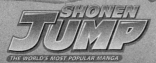

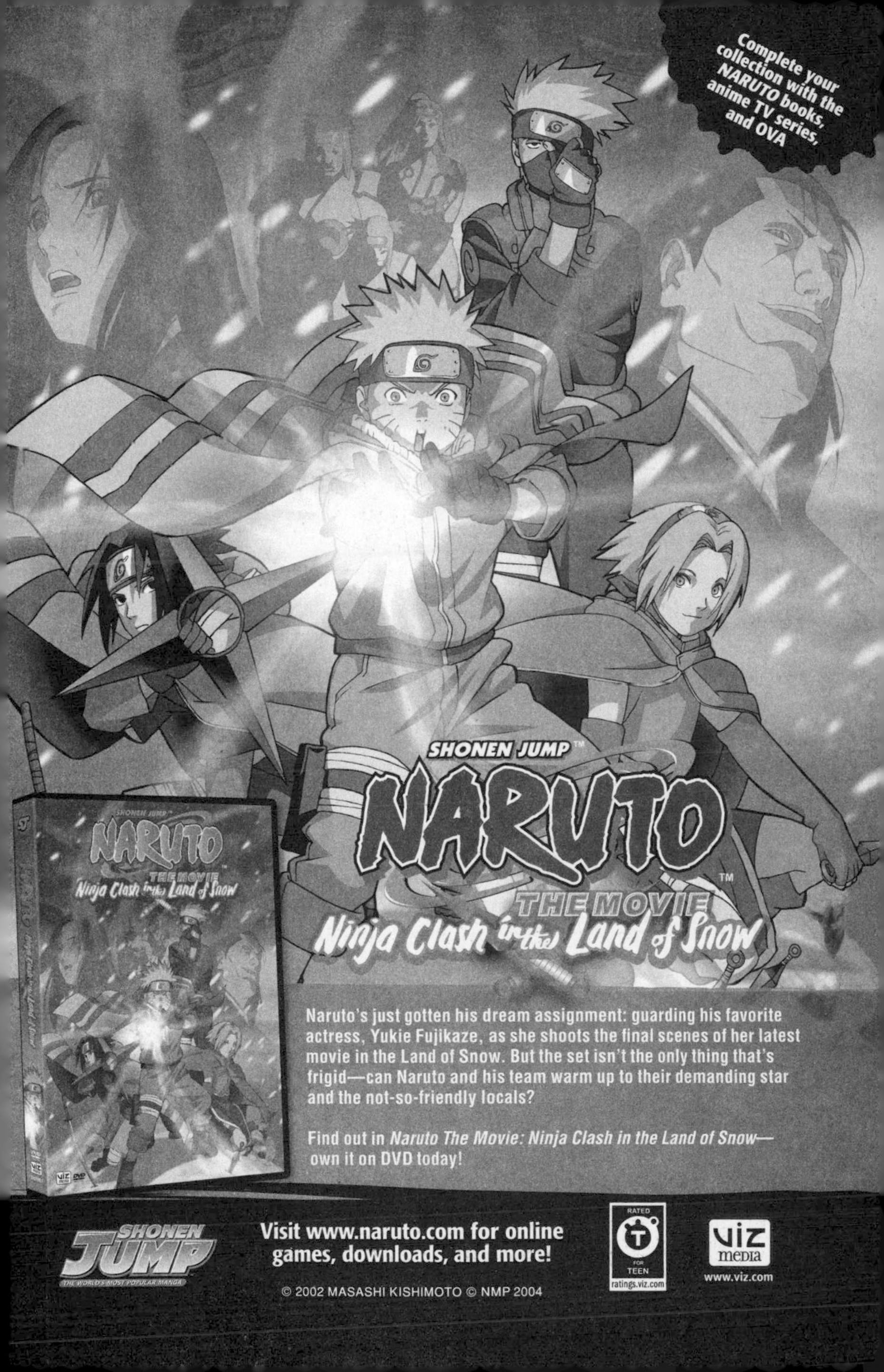
Complete your collection with the NARUTO books, anime TV series, and OVA
SHONEN JUMP™
NARUTO™
THE MOVIE
Ninja Clash in the Land of Snow
Naruto's just gotten his dream assignment: guarding his favorite actress, Yukie Fujikaze, as she shoots the final scenes of her latest movie in the Land of Snow. But the set isn't the only thing that's frigid—can Naruto and his team warm up to their demanding star and the not-so-friendly locals?
Find out in Naruto The Movie: Ninja Clash in the Land of Snow—own it on DVD today!
SHONEN JUMP
THE WORLD'S MOST POPULAR MANGA
Visit www.naruto.com for online games, downloads, and more!
© 2002 MASASHI KISHIMOTO © NMP 2004
RATED T FOR TEEN
ratings.viz.com
viz media
www.viz.com

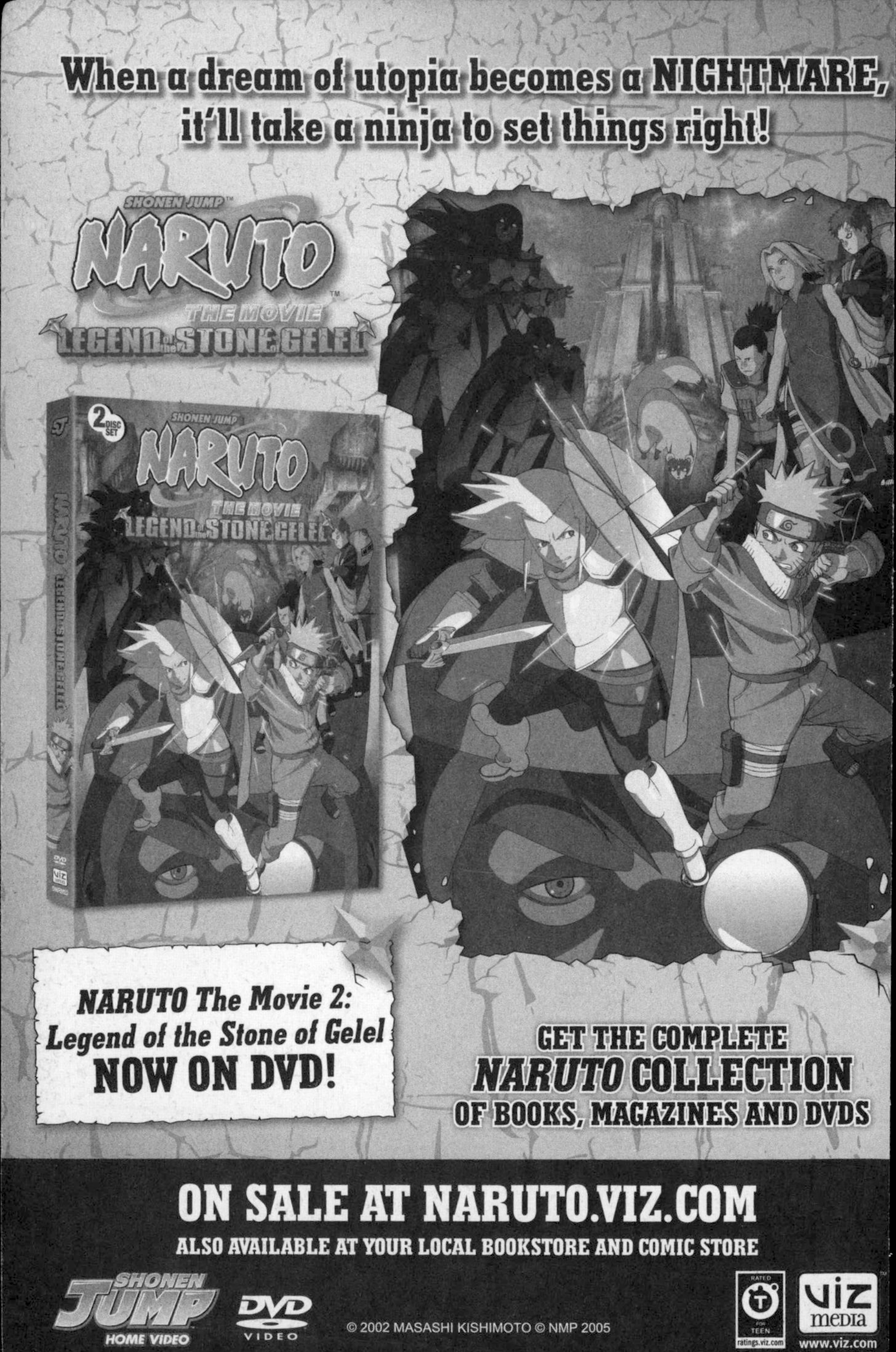
When a dream of utopia becomes a NIGHTMARE, it'll take a ninja to set things right!
SHONEN JUMP
NARUTO
THE MOVIE
LEGEND of the STONE of GELEL
2 DISC SET
SHONEN JUMP
NARUTO
THE MOVIE
LEGEND of the STONE of GELEL
NARUTO The Movie 2: Legend of the Stone of Gelel NOW ON DVD!
GET THE COMPLETE NARUTO COLLECTION OF BOOKS, MAGAZINES AND DVDS
ON SALE AT NARUTO.VIZ.COM
ALSO AVAILABLE AT YOUR LOCAL BOOKSTORE AND COMIC STORE
SHONEN JUMP HOME VIDEO
DVD VIDEO
© 2002 MASASHI KISHIMOTO © NMP 2005
RATED T FOR TEEN
ratings.viz.com
viz media
www.viz.com

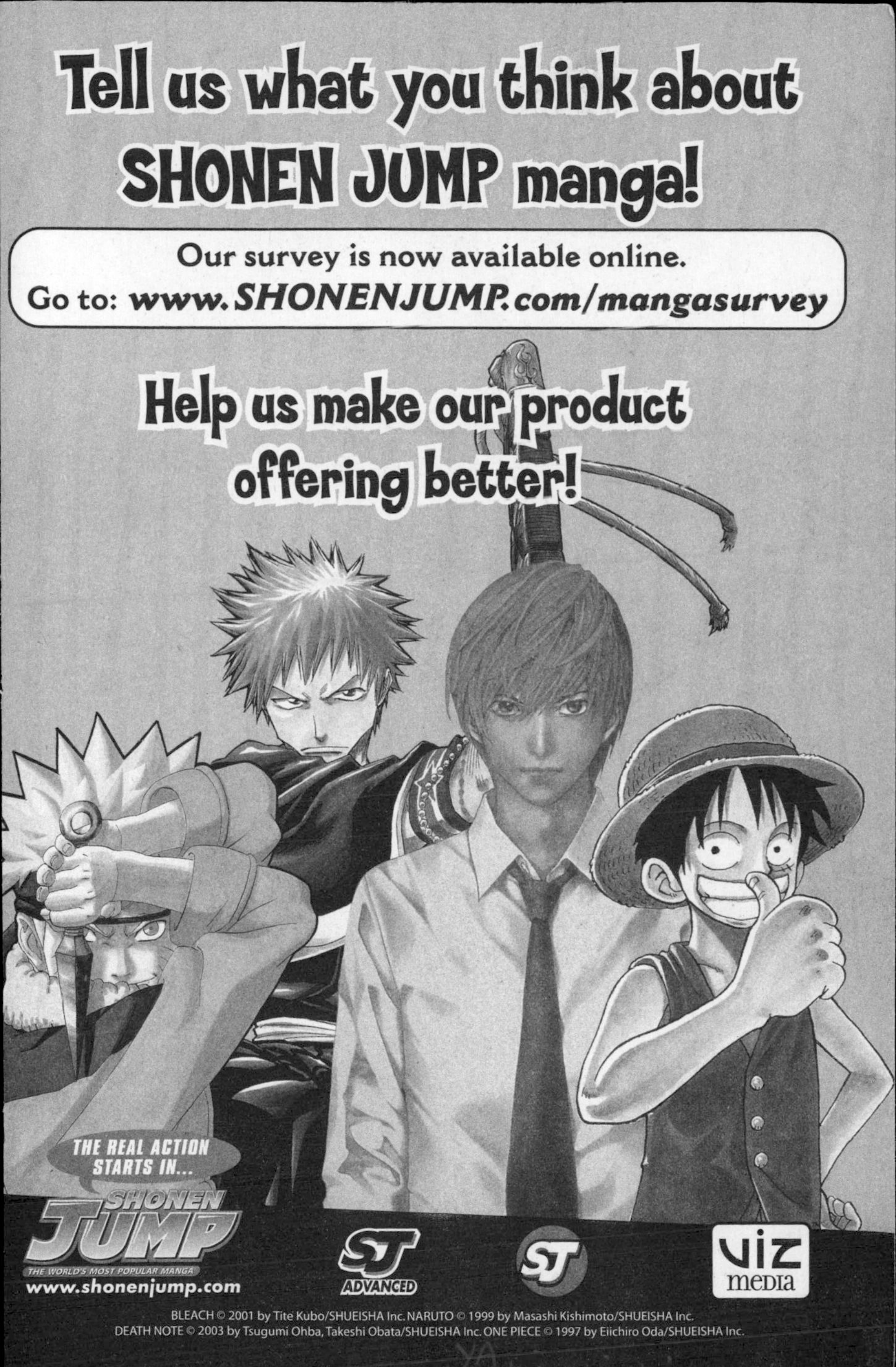
Tell us what you think about SHONEN JUMP manga!
Our survey is now available online.
Go to: www.SHONENJUMP.com/mangasurvey
Help us make our product offering better!
THE REAL ACTION STARTS IN...
SHONEN JUMP
THE WORLD'S MOST POPULAR MANGA
www.shonenjump.com
SJ ADVANCED
SJ
VIZ media
BLEACH © 2001 by Tite Kubo/SHUEISHA Inc. NARUTO © 1999 by Masashi Kishimoto/SHUEISHA Inc.
DEATH NOTE © 2003 by Tsugumi Ohba, Takeshi Obata/SHUEISHA Inc. ONE PIECE © 1997 by Eiichiro Oda/SHUEISHA Inc.

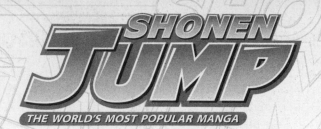
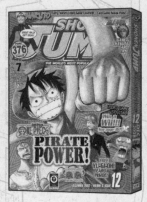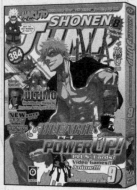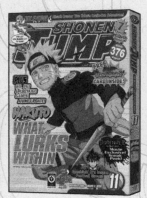

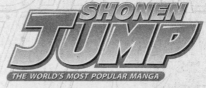

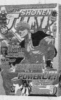

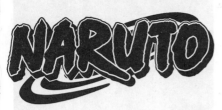

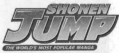